DECODING NICEA

BY PAUL F. PAVAO

The Greatest Stories Ever Told® • Selmer, Tennessee

DECODING NICEA

by Paul F. Pavao

ISBN, Print edition: 978-0-9888119-9-7

Published by:

The Greatest Stories Ever Told
P.O. Box 307
Selmer, TN 38375
admin@Christian-History.org
http://www.Christian-History.org

History is, by definition, the most exciting
stories and interesting facts of all time.

Early Christian Quotations

All quotations from the early church fathers are taken from:

Coxe, A. Cleveland, ed. *The Ante-Nicene Fathers*. Grand Rapids, MI: Christian Classics Ethereal Library, 1886. web. Accessed June 15, 2007.

Schaff, Philip, ed. *The Nicene and Post-Nicene Fathers*. Series 1 and 2. Grand Rapids, MI: Christian Classics Ethereal Library, 1890. web. Accessed June 15, 2007.

Language, grammar, and even word order have been adjusted minimally, as needed, for ease of reading. Extreme care has been taken not to adjust the meaning of any citations.

I have referenced early Christian writings by their most common titles. All writings and authors can be found with a search at the Christian Classics Ethereal Library: <http://www.ccel.org/fathers>

Scripture Quotations

Unless otherwise noted, Scripture quotations by the author are taken from the King James Version and adjusted to conform to modern language.

The vast majority of Scripture quotations in this book are made by the early church fathers themselves. These quotations are translated by *The Ante-Nicene Fathers* and *The Nicene and Post-Nicene Fathers* series. Where these deviate from popular English translations, usually due to the use of the Septuagint[1] by the early church fathers, the unique translations are duly noted in the text or in footnotes.

Footnotes

I have chosen footnotes over endnotes because I prefer them myself when I read. Jesus said, "Whatever you would have people do for you, do the same for them,"[2] so I have given you footnotes. I'm trying to set the record straight, so I have carefully referenced my sources. I am trying to write for "everyman," so I have included copious definitions and explanations.

---

[1] The Septuagint or "LXX" is a Greek translation of the Hebrew Scriptures (Old Testament) made between 200 BC and the birth of Jesus.

[2] Matthew 7:12. A footnote!

Table of Contents

Appendices

Reference Information

Historical Documents

About the Author

Paul Pavao is first and foremost a husband, father, and follower of Jesus Christ. However well or poorly I may perform any of those roles, they are the center of my life and what I most hope to be remembered for.

From the day I read about it, I have longed to "be devoted to the apostles' teaching, fellowship, the breaking of bread, and prayers" and to "pursue righteousness, faith, love, and peace along with those who call on the Lord out of a pure heart."[3]

I love history.

> *History is, by definition, the most exciting stories and interesting facts of all time.*

I have combined my love of history with my passion for the church of Jesus Christ. I study history with one goal in mind. I want to know the secret of the incredible power behind the boasting of Paul the apostle and the churches that he started.

> *Among us you will find the uneducated, craftsman, and old women, who, if they are unable in words to prove the benefit of our doctrine, yet by their deeds exhibit the benefit arising from their persuasion of its truth.[4]*

> *[Even] our boys and young women treat the crosses and tortures with contempt. They endure wild beasts and every other punishment with the inspired patience of suffering.[5]*

---

[3] Acts 2:42. 2 Timothy 2:22.

[4] Athenagoras. *A Plea for the Christians*. 11. AD 177.

[5] Minucius Felix. *The Octavius*. 37. AD 160-230.

Acknowledgments

There is no way to acknowledge my debt to everyone. My apologies to all those I missed, whether still on the earth or among that "great cloud of witnesses."

My parents, who told me I could learn anything and who made everything interesting, gave me my love for learning.

Mr. Shea, my twelfth-grade European history teacher at Kaiserslautern American High School, and Gene Edwards, author of *Revolution: The Story of the Early Church*, inspired my interest in history as storytelling.

David Bercot, author of *Will the Real Heretics Please Stand Up*, let me know that we had writings from the early apostolic churches, and Dan McAlister gave me my first copy of *The Ante-Nicene Fathers*, volume one. I still have that underlined, highlighted, and beat up copy.

My wife, Lorie, and our six children have given up many hours and days with their husband and father to let me—no, to encourage me to—research and write.

My daughter-in-law, Esther, has put innumerable hours into the cover and all the labor of publishing a book.

Rose Creek Village is not just my church, but my home and family. Rose Creek Village is not an organization; it is many individuals and families who have given up the American dream to find out that Jesus is the same today as he was 2,000 years ago.

A thousand others have loved, encouraged, and supported me. Best of all, they've listened to me without looking bored.

Above all, I want to acknowledge the God of heaven and his *Logos*, King Jesus our Lord, who has been proving for 2,000 years that his people really can't be conquered ... and that it has nothing to do with organizations. Every time the world seems enveloped in darkness, the bright light of Jesus Christ has found a way to dispel it.

Dedication

To my brothers and sisters in Christ,

You are those to whom I have committed my life and for whom I have lived until this day.

I wrote this book in English—your English—so you can have what is yours. I filled it with stories—true stories—so you can enjoy what is yours.

Shake yourself from the dust.
Arise!
Take your place, oh Jerusalem.
Remove the chains that are around your neck,
    oh captive daughter of Zion;
For this is what the Lord says,
    " ... You shall be redeemed without money."
                                    ~ Isaiah 52:2-3

Part I:

The Council of Nicea:

The Story

Chapter 1:
The Greatest Story on Earth

The Council of Nicea was one of the most momentous events in human history, or at least in the history of western civilization.

The Council of Nicea was first and foremost an attempt by the Roman emperor Constantine the Great to keep his empire from splitting. Having just overthrown his co-emperor Licinius,[6] he was horrified to find the religion he had just rescued and raised to national prominence in shreds.

> When ... I had been victorious over my enemies, I thought that nothing more remained but to return thanks to him ... As soon as I heard that news which I had least expected to receive—I mean the news of your dissension—I judged it to be of no secondary importance ... I immediately sent to require your presence.[7]

---

[6] It was typical in the fourth century for the Roman empire to have two emperors, one in the east and one in the west. The goal, in fact, was a "tetrarchy," or rule of four, with one Augustus and one Caesar in each half of the empire, the Augustus outranking the Caesar.

[7] "Constantine's Address to the Council Concerning Peace." Eusebius. *Life of Constantine*. III:12.

'Their presence' did far more than bring unity to a divided religion. In fact, unity would have to wait 58 years for another emperor bent on peace. But the Council of Nicea did bring other things.

There, for the first time, Christian bishops were welcomed as guests of the emperor. There, for the first time, a Roman emperor acknowledged himself as not just tolerant of Christianity, but a Christian himself.

When Constantine took his seat among the bishops at Nicea, a state government and the government of the Christian church became joined for the first time.

And the world would never be the same again.

The Story of Nicea

History is, by definition, the most exciting stories and interesting facts of all time. Christian history, then, is the most exciting stories and interesting facts of the last 2,000 years.

The story of Nicea is perhaps the most interesting of all.

This book tells that story, and in the process it deals with the currently popular myths and rumors about this fascinating piece of western history. The story, in and of itself, answers ...

- Why should I care about the Council of Nicea?
- What impact did Nicea have on western civilization?
- Did the Council of Nicea invent the Trinity, throw out gnostic gospels, and change the Sabbath day?
- Who was Constantine and why was he involved?
- Was Constantine a Christian?

As a bonus, we will also address related issues, like:

- Where did we get our Bible?
- What was the pre-Nicene church like? Was it already Roman Catholic?

And most of all, this book will tell you *how to know who's telling you the truth.*

The Da Vinci Code

A lot of the interest in the Council of Nicea was fueled by the publication of Dan Brown's bestseller, *The Da Vinci Code*. In it, Brown claimed:

- "Until *that* moment in history, Jesus was viewed by his followers as a mortal prophet" (emphasis his).[8]
- "The Bible, as we know it today, was collated by the pagan Roman emperor Constantine the Great."[9]
- "More than *eighty* gospels were considered for the New Testament, and yet only a relative few were chosen for inclusion."[10]

Are Dan Brown's claims true? How do we know? Where did he get his information, and who sorts out what **really** happened at Nicea?

You will be handling the original writings of the participants, and you will never wonder again.

The Council of Nicea for Christians

But those are just the secular questions. Long before *The Da Vinci Code* was published, the Council of Nicea was important to Christians. It produced the Nicene Creed,[11] a version of which is recited on a weekly basis in Roman Catholic, Eastern Orthodox, and even many Protestant churches.

To the Eastern Orthodox the Council of Nicea is the first great ecumenical council of the seven considered to carry divine authority. The Roman Catholic Church attributes divine authority to it as

---

[8] *The Da Vinci Code*. p. 253. Emphasis his.
[9] *ibid.* p. 252
[10] *ibid.* Emphasis his.
[11] The Nicene Creed is given in Appendix G.

well. Major Protestant denominations hold its creed as essential to orthodoxy.

More radical Protestants claim that Nicea marks the fall of the free church. There, they say, the church married the world, birthed the papacy, inaugurated the split between clergy and laity, began to persecute the free churches, causing the world and Christianity to fall into the Dark Ages.

Who is right and how do we know?

Getting the Facts About the Council of Nicea

The events surrounding the Council of Nicea are not shrouded in mystery. The sources are few, well-known, easy to obtain, and agreed upon by all historians, both Christian and secular.

The problem is, rumors are a lot more fun.

If you're one of those who prefer facts to rumors, I will put the history in your hands. If you're a Christian, the story of Nicea is both exciting and intriguing. It provides important insight into the foundations of your faith and the issues and sources that were important to early Christians.

Even if you are not a Christian, the Council of Nicea marks a dramatic shift in world history. While the influence of Christians had been growing steadily for almost 300 years by the time of Nicea, it was only afterward that Christianity played a major role in world government.

Unfortunately for those that are looking for a way to write off Christianity or increase the historical importance of gnosticism,[12] the council did not change Christian orthodoxy in any way. It simply formalized a political influence for Christian leaders that Constantine was in the process of bestowing upon them anyway.

---

[12] Gnosticism was an early competitor to the teachings of the apostles. By the middle of the second century, gnostic teachers were removed from all apostolic churches, and by the Council of Nicea they had no influence on the churches whatsoever. See Chapter 12 for a thorough description of gnosticism.

Chapter 2:

How Do We Know Anything About Nicea?

- "The Council of Nicea threw out hundreds of gnostic gospels."
- "The Council of Nicea was divinely inspired."
- "The Council of Nicea made the church worldly."
- "The Council of Nicea was good."
- "The Council of Nicea was bad."

Thousands of voices vie for our attention. They stand at virtual street corners on the World Wide Web, each hawking their own particular message. In the case of the Council of Nicea, *The Da Vinci Code's* Leigh Teabing pleads his case against Constantine and the bishops gathered with him in public cinemas, and we pay to listen to him. Books are written questioning the Christian view of Jesus and the church, not just by Dan Brown, the author of *The Da Vinci Code*, but also by Hugh Schonfield (*The Passover Plot*); Baigent, Leigh, and Lincoln (*Holy Blood, Holy Grail*); and Bart Ehrman (*Judas Iscariot: A New Look at Betrayer and Betrayed*).

What's true? Who says? How do we know whom to believe?

Many people don't think about where history comes from. The textbooks we studied in public school didn't give extensive references; or, if they did, we paid no attention to them. We just believed whatever the textbooks said!

Now, though, we have the internet. History is suddenly up for grabs:

- "The founding fathers of the United States were Christian."
- "The founding fathers were Deist."
- "The founding fathers wanted a clear separation of church and state."
- "The founding fathers wanted the government to be Christian; it's only specific denominations that have to be separate."

It's not only the Council of Nicea that causes controversy.

There is a solution to the problem. There is a right way to learn and pass on history, and you can easily find out who's doing it the right way.

Primary and Secondary Sources

Primary sources are reports from someone who was there. There may be great and astonishingly accurate Christian histories written today, but they can never be anything but secondary sources *because the authors weren't there.*

Eye-witnesses have to be taken with a grain of salt, but they are the only ones who can report on what happened. If we have no eye-witnesses, or at least contemporary accounts from people who actually talked to the eye-witnesses, then all we have is speculation and not reliable history.

In the case of the Council of Nicea, we have several eye-witnesses, and we also have one fourth-century and three fifth-century histories[13] whose authors were privy to sources that we are not. Those histories preserve most of our primary sources and establish, with the surrounding sources mentioned below, that we have a reliable account of the proceedings of the Council of Nicea.

Primary sources for the Council of Nicea are:

- A letter written at the end of the council by the historian Eusebius to his church in Caesarea, preserved in his *Life of Constantine.*[14]

- A description of the proceedings by Eusebius, who participated in the council, also preserved in *Life of Constantine.*

- Letters from Constantine and from the council passing on the council's decisions to the churches.[15]

- A list of 20 "canons"—ecclesiastical rules—passed by the council. That list circulated and is found in several histories and in manuscripts preserved from the fourth and fifth centuries.[16]

- A short account of some events of the council contained in writings by Athanasius, who attended as a young advisor before he was bishop.

- A letter by a bishop named Eustathius, preserved in *The Ecclesiastical History of Theodoret.*[17]

Every one of these sources can be found in the three series, *Ante-Nicene Fathers* and *The Nicene and Post-Nicene Fathers,* Series 1 and Series 2. These are available through any Christian bookstore, on Amazon, and most inexpensively, through Christian Book Distributors.[18]

---

[13] AD 325, when the Council of Nicea occurred, is early fourth century.

[14] Appendix I.

[15] Appendices H and J.

[16] Chapter 7.

[17] I:7.

[18] <http://www.christianbook.com>.

Better yet, they are available for free reading on the internet at *The Christian Classics Ethereal Library*[19] or at any public library.

You don't have to wonder about what is being said in this book. You can look up every reference I give.

There are not any other primary sources. Everything else said about the Council of Nicea that is not from these sources is speculation or wishful thinking.

Further, what we read in these primary sources is strongly confirmed by other things that we know ...

Surrounding Events

On top of these sources for the Council of Nicea, we also have innumerable primary sources for the events before and after Nicea.

There are many letters between bishops both before and after Nicea. There are letters and decrees of emperors. There are the four histories I mention above. There are secular histories as well; Ammianus Marcellinus, for example, is often leaned on by Christian historians. Even Julian the Apostate, the only non-Christian emperor after Nicea, who reigned as Augustus from 360 to 363, left letters discussing Christianity less than 40 years after Nicea.

Knowing these surrounding events helps us know whether the sources we have for Nicea are reliable.

For example, if Dan Brown was correct, then we should find that many of the letters written by bishops before Nicea discuss gnosticism, gnostic gospels, and what to do about them. We should at least find the bishops discussing the canon.[20]

---

[19] <http://www.ccel.org/fathers>

[20] "The canon," from the Latin word for "rule," is the list of books which are regarded as Scripture by a religion (in this case, Christianity). A canon is also an official ecclesiastical decision of a council.

> ### The Glossary
>
> Most rare, ancient, or ecclesiastical words are defined in footnotes, at least the first time they occur. Appendix A is a glossary to help you with such terms. You might want to stick a bookmark in it!
>
> The abundant use of source material, which I regard as important, means that such terms will occasionally occur. I have replaced those with more modern terms where possible.

This is not what we find. Which books belong in the Bible rarely comes up. Eusebius Pamphilus discusses it in his *Ecclesiastical History* in 323. What he says lines up closely with lists given by Origen around 230, almost a full century earlier, and an anonymous Muratorian Fragment, generally dated to AD 170. None of these lists even mention gnostic gospels such as the Gospel of Thomas.[21]

In fact, as early as AD 185, almost a century and a half before Nicea, Irenaeus, perhaps the most respected and well-known bishop of his time, said there were only 4 Gospels.[22] His famous work, *Against Heresies*, indicates that the gnostics contested this, but also that they were outside and separate from the apostolic churches who would later send bishops to the Council of Nicea.

The writings from the times surrounding Nicea discuss what we know Nicea to be about: the divinity of Christ; whether the term begotten or created should be applied to him; whether his generation from the Father was eternal or occurred in time; whether he existed before he was begotten; and, of course, whether that controversial term *homoousios* should be admitted to common use in the churches.[23]

---

[21] Appendix L gives all the lists of canonical books created before and around the time of Nicea. They are remarkably consistent.

[22] *Against Heresies*. III:11:8.

[23] *Homoousios* means "one in substance," It's a central term in the Nicene Creed, and it was crucial to the controversy after Nicea. I'll introduce the term

Thus, the surrounding events verify that traditional history is accurate. The Council of Nicea convened to condemn the doctrines of Arius—who taught that the Son of God was created and did not exist prior to his creation—and to consider the day on which Easter/Passover should be celebrated. The council also took care of some miscellaneous ecclesiastical issues, none of which had anything to do with the books of the Bible.

This does not mean there's nothing to learn! There are significant details of the controversy that are not well known. Fascinating questions that we will answer include:

- Why did Arius' views receive such a wide hearing?
- What significant detail of the Nicene Creed slips beneath our notice no matter how many times we repeat it?
- Who is really responsible for ending the Arian Controversy?

This brings us to our final source for the Council of Nicea.

Pre-Nicene History

There is no doubt that the gnostics existed and had their own Gospels very early in the history of the church. There is no doubt that during the time of the apostles, at least some of the gnostics were *in* the apostolic churches. We know this because there are letters from the apostles condemning gnostic tenets and making it clear that some in the church held to them.[24]

However, the same sort of writings that make up the New Testament make it clear that gnosticism was driven out of the churches by the mid-second century. If there were disputes over which books the church should treat as Scripture, those disputes were settled in the second century. Except for a few books like James, Hebrews, First Clement, and the Shepherd of Hermas, the canon

---

in Chapter 4, discuss its importance to the opponents of Nicea in Chapter 9, and give you a thorough explanation and history of the term in Chapter 15.

[24] e.g., 1 Corinthians 15 and the three epistles of John

was settled by the time the Muratorian Fragment, the first known attempt to list all the books of the Bible, was written in the mid-second century. Further, the books that were quoted in second-century Christian writings confirm that, in general, there was no dispute over which books constituted the canon of the apostolic churches.

Second-century gnostic writings abound. They existed, and they were obviously read and used by gnostic sects. However, since gnostic sects were no longer part of the community of apostolic churches, the only reference we find to them in the writings of the apostolic churches are arguments against them as outsiders. They no longer had a place in the apostolic churches.

By the mid-third century, the church was no longer even discussing such writings. Apparently, the gnostics had lost their ability to have any influence at all in Christian congregations.

Modern supporters of gnostic writings argue that gnostics were real Christians possessing an authentic alternative message from Christ. I don't agree with that, but it's irrelevant to the Council of Nicea. The Council of Nicea was conducted by bishops of the apostolic churches, not bishops of gnostic sects. There were no gnostics at Nicea. They had been gone from the apostolic churches for around two centuries.

The same is true of other rumors surrounding Nicea. Dan Brown states, and internet rumors abound, that the divinity of Jesus was invented at Nicea by a vote of the bishops present. This is easily resolved by looking at pre-Nicene history.

Numerous writers look directly at the subject of the divinity of Christ. Tertullian's *Against Praxeas*, written around AD 210, is a 26,000 word treatise exclusively discussing and defending the divinity of Christ. Origen, in AD 225, devotes the first three chapters of his *De Principiis* to the Trinity; one chapter each to the Father, Son, and Holy Spirit. Even earlier, Justin Martyr devotes several chapters of his *Dialogue with Trypho, a Jew* to showing that "there is ... another God and Lord subject to the Maker of all things."[25]

One of the earliest of all post-New Testament Christian writers, Ignatius, said to have been appointed as bishop of Antioch—the apostle Paul's home church—by the apostles, begins his letter to the church at Ephesus by commenting that Christians are "elected through the true suffering by the will of the Father and Jesus Christ, our God." His letter dates to either AD 107 or 116.

Thus, the history prior to Nicea makes it impossible that the divinity of Jesus was being invented at the council in 325. Instead, by AD 185, Irenaeus could boast that the faith of the apostolic churches was the same throughout the world, as though the Church "had only one mouth."[26] Irenaeus regularly refers to Jesus as God.[27]

Conclusion

We are not left wondering what happened at Nicea. We don't have to wrestle with rumors or wonder who is telling us the truth.

If you have access to the internet, it would be good to actually bookmark the Christian Classic Ethereal Library at www.ccel.org/fathers. That is their church fathers section, and it will give you free access to the three series I mentioned above.

Now that we know where our story comes from, let's look at how we got from the babe in a manger to more than 250 bishops sitting with the emperor of the greatest empire on earth.

---

[25] *Dialogue with Trypho, a Jew.* 56.
[26] *Against Heresies.* I:10:2.
[27] e.g., *Against Heresies.* III:6:1.

Chapter 3:
Christianity Before Nicea

The generally accepted dates for Jesus' birth are between 6 and 4 B.C. Since B.C. means "Before Christ," this seems counterintuitive, but it is easily explained.

Prior to the sixth century, calendars were not dated from Jesus' birth. Years were given by the year of the reign of whichever king was in power at the time. For example, *The Ecclesiastical History of Socrates Scholasticus*, written in the mid-fifth century and cited regularly in this book, assigns years for the events surrounding Nicea by the year of the reign of Constantine I and his son Constantius II.

A man named Dionysius Exiguus created the term and the idea of *Anno Domini*, which means "year of our Lord" and from which we get our AD numbering system for our years. He did not create this system until 525, and he was unable to accurately determine the year that Jesus was born.

Historical sources are clear that King Herod the Great, under whose reign Jesus was born, died in 4 B.C. Since Matthew tells us that Herod killed all the children under two years old in Bethlehem in an attempt to ensure that he killed Jesus as well (Matt. 2:16-18), Christian historians back his birth up another two years from 4 B.C.

This is how the dates 6-4 B.C. are obtained for Jesus' birth.

The dates of his death are more easily fixed because Luke tells us exactly when John the Baptist began baptizing, which was the 15th year of the reign of Tiberius Caesar. He also gives us the name of several tetrarchs, so that the time frame can be reasonably established at around AD 28 or 29.

Thus, Jesus' death is usually assigned to AD 33 because that allows the three Passovers mentioned by the Gospel of John and Passover would have fallen on the right day of the week that year.

Once Jesus died and rose again, the apostles began to spread the Gospel throughout the empire.

The Resurrection of Jesus Christ

It should be obvious that many, if not most, secular historians do not believe that Jesus really rose from the dead. Personally, I find the apostles to be the most powerful evidence there is of Jesus' resurrection. All of the apostles except John were eventually put to death for their testimony.

It would be easy to pick a second best piece of evidence for the resurrection: Christians. The name of Jesus Christ has been transforming people's lives and bringing them into fellowship with God for 2,000 years despite strenuous efforts by skeptics to discredit his resurrection on an intellectual basis. The incredible power of his name has been, is now, and always will be the strongest ongoing evidence for the resurrection and divinity of our Lord Jesus Christ.

There is no evidence that the apostles nor any of their successors set about to create an organization or hierarchy to unite the churches. On the contrary, Christian apologists of the pre-Nicene era regularly pointed to the unity of the independent Christian churches and their agreement on important points of theology as proof that they had each, individually, carefully preserved the faith that had been taught to them by the apostles. This argument would have meant nothing at all if each of those churches were being controlled by or received their theology from a central, ruling organization.[28]

The churches were likely relatively small throughout the second century, though they were found all over the world. Persecution was intermittent, but could arise at any time because Christians refused to sacrifice to the Roman gods, a public obligation for everyone in the Roman empire except Jews, who had a special exemption (an exemption that was likely not always honored).

By the third century, though, Tertullian, a Christian apologist, could argue that if the emperor were to banish all Christians from his empire he would have no subjects left to rule over. While this is a gross exaggeration, it does make it clear that he understood Christianity to be both widespread and popular. I have read estimates that suggested that 10% of Roman residents were Christian by the end of the third century, but there is no way to know how accurate that number is.

It is clear that churches were becoming much larger by the end of the third century. Writings from that period begin to describe seating arrangements for official members, for those being instructed in the faith, for those under church discipline, and for the clergy.

It is also easy to see the increase in the power and position of church leaders in the third century. In the mid-second century, Justin's *First Apology*, with its description of early Christian baptism and an early Christian worship service could leave you wondering whether there were any official leaders at all in Rome at the time. While there are plenty of other writings making it clear that there were church leaders in Rome in the mid-second century, no description of third century Christianity would be possible without bishops and elders, who were already holding church councils and disputing among themselves.

---

[28] This thought is developed and proven in Chapter 18: Was the Pre-Nicene Church Roman Catholic?

Thus it was a larger, more centralized, and more organized Christianity that would face the dawning of the fourth century and the most momentous events in the history of the church of Jesus Christ.

Heresies

No description of early Christianity would be complete without addressing the various heresies, especially in a book about the Council of Nicea.

There are two myths that we are going to have to dispel here.

Gnosticism

The first myth is that gnosticism played any role in Christianity after the second century.[29]

Gnosticism is a very general term applied to a wide variety of groups that would have called themselves Christian but who held to beliefs very different than anything we know as Christian today. While those groups could be very different from one another, there were some consistent characteristics.

- The true God is unknowable, but he has certain "emanations," called "aeons," who interact with people.

- The God who made the world was indeed the God of the Jews, but he was not the true God. Instead, he was an ignorant and accidental by-product of one of the aeons.

- All physical creation, because it was the product of this ignorant God of the Jews, should not have happened and is not good.

- Since all of the physical creation is bad, there is no redemption of the body, and Christ did not come in the flesh, even if he happened to temporarily inhabit the physical body of Jesus of Nazareth.

---

[29] Gnosticism is more fully discussed in Chapter 12.

- Jesus' death was not redemptive, but was only the failed end of his ministry. The Christ spirit left him and continues to lead people to true redemption through spiritual knowledge that would eventually lead men's spirits to the fullness of God (the *pleroma*).[30]

The saving knowledge, or *gnosis*, from which we get the word "gnostic," varied. Each gnostic teacher had his own special revelation, and coming up with new revelation was highly prized among the gnostics.

> Every one of them generates something new, day by day, according to his ability. For no one is deemed perfect who does not develop among them some mighty fictions.[31]

Gnostics, it appeared, thrived even in the first century. Paul addresses standard gnostic teaching in 1 Corinthians 15. There he says there are some among the Corinthians saying "there is no resurrection of the dead" (1 Cor. 15:12) The apostle John has even more references to gnosticism. It is clear that gnostics are "those who are trying to seduce you" in 1 John 2:26, and it is almost certain that Diotrephes, who refused to receive John, was a gnostic teacher who gained leadership of one of John's churches (3 Jn. 9).

Not long after, Ignatius, a bishop of the church in Antioch, Paul's home church, wrote a series of letters on his way to martyrdom in Rome in either AD 107 or 116. His letters give instructions on stopping the influence of the gnostics, who are clearly still inside the churches. His primary emphasis is that nothing should be done apart from the bishop of each church, which

---

[30] The history of gnosticism is complicated, but the points outlined here are not controversial. Both supporters and opponents agree these things are basic to gnosticism. Irenaeus, Tertullian, and Hippolytus, writing between AD 185 and 230, have thorough descriptions of many branches of gnosticism. I've compared gnostic writings such as the *Gospel of Mary Magdalene*, which is mildly gnostic, and the *Apocryphon of John* and the *Pistis Sophia*, both thoroughly gnostic writings, and they verify that the description of Irenaeus and the others is accurate.

[31] Irenaeus, *Against Heresies* I:18:1

makes his letters noticeably unique—and a bit shocking to Protestants—among the very early Christian writings.

Ignatius' letters, however, are the last reference to gnostics *in* the church. Numerous apologies [i.e., defenses of Christianity] are directed at gnostic schools *outside* the church in the late second and early third centuries.[32] Apparently, Ignatius' pleas had been heard, and the gnostics found no more room in the churches.

After Hippolytus *Refutation of All Heresies* in AD 225, almost nothing is heard of the gnostics from Christian circles. There are no more apologies directed against them, and they are never mentioned in the years surrounding Nicea.

As mentioned in the introduction, Dan Brown's *Da Vinci Code* claims that the Council of Nicea threw out numerous gnostic books in favor of books that claimed that Jesus was God. As we shall see throughout our narrative, the early Christians never doubted the divinity of Jesus Christ, and they spoke about it both often and in depth.[33]

Gnostics did deny the divinity of Jesus, and they even denied that he was actually the Christ. Instead, they taught that Christ was an aeon that rested upon the man Jesus during his lifetime. The gnostics, however, were out of the churches by the mid-second century, and they were no longer a threat by the mid-third century.

The Trail of Blood

The second myth that we must refute here is the allegation that there were free churches, separate from the catholic and apostolic churches,[34] which held beliefs closer to modern Protestant beliefs; especially salvation by faith alone, sacraments that are purely

---

[32] The most well-known are Irenaeus' *Against Heresies* (c. 185), Tertullian's *Prescription Against Heretics* (c. 210), and Hippolytus' *Refutation of All Heresies* (c. 225)

[33] See especially chapters 16 and 17.

[34] "Catholic" originally just meant universal. See Chapter 15 for a description of what the "holy, catholic, and apostolic" church was to Nicene and pre-Nicene Christians.

symbolic (primarily baptism and the Lord's Supper), and clergy with less authority.

In 1931, Baptist minister Dr. James Milton Carroll published a booklet called *The Trail of Blood*. It attempted to trace the history of the Baptists all the way back to the apostles through numerous Christian groups that existed outside of the catholic churches.

E.H. Broadbent published a much more comprehensive book with a similar idea the same year, titled *The Pilgrim Church*. The problem is, their information is not accurate.

Other than the gnostics, whose beliefs were nothing like anything we know as Christianity and who were indeed driven out by apostolic Christians, there was very little division in the early churches. Pre-Nicene Christians loved to point to the unity of the churches as evidence of their divine origin and faithful adherence to apostolic teaching.

There were two notable divisions, both cited in *The Pilgrim Church*, in pre-Nicene Christianity. There was nothing Protestant about them, however, except their separation from the catholic churches. In all the categories mentioned above—salvation, the sacraments, and the role of the clergy—their beliefs were exactly similar to the catholic churches.

The Montanists

About 156, a man by the name of Montanus claimed to be a prophet in Phrygia. One of the churches there judged his prophecies to be false. He refused to repent, so they allowed him to appeal to other churches, but they, too, judged him a false prophet. Montanus still refused to repent and with two women who claimed to be prophetesses, Maximilla and Prisca, he started his own movement.

We are fortunate that one of the most prolific of the early Christian writers, Tertullian, joined the Montanist movement, at least for a time. We have writings from both his time as a catholic and his time as a Montanist. Thus, we have great source for the differences between the Montanists and the apostolic churches.

The Montanists were much stricter than catholic churches. A person who committed a major sin after baptism, such as adultery or murder, could not be readmitted to fellowship. They could repent, but only God could forgive such a person. The church could not.

Further, they believed that the Holy Spirit had only temporarily allowed Christians to remarry after a spouse died. Like the temporary allowance for divorce under the old covenant because of the hardness of the human heart (Matt. 19:7-8), the Holy Spirit had granted the church time to grow up and become more holy. Now, during the last half of the second century when Montanus was prophesying, all Christians were expected to remain unmarried if a wife or husband died.

Otherwise, the Montanists held to all the same doctrinal views as the catholic churches.

The Novatians

The second, and only other, major division in the pre-Nicene churches came from an elder named Novatian. After one particular persecution in the mid-third century, the Roman church readmitted certain Christians that had sacrificed to the Roman gods during the persecution. Novatian objected.

The timing of Novatian's objection needs to be considered. Novatian's objections came out after Fabian, bishop of Rome, was martyred in AD 250. Novatian objected to not being appointed in Fabian's place, and he found other bishops in the area to consecrate him in the place of Cornelius, Fabian's legitimately appointed successor. His ordination was not recognized as lawful by anyone, and so Novatian's church became a separate movement.

The Novatianist movement thrived. Like the Montanists, however, it had only that one major difference with the Catholic churches. They refused to readmit a Christian that had lapsed during persecution even if he repented. Also like the Montanists, they refused to readmit Christians who had committed a major sin after baptism.

The story is told of a Novatian bishop who was invited to the Council of Nicea. The emperor Constantine asked the bishop, whose name was Acesius, why the Novatians remained separate from the catholic churches since they were in agreement on the issues addressed at Nicea. When told of Novatian opinions, the emperor remarked, "Place a ladder, Acesius, and climb to heaven alone."[35]

The Novatians remained so theologically aligned with the catholic churches that at the Council of Nicea it was determined that if a Novatian bishop repented and returned to the catholics, he would be allowed to keep his office.[36]

Novatians were also known as the *Cathari*, the Greek word for "pure," though they are not to be confused with the Cathars of later medieval history, who were descendants of the mostly Zoroastrian heresy known as the Manichaeans.

Nicene Era Heresies

The debates over the Council of Nicea would spawn several other heretical groups, such as the Macedonians and the Eunomians.[37] Their most outstanding feature was that they opposed the Council of Nicea and specifically the term *homoousios* ("one in substance") that was inserted in the Nicene Creed. The Macedonians were also known as *pneumatomachi*, or "enemies of the Spirit," because they denied that the Holy Spirit was a person.

Such heresies will be discussed more in Chapters 8 and 9. I believe it is fair to say that they were spawned more because of personalities and the desire for power than for any real doctrinal convictions.

The Great Persecution

In AD 303, the emperor Diocletian—spurred on by his general Galerius who would succeed him as emperor in 305—ordered an empire-wide persecution to be carried out against the Christians.

---

[35] *Ecclesiastical History of Socrates Scholasticus*. I:10.

[36] Canon 8. See Chapter 7.

[37] The glossary, Appendix A, has descriptions of the Macedonians and Eunomians as well as the other groups mentioned in this chapter.

That persecution became known as the Great Persecution, and it lasted until 311.

Rome was ruled by four emperors at the time: one Augustus and one Caesar each in the west and in the east. It is difficult to determine how much the other emperors enforced the edict, especially in the west. What we do know is that extensive persecution did occur in the east, most church buildings were destroyed, and many bishops were tortured and killed.

In AD 311 Galerius gave up his attempt to end Christianity, and he issued the Edict of Toleration, ending the persecution. That same year he died of a horrible illness that Christians universally attributed to the judgment of God.

A year later, in the west, the emperor Constantine had his famous vision of a cross with the words, "In this sign, conquer," written under it. He emblazoned the symbol he had seen, a combination of the Greek letters X and P—*chi* and *rho*, the first two letters of "Christ" in Greek—on his soldiers' shields, and marched into battle to defeat his western co-emperor, Maxentius.

The eastern Augustus, Licinius, had appointed Maximinus as Caesar after Galerius' death. Maximinus soon tried to overthrow Licinius, but he was defeated and deposed. Licinius then defeated Maximinus in civil war. In 313 he issued the Edict of Milan together with Constantine, making Christianity a legal religion and ordering the restoration of all possessions and buildings taken from the Christians.

This symbol Constantine saw is called a *labarum*.

Courtesy of Wikimedia Commons. Public Doman image.[30]

From then on, Constantine became known as a supporter of the Christians and a Christian himself.[39] A decade later, in 324, when Licinius began persecuting Christians again, Constantine seized the opportunity to overthrow him, put him to death, and became sole ruler of the Roman empire.

Upon his return from victory over Licinius, he was stunned to find the religion he had so avidly supported on the brink of tearing his empire in half.

---

[38] Jastrow. Wikimedia Commons. Accessed 8 Apr. 2011. <http://commons.wikimedia.org/wiki/File:Chi_Rho_Montrejeau_MNMA_Cl22 392.jpg>.
[39] Whether Constantine was really a Christian is discussed in Chapter 14.

Chapter 4:
The Council of Nicea

In AD 324, Constantine I, the emperor of the western Roman empire, defeated Licinius, emperor in the east, and put him to death, bringing the vast Roman empire under his sole rule.

When he returned from his triumph, he was horrified to find that the religion he had supported and embraced—the religion into which he had led the majority of his subjects—was on the brink of tearing his newly united empire in half.

The Arian Controversy

Around AD 318, Arius, an elder in Alexandria in Egypt, told his bishop, Alexander, that he believed that Jesus was created from nothing and had no existence prior to being created.

By the fifth century, his words had become infamous. Theodoret says:

> Arius, in direct opposition to the truth, affirmed that the Son of God is merely a creature or created being, adding the famous dictum, "There once was a time when he was

not," with other opinions which may be learned from his own writings.[40]

Alexander immediately took offense, and a controversy raged between Arius and Alexander that continued for several years. Alexander, despite urgings from other elders and surrounding bishops, took no punitive measures toward Arius at first. Finally, in 321, he gathered more than 100 bishops from Egypt and surrounding countries and excommunicated him.

Icon[41] of Arius

Wikimedia Commons. Public Domain.[42]

Arius, however, was not moved. He went north to Nicomedia, where he found a sympathetic ear in Eusebius, the bishop of Nicomedia.

---

[40] *Ecclesiastical History of Theodoret*. I:2. Several of Arius' letters can be found in Appendix D.

[41] An icon is a religious image used as a focal point for worship primarily by the Orthodox Churches. The Orthodox are the descendants of the eastern catholic churches, which will be explained further in Chapter 8. Personally, I have some strong opinions about the use of icons in worship, but that is not pertinent to this book.

[42] Unknown author. Wikimedia Commons. Accessed 24 Mar. 2011. <http://commons.wikimedia.org/wiki/File:Arius.gif>.

Nicomedia, in modern Turkey, held the imperial court, making it one of the more important cities in the empire. As a result, Eusebius was one of the most influential bishops in the east.

> At this time, Eusebius possessed great influence because the emperor resided at Nicomedia. ... On this account, therefore, many of the bishops attended Eusebius' court.[43]

While Eusebius convinced bishops, Arius taught his doctrine to merchants and to children in the marketplace.

> Confusion prevailed everywhere. One could see not only the prelates of the churches engaged in debates, but the people divided as well, some siding with one party and some with the other. This affair was carried out to so disgraceful an extent that Christianity became the subject of popular ridicule, even in the theaters.[44]

Eusebius and Eusebius

It's important not to confuse Eusebius of Nicomedia with Eusebius Pamphilus, bishop of Caesarea, who wrote a church history in 323, just two years before the Council of Nicea.

Both Eusebiuses would play crucial roles at the council. The bishop of Nicomedia led the Arian faction and was exiled for a short time for refusing to subscribe to the condemnation of Arius. The bishop of Caesarea recorded the proceedings and provided the "rule of faith" that was adapted to become the Nicene Creed.

Apparently, Eusebius and Arius were convincing because the controversy spread so widely that the emperor Constantine the Great feared that it would split his empire.

> The partisans of Arius deemed it prudent to seek the favor of bishops of other cities and sent legations to them. They also sent a written statement of their doctrines to

---

[43] *Ecclesiastical History of Socrates Scholasticus.* I:6.
[44] *ibid.*

them, requesting of them that if they considered such sentiments to be of God, they would indicate to Alexander that he should not trouble them. ... This precaution was of no small advantage to them, for their tenets became universally disseminated, and the questions they had started became matters of debate among all the bishops.[45]

Constantine the Great Intervenes

Constantine had just united his empire by overthrowing and executing Licinius, his co-emperor in the east. He was not about to let the empire be torn apart by a dispute among Christians.

> Finding, then, that the whole of Africa was pervaded by an intolerable spirit of mad folly, through the influence of those who ... had presumed to rend the religion of the people into diverse sects; I was anxious to check this disorder ... For while the people of God, whose fellow-servant I am, are thus divided amongst themselves by an unreasonable and pernicious spirit of contention, how is it possible that I shall be able to maintain tranquility of mind?[46]

First, he wrote a letter and sent it by the hand of the aged and respect bishop of Cordova in Spain, Hosius. The letter, which Eusebius says was delivered by Hosius in person, asked both Alexander and Arius to stop their feuding over the matter. Constantine argues that the issue was not of enough consequence to divide the church:

> Exhibit, both of you, an equal degree of forbearance. ... It was wrong in the first instance to propose such questions as these, or to reply to them in the second instance.[47]

---

[45] *Ecclesiastical History of Sozomen.* I:15.
[46] "Constantine's letter to Alexander the Bishop and Arius the Presbyter." Eusebius. *Life of Constantine.* II:66,72. Appendix E contains the entire letter.
[47] *ibid.* II:69.

THE COUNCIL OF NICEA

He even appeals to the unity of the philosophers in order to check the division of the church:

> You know that philosophers, though they all adhere to one system, are yet frequently at issue on certain points, and differ, perhaps, in their degree of knowledge. Yet they are recalled to harmony of sentiment by the uniting power of their common doctrines. If this be true, is it not far more reasonable that you, who are the ministers of the Supreme God, should be of one mind respecting the profession of the same religion?[48]

Though he asks them to drop it, he acknowledges that Arius' position is clearly in the wrong:

> You, Arius, inconsiderately insisted on what ought never to have been conceived at all, or, if conceived, should have been buried in profound silence.[49]

Neither Alexander nor Arius backed down.

Here it would be good to pause and consider whether Constantine's assertion—and the bishop Hosius' opinion, for he delivered the letter—is accurate. Should this issue just have been dropped? Was it of such importance that the church couldn't just let each church or church leader make their own personal decision on the matter? Was Arius even wrong? Or is it possible he was the one adhering to the apostolic faith?

And if he was wrong, how do we know?

In order to answer those questions, we need to examine first what exactly he taught.

What Was Arianism?

It is commonly said that the Council of Nicea was called to determine whether Jesus was God.

---

[48] *ibid.*
[49] *ibid.*

If we had only one sentence to describe Nicea, and if we were speaking with people who knew nothing at all about the council, then that description would be close enough. Arius denied that Jesus was God, and this did not agree with the historical position of the church.

But if we really want to understand Nicea, then that description will not suffice.

It would be more accurate to say that the Council of Nicea met to determine *what the Son of God was made of*.

Was the Son of God "Made"?

Why would Arius suggest that the Son of God was created? Was he simply a loose cannon dreaming up new doctrines?

Worse, was he really able to convince bishops all over the eastern half of the Roman empire—men who outranked him in the ecclesiastical hierarchy—that Jesus was created on the basis of nothing more than his persuasive reasoning?

Far from it. Arius got his idea from Scripture.

In the early centuries of the church, including the fourth century when the Council of Nicea was held, it seemed obvious to the churches that Proverbs 8:22-31 was a reference to the Son of God. There, Wisdom speaks as a person, and it makes statements like these:

- Before the mountains were settled, before the hills, I was brought forth. (v. 25)
- When [God] prepared the heavens, I was there. (v. 27)
- When he established the foundations of the earth, then I was next to him ... rejoicing in the habitable parts of the earth, and my delight was in the sons of men. (vv. 29-31)

Who is this Being that was with God before anything was created? Who established the foundations of the earth with him?

The answer to that question is given in the Gospel of John.

In the beginning was the Word, and the Word was with God, and the Word was God ... And the Word became flesh, and dwelt among us. (Jn. 1:1,14, NASB)

It seemed readily apparent to the early Christians that Wisdom of Proverbs 8 was the Word of John 1. Jesus, the Word and Son of God, was with God in the beginning.

But Proverbs 8 also has an interesting and surprising statement in it; one that would provide the impetus for Arius' radical idea.

We have to remember that the Christians in the eastern half of the Roman empire still spoke Greek. They did not read the old covenant Scriptures in their original Hebrew. They read a Greek translation of the Hebrew Scriptures called the Septuagint (LXX for short) that many of them believed to be inspired.

In the LXX Proverbs 8:22 reads like this:

> The Lord created me the beginning of his ways for his works.

In Arius' mind, if Christians were going to quote Proverbs 8 as applying to Jesus, then Jesus was created. And if he was created, then he must have had a beginning.

Isn't Wisdom a She?

If you read Proverbs, you will see that when Wisdom is personified, it is personified as a woman. There's a simple reason for this.

In almost every western language, except English, all words have gender, not just living things. In German, for example, my table is masculine, my house is neuter, and its walls are feminine. In Spanish, my dinner table is feminine.

Gender applies to pronouns, too. If I hang a picture on my wall in German, I am hanging it on her. If I pour coffee, I am pouring him, not it.

Wisdom is feminine in both Hebrew and Greek. Thus, it could only be personified as a woman, and it had to be referred to as she. Such terminology, a matter of grammar only, did not stop early Christians from applying Proverbs 8 to Christ often and consistently both before and after the Council of Nicea.

In the Beginning

Surprisingly enough, at least to modern Christians, Arius' contemporaries did not object as much to Arius' use of the word "created," as they did to the conclusions he drew from it. They couldn't really object to "created" because they agreed that Proverbs 8:22 was a reference to the Son of God.[50]

Their main objection was to Arius' conclusion. Arius reasoned that if the Scriptures say that the Son of God was created, then he must have had a beginning. And before that beginning, he did not exist.

> We say, believe, have taught, and do teach that the Son ... subsisted before time and before ages as perfect God, only-begotten and unchangeable, and that before he was begotten or created or purposed or established he did not exist. ... We are persecuted because we say that the Son has a beginning, but that God was without beginning. ... We say this because he is neither part of God nor part of his essential being.[51]

As you can see, Arius didn't object to calling Jesus God, nor did he care whether the term "created" was used or not. He was fine with "begotten or created or purposed or established." No matter what you called it, Arius was convinced that the Son did not exist prior to this happening.

And it was to this that orthodox Christians objected.

> Although it is once said in Scripture, "The Lord created me the beginning of his ways on account of his works" [*Prov. 8:22*] yet it would do us well to consider the meaning of the phrase and not ... jeopardize the most important doctrine of the church from a single passage! ... For although [the Scripture] says that he was created, it is not as if he were saying that he had arrived at existence from

---

[50] See Chapter 15.
[51] "Letter of Arius to Eusebius, Bishop of Nicomedia." *Ecclesiastical History of Theodoret.* I:4.

what did not exist, nor that he was made of nothing like the rest of the creatures.[52]

Here Eusebius of Caesarea acknowledges that the Scripture uses the term "created" in reference to the Son (though only once), but he objects to the idea that it means that the Son was made from nothing like all other creatures.

So what did the word "created" imply?

Alexander, the bishop who excommunicated Arius, explains it like this:

> How can he be the only-begotten if he is reckoned among the created things? And how could he have had his existence from non-entities, since the Father has said, "My heart has emitted a good Word" [*Ps. 45:1, LXX*], and, "I begat you out of my bosom before the dawn"? [*Ps. 110:3, LXX*].[53]

I have been careful to include these citations from the bishops who led the condemnation of Arius because the real subject of Nicea is so unfamiliar to modern Christians. It is difficult, if not impossible, to find a thorough explanation of the real dissension between Arius and the orthodox bishops in language that is understandable to laymen.

Having cited these two bishops, however, I will leave a more thorough proof and explanation of the real controversy and the orthodox view of the Trinity to chapters 16 and 17. Here I will give you a brief and, hopefully, easily understandable version of the real issue.

---

[52] Eusebius. *Against Marcellus* as cited by *The Ecclesiastical History of Socrates Scholasticus*. II:21.

[53] "The Epistle of Alexander, Bishop of Alexandria." *The Ecclesiastical History of Socrates Scholasticus*. I:6.

What Was Jesus *Made of?*

What an odd question! Who has ever conceived of such a question?

Every bishop at the Council of Nicea conceived of and discussed that question.

Arius—and at the council itself, Eusebius of Nicomedia—claimed that the Son of God was made from nothing. If that is true, then whatever "substance" that the Son consists of is a created substance.

Our earth and our bodies are made from atoms that did not exist prior to the creation. Even the angels and our own human souls did not exist prior to the creation. The Arians were arguing that, like us, Jesus was originally formed from nothing, and he was therefore made from some sort of created substance.

To those familiar with the teaching of the churches, the faith that they believed was given to them by the apostles, this was a horrifying thought. Created substances are by their nature not eternal. They had a beginning, and any substance with a beginning can also have an end.

> [We] teach that matter is one thing and God another and that they are separated by a wide interval. For the Deity is uncreated and eternal ... while matter is created and perishable.[54]

If Jesus consisted of some created substance, then he was not eternal ... and he was therefore not divine.

Rejecting this, the Council of Nicea argued that the Son was created from an uncreated substance—the *substance of God.*

The Substance of God

In the quote from Alexander above, you will notice that Alexander quotes two passages from the LXX that read like this:

---

[54] Athenagoras. *A Plea for the Christians.* 4. AD 177.

- My heart has emitted a good Word. (Ps. 45:1)

- I begat you out of my bosom before the dawn. (Ps. 110:3)

Alexander was not making new use of these verses. They are quoted extensively by Christians long before Nicea.[55]

To those early Christians, Jesus was *literally* the Word of God. Before the beginning he had been inside of God, and then, prior to the creation, he was "emitted" from the Father's heart, or, as Psalm 110:3 puts it, he was begotten out of the Father's bosom.

Athenagoras, whom we quoted earlier and who wrote some 150 years before the Council of Nicea, explains:

> He is the first product of the Father, not as though he was being brought into existence, for from the beginning God ... had the Word in himself.[56]

We are even fortunate enough to have a comment on this matter from Theophilus, the seventh bishop of Antioch, which was the apostle Paul's home church!

> When God wished to make all that he determined, he begot this Word ... the firstborn of all Creation [*Col. 1:15*] ... This is what the holy Scriptures teach us, as well as all the Spirit-bearing men, one of whom, [the apostle] John says, "In the beginning was the Word, and the Word was with God" [*Jn. 1:1*], showing that **at first God was alone, and the Word was in him**.[57]

In this way the Christians prior to and at Nicea argued that the Son of God was not created from nothing; instead, he was begotten from the uncreated substance of God.

He did not have a beginning; he had always existed *inside of God* as God's Word.

This is why the Council of Nicea worded its creed so carefully:

---

[55] Numerous citations are given in Chapter 15.

[56] *A Plea for the Christians.* 10.

[57] *To Autolycus.* II:22. c. AD 168. Emphasis added.

> We believe in one God, the Father Almighty ... and in one Lord, Jesus Christ, the Son of God, the only-begotten of the Father, that is, *of the substance of the Father*, God from God, Light from Light, true God from true God; begotten, not made, *one in substance with the Father* ...
>
> But the holy catholic hand apostolic church anathematizes those who say, "There was a time when he did not exist," and, "He did not exist before he was begotten," and, "He was made from what did not exist," and those who assert that he is of some other substance or essence than the Father, that he was created, or is susceptible to changing.[58]

The council actually put the comment about the substance of the Father in their creed *twice*. And if anyone still missed the point, they included very specific condemnations, known as *anathemas*, at the end. In those anathemas, for the third time in a creed of only 188 words, they included the word "substance."

The issue was not as simple as "Is Jesus God?" Note in the quote above that the Nicene Creed nowhere directly calls Jesus God. The council did focus on his *divinity*, but the terminology, calling Jesus "God," they did not think to bring up.

He is the Word of God, made from the substance of God, and thus he is "God from God ... true God from true God." The council was satisfied, however, with stating that the one God is the Father Almighty. He has a Son—begotten from his own substance and not created from nothing—but the Father alone is called the one God in the Nicene Creed.

> Do not let anyone think it is ridiculous that God should have a Son ... The Son of God is the Word of the Father.[59]

---

[58] Appendix G. Emphasis mine.
[59] Athenagoras. *A Plea for the Christians*. 10. AD 177.

Two Gods?

If the Father is the one God, and yet the one God has a divine Son, then an obvious question arises. Doesn't that make two Gods?

In fact, that is exactly what orthodox Christians were accused of by both Jews and those who followed a heresy known as Sabellianism, which teaches that God is only one person, not three.[60]

> They are constantly throwing out against us that we are preachers of two gods and three gods.[61]

Tertullian, the author of that quote, goes on:

> I confess that I call God and his Word—the Father and the Son—two. For the root and the tree are distinctly two things, but correlatively joined; the spring and the river are also two forms, but indivisible ... Everything which proceeds from something else must necessarily be second to that from which it proceeds ... Nothing, however, is foreign to that original source from which it derives its own properties. Similarly, the Trinity, flowing down from the Father through intertwined and connected steps, does not at all disturb the Monarchy [*i.e., the single/one rule or reign of God*].[62]

Finally, after using such illustrations to explain the unity of the Father and the Son, he explains why it is the Father that is called the one God. This explanation is from long before Nicea, but it is apparent that the bishops at Nicea knew this teaching because they followed it in their creed.

---

[60] In this view, the one God "acts out" the roles of Father, Son, and Holy Spirit like an actor might play three roles in a play. It was also called *patripassianism*, because mainstream Christians said Sabellianism taught that the Father suffered. Today it is more commonly called modalism.

[61] Tertullian. *Against Praxeas*. 3. c. AD 210.

[62] *ibid.* 8.

Inasmuch as this Son is undivided and inseparable from the Father, so he is reckoned to be in the Father, even when he is not named. ... He is the only God, but in company with his Son, with whom "he stretches out the heavens alone" [*Is. 44:24*].[63]

All of this will be explained more carefully in chapters 16 and 17. There we will also look at exactly ***when*** pre-Nicene and Nicene Christians referred to Jesus as God ... and when they did not.

First, though, we now understand the issue addressed at Nicea well enough to go on with our story.

The Council of Nicea

Neither Constantine's letter[64] nor the intervention of Hosius, bishop of Cordova in Spain, was enough to get Alexander or Arius to back down.

The evil had become too strong both for the exhortations of the emperor and the authority of him who was the bearer of his letter, for neither Alexander nor Arius were softened by this appeal. In addition, there was incessant strife and tumult among the people.[65]

When Constantine saw that diplomacy had failed, he exerted some imperial muscle. He called all the bishops of the empire to the resort town of Nicea, south of the Black Sea and just east of the Sea of Marmara.

Nor was this merely the issuing of a bare command but the emperor's goodwill contributed much to its being carried into effect. For he allowed some the use of the public means of conveyance, while he afforded to others an ample supply of horses for their transport.[66]

---

[63] *ibid.* 18.

[64] Appendix E.

[65] *Ecclesiastical History of Socrates Scholasticus.* I:8.

[66] Eusebius. *Life of Constantine.* III:6.

Thus began what may well be the most influential event in the history of Christianity.

Constantine's on Humility in Doctrine

Constantine may or may not have been a humble man himself, and I'm not sure his advice applies to a doctrine as central as the divinity of the Son of God, but Constantine's plea to Alexander and Arius for humility seems profound to me:

> For how very few are there able either accurately to comprehend or adequately to explain subjects so sublime and complex in their nature? Or, granting that one were fully competent for this, how many people will he convince? Or who ... in dealing with questions of such subtlety as these, can secure himself against a dangerous degradation of the truth?

> It is therefore incumbent on us in these cases to be sparing of our words. We may find that we ourselves are unable, through the feebleness of our natural faculties, to give a clear explanation of the subject before us. Or, on the other hand, we may find that the slowness of our hearers' understandings disables them from arriving at an accurate apprehension of what we say.

> By one or the other of these causes the people may be reduced to the alternative either of blasphemy or schism.

Why Was Arian Influence So Widespread?

The rapid spread of Arian doctrine, especially when it has so little support in Pre-Nicene Christian tradition, is, on the surface, surprising.

There are three reasons that their influence would be so strong.

1. Arianism Was Not as Heretical to Pre-Nicene Christians as It Is to Us

The first and simplest is that Arianism was not such a great departure from early Christian doctrine that it would arouse great opposition. Remember, Arius received no discipline for his views for around 3 years, despite the fact that he was an elder, leading a portion of the church in Alexandria under a bishop with whom there was a lot of animosity.

As explained above, the idea that the Son was created was not in and of itself heretical or even unorthodox. To the Pre-Nicene mind, it was *scriptural*, being stated in those terms in Proverbs 8:22. The difference between Arianism and orthodoxy was that orthodox Pre-Nicene belief specified that before his "creation"—better described as his birth or generation—he already existed inside of God as God's Word. Arius did not allow this, saying that the generation of the Son marked his beginning, before which he did not exist at all.

On the other hand, Arius affirmed most important Pre-Nicene terms. He agreed that the Son was the Word and Wisdom of God; he affirmed that the Son was not like other creatures; and he was willing to, and often did, refer to the Son as God.

In the end, though, his defense of the statement, "There was a time when the Son was not," is what would get him exiled. The phrase was specifically anathematized in the Nicene Creed.

> We are persecuted because we say that the Son has a be-
> ginning, but that God is without beginning ... and like-
> wise because he said he is of the non-existent.[67]

2. The School of Lucian

The second reason that Arianism was able to spread so widely is that Arian doctrine was not the invention of Arius.

Lucian of Antioch was an elder who is known to have led a theological school at Antioch in the late third century. It is very likely that he trained many of the leading proponents of Arianism, including Eusebius of Nicomedia and Theognis of Nicea, two men who were exiled for refusing to assent to the condemnation of Arius. He also taught Arius himself. Eusebius of Caesarea, the histo-

---

[67] "The Letter of Arius to Eusebius, Bishop of Nicomedia." *The Ecclesiastical History of Theodoret.* I:4. Given in full in Appendix D.

rian, speaks of him in the most glowing terms, saying he was "a most excellent man in every respect, temperate in life and famed for his learning in sacred things."[68]

Sources agree that despite his admirable manner of life and despite **probably** not holding to the doctrines of Paul of Samosata (who taught that Jesus was merely an exalted man), he and his school were excommunicated for at least 17 years, and probably more, before being restored. Finally, in 311 or 312 he was martyred at the very end of the Great Persecution.

Despite such important influence, we know almost nothing else about him, not even what he taught!

The *Catholic Encyclopedia* says:

> In the minds of practically all writers ... he has the unenviable reputation of being the real author of the opinions which afterwards found expression in the heresy of Arius."[69]

Philip Schaff, editor of *The Nicene and Post-Nicene Fathers*, writes:

> He was held in the highest reverence by his disciples and exerted a great influence over them even after his death. Among them were such men as Arius, Eusebius of Nicomedia, Asterius, and others who were afterward known as staunch Arianists.[70]

Again, despite all this, no one can say with any certainty what he taught. Schaff, in writing his "Prolegomena" to *The Ecclesiastical History of Eusebius* says that Lucian taught "the creation of the Son, the denial of his co-eternity with the Father, and his im-

---

[68] Eusebius. *Ecclesiastical History*. IX:6:3.

[69] Healy, Patrick. "Lucian of Antioch." The *Catholic Encyclopedia*. <http://www.newadvent.org/cathen/09409a.htm>.

[70] "The Outbreak of the Arian Controversy. The Attitude of Eusebius." *The Nicene and Post-Nicene Fathers*. Series 2, Vol. I.

mutability[71] acquired by persistent progress and steadfastness."
However, he also adds that this is "according to Harnack." In *History of the Christian Church* he writes:

> The charge brought against him and his followers is that
> he denied the eternity of the Logos [*Greek for "Word"*] and
> the human soul of Christ (the Logos taking the place of
> the rational soul). Arius and the Arians speak of him as
> their teacher. ... Baronius defends his orthodoxy, other
> Catholics deny it. ... The contradictory reports are easily
> reconciled by the assumption that Lucian was a critical
> scholar with some peculiar views on the Trinity and
> Christology which were not in harmony with the later Ni-
> cene orthodoxy, but that he wiped out all stains by his he-
> roic confession and martyrdom.[72]

That testimony is a hundred years old. The *Catholic Encyclo-pedia* says:

> In his Christological system — a compromise between
> Modalism and Subordinationism — the Word, though
> Himself the Creator of all subsequent beings was a crea-
> ture, though superior to all other created things by the
> wide gulf between Creator and creature.[73]

The *Catholic Encyclopedia* gives no source for this.

The answer to all this? There is little doubt, it seems, that Lucian really did teach many of the leading proponents of Arianism.
On top of this, Arianism, to the Pre-Nicene mind, was close
enough to orthodoxy to be given credence if it were framed in the
right terms.

---

[71] Immutability means that he never changes. Schaff is saying that Lucian believed that the Son became unchangeable during his life on earth by progress in
obedience to God.

[72] *History of the Christian Church*. Vol. II, sec. 194. Parentheses original.

[73] Healy, Patrick. "Lucian of Antioch." The *Catholic Encyclopedia*. Accessed
March 8, 2011. <http://www.newadvent.org/cathen/09409a.htm>.

A very strong indication that this was so is that Arius, in a letter to Alexander during the time of his excommunication, lists Eusebius of Caesarea as a supporter. Schaff gives a long argument that Arius' claim is an accurate one, but then he sums up his argument with a very poignant statement:

> When we examine the Caesarean creed which Eusebius presented to the Council as a fair statement of his belief, we find nothing in it inconsistent with the acceptance of the kind of Arianism which he defends in his epistle to Alexander, and which he evidently supposed to be practically the Arianism of Arius himself.[74]

If Arius could convince even Eusebius of Caesarea—a devoted student of history who consistently denied that the Son had a beginning—that his doctrines were orthodox and in line with the tradition that came from the apostles, then it should not surprise us that he was also able to convince many others.

3. Sabellianism Was a More Influential and Persistent Enemy

Arianism had another advantage. It was the polar opposite of *Sabellianism*, a heresy that the church had been battling for over a century.

Sabellius, from whom Sabellianism gets its name, was an early-third-century teacher who was excommunicated for denying the three persons of the Trinity. To Sabellius, God was just one divine person revealing himself three ways, in much the same way as an actor might play three roles in a play.

Sabellianism was simpler than the apostolic version of the Trinity. As such, it was popular. Very popular.

Around AD 210, Tertullian says that *the majority* of believers were "simple" and could not understand "the order of the three in one."[75]

---

[74] "The Outbreak of the Arian Controversy. The Attitude of Eusebius." *The Nicene and Post-Nicene Fathers*. Series 2, Vol. I. Emphasis mine.
[75] *Against Praxeas*. 3.

The majority of believers in pre-Nicene Christianity had come out of paganism. They had come from a religion of many Gods to Christianity, a religion of only one God. How could this one God also have a Son? And how could this Son also be God?

Sabellianism was easy to understand. An actor can play three roles in a play and still be one person. God can reveal himself as the Father in creation, as the Son in redemption, and as the Holy Spirit in the church, yet still be one God. Simple.[76]

But just because it's easy doesn't make it true. We should not be surprised that the truth about God is somewhat difficult for humans to understand!

Nonetheless, the ease of the Sabellian doctrine made it popular, even among church leaders. Bishops and elders alike, even if they did not embrace Sabellianism, did let it influence them.

This gave Arianism a leg up.

> There was ... very good reason for laying particular stress upon the subordination of the Son over against Sabellianism, which was so widely prevalent during the third century, and which was exerting an influence even over many orthodox theologians who did not consciously accept Sabellianistic tenets.[77]

As long, then, as Arius and his supporters were careful in their wording so as not to tramp upon apostolic tradition in any obvious way, Arianism held appeal to those who opposed Sabellianism.

The combination of all three influences—the nearness of Arianism to orthodox tradition, the ground laid by the teaching of Lucian in the late third century, and Arianism's appeal as a distant

---

[76] Today Sabellianism is called modalism in scholastic circles. Several denominations, the United Pentecostal Church being the largest, still hold to it. Popularly, it is known as the "Jesus only" doctrine because modern modalists like to say, "Jesus is the Father, is the Son, and is the Holy Spirit."

[77] "The Outbreak of the Arian Controversy. The Attitude of Eusebius." *The Nicene and Post-Nicene Fathers*. Series 2, Vol. I. Emphasis mine.

alternative to Sabellianism—was apparently enough to allow Arianism to take strong root in the churches of the Roman empire.

The reasons we have just given are made more credible by the fact that Arianism found support almost exclusively in the east, where Lucian's school at Antioch would have had the most influence. Most of the times that Athanasius, the post-Nicene champion of the Nicene Creed, was banished from his home in Alexandria, he fled to the west.[78] There he found the support of the influential bishop of Rome, and council after council ruled—obviously to little effect—on his behalf.

The Arian controversy and the divide between east and west were a threat not only to the unity of the church but to the unity of the Roman empire as well.

The Arrival of the Bishops

On June 14, 325 bishops began arriving from all parts of the empire. They received a truly royal welcome.

Eusebius describes the arrival of the bishops:

> As soon ... as the imperial injunction was generally made known, every one of [the bishops] hastened there with the utmost willingness ... Now when they were all assembled, it appeared evident that the proceeding was the work of God, inasmuch as men who had been most widely separated—not merely in sentiment but also personally and by difference of country, place, and nation—were here brought together and comprised within the walls of a single city, forming as it were a vast garland of priests, composed of a variety of the choicest flowers.
>
> In effect, the most distinguished of God's ministers from all the churches which abounded in Europe, Libya, and Asia were here assembled.[79]

---

[78] See Chapter 10.

[79] The terminology here covers all of the ancient Roman empire: southern Europe, north Africa, and the Middle East, respectively.

... the number of bishops exceeded two hundred and fifty, while that of the elders and deacons ... [and] the crowd of acolytes[80] and other attendants was altogether beyond computation. Of these ministers of God, some were distinguished by wisdom and eloquence, others by the gravity of their lives and by patient fortitude of character, while others united in themselves all these graces. There were among them men whose years demanded veneration; others were younger, and in the prime of mental vigor; and some had but recently entered on the course of their ministry.

Ample provision was made daily for the maintenance of all by the emperor's command.[81]

As you can see, Eusebius, who was there, puts the number of bishops at more than 250. Later writers universally say there were 318, but there's no authority for this. Even Athanasius, who was also there but as a deacon and advisor, doesn't give 318 as a number until the end of his life. It is very likely that this figure was adopted from Genesis 14:14, where Abraham took 318 men to free his nephew Lot. The number had symbolic significance to the early Christians because its letters in Greek seemed to symbolize both Jesus' name and the cross.[82]

While it's impossible to know the exact number, a general number is not hard to determine. Theodoret preserves a passage from Eustathius, bishop of Antioch, that gives the number as "about" 270.[83] Constantine, in his letter to the church in Alexandria immediately after the council, says there were over 300.[84] Over 250 and less than 325 would be an accurate figure.

The council would continue for approximately 10 weeks, with final decisions made around August 25, 325.

---

[80] An assistant to a clergyman.

[81] Eusebius, *Life of Constantine* III:6-9

[82] *Letter of Barnabas*. 9.

[83] *ibid.* I:7.

[84] *Ecclesiastical History of Socrates Scholasticus*. I:9.

> **Mythbusting**
>
> I read on the internet recently that Sylvester, the bishop of Rome, did not show up in Nicea because he disagreed with the proceedings.
>
> This is not true. Theodoret, the fifth-century historian, agrees with Eusebius, and writes:
>
> *The bishop of Rome, on account of his advanced age, was absent, but he sent two elders to the council with authority to agree to what was done.*[85]
>
> Further, the Nicene champion Athanasius[86] would repeatedly find a home in the church at Rome during his banishments under Constantius II. In other words, neither Sylvester nor his successors ever opposed the Nicene Creed.

Debates in the Courtyard

The first few days were apparently unscheduled, and the bishops and their companions were apparently anxious to test their theological muscle:

> Many of the laity were also present, who were practiced in the art of dialectics[87] and each eager to advocate the cause of his own party. Eusebius, bishop of Nicomedia ... together with Theognis and Maris ... were powerfully opposed by Athanasius, a deacon of the Alexandrian church who was highly esteemed by Alexander his bishop ...
>
> Now a short time previous to the general assembling of the bishops, the disputants engaged in preparatory logical contests before the multitudes.[88]

---

[85] *The Ecclesiastical History of Theodoret.* I:6.

[86] More on Athanasius in Chapter 10.

[87] A form of argument meant to lead both sides to agreement rather than pronouncing one the winner over the other.

[88] *Ecclesiastical History of Socrates Scholasticus.* I:8.

I hope that you find this no better a way to find the will of God than I do. It's frightening to think that this was the atmosphere as the council began. There is nothing about this that makes it seem like the participants were ready to lay down their opinions and seek the will of God.

Fortunately, God is in more control of things than we humans typically care to believe, and he provided intervention to get things on a better keel.

> When many were attracted by their interesting discussions, one of the laity, a confessor,[89] who was a man of unsophisticated understanding, reproved these reasoners, telling them that Christ and his apostles did not teach us dialectics, art, nor useless subtleties, but simplemindedness, which is preserved by faith and good works.
>
> As he said this, all present admired the speaker and assented to the justice of his remarks, and the disputants themselves, after hearing his plain statement of the truth, exercised a greater degree of moderation.[90]

The Remainder of the Deliberations That We Know About

Here the details get a bit hazy. Eusebius, who furnishes with the only blow-by-blow account of the actual proceedings jumps straight from these debates occurring "a short time previous to the general assembling of the bishops" to "the appointed day ... on which the council met for the final solution of the questions in dispute."

A note in *The Nicene and Post-Nicene Fathers* translation of Eusebius' *Life of Constantine* suggests that this "appointed day ... for the final solution" was the last day of the council.

Personally, I find it impossible to believe that the discussions that Eusebius goes on to describe all happened in one day. I also find it hard to believe that Eusebius skipped over most of the 10

---

[89] A person who had stood for Christ during persecution.
[90] *ibid.*

weeks that the bishops and their companions were in Nicea to describe only one day of the council.

If the *Nicene and Post-Nicene Fathers* note were correct, then all the following had to happen on one day:

- Eusebius of Caesarea and the emperor each gave an opening speech.

- The emperor opened the floor to the bishops, and they broke into dispute.

- The emperor intervened, listening to each bishop carefully, and oversaw their discussion until it reached a point of peace.

- Eusebius presented the rule of faith of the church at Caesarea.

- The emperor asked for *homoousios* to be added to the creed.[91]

- The bishops talked about it and worked out the wording of the Nicene Creed.

- Eusebius of Caesarea at least, and most likely others, asked about the meaning of each phrase of the creed and "resisted the introduction of certain objectionable expressions until the last moment."

- Once the Arian dispute was resolved, the bishops took up the 200-year-old dispute between the eastern and western churches over the day on which Passover should be celebrated.

- While the time frame of the drawing up of the canons is not given anywhere, it seems safe to assume they com-

---

[91] "One in substance." The importance of the term is described briefly above and much more thoroughly in Chapters 9 and 16.

posed the canons only after the two most important issues of the council were resolved.[92]

This is not just a large amount of debating and decision-making to happen in one day; it is an impossible amount. In the fourth-century Middle East, especially in an imperial court, diplomacy and decorum would have added many words in the midst of more pertinent discussion.

It seems at least safest, and possibly necessary, to conclude that "the appointed day ... for the final solution" was the appointed day to *begin* the final solution, not the last day of the council.

The Role of *Apostolic* Tradition

We have to remember that this "resolution" of the Arian controversy was simply the council's decision and declaration. Not everyone accepted it, and the conflicts between sides would not end for 58 years.

We also have to remember that the doctrines of Arius really didn't stand a chance. These bishops—and their companions—obviously had strong opinions and liked a good debate, but the tradition of the church on the substance of the Father and Son was long-standing and unanimous.[93]

Tradition was important in the fourth century. Novelty was the ultimate theological crime. As far as Pre-Nicene Christians were concerned, elders and bishops had just one theological function: to preserve the truth that they had received from the apostles ... *unchanged*.

> The question the Fathers considered was not what they supposed Holy Scripture might mean, nor what they, from à priori arguments, thought would be consistent with the mind of God, but something entirely different, to wit, what they had received. They understood their posi-

---

[92] Canons are ecclesiastical rules. Chapter 7 has a list and explanation of the 20 canons of Nicea.

[93] See Chapter 15.

tion to be that of witnesses, not that of exegetes. They recognized but one duty resting upon them in this respect— to hand down to other faithful men that good thing the Church had received according to the command of God. The first requirement was not learning, but honesty. The question they were called upon to answer was not, What do I think probable, or even certain, from Holy Scripture? but, What have I been taught, what has been entrusted to me to hand down to others?[94]

This was not a new idea in the fourth century. Unlike today, the early churches could stand on what was handed down from the apostles. It was entirely believable that the apostles could train men to hold to the basics of the faith and that those leaders could accurately pass that faith to other leaders.

We've probably all played the telephone game, where a group at a party passes a statement or idea around a room by whispering from one person to another. It's always funny to see how different the end result is from the message that the first person passed to the second.

But in a short chain, we would not get those results. Two or three people can accurately pass a message that twenty or thirty people cannot. Over a hundred years, the beliefs of a church don't change much, especially when they know their job is to preserve their faith unchanged, and they are comparing those beliefs to those of other churches started by the apostles. When they devote themselves together to preserving the teachings of the apostles unchanged, they can succeed, at least for a time and possibly for centuries.

> We refer them to that tradition which originates from the apostles, which is preserved by means of the succession of elders in the churches ... We are in a position to reckon up those who were, by the apostles, instituted bishops in the churches and the succession of these men to our own

[94] Schaff, Philip. "The First Ecumenical Council: Historical Introduction." *The Nicene and Post-Nicene Fathers*. Series II, Vol. XIV.

times ... In this order and by this succession the ecclesiastical tradition from the apostles and the preaching of the
truth have come down to us.[95]

Since the Lord Jesus Christ sent the apostles to preach, no
others ought to be received as preachers than those whom
Christ appointed ... All doctrine which agrees with the
apostolic churches, those molds and original sources of
the faith, must be considered truth, as undoubtedly containing that which the churches received from the apostles
... whereas all doctrine must be prejudged as false which
smells of dissimilarity to the truth of the churches and
apostles of Christ and God.[96]

The job of these successors was to preserve the truth unchanged, neither adding to it nor taking away.

Earnestly contend for the faith which was once delivered
to the saints. (Jude 3)

For the faith being ever one and the same, one who is able
at great length to discourse concerning it does not make
any addition to it, nor does one who can say but little di-
minish it. It does not follow that because men are en-
dowed with greater or lesser degrees of intelligence that
they should change the content [of the faith] itself.[97]

Arius and Eusebius were very skillful at arguing their position
scripturally. We have a number of letters from them to indicate
that, and the rapid spread of Arianism makes it clear that they
seemed convincing to their contemporaries.

A certain one of the elders ... whose name was Arius, possessing no small amount of logical ingenuity ... [drew] this
inference from his novel train of reasoning.[98]

---

[95] Irenaeus. *Against Heresies*. III:2:1, III:3:1, III:3:3. c. AD 185.
[96] Tertullian. *Prescription Against Heretics*. 21. c. AD 210.
[97] Irenaeus. *Against Heresies* I:10:2-3. c. AD 185.
[98] *Ecclesiastical History of Socrates Scholasticus*. I:5.

But the very novelty of his reasoning, even if it could claim support for a few decades because of Lucian, made his position hopeless at a council of bishops that included a man like Eusebius, thoroughly familiar with the teaching of the fathers back to the beginning. Because of this, Athanasius tells us that the Arians knew they didn't have a leg to stand on:

> Eusebius [of Nicomedia] and his fellows endured indeed, as not daring to contradict, being put to shame by the arguments which were urged against them.[99]

Thus, we see that the debate at Nicea was not about whether Arius was correct. The Arian supporters, led by Eusebius of Nicomedia, did not 'dare to contradict.' The real problem facing the council was how to phrase a creed in such a way that everyone would know that Arius' doctrines were rejected by the church.

It was one thing for bishops at a council to determine that Arius teachings were novel and false. That was easy. It was quite another to frame a short, memorable creed that would allow the average Christian both to recognize Arianism and reject it as heresy.

> The almost unanimous horror of the Nicene Bishops at the novelty and profaneness of Arianism condemns it irrevocably as alien to the immemorial belief of the Churches. But it was one thing to perceive this, another to formulate the positive belief of the Church in such a way as to exclude the heresy; one thing to agree in condemning Arian formulæ, another to agree upon an adequate test of orthodoxy. This was the problem which lay before the council.[100]

---

[99] *Defense of the Nicene Definition.* 20.
[100] Schaff, Philip. "Prolegomena: Life of St. Athanasius and Account of Arianism." *The Nicene and Post-Nicene Fathers.* Series II, vol. IV.

Constantine's Role at the Council

The bishops gathered in the largest building of the palace. They sat, and slowly the assembly quieted in expectation of the arrival of the emperor.

The emperor entered. Three members of the royal family and friends who held to the Christian faith accompanied him. His soldiers were conspicuously absent. He was in full imperial dress, purple robes adorned with precious gems, so that Eusebius describes him as being "like a heavenly messenger of God." He even comments that the emperor was the tallest person in the room.

The bishops rose quietly to acknowledge his entrance, and they all stood quietly as a golden chair was brought for the emperor. As an act of humility (*that I have difficulty appreciating*), he awaited a gesture from the bishops before taking his seat. Only after the emperor sat down did the bishops follow suit.

Then "the bishop who occupied the chief place in the right division of the assembly"—almost universally believed to be Eusebius himself—rose and delivered a short speech to the emperor, primarily giving thanks to God for him.

Constantine followed Eusebius' speech with his own. The speech explained to the bishops how surprised and distressed Constantine was to find that after uniting his empire by overthrowing Lucinius, an enemy of the Christians, there was dissension in the ranks of the Christians. So he exhorted them, by the grace of God, "to discard the causes of that disunion which has existed among you."[101]

Constantine then gave permission for the bishops to give their opinions, and they immediately set about ignoring the exhortation of the emperor.

> On this some began to accuse their neighbors, who defended themselves and recriminated in their turn. In this manner numberless assertions were put forth by each par-

---

[101] The speech is given in full in Appendix F.

ty, and a violent controversy arose at the very com-
mencement.[102]

Amazingly, it was Constantine himself who had to calm the
bishops down:

> The emperor gave patient audience to all alike and re-
> ceived every proposition with steadfast attention. By oc-
> casionally assisting the argument of each party in turn, he
> gradually disposed even the most vehement disputants to
> a reconciliation. At the same time, by the affability of his
> address to all and his use of the Greek language, with
> which he was not altogether unacquainted, he appeared
> in a truly attractive and amiable light, persuading some,
> convincing others by his reasonings, praising those who
> spoke well, and urging all to unity of sentiment, until at
> last he succeeded in bringing them to one mind and
> judgment respecting every disputed question.[103]

To me, this is embarrassing, and I have to pause to discuss this
here ...

Excursus on Unity and Peaceful Harmony

I have made every effort to give you an accurate and unbiased
history of the Council of Nicea in this book, but I cannot give you
a disinterested one. I am a Christian, and the kingdom of God is
my concern. It will do you no good to know things that don't produce results in your life.

Here were nearly 300 bishops, many of whom had withstood
prison and torture on Christ's behalf, the very men who were
commissioned to carry the apostles' message down through the
generations, and these same men were parading the inability of the
leaders of Christ's church to get along in front of the onlookers at
the emperor's resort city.

The apostle Paul wrote:

---

[102] Eusebius. *Life of Constantine*. III:13.
[103] *ibid.*

Dare any of you, having a matter against another, go to law before the unjust and not before the saints? ... I speak this to your shame. (1 Cor. 6:1,5)

There have been a lot of negative things said about Constantine, by me as well as by others. But dare we blame Constantine for this state of affairs?

The unjust emperor, who had just put Licinius to death, now had to use diplomacy and kindness to settle bishops who had already needed to be called to the royal resort city in order to prevent an empire-wide church split; yet they were not embarrassed!

So, once the emperor had settled these bishops down and persuaded them with his reasonings, they were ready for a more amiable discussion of the issues.

The Nicene Creed

In his letter back to Caesarea,[104] Eusebius tells us that he presented the rule of faith[105] of the church at Caesarea to everyone in the presence of the emperor. This statement of faith, which reads as follows, received, according to Eusebius, "universal approbation."

We believe in one God, the Father Almighty, Maker of all things visible and invisible;

And in one Lord, Jesus Christ, the Word of God—God of God, Light of Light, Life of Life—the only-begotten Son, born before all creation, begotten of God the Father, before all ages, by whom also all things were made; who on account of our salvation became incarnate and lived among men; and who suffered and rose again on the third

---

[104] Appendix I.

[105] Before Nicea each church had their own "rule of faith," a short statement of beliefs learned and recited at baptism. A history of the rule of faith can be found on my website, *Christian History for Everyman*. <http://www.christian-history.org/rule-of-faith.html>.

day, ascended to the Father, and shall come again in glory to judge the living and the dead.

We believe also in one Holy Spirit.

We believe in the existence and subsistence of each of these: that the Father is truly Father, the Son truly Son, and the Holy Spirit truly Holy Spirit; even as our Lord also, when he sent forth his disciples to preach the Gospel, said, "Go and teach all nations, baptizing them in the name of the Father, and of the Son, and of the Holy Spirit.[106]

The emperor urged the bishops to consent to this, but he also pushed for the insertion of the word *homoousios.*[107]

Our most pious emperor ... exhorted all present to give [these articles of faith] their assent ... with the insertion, however, of that single word, *homoousios,* an expression which the emperor himself explained as not indicating corporeal affections or properties.[108]

What is an emperor doing caring so much about an issue of church doctrine, that he would push for something like a declaration that the Father and the Son were of one substance? Why would he be explaining to bishops that a technical term like *homoousios* doesn't indicate "corporeal affections or properties"?

It has been suggested that Hosius, an advisor to the emperor, taught the term and its importance to the emperor. It was not a new term; second and third-century Christians discussed the substance of God on a regular basis.[109] Hosius, and any other well-taught bishop, would have been familiar with the term "substance" (*ousios* in Greek).

---

[106] *The Ecclesiastical History of Socrates Scholasticus.* I:8. The entire letter is in Appendix K.

[107] "Same substance." The meaning and importance of *homoousios* are discussed in Chapters 9 and 17.

[108] *The Ecclesiastical History of Socrates Scholasticus.* I:8.

[109] Numerous citations given in Chapter 13.

Athanasius tells us that the term *homoousios*, "one in substance," was suggested during the discussions in the council because Eusebius of Nicomedia and the other Arians had come up with ways to redefine all other terminology that the council used. The intent of the Arian bishops was to agree to the Nicene terminology, then reinterpret it so that they could still hold to the belief that the Son of God had a beginning.[110]

In fact, *homoousios* proved to be the perfect word. As we shall see in Chapter 9, it was the term *homoousios* which the Arians could never swallow. They battled against it until they were finally conquered by the emperor Theodosius in AD 383.

However the term originated, Eusebius of Caesarea, the only eyewitness to this part of the proceedings that left us a report, tells us that it was Constantine who finally championed the inclusion of the term *homoousios*.

Whether it was necessary to do so even at Nicea was debated by the bishops. Eusebius makes it clear that he himself asked about the term. In fact, it does not appear that he embraced it with great enthusiasm, remarking in his letter to Caesarea that "we do not cavil" at the word *homoousios*. This is hardly rousing support.

Nonetheless, Eusebius agreed, and he says it was the bishops who convinced him, not Constantine, though he was also open because he knew *homoousios* had been used by eminent writers in the church's past.

In this way, the council agreed to the addition of *homoousios* to its creed.

Even then, *homoousios* was not enough, in the council's opinion, to completely stop Arius. So they added a section at the end specifically anathematizing statements that were in common use among the Arians.

The creed the council decided upon in AD 325 is as follows. The one quoted in churches today is slightly modified, with some

---

[110] Athanasius. *Defense of the Nicene Definition*. 19.

phrases added later in the fourth century and approved at the Council of Chalcedon in 451.[111]

> We believe in one God, the Father Almighty, Maker of all things visible and invisible;
>
> And in one Lord Jesus Christ, the Son of God, the only-begotten of the Father; that is, of the substance of the Father; God of God and Light of light; true God of true God; begotten, not made, one in substance [*homoousios*] with the Father; by whom all things were made, both which are in heaven and on earth; who for the sake of us men, and on account of our salvation, descended, became incarnate, and was made man, suffered, arose again the third day, ascended into the heavens, and will come again to judge the living and the dead.
>
> Also in the Holy Spirit.
>
> But the holy, catholic,[112] and apostolic church anathematizes those who say, "There was a time when he was not"; "He was not before he was begotten"; "He was made from that which did not exist"; and those who assert that he is of other substance or essence than the Father, that he was created, or is susceptible to change.

What the Creed Means

We are indeed fortunate to have Eusebius' letter back to Caesarea. He tells us that he "did not neglect to investigate the distinct sense of the expressions."

Here is what the bishops of Nicea told Eusebius about each phrase:

---

[111] Both versions of the creed are given in Appendix G.

[112] "Catholic" here simply means universal. It was a reference to the united churches that were descended from the apostles. "Holy, catholic, and apostolic" is explained in Chapter 15.

Begotten, Not Made

Rejecting the term "made" was something new. As pointed out above, Proverbs 8:22—in the Septuagint[113]—used the term "created," and it was universally understood to refer to the generation of the Son before the beginning. Thus, the council was rejecting wording that was used in Scripture!

"Created" was not the preferred term. By the time of the Council of Nicea Christians almost exclusively used "begotten" or "generated," not "created" or "made." Apparently the bishops thought it was worth banning the terms in order to leave no room for Arius and others who used the terms in a way that contradicted traditional understanding of the generation of the Son.

It's hard to say how important it was to ban "made." Arius didn't care what term was used. Whether the son was generated, established, or begotten, Arius still insisted he had a beginning before which he did not exist.

Nonetheless, the council banned the term, though it was not so much the word "made" that was rejected, but the Arian understanding of that word.

Eusebius asked for "the distinct sense" of the phrase, and he describes the answer he received:

> On the same grounds we admitted also the expression "begotten, not made." "For 'made,'" they said, "is a term applicable in common to all the creatures which were made by the Son, to whom the Son has no resemblance. Consequently he is no creature like those which were made by him, but is of a substance far excelling any creature. The Divine Oracles teach that this substance was be-

---

[113] The Septuagint was a Greek translation of the Hebrew Scriptures, so named because it was believed to have been translated by 70 Jewish scholars under Ptolemy, king of Egypt. It is also known as the LXX.

gotten of the Father by such a mode of generation as cannot be explained nor even conceived by any creature."[114]

There was no way anyone would disagree with this explanation. It could perhaps be argued that it was inappropriate to ban a term used in Proverbs 8:22, but even Arius would not deny the wording of the explanation that was given to Eusebius.

Homoousios, One in Substance

We will leave a more thorough discussion of *homoousios* to Chapter 15, but it's worth looking at the council's explanation of the term here.

> That he is one in substance [*homoousios*] with the Father, then, simply implies that the Son of God has no resemblance to created things but is in every respect like the Father only who begot him; that he is of no other substance or essence but of the Father. To this doctrine, explained in this way, it appeared right to assent, especially since we knew that some eminent bishops and learned writers among the ancients have used the term *homoousios* in their theological discourses concerning the nature of the Father and the Son.[115]

There's nothing new here that has not already been explained.

Anathemas

The anathemas[116] at the end of the creed are no longer recited by any churches. Arius' views disappeared from mainstream churches after the fourth century, rendering them unnecessary.

---

[114] *The Ecclesiastical History of Socrates Scholasticus.* I:8. The entire text of the letter is given in Appendix I. The verses of "the Divine Oracles" that teach that "this substance was begotten by the Father" are covered thoroughly in Chapter 15.
[115] *ibid.*
[116] Curses or condemnation

The barbarian tribes that conquered Rome and the western Roman empire in the fifth century had remained Arian, being outside of the Roman empire and out of touch with the controversy raging within. Later, however, they would embrace the Roman bishop as the primary authority in the church even as they were conquering Rome itself.

As they embraced the Nicene faith, Arianism disappeared until revived by Charles Russell and the Jehovah's Witnesses in the early 20th century.

Thus, the anathemas have served no real purpose since the end of the fourth century.

Eusebius gives no report from the council on the anathemas. Apparently, he was more open to these, and he simply explains why he embraced them:

> We have also considered the anathema pronounced by them after the declaration of faith inoffensive because it prohibits the use of illegitimate terms from which almost all the distraction and commotion of the churches have arisen. Accordingly, since no divinely-inspired Scripture contains the expressions, "of things which do not exist" and "there was a time when he was not" and the other phrases that are listed, it seemed unjustifiable to utter and teach them. In addition, this decision received our sanction all the more from the consideration that we have never before been accustomed to employ these terms.[117]

In this way, the Arian controversy was resolved, at least as far as the council was concerned.

The Paschal Controversy

Having successfully dealt with Arius, the council was ready to move on to a much older controversy.

---

[117] *ibid.*

But before this time another most virulent disorder had existed, and long afflicted the Church; I mean the difference respecting the salutary feast of Passover. For while one party asserted that the Jewish custom should be adhered to, the other affirmed that the exact recurrence of the period should be observed, without following the authority of those who were in error [*i.e., the Jews*] and strangers to gospel grace.[118]

First, though, we need to pause to discuss whether all the bishops, even those few that supported Arius, caved in and agreed with the council, whether any were excommunicated, and who those bishops might be.

---

[118] Eusebius. *Life of Constantine*. III:5.

Chapter 5:
Who Was Condemned at Nicea?

There is no doubt that Arius himself was condemned, excommunicated, and exiled at the Council of Nicea.

The question that is very difficult to answer is whether any bishops were condemned with him, and, if so, which ones.

Arius was merely an elder. He would have gotten nowhere had he not had the support of Eusebius, bishop of Nicomedia. Sozomen tells us that there were 16 other bishops supporting Arius at the beginning of the council, but "eventually the majority of these yielded assent to the general view."[119]

The question is, which ones did not?

Who Was Disciplined at Nicea?

Eusebius of Nicomedia's behavior after the council makes it clear that he remained an avid supporter of the doctrines of Arius. It is also clear, however, that at some point he repudiated the teachings of Arius to end an exile imposed upon him by Constantine.

---

[119] *Ecclesiastical History of Sozomen.* I:20.

There is an extant letter from the council back to the church in Alexandria that mentions that only two less significant bishops, Theonas of Marmarica and Secundus of Ptolemais, stood their ground on Arius' side and were excommunicated. However, there are several later testimonies that Eusebius of Nicomedia and Theognis of Nicea—the very city in which the council was held—were removed from office, but it seems extremely unlikely that this would go unmentioned in a letter to Alexandria that mentions the excommunication of two lesser bishops.

Nonetheless, even Socrates Scholasticus, who preserves the letter from the council I just mentioned, says that five bishops refused to sign the creed, and he says that it was Eusebius of Nicomedia and Theognis, the bishop of Nicea, who were exiled with Arius. He even includes their letter of recantation when they were recalled from exile.

> We having been sometime since condemned by your piety, without a formal trial, ought to bear in silence the decisions of your sacred adjudication. But since it is unreasonable that we by silence should countenance calumniators against ourselves, we on this account declare that we entirely concur with you in the faith; and also that, after having closely considered the import of the term consubstantial [*homoousios*], we have been wholly studious of peace, having never followed the heresy.[120]

It's also important to note that we are told that Eusebius (of Nicomedia) and Theognis were condemned only after refusing to agree with the condemnation of Arius, which they did because they disagreed that Arius held the opinions assigned to him. (This is incorrect; see Arius' letters in Appendix D.)

> We subscribed the declaration of faith; we did not subscribe the anathematizing; not as objecting to the creed, but as disbelieving the party accused to be such as was represented, having been satisfied on this point, both

---

[120] *Ecclesiastical History of Socrates Scholasticus.* I:14.

from his own letters to us, and from personal conversations.[121]

What should we conclude?

Most historians today seem to believe that Eusebius of Nicomedia and Theognis were exiled a few months after the council for maintaining contact with Arius, Theonis, and Secundus, who were exiled at the council. Eusebius and Theognis were then recalled in AD 328. Their letter of recantation also mentions the recall of Arius, which also happened that year, although Athanasius managed to see to it that Arius was unable to reach Alexandria until near the time of his death in 336.

There is no way to determine whether Maris of Chalcedon was ever actually exiled as Socrates Scholasticus claims.

Other Testimonies

All the testimonies conflict. No two agree on who was condemned at Nicea. Again, it seems to me that the most reliable testimony will be the letter from the council itself, but here is a list of what else we have to work with.

Eusebius Pamphilus of Caesarea

Eusebius of Caesarea says the creed received "the signature of every member." He doesn't mention anyone being exiled.[122] (*Life of Constantine* III:14).

Eusebius was at the council and was a major player in the discussions, so his testimony carries weight. Nonetheless, his description of the council is in *Life of Constantine*, not in his church history, so there was no reason for him to be terribly specific about anything except the emperor's role in the council. His emphasis is that the emperor was extremely gracious in bringing the bishops to a unanimous decision. The fact that they had to expel

---

[121] *ibid.*

[122] *Life of Constantine*. III:14.

Arius and two, four, or five of his supporters in order to obtain that unanimity would not have been required to be mentioned.

Letter of the Council of Nicea to Alexandria

Their letter is preserved in *The Ecclesiastical History of Socrates Scholasticus* I:9. It states:

> So contagious has his pestilential error proved, as to drag into perdition Theonas, bishop of Marmarica, and Secundus of Ptolemais; for they have suffered the same condemnation as [Arius].

Letter of Recantation from Eusebius of Nicomedia and Theognis of Nicea

Some of this was quoted above. It is preserved in *Ecclesiastical History of Socrates Scholasticus* I:14:

> We having been sometime since condemned by your piety, without a formal trial, ought to bear in silence the decisions of your sacred adjudication. But since it is unreasonable that we by silence should countenance calumniators against ourselves, we on this account declare that we entirely concur with you in the faith; and also that, after having closely considered the import of the term consubstantial [*homoousios*], we have been wholly studious of peace, having never followed the heresy.
>
> After suggesting whatever entered our thought for the security of the churches, and fully assuring those under our influence, we subscribed the declaration of faith; we did not subscribe the anathematizing; not as objecting to the creed, but as disbelieving the party accused to be such as was represented, having been satisfied on this point, both from his own letters to us, and from personal conversations.
>
> But if your holy council was convinced, we, not opposing but concurring in your decisions, by this statement give them our full assent and confirmation: and this we do not as wearied with our exile, but to shake off the suspicion of heresy.

> If therefore ye should now think fit to restore us to your presence, you will have us on all points conformable and acquiescent in your decrees: especially since it has seemed good to your piety to deal tenderly with and recall even him who was primarily accused. It would be absurd for us to be silent, and thus give presumptive evidence against ourselves, when the one who seemed responsible has been permitted to clear himself from the charges brought against him. Vouchsafe then, as is consistent with that Christ-loving piety of yours, to remind our most religious emperor, to present our petitions, and to determine speedily concerning us in a way becoming yourselves.

This letter, as pointed out above, mentions the recall of Arius, which must also have happened in 328, though Arius' letter of recantation wasn't written until 335, and he wasn't officially reinstated until the council of Jerusalem in 336.

As said above, most historians seem to believe Eusebius and Theognis were exiled shortly after Nicea, which would be why the letter from the council to Alexandria doesn't mention their discipline.

Socrates Scholasticus

Socrates says that five of the bishops "would not receive [the Nicene Creed], objecting to the term *homoousios*."[123] Those five are:

- Eusebius of Nicomedia
- Theognis of Nicea
- Maris of Chalcedon
- Theonis of Marmarica
- Secundus of Ptolemais

---

[123] *Ecclesiastical History of Socrates Scholasticus*. I:8.

Socrates' history is very confused, however. A few sentences later, he says that Eusebius and Theognis and their followers were sent into exile along with Arius. He then adds that they recanted in writing a short time after their banishment, and he includes a letter of recantation that he apparently had in his possession. He does not explain why nothing was done with the other three unless he is including them in the "followers" of Eusebius and Theognis.

Worse, he then appends the letter from the council to the church of Alexandria, stating that only Theonis and Secundus were condemned!

Sozomen

Sozomen, writing in the fifth century like Socrates, mentions by name 4 of the 5 bishops given by Socrates Scholasticus, and says they agreed to the creed and anathemas. He leaves out Theonis of Marmarica from Socrates' list. He states that Eusebius of Nicomedia and Theognis refused to agree to the exile of Arius, and that Constantine removed them from office and made them leave the cities of which they were bishops.[124]

Theodoret

Theodoret gives a list of Arian supporters that also includes 4 of the 5 mentioned by Socrates Scholasticus.[125] He does not include Maris of Chalcedon.

According to Theodoret, all of these supporters of Arius rushed to condemn him when they saw Eusebius of Nicomedia's writings torn up by the council so that they would not lose their positions as bishops. He says only Theonis and Secundus were honest in their support of Arius and were excommunicated.[126] Thus, his testimony is the only one that agrees with the council's letter to Alexandria.

---

[124] *Ecclesiastical History of Sozomen.* I:21.
[125] *Ecclesiastical History of Theodoret.* I:5.
[126] *ibid.* I:7.

Conclusion

The supporters of Arius realized early that they could not win the battle with the rest of the bishops. According to Athanasius, they chose to attempt to twist Nicene terminology to their system, winking at each other over their schemes rather than participating in the discussion.

At the end, it appears that all but Theonis and Secundus opted to agree with the council to avoid punishment, then regroup their offense afterward.

The above is interesting history, but which bishops were condemned has little bearing on post-Nicene history. All the bishops mentioned above supported Arius after the council, and all were reinstated and held power once Constantius II became emperor.

Let us now return to the proceedings and look at the other major issue addressed by the council, the Paschal controversy.

Chapter 6:
The Paschal Controversy

Polycarp, the aged and respected bishop of Smyrna, was in Rome. It was spring, around the year 160, and the Italian weather was beautiful.

He was around 80 years old, and attendants helped him across the threshold into the home of Anicetus, bishop of Rome.

Rome was the most prestigious church in the world. It was not only founded by Paul, but Peter had lived there as an elder for many years before Nero had him crucified, upside down at Peter's request. He felt unworthy to die in the same manner as his Lord.

Now, though, Anicetus had an issue with Polycarp. It was Saturday, the day before *Pascha*, the Christian version of Passover, the celebration of the resurrection of Christ. In preparation, the Roman church was fasting, but the Smyrneans, and Polycarp himself, were not.

Quartodeciman

Quartodeciman is Latin for 14. After the Council of Nicea decided that Passover should be celebrated on Sunday each year rather than on whatever day of the week Nisan 14 happened to fall on, those who refused to comply became known as quartodecimans. The name has anachronistically been applied backward to the controversy even before Nicea.

The second century was a time of great unity and joy in the churches. They did everything together. Having vanquished the gnostic heretics, the apostolic churches proclaimed their Gospel together as if they had "but one soul and one and the same heart." They proclaimed the teaching of the apostles and handed them down "with perfect harmony, as if they possessed but one mouth."[127]

Anicetus, then, was shocked at the distinction he was now witnessing. Why did the Smyrneans not fast with the Romans in preparation for the greatest of all days, the great feast of *Pascha*?

"John, and other apostles, as well," Polycarp explained to Anicetus, "taught us this tradition. The Lord Jesus Christ suffered on the Passover day, Nisan 14 by Jewish reckoning, and so we celebrate that day as we have been taught by the apostles."

Anicetus was not sure what to do. The tradition of celebrating *Pascha* on the Lord's day, the first day of the week when Jesus rose from the dead, had come to them from Peter and Paul. How could they do otherwise? Yet here was Polycarp, possibly the last bishop alive who actually knew the apostles. As Peter and Paul were the greatest of apostles in their day, so Polycarp was greatest of bishops in this day.

But Anicetus' flock knew that there was disparity in practice between the Smyrneans and the Romans. Something must be done.

The Christian spirit and affection was strong in those days. From great to small, Christians were known for their bravery. Not just men, but women and children scorned the punishment of Roman persecutors, passing judgment on their judges by their joy in facing death, and knowing that every drop of blood they shed was seed. "The more often you mow us down, the more of us there are," they would boast.[128]

---

[127] Irenaeus. *Against Heresies*. I:10:2.
[128] Tertullian. *Apology*. 50. c. AD 210.

The early Christians were not just brave but even poetic in their sufferings:

> It's a beautiful thing to God when a Christian does battle with pain.
>
> When he faces threats, punishments, and tortures by mocking death and treading underfoot the horror of the executioner; when he raises up his freedom in Christ as a standard before kings and princes; when he yields to God alone and, triumphant and victorious, he tramples upon the very man who has pronounced sentence upon him.
>
> God finds all these things beautiful.[129]

Warmed by that Christian spirit, Anicetus asked his venerable fellow bishop to appear in the gathering the following morning.

Each first day Sunday—the Christians in Rome, and indeed all over the world, would gather early, before the day's work commenced, and break bread and drink wine in remembrance of the Lord's death, as he had commanded. They did not kneel, for the first day was the Lord's day,[130] the day of resurrection, and thus it was to be celebrated with joy. When they prayed, they raised their hands, making their whole bodies a sign of the cross and expecting acceptance at the throne of God because of the precious blood of Christ, who had died on their behalf.

This first day the bishop of Rome handed the bread to Polycarp to break.

Polycarp offered prayer to God in heaven, thanking him that as the wheat was gathered from every hillside to be ground together into one loaf, so the people of God had been gathered from every place to become one body for the Son of God to dwell in.

---

[129] Minucius Felix. *The Octavius.* 37. c. AD 200.

[130] Seventh Day Adventists and other modern groups have questioned whether the Lord's Day was really Sunday. Entire books have been written arguing that the Lord's Day was another term for the Sabbath. No one, however, who has actually read the early Christian writings could believe this to be true. See Chapter 13.

He then broke the loaf, gave it to the servants of the congregation, and they ate the food that they called "the medicine of immortality."[131]

Polycarp repeated the prayer with the cup, filled with wine that had been crushed from grapes from many clusters.

And as they finished, the two bishops looked at one another, knowing that without breaking the tradition of their forefathers in the faith, they had preserved that one loaf and that one cup that is the church of Jesus Christ.

The Unity Broken

Anicetus and Polycarp were filled with fervency and love for God. Their successors could not find it in themselves to follow suit.

Thirty-five years later, Victor was bishop of Rome, and he could not understand the practice of his brothers in Asia Minor. Every church in the world celebrated Passover on the first day following the first new moon after the vernal equinox (March 20 or 21). Every church, that is, except those in Asia Minor.

Polycrates was bishop of the church in Ephesus, which was founded by Paul and therefore the most important episcopal seat in Asia Minor. Victor wrote to him and demanded that he conform to the practice of the church universal.

Polycrates was offended. He wasted no time in responding to this brash bishop in Rome:

> We observe the exact day; neither adding, nor taking away. For in Asia also great lights have fallen asleep, who will rise again on the day of the Lord's coming ... Among these are Philip, one of the 12 apostles, who fell asleep in Hierapolis ... John, who was both a witness and a teacher, who reclined upon the bosom of the Lord ... And Polycarp in Smyrna, who was a bishop and martyr. All these observed the 14th day of the Passover according to the Gos-

---

[131] Ignatius. *Letter to the Ephesians*. 19. c. AD 110.

pel, not deviating in any way, but following the rule of faith.

> I ... who have lived 65 years in the Lord, have met with brothers throughout the world, and who have gone through every Holy Scripture, am not frightened by terrifying words, for those greater than I have said, "I must obey God rather than man" [*Acts 5:29*].[132]

Victor couldn't believe it. Enraged, he fired off letters to churches all over the empire declaring the churches in Asia Minor excommunicated.

He did not get the response he expected. Bishops were horrified. They, too, sat down and wrote but they urged him "to consider the things of peace and of neighborly unity and love."[133]

Eusebius, the historian who was at the Council of Nicea, tells us that he has seen some of these letters, "sharply rebuking Victor."[134]

One of Victor's letters made it to barbarian Gaul, where Irenaeus, a disciple of Polycarp's at Smyrna, was serving as a missionary and bishop of a number of churches he had either begun there or was overseeing. Irenaeus remembered Polycarp. He had sat under his teaching as a young man. He remembered the story of Polycarp's visit to Anicetus, and Irenaeus knew what he had to do.

> This variety in [the Passover's] observance did not originate in our time, but long before that in that of our ancestors. It is likely that they did not hold to strict accuracy, and thus they formed a custom for their posterity according to their own simplicity and unique mode. Yet all of those nonetheless lived in peace, and we also live in peace

---

[132] Eusebius. *Ecclesiastical History*. V:24.

[133] *ibid.*

[134] *ibid.*

with one another. The disagreement in regard to the fast *confirms* the agreement in the faith.[135]

In addition to this reasoning, he appealed to Victor's predecessors at Rome. He refers to five previous Roman bishops by name, going back over 70 years to AD 116, who were "at peace with those who came to them from the parishes in which [Nisan 14] was observed."[136]

What could Victor say? His appeal was to the tradition handed down to him. Now Irenaeus, whose name in Greek means peace, was pointing out that Rome's tradition included peace with those who disagreed concerning the Passover.

Irenaeus corresponded with the other churches as well, and the church—one, holy, catholic, and apostolic—had dodged the spear of division again.

Passover or Easter?

Many history books, as well as the translations of the fourth and fifth-century historians—Eusebius, Socrates, Sozomen, and Theodoret—continually use "Easter" to refer to the feast in question. All these writings, however, were originally in Greek, and they all use *Pascha* as the word for the feast. *Pascha* is the word used in the Septuagint, the Greek translation of the Hebrew Scriptures, for Passover. It should not be translated "Easter."

The Council of Nicea

A century later the church was weaker. As they battled over Arianism, the Trinity, and modalism, so they continued the battle over the feast of Passover and the fast before it. Eusebius tells us:

> Before this time another most virulent disorder had existed and long afflicted the Church. I mean the difference re-

---

[135] *ibid.* Emphasis mine.
[136] *ibid.*

specting the health-giving feast of Passover. ... The people were divided everywhere because of this ... No one appeared who was capable of devising a remedy for the evil because the controversy continued equally balanced between both sides.[137]

Because the Church could not produce another Anicetus, Polycarp, or Irenaeus, they had to be satisfied with a Roman emperor, Constantine:

Constantine appeared to be the only one on earth capable of being his minister for this good end. For as soon as he was made acquainted with the facts which I have described, and perceived that his letter to the Alexandrian Christians [Alexander and Arius] had failed to produce its due effect, he at once aroused the energies of his mind and declared that he must pursue to the utmost this war also against the secret adversary who was disturbing the peace of the Church.[138]

For good or for bad, Constantine's intervention was effective, at least in Nicea.

Once the bishops had managed to agree on Arius, they were apparently in an affable mood for the Passover controversy.

Eusebius ties the unity concerning the Nicene Creed to agreement on the Passover celebration and its preceding fast:

The result was that they were not only united concerning the faith, but the time for the celebration of the health-giving feast of Passover was agreed on by all. ... Then the emperor, believing that he had thus obtained a second victory over the adversary of the Church, proceeded to solemnize a triumphal festival in honor of God.[139]

It is unlikely that the bishops were in any mood for fighting over Passover after getting through the difficult, emotional drama

---

[137] *Life of Constantine*. III:5.

[138] *ibid.*

[139] *Life of Constantine*. III:14.

of Arianism and the use of *homoousios*. Celebrating on Sunday rather than Nisan 14 was by far the more common practice, and 200 years of holding out on the basis of tradition against another good, solid tradition had to be exhausting. We have no record of the discussion that ensued, but it seems likely that it was not difficult or long.

There were more issues to consider, but none so major as Arianism or Passover. These were summed up in 20 canons.[140] One, the issue of the Melitians who had formed a schism in Egypt over communing with those who fell away during persecution, was either so minor or so local that it was not even covered in a canon but simply addressed with a letter to the church in Alexandria.[141]

The Canons of Nicea

The 20 canons of Nicea mostly concern minor topics. A couple are significant, however, providing solid historical clarity on the subject of the papacy and Christian involvement in war.

With 20 topics to cover, we will give them their own chapter.

---

[140] Ecclesiastical rules. In this case the decisions of a council.
[141] Appendix H.

Chapter 7:
The Canons of the Council of Nicea

Perhaps the simplest way to dispel all the myths associated with the Council of Nicea is to look at the 20 canons that the Council of Nicea issued. These and the creed are the only decisions made at Nicea.

These canons are provided for your information. Some of them are not of much interest to us today, but two at least should cause modern Christians to take note:

- Canon 6 makes it clear that there was no pope in the fourth century. The history prior to Nicea establishes this clearly as well, but Canon 6 finalizes the argument in one short paragraph. I am really not sure how the Roman Catholic Church can argue for the historicity of the papacy if the public knows about Canon 6 of Nicea.

- Canon 12 assigns banishment from communion *for up to 13 years* for Christians who join the military 'like dogs returning to their own vomit.' Again, Christian history prior to Nicea makes it clear that when Christians first heard the Gospel they did not kill, neither in war nor through the courts, but Canon 12 brings it to our attention in a public decision from the most well-known church council of all time.

Do not think that the Council of Nicea made any dramatic new decisions that conflict with earlier church history. It is not true.

At the Council of Nicea we can see the influence of 300 years of gradual change in the church. We can see the effect of the continued increase in the authority and centrality of the clergy. But there is nothing in these canons or in the Nicene Creed that indicates the Council of Nicea sent the church in any new directions. Every decision, and the creed itself, can be justified historically or shown to be the result of development over time.

The new relationship between the emperor and the bishops did cause dramatic change. The massive influx of new believers, almost all nominal and simply following the emperor into the new state religion, did dramatically change the church. Violence, intrigue, and new ways of dealing with the new problems followed rapidly on the heels of Nicea. Corruption in the leadership of the church multiplied rapidly because so many more church members meant bishops had much more power and influence.

But none of these things can be attributed to decisions made at the council. These changes were not planned. They simply happened as the inevitable result of the emperor favoring the Christian religion.

Those of you who are deeply interested in the time period will get a good feel for the state of the churches and their structure during the Nicene period by reading through the canons and my comments. Others of you may want to leave this chapter for reference only and go directly to Chapter 8. You may not want to skip Canons 6 and 12, however, which reference the pope and serving in the military, issues which are discussed among Christians to this day.

In addition, Canon 3 gives some insight into problems with clerical celibacy, which was not mandatory in the third and fourth centuries, but was common.

Sources for the 20 Canons

Rufinus, a late fourth-century historian, gives the earliest copy of the text of the canons, though his are in Latin. Twenty years later, Gelasius, the bishop Cyzicus, gave the text of the canons in his history of Nicea. Finally, numerous manuscript copies of the canons were made in the fourth and fifth centuries, some of which are preserved in museums today.

The Text of the 20 Canons of Nicea

These 20 canons are readily available to the public both in books and on the internet. I got my text from *The Nicene and Post-Nicene Fathers*, series 2, volume 14, which is published by both Hendrickson and Eerdmans Publishers. I have updated the language and punctuation, as the series was translated over 100 years ago.

Canon

The word "canon" is from a Latin word simply meaning a rule. Over time, canon has come to carry a very ecclesiastical connotation, but basically it's just a rule. It's used primarily of decisions from a council, like these, or of the books chosen to be included in the Bible.

Canon 1

If anyone in sickness has been subjected by physicians to a surgical operation, or if he has been castrated by barbarians, let him remain among the clergy; but, if any one in sound health has castrated himself, then it is good that such a one, if enrolled among the clergy, should cease, and that from now on no such person should be promoted. But, as it is evident that this is said of those who willfully do the thing and presume to castrate themselves, so if any have been made eunuchs by barbarians, or by their masters, and should otherwise be found worthy, such men the canon admits to the clergy.

There was a very strong emphasis on celibacy in the early churches. Although even the Roman Catholic church did not mandate celibacy for church leaders until the 12th century, the emphasis on denying the urges of the flesh, even in marriage, dates back at least to the second century, when Justin Martyr mentions that "even if we marry, it is only for the purpose of producing children."[142]

In the third century Origen discusses the qualification that elders have but one wife. Today, we would understand that to mean that polygamy is forbidden, or perhaps that a church leader should never divorce and remarry. In Origen's time, however, it is clear that bishops *were not to remarry even after their wives died.*

Origen does not argue for this. He discusses it as though it was simply normal procedure for every church that all Christians knew about. This requirement has to predate Origen long enough for it to become standard in the churches, thus making it a second-century practice.

The issue, clearly, was that church leaders should lead the way in proving they can overcome the temptations of the flesh, especially in this universally difficult area of sexual desire.

With all the emphasis on lifelong sexual control, young men having difficulty in this area, rather than marrying as the apostle Paul recommends, would occasionally castrate themselves.

The Council of Nicea determined that those who had castrated themselves should not be bishops or elders.

Excursus on Celibacy

I have to weigh in on this. It is clear from history, both modern and medieval, and from these very canons (see Canon 3), that the emphasis on celibacy has led to horrific immorality, often involving boys.

If you read through the comments on Canon 3, you'll see a story recounted by Sozomen of what happened when the Council of Nicea discussed requiring celibacy of all clergy, even if they were married. A wise Christian talked them out of it, warning that imposed celibacy would lead to immorality.

---

[142] *First Apology.* 29.

If church leaders are going to be an example for the flock, they should be an example of what the Scriptures teach, *not what we wish were true about the human condition.* Jesus said that lifelong virginity is a gift that *some* have (Matt. 19:9-12). Paul said that those who burn with passion should marry, not spend their lives trying to overcome it (1 Cor. 7:9). He agrees with Jesus that the single life is for those that have a gift for it (1 Cor. 7:7).

Thus, marrying and living a faithful married life is as good an example to the church as remaining unmarried.

Finally, it seems to me that the Scriptures teach that being married is a *requirement* for elders and bishops, not just an option (cf. 1 Tim. 3:2,4; Tit. 1:6). A lifelong virgin may show great self-control, but according to the Scriptures, he is not qualified to be an elder. He is going to have to serve the church in some other capacity.

Here I do have to point out, especially after having commented on the importance of the ancient tradition of the church,[143] that celibacy was honored among Christians from at least the second century. I am venturing out on a limb by suggesting that this was a result of an overemphasized and unhealthy asceticism rather than apostolic tradition. I am willing to take that risk because the Scriptures do not seem to me to share that early Christian emphasis on celibacy and because such asceticism was revered in Greek philosophy as well. There is no doubt that Greek philosophy, being the most esteemed spiritual path in Roman culture, had an influence on most of the early Christian writers whose writings are still extant.

Excursus on Clergy

I am convinced that knowing that the church is not an organization, but a family, to be critically important, especially in our time. Because of this, I think it is important to comment on the word "clergy" as well.

---

[143] Chapter 4

"Clergy" is not a term that would have been used in the first or second centuries. It implies a separation between leaders and non-leaders that did not exist in the apostolic period and immediately thereafter. Even as late as AD 200, Tertullian described Christian leaders in this way:

> The tried men of our elders preside over us, obtaining that honor not by purchase, but by established character.[144]

Leaders of the earliest churches earned the right to lead by living an exemplary life before the church. In the environment of the early churches, this meant that the people you were leading were your friends. If you did not grow up with them physically, you certainly had grown up with them spiritually. You were not "clergy" to those people; you were Joe or Bill or Clement or Irenaeus.

Canon 15 addresses clergy moving from church to church. The council forbade this, but it remained a common occurrence. It was an indication of the growing separation between the clergy and the Christians they purported to lead.

That separation has continued until today, when pastors, whether Catholic or Protestant, are almost always strangers to a congregation when they begin to lead it. No one in the congregation knows their lives, their struggles, or their personalities. It is as though they alone are not in need of teaching, exhortation, and oversight.

Jesus said that a good shepherd knows his sheep by name (Jn. 10:3) and that if one from a flock of 100 leaves, the shepherd will leave the 99 to find that one. Today, if one person leaves, it is unlikely that the shepherd[145] would even know, much less go after that person.

We need to pray for good shepherds, and if you are a shepherd, know that you will receive a stricter judgment (Jam. 3:1).

---

[144] *Apology*. 39.

[145] In the early churches, the bishops and elders were the shepherds. There was not a separate office of pastor. That term was not separated from bishop or elder until the Reformation in the 16th century. See Appendix C.

Jeremiah 23 begins with, "Woe to the pastors that destroy and scatter the sheep of my pasture." It would do us good, especially if we claim to be Bible believers, to qualify our shepherds with the tests approved by the apostle Paul rather than with finals approved by a theological seminary! (1 Tim. 3:2-7; Tit. 1:5-9).

Canon 2

> *Forasmuch as, either from necessity or through the urgency of individuals, many things have been done contrary to the ecclesiastical canon, so that men just converted from heathenism to the faith, and who have been instructed but a little while, are immediately brought to the spiritual laver, and as soon as they have been baptized, are advanced to the office of bishop or the office of elder, it has seemed right to us that for the time to come no such thing shall be done. For to the catechumen[146] himself there is need of time and of a longer trial after baptism. For the apostolic saying is clear, "Not a novice; lest, being lifted up with pride, he fall into condemnation and the snare of the devil" [1 Tim. 3:6] But if, as time goes on, any sensual sin should be found out about the person, and he should be convicted by two or three witnesses, let him cease from the clerical office. And whoever transgresses these will imperil his own clerical position, as a person who presumes to disobey the great synod.*

This canon forbids men from becoming bishops or elders immediately after baptism.

This is not as strange as it may sound to our ears. By the fourth century new converts would often be trained in the faith for a year or more before being baptized. During this time, they were

---

[146] A person being *catechized*, or instructed in the faith. This happened prior to baptism. Catechumens were not yet baptized and not yet admitted to communion.

called "catechumens," from the word "catechize," which means to instruct in basic doctrines.

Over the course of one to three years, it would be easy for a gifted man to distinguish himself so that a church might want to appoint him as an elder or even a bishop.

Of course, there could also have been problems with the office of bishop being purchased by a wealthy convert, although this was much more likely to happen *after* Nicea when bishops had political clout and most Roman citizens were nominally Christians and subject to the bishop.

The council forbade this rapid rise to power.

This canon, too, makes a comment about "sensual sin." With Canon 3 it seems evident that there was a problem with sexual sin among the clergy, something I attribute both to the high honor in which celibacy was held and to the excessive adoration given to the "clergy."

Note also that the council refers to itself as "the great synod." I suppose it's unavoidable that such a collection of bishops seated with the emperors would have a high, though perhaps not exaggerated, opinion of their own power and authority.

Canon 3

> *The great synod has stringently forbidden any bishop, elder, deacon, or any one of the clergy whatever, to have a subintroducta dwelling with him, except only a mother, or sister, or aunt, or such persons only as are beyond all suspicion.*

A "subintroducta" is simply a woman living with a clergyman as a housekeeper or in some other supposedly platonic role.

The Greek word is *suneisaktos*, and there is some confusion about its literal meaning, but no confusion about what's being talked about here. Leaders of the church should not have a single woman living in their house unless it's a close relative who is above suspicion.

I exchanged emails once with a church history professor who had written on the internet that this canon "ruled that married men who became priests must abstain from sexual intercourse with their wives."

> I can see how the word subintroducta could cause confusion. ... All the articles and references I have read, however, indicate that in the fourth century church it was used to refer to live-in females in a marriage relationship or something resembling it.

This makes no sense in the context of canon 3, and it is answered effectively by Hefele's comment on Canon 3 given in *The Nicene and Post-Nicene Fathers*:

> If by the word suneisaktos was only intended the wife in this spiritual marriage, the Council would not have said, any suneisaktos, except his mother, etc.; for neither his mother nor his sister could have formed this spiritual union with the cleric.147

On top of this, Sozomen the historian says that requiring clergy to abstain from intercourse with their wives was discussed at the council and rejected:

> The Synod enacted laws which were called canons. While they were deliberating about this, some thought that a law ought to be passed enacting that bishops and elders, deacons and subdeacons, should hold no sexual relations with the wife they had espoused before they entered the priesthood. But Paphnutius, the confessor,[148] stood up and testified against this proposition. He said that marriage was honorable and chaste and that cohabitation with their own wives was chastity. He advised the synod not to frame such a law, for it would be difficult to bear, and might serve as an occasion of incontinence to them and their wives. He also reminded them that according to the ancient tradition of the church, those who were unmarried when they took part in the communion of sacred or-

---

[147] *The Nicene and Post-Nicene Fathers.* Series II, Vol. 14.

[148] A person who had endured persecution because of the faith.

ders were required to remain so, but that those who were married were not to put away their wives.

Such was the advice of Paphnutius, although he was himself unmarried, and in accordance with it, the Synod concurred in his counsel, enacted no law about it, but left the matter to the decision of individual judgment and not to compulsion.[149]

Further, the word *subintroducta* is used in a letter written by the Synod of Arles in AD 268, which condemned Paul of Samosata and deposed him as bishop of Antioch.[150] They describe the subintroductae of Paul of Samosata and the elders he had appointed, making it clear that these are not wives. They also mention that such a practice has led to disgrace even among catholic bishops:

> And there are the women, the *subintroductae*, as the people of Antioch call them, belonging to [Paul of Samosata] and to the elders and deacons that are with him. ... We know, beloved, that the bishop and all the clergy should be an example to the people of all good works, and we are not ignorant how many have fallen or incurred suspicion through the women whom they have thus brought in. So that even if we should allow that he commits no sinful act, yet he ought to avoid the suspicion which arises from such a thing, lest he stumble someone or lead others to imitate him. For how can he reprove or admonish another not to be too familiar with women ... when he has himself sent one away already, and now has two with him, blooming and beautiful, and takes them with him wherever he goes ... ?[151]

I think that's a clear enough picture of what the Council of Nicea was trying to end.

---

[149] *Ecclesiastical History of Sozomen*. I:23.

[150] See Canon 19 for a description of Paul of Samosata.

[151] Eusebius. *Ecclesiastical History*. VII:30:12-14.

Excursus on Holiness and Church Leaders

Don't let modern experience deceive you. It is a surprise and a new development that such immorality would be widespread, an immorality I blame on an overemphasis on avoiding sexual pleasure, even if a person is married. By the late third century, this emphasis would have been very strong.

Overall, before the church obtained political influence and public popularity during Constantine's reign, the bishops and elders of the catholic churches were noted for good works. One of the strongest defenses of the faith employed by pre-Nicene churches was the exemplary lives of their members and especially their leaders. As late as AD 230 or so, Origen offered to compare any set of church leaders with any set of Roman public leaders, claiming that the worst of the Christian leaders would prove to lead a life superior to that of the best of the public leaders.[152]

Canon 4

It is by all means proper that a bishop should be appointed by all the bishops in the province. If this should be difficult, either on account of urgent necessity or because of distance, three at least should meet together, and the assent of the absent [bishops] should be given and communicated in writing, then the ordination should take place. But in every province the ratification of what is done should be left to the metropolitan.

This was direction on the ordination of a bishop. They should be appointed by all the bishops of a province, but at a minimum three. This should be ratified by the metropolitan.

A metropolitan is the bishop of a city whose authority extended to surrounding towns or even entire provinces. Canon 6 makes it clear that the bishops of Alexandria, Rome, and Antioch had

---

[152] *Against Celsus.* III:30.

authority over at least an entire country. In either case, a metropolitan was the leading bishop of a group of bishops.

Canon 5

*Concerning those, whether of the clergy or of the laity,
who have been excommunicated in the several provinces,
let the provision of the canon be observed by the bishops
which provides that persons cast out by some be not readmitted by others. Nevertheless, inquiry should be made
whether they have been excommunicated through cap-
tiousness,[153] contentiousness, or any such like ungracious
disposition in the bishop. And, that this matter may have
due investigation, it is decreed that in every province synods shall be held twice a year, in order that when all the
bishops of the province are assembled together, such questions may by them be thoroughly examined, that so those
who have admittedly offended against their bishop, may be
seen by all to be for just cause excommunicated, until it
shall seem appropriate to a general meeting of the bishops
to pronounce a milder sentence upon them. And let these
synods be held, the one before Lent,[154] (that the pure Gift
may be offered to God after all bitterness has been put
away), and let the second be held about autumn.*

This directly pertained to the matter of Arius and Alexander.
Alexander, the bishop of Alexandria, excommunicated Arius, but
he was received by Eusebius, the bishop of Nicomedia.

Such a situation happened a century earlier with Origen, who
was also excommunicated by the bishop of Alexandria, although
that was probably a matter of jealousy. Origen was a respected
teacher both in the church on spiritual subjects and out of it in

---

[153] "Marked by a disposition to find and point out trivial faults." (*The Free Dictionary*).

[154] The term Lent was already being applied to the fast that preceded Passover.
See Chapter 6.

secular subjects. Once, while traveling, the church at Caesarea asked him to speak at a gathering of the church. The bishop of Alexandria objected to this, saying that only an elder or bishop should be teaching the church in a meeting. So the next time Origen came through, the bishop of Caesarea ordained Origen as an elder. The bishop of Alexandria then excommunicated him, and Origen remained a part of the church in Caesarea for the rest of his life.

This canon forbids such pettiness between churches and demands that they resolve such issues in local synods.

Canon 6

Let the ancient customs in Egypt, Libya and Pentapolis prevail, that the Bishop of Alexandria have jurisdiction in all these, since the like is customary for the Bishop of Rome also. Likewise in Antioch and the other provinces, let the churches retain their privileges. And this is to be universally understood, that if anyone be made bishop without the consent of the metropolitan,[155] the great Synod has declared that such a man ought not to be a bishop. If, however, two or three bishops shall from natural love of contradiction, oppose the common assent of the rest, it being reasonable and in accordance with the ecclesiastical law, then let the choice of the majority prevail.

The main purpose of this canon is most likely to stifle the Melitian schism.

Melitius was a bishop of Lycopolis in Egypt who, like the *Cathari* (see Canon 8), objected to the readmission of Christians who had lapsed during persecution. He began ordaining bishops who agreed with him in other cities. After the council was over,

---

[155] A bishop of a large city who had authority over other cities or even entire provinces.

the bishops sent a letter to the church at Alexandria specifically condemning the Melitians.[156]

Nonetheless, this canon rings down through the centuries because of the later claim of the bishop of Rome to authority over the entire church.

This increase in the levels of hierarchy and in the power held by those at the top levels of the hierarchy happened gradually over time. Eventually, after Rome fell to the barbarians in the fifth century, the bishops of Constantinople and Rome would battle over who would be the highest bishop of all.

Rome did not win that battle. Political separations between the barbarian-controlled west and the emperor-controlled east led to the Roman bishop carrying primary power in the west only. When those political separations waned, and the battle for supreme power in the church raged again, east and west separated into what is now known as the Roman Catholic and Eastern Orthodox churches. "The pope," as he is now known, has only ever held full power in the west and that remains true until this day.

This canon makes it clear that the bishop of Rome was not "pope" at the time of Nicea. In fact, he carried no more authority than the bishop of Alexandria, although this authority was clearly great.

Recently, I listened to a Catholic theologian explain that this canon really just says that it is customary for the bishop of Rome to grant the bishops of Alexandria and Antioch authority over large areas. Rather than answer that, I will simply let the wording of the canon argue for itself against such an unusual interpretation. The wording is accurate enough that even newadvent.org, the home of the *Catholic Encyclopedia*, uses the translation given above.[157]

_____

[156] The letter is given in full in Appendix H.
[157] "First Council of Nicea." *New Advent*. Accessed March 11, 2009. <http://www.newadvent.org/fathers/3801.htm>.

Canon 7

Since custom and ancient tradition have prevailed that the Bishop of Aelia [i.e., Jerusalem] should be honored, let him, saving its due dignity to the Metropolis, have the next place of honor.

The bishop of Jerusalem was not a metropolitan,[158] but the council states that tradition dictates that he should have second place next to his metropolitan.

Canon 8

Concerning those who call themselves Cathari, if they come over to the catholic and apostolic Church, the great and holy synod decrees that they who are ordained shall continue as they are in the clergy. But it is before all things necessary that they should profess in writing that they will observe and follow the dogmas of the catholic and apostolic Church; in particular that they will take communion with persons who have been twice married and with those who having lapsed in persecution have had a period [of penance] laid upon them and a time fixed [for returning to fellowship], so that in all things they will follow the dogmas of the catholic Church. Wherever, then, whether in villages or in cities, all of the ordained are found to be of these only, let them remain in the clergy, and in the same rank in which they are found. But if they come over where there is a bishop or elder of the catholic Church, it is apparent that the bishop of the church must have the bishop's dignity; and he who was named bishop by those who are called Cathari shall have the rank of elder, unless it shall seem fit to the bishop to admit him to partake in the honor of the title. Or, if this should not be

---

[158] A bishop of a large city who had authority over other cities or even entire provinces.

satisfactory, then shall the bishop provide for him a place as chorepiscopus[159] *or elder, in order that he may be evidently seen to be of the clergy, and that there may not be two bishops in the city.*

The *Cathari* are more commonly known as the Novatianists today. The Novatianists were descendants of an elder by the name of Novatian who had been passed over as bishop of Rome about 75 years before Nicea, most likely because he had received a "clinic baptism." What that means is that before the church was ready to baptize him, Novatian fell into a deathly illness. Due to the illness, the church baptized him to ensure that he would not die unbaptized.

Obviously, he recovered from his illness, and he was offended that Cornelius was selected as bishop in AD 251 rather than himself. He got himself proclaimed bishop by three minor Italian bishops, but his office was recognized by no one.

Undeterred, he formed his own church in Rome, only the second major split that the church had experienced in its history, the first being the Montanists in the late second century.

Novatianist congregations spread, calling themselves the *Cathari*, from the Greek word for pure or clean. They adopted this name after the persecution under Decius in the 250's. During that persecution, the churches having grown larger and in some ways weaker over the previous century, many fell away, either offering sacrifices to the Roman idols or purchasing a certificate that said they did. Some of these lapsed Christians repented once the persecution ended. While the catholic churches welcomed them back after a period of penance, Novatianist congregations refused to do so. Thus, they were "the pure," while the catholic congregations, to the Novatianists, were impure.

Seventy years later, during the time of Constantine, persecution of Christians in the Roman empire virtually came to an end. It would not be long before the *Cathari* simply returned to the catho-

---

[159] A rural bishop who was subject to the bishop of the nearest city.

lic churches, having no real differences beside their treatment of Christians that lapsed during persecution and, similarly, their willingness to readmit Christians after major sin.

That return to the catholic churches had begun already, and Canon 8 of Nicea explains how to deal with both individuals and churches that returned to catholicity. Novatian elders were to retain their position as elder if they would agree to take communion with those who had lapsed during persecution and been through a time of penance.

The phrase "twice married" here is almost certainly a reference to those who married again after their spouse had died. The Montanists had forbidden such second marriages to everyone, and remarriage after the death of a spouse had been forbidden to bishops and elders even in the catholic churches for at least a century. The third-century churches—and, some would argue, even the apostles—understood the reference to "the husband of one wife" as a qualification for the position of elder in this way (1 Tim. 3:2).

With those being the only differences, it was apparently no problem to receive *Cathari* clergy back into the catholic churches in their ordained positions, with the exception being that if there were already a catholic bishop, the *Cathari* bishop would enter the catholic church as either an elder or a "chorepiscopus." A chorepiscopus was a bishop of a rural congregation who served under the metropolitan.[160] The office of chorepiscopus was invented in the third century and discontinued by the ninth.

Canon 9

If any elders have been advanced without examination, or if upon examination they have made confession of crime, and men acting in violation of the canon have laid hands upon them, notwithstanding their confession, such

---

[160] A bishop of a large city who had authority over other cities or even entire provinces.

the canon does not admit; for the Catholic Church re-quires that which is blameless.

This canon provides that if an elder is found to have committed a crime, but it's not found out until after he's ordained, he must be removed from office. It doesn't matter whether the crime was simply unknown or if he was ordained despite the crime. If he's a criminal, he cannot be an elder and must be removed from his position.

Canon 10

If any who have lapsed have been ordained through the ignorance, or even with the previous knowledge of the ordainers, this shall not prejudice the canon of the Church; for when they are discovered they shall be deposed.

Canon 10 is similar to Canon 9, but it concerns those who lapsed during persecution. Even after repentance and penance, such a person can never be elder and must be deposed if they were somehow ordained.

Canon 11

Concerning those who have fallen without compulsion, without the spoiling of their property, without danger or the like, as happened during the tyranny of Licinius, the Synod declares that, though they have deserved no clemency, they shall be dealt with mercifully. As many as were communicants,[161] if they heartily repent, shall pass three years among the hearers[162]; for seven years they shall be

---

[161] Those in good standing and thus admitted to communion

[162] Those who have neither been baptized nor admitted to training classes for baptism. These were merely "hearers," determining whether they wanted to be Christians.

prostrators;[163] *and for two years they shall communicate with the people in prayers, but without oblation.*[164]

If a person sacrificed to the Roman gods at the mere threat of persecution, without anything even being done to them, then they would be banned from communion for 12 years.

This involved sitting for three years with the "hearers," which are those who are considering the Christian faith, but who are neither baptized nor admitted to "catechism," or basic teaching, in preparation for baptism. After that, it was seven years with the "prostrators," those who were banned from communion for some sin. Finally, they would be allowed to sit with the full members for prayer, but they would not be allowed to eat the bread or drink the wine of the Eucharist, which they refer to here as an "oblation."[165]

Canon 12

As many as were called by grace and displayed the first zeal, having cast aside their military belts, but afterwards returned like dogs to their own vomit—so that some even spent money and by means of gifts regained their military stations—let these, after they have passed the space of three years as hearers,[166] *be for ten years prostrators.*[167]

---

[163] Those under penance. These are baptized Christians who are not admitted to communion until their time of penance is over.

[164] "Oblation" is a reference to communion (or Eucharist, which means *thanksgiving*). The early churches considered the bread and wine of communion to be an offering, though it was not in any way a "re-offering" of Christ's sacrifice on the cross. (See comments on Canon 18). Those allowed to communicate in prayers, but without oblation, were those who could pray with the regular members, but they could not take communion.

[165] See note 153.

[166] Those who have neither been baptized nor admitted to training classes for baptism. These were merely "hearers," determining whether they wanted to be Christians.

But in all these cases it is necessary to examine well into their purpose and what their repentance appears to be like. For as many as give evidence of their conversions by deeds, and not pretense, with fear, tears, perseverance, and good works, when they have fulfilled their appointed time as hearers, may properly communicate in prayers; and after that the bishop may determine yet more favorably concerning them. But those who respond with indifference and who think the form of entering the Church is sufficient for their conversion must fulfill the whole time.

I mentioned this one at the top of the page.

The punishment for joining the military is even more severe than for denying Christ without being persecuted! For joining the military, years eleven and twelve are still with the prostrators, and there's a thirteenth year in addition.

And remember, this is Constantine's military! The emperor Constantine was at this council!

I've heard lots of arguments from people who do not want to believe that the early church was against military service, but it's not a doubtful issue. The Christian writings before Nicea are universal on the subject from the very beginning. For example, even as early as AD 150, Justin Martyr subjoins a letter to his *First Apology* that is supposedly from Marcus Aurelius describing his experience with Christians. It says:

> I summoned those among us who go by the name of Christians ... They began the battle, not by preparing weapons, arms, nor bugles, for such preparation is hateful to them, on account of the God they bear about in their conscience.

More directly, Justin writes:

---

[167] Those under penance. These are baptized Christians who are not admitted to communion until their time of penance is over.

We who formerly used to murder one another do not only refrain from making war on our enemies but also, so that we may not lie nor deceive our examiners, willingly die confessing Christ.[168]

You will find nothing contrary in any writings of the church prior to Nicea.

Think about it a moment. If Christians are forbidden to do violence to their own enemies, turning the other cheek and praying for their persecutors, then why would they do violence to the enemies of others? We are foreigners and travelers in this world. Why would we fight for an earthly government that is not our own, when we will not make war on behalf of the heavenly government that is our own?

My kingdom is not of this world. If my kingdom were of this world, then my servants would fight. (Jn. 18:36)

Finally, there are those who claim that Canon 13 was only given to prevent Christians from sacrificing to idols. Such claim that sacrificing to idols was necessary to enter the military, and this was the only reason the church forbade military service in the Roman empire.

What they forget is that the emperor Constantine was at this council. He was in charge of the military. He had already decreed that persecution against Christians should stop and that all seized property should be returned to the church. He had favored Christianity openly, painting crosses on his soldiers' shields. If the issue was sacrifices to the Roman gods, Constantine could simply have decreed that such sacrifices were not necessary for Christians.

That was if such sacrifices were even necessary. It seems clear that by AD 325 Constantine, the only Roman emperor, would not have required pagan sacrifices of anyone entering the military.[169]

---

[168] First Apology 39

[169] See Chapter 14 for a discussion of Constantine's leaning toward Christianity.

This book is not about Christianity and war, so I will resist the temptation to speak further on the matter. Suffice it to say that the early Christians universally taught that Christians should never engage in warfare, and Canon 12 of the Council of Nicea confirms this with the most severe penalties.

Obviously, after Nicea this would not be able to continue. Eventually, almost everyone in the Roman empire was at least nominally Christian, including the emperor himself, so it would have been impossible to continue to ban military service for Christians.

Of course, that is not a minor change! The fourth century was a time of drastic change, and for Christians to begin killing— please pause to think about that word and what it means—is one of the most major changes that occurred with the Christianization of the Roman empire.

"The Form of Entering the Church"

One more thing must be commented on. Canon 12 states, "Those who respond with indifference and *who think the form of entering the Church is sufficient for their conversion* must fulfill the whole time."

Constantine had already begun urging his people to convert to Christianity. The ranks of the churches were already swelling with those who were Christians in name only.

> From the time of Constantine church discipline declines; the whole Roman world having become nominally Christian, and the host of hypocritical professors[170] multiplying beyond all control.[171]

The bishops of Nicea, commendably, wanted something more than simply attending the church, and they would not admit to

---

[170] A person who "professes" Christianity.

[171] Schaff, Philip. *History of the Christian Church.* Vol. III, section 1.

communion those who were deceived into thinking that merely entering the church is sufficient for conversion.

The one mark they mention here of those who are not really converted is an indifferent response to the church's discipline. Interestingly enough, Martin Luther said something very similar 1200 years later. (This quote does not constitute an endorsement of the doctrines of Martin Luther!)

> He who cannot, by the gracious and lovely message of God's mercy so lavishly bestowed upon us in Christ, be persuaded in a spirit of love and delight to contribute to the honor of God and the benefit of his neighbor, is worthless to Christianity, and all effort is lost on him.[172]

Canon 13

Concerning the departing [i.e., dying], the ancient canonical law is still to be maintained; to wit, that, if anyone be at the point of death, he must not be deprived of the last and most indispensable Viaticum.[173] But, if anyone should be restored to health again who has received the communion when his life was despaired of, let him remain among those who communicate in prayers only. But in general, and in the case of any dying person whatever asking to receive the Eucharist, let the Bishop, after examination is made, give it him.

This canon allowed for the giving of the Eucharist—communion—to anyone that was in danger of dying. The word *viaticum* is from a Latin word that means "food for the journey."

---

[172] Luther, Martin. "First Sunday After Epiphany." *Complete Sermons of Martin Luther.* Grand Rapids, MI: BakerBooks, 2007. Vol. IV, p. 11.
[173] *Viaticum* could mean any ecclesiastical service provided for a dying person, but in the context of Canon 13 the "last and most indispensable *Viaticum*" is clearly the Eucharist (communion).

The explanation in *The Nicene and Post-Nicene Fathers*[174] says that the term *viaticum* could be applied to any ecclesiastical service given to the dying person, including baptism or a blessing, but it primarily applied to the Eucharist, which, of course, is actually food and better suited to the term.

If the person recovered, his banning from communion would be reinstated until his time of penance was over.

Canon 14

> *Concerning catechumens*[175] *who have lapsed, the holy and great Synod has decreed that, after they have passed three years only as hearers, they shall pray with the catechumens.*

Catechumens were given less punishment than baptized Christians for lapsing. Of course, they still had to be approved by the elders of the church for baptism.

There is a famous story concerning the martyrdom of several catechumens in Tertullian's time, around AD 200, much of it written by the martyrs themselves. That story is available online at *Christian History for Everyman* <http://www.christian-history.org/perpetua-and-felicitas.html>.

Canon 15

> *On account of the great disturbance and discords that occur, it is decreed that the custom prevailing in certain places contrary to the canon must wholly be done away with, so that neither bishop, elder, nor deacon shall pass from city to city. And if anyone, after this decree of the holy and great Synod, shall attempt any such thing or continue in any such course, his proceedings shall be utterly*

---

[174] Series II, Vol. 14.

[175] Those who are being *catechized*, trained in the basics of the faith in preparation for baptism.

void, and he shall be restored to the church for which he was ordained bishop or elder.

This canon is probably directly a result of Eusebius of Nicomedia receiving Arius from Alexandria after he had been excommunicated. As mentioned above (Canon 5), a similar situation happened with Origen a hundred years earlier.

Apparently, church leaders moving from place to place, and the potential jealousies it brought about, was a common problem in some areas of the empire. The council forbade it from happening any more.

This, too, is something we modern Christians should take note of. Church leaders did not move around in the early churches. This was true largely because they became leaders not by attending seminary and obtaining a theological degree, but by living an exemplary Christian life in a congregation. That congregation would then choose that godly person as a leader, much as the congregation in Jerusalem chose Stephen and Philip in Acts 6.

Tertullian describes this procedure around AD 210:

> The tried men of our elders preside over us, obtaining that honor not by purchase, but by established character.[176]

Canon 16

Neither elders, nor deacons, nor any others enrolled among the clergy, who—not having the fear of God before their eyes, nor regarding the ecclesiastical canon—shall recklessly leave from their own church, ought by any means to be received by another church; but every constraint should be applied to restore them to their own parishes. If they will not go, they must be excommunicated. And if anyone shall dare surreptitiously to carry off and in his own church ordain a man belonging to another, without the consent of his own proper bishop, from whom alt-

---

[176] *Apology.* 39.

hough he was enrolled in the clergy list he has seceded, let the ordination be void.

Canon 16 simply requires all churches to enforce Canon 15.

Canon 17

Forasmuch as many enrolled among the clergy, following covetousness and lust of gain, have forgotten the divine Scripture, which says, "He has not loaned his money for interest" [Ps. 15:5], and in lending money ask the hundredth of the sum[177], the holy and great synod thinks it just that if after this decree any one be found to receive interest, whether he accomplish it by secret transaction or otherwise, as by demanding the whole and one half, or by using any other contrivance whatever for filthy lucre's sake, he shall be deposed from the clergy and his name stricken from the list.

The council forbade church leaders from loaning out money at interest. The penalty is being permanently defrocked. I'm also pretty sure that "stricken from the list" means losing whatever support the person was receiving from the church. I don't know what the job market was like in the Roman empire in the early fourth century, but I suspect that losing your support could create a big need for someone who had been an elder or bishop for any length of time.

It mentions even one percent interest, but at the end it addresses those who have loaned out money expecting an additional fifty percent upon repayment.

Note that the council says there are "many enrolled among the clergy" who have loaned out money at interest for the purpose of

---

[177] A note here by the editors of *The Nicene and Post-Nicene Fathers* says that the "hundredth of the sum" was monthly interest. I don't know how they know this.

"covetousness and lust of gain." This is quite an indictment, and it indicates that corruption was a problem even before Nicea.

Canon 18

> *It has come to the knowledge of the holy and great synod that, in some districts and cities, the deacons administer the Eucharist to the elders, whereas neither canon nor custom permits that they who have no right to offer[178] should give the Body of Christ to them that do offer. And this also has been made known, that certain deacons now touch the Eucharist even before the bishops. Let all such practices be utterly done away, and let the deacons remain within their own bounds, knowing that they are the servants of the bishop and the inferiors of the elders. Let them receive the Eucharist according to their order, after the elders, and let either the bishop or the elder administer to them. Furthermore, let not the deacons sit among the elders, for that is contrary to canon and order. And if, after this decree, any one shall refuse to obey, let him be deposed from the diaconate.*

In earlier centuries, bishops and elders were *compared* to the high priest and priests—or, more generally, the Levites—of the Old Testament. By the third century, however, we find Cyprian actually referring to elders as priests.

This can't possibly be a good thing. The Scriptures make no reference to elders as a priesthood, but they regularly refer to all believers as priests, using terms like "a royal priesthood" and "kings and priests to our God."[179]

---

[178] The early churches, even before Nicea, referred to the Eucharist, or communion, as an offering, though this did not mean that Christ himself was being offered again. See the comments on this canon for further explanation and one citation.

[179] e.g., 1 Peter 2:9. Revelation 1:6.

As far as treating the bread and wine of the fellowship meal as an offering, it appears that the churches did so from very early times. Justin Martyr, who is probably the least "ecclesiastical" early Christian writer of the second century, wrote:

> God speaks by the mouth of Malachi ... about the sacrifices presented by you [Jews] at that time: "I have no pleasure in you," says the Lord, "and I will not accept sacrifices at your hands ... my name has been glorified among the Gentiles, and in every place incense is offered to my name and a pure offering. For my name is great among the Gentiles," says the Lord, "but you profane it" [*Mal. 1:10-12*].
>
> He, then, speaks of those Gentiles—namely us [Christians]—**who offer sacrifices to him in every place; in other words, the bread of the Eucharist and also the cup of the Eucharist,** affirming both that we glorify his name and that you profane it.[180]

Protestants today would object to the idea that Christ is being offered again in the Eucharist, but this is not what Justin is suggesting. It's unlikely that the bishops at Nicea were suggesting that, either. Instead, the Eucharist was an offering in the same sense that we offer ourselves, as Paul commands us in Romans 12:1, or in the sense that we offer "sacrifices" of praise and thanksgiving when we sing and pray to God.[181]

Nonetheless, the idea that the Eucharist could be offered only by "priests"—bishops and elders—was firmly established by the fourth century. Thus, the council is appalled that deacons would handle the bread and wine of the Eucharist before the bishops and elders, and they decree that this must not continue.

Further, they forbid the deacons to sit among the elders. Special places for each "rank" of Christian in the meetings was also common by this time. The *Constitutions of the Holy Apostles*, a document that took a century to compile, gives a seating pattern

---

[180] *Dialogue with Trypho, a Jew*. 41. Emphasis mine.
[181] Hebrews 13:15

that separates not just the clergy, but also the catechumens, hearers, penitents, and the regularly baptized members.[182]

Canon 19

Concerning the Paulianists[183] who have flown for refuge to the Catholic Church, it has been decreed that they must by all means be rebaptized; and if any of them who in past time have been numbered among their clergy should be found blameless and without reproach, let them be rebaptized and ordained by the bishop of the catholic church; but if the examination should discover them to be unfit, they ought to be deposed. Likewise in the case of their deaconesses, and generally in the case of those who have been enrolled among their clergy, let the same form be observed. And we mean by deaconesses such as have assumed the habit, but who, since they have no imposition of hands, are to be numbered only among the laity.

Paulianists are followers of Paul of Samosata, who was bishop of Antioch from AD 260 (or possibly a year or two earlier) until AD 268, though he was not finally deposed until 272 because he was also a *procurator ducenarius* (a minor official) for Zenobia, the queen of Palmyra, and she would not stand for his humiliation.

Paul of Samosata denied the divinity of Christ, teaching that he had the divine *Logos* within him more than any previous person, but he was not divine by nature. He did not treat the *Logos* nor the Holy Spirit as separate persons, but as powers that proceeded from God. And, of course, that power that was the *Logos* was not Jesus himself, but was simply a power that Jesus received at birth.

---

[182] Book II, Section 7.

[183] Followers of Paul of Samosata, who was excommunicated in the third century for teaching that Jesus was merely an exalted human. Further explanation in the comments.

Paulianists continued this heresy, which Eusebius described as an innovation. It is true that one can find no such teaching in the Scriptures or inside the catholic churches of the second century. This heresy is very close to what the Ebionites, a very early Christian sect that kept the Law like Jews, taught. They believed that Jesus did not receive the power of the *Logos* until his baptism, which is slightly different than the Paulianists. The Ebionites were never in the catholic churches, though some argue that they are a Judaizing segment of the original apostolic church in Jerusalem.

Deaconesses

There are many references to deaconesses in early Christian writings. They assisted with many services that required a woman, such as helping with dressing and undressing for baptisms and visiting sick, elderly, or incarcerated women.

The council notes for us that deaconesses have not had hands laid upon them, and they are not considered clergy.

I did read comments on this canon that state that the council was *removing* clerical status from *only* these Paulianist deaconesses, but I don't believe Canon 19 can be read that way, nor do I believe there's any indication that any other deaconesses had hands laid upon them or were considered clergy.

Canon 20

Forasmuch as there are certain persons who kneel on the Lord's Day and in the days of Pentecost, therefore, to the intent that all things may be uniformly observed everywhere, it seems good to the holy synod that prayer be made to God standing.

The Lord's Day is the first day of the week. Ignatius tells us, as early as AD 110, that even Jews converted to Christ were "no longer observing the Sabbath, but living in observance of the

Lord's Day, on which also our life has sprung up again by him and by his death."[184]

We will leave a further proof of this for Chapter 12, where we will address the myth that Constantine changed the Sabbath to Sunday. He did not. On the contrary, the Council of Nicea never addressed the Sabbath because it had been settled among Christians for at least 200 years. The reason we argue about the issue today is because we have lost a very crucial understanding of the Law, and especially Jesus' treatment of the Law in Matthew 5, that was known to all the early church, but we will save that discussion for Chapter 12.

The idea that Christians should not kneel on Sundays is a very early tradition. Tertullian, around AD 200, mentions it as a tradition so ancient and so established that it is likely to be apostolic.

> We count fasting or kneeling on the Lord's Day to be unlawful ... If for these and other such rules you insist on having positive Scripture injunction, you will find none. Tradition will be held forth as the originator of them, custom as their strengthener, and faith as their observer. That reason will support tradition, custom, and faith, you will either perceive yourself or learn from someone who has. ... If I nowhere find a law, it follows that tradition has given the fashion in question to custom, to find subsequently the apostles' sanction, by the true interpretation of reason. These instances, therefore, will make it sufficiently plain that you can vindicate the keeping of unwritten tradition established by custom, the proper witness for tradition **when demonstrated by long-continued observance.**[185]

I do not give you this quote from Tertullian to argue that we must hold to every tradition that is handed down to us. Our Lord Jesus warned that it is possible to void God's commands by the traditions of men (Mk. 7:13). We should not just hold to any tradition delivered to us. I quote Tertullian simply to show you that

---

[184] *Letter to the Ephesians*. 9.
[185] *De Corona*. 3-4. Emphasis mine.

even in AD 200, the idea that we should not kneel on Sunday had been established for so long that Tertullian could not find its origin. Further, he expected that none of his readers would be able to name an origin, either.

When you are writing barely over a century after the last apostle died, you can present a strong case that the tradition whose origin you cannot remember is old enough to have come from the apostles themselves. Today, such an argument would be ludicrous. There are thousands or millions of other possible origins for modern traditions beside the apostles. In AD 200, however, a very ancient tradition could be so likely to have come from the apostles as to be worth holding to.

We learn something else from Tertullian's quote. What mattered to the early churches was not just a scriptural origin, but *any apostolic origin, whether directly from Scripture or not.*

This is suggested by the Scriptures themselves. Paul told the Thessalonian church, "Hold the traditions which you have been taught, whether by word or by our letter" (2 Thess. 2:15) But remember, this is a reference to traditions that come from *the apostles.*

The New Testament writings themselves were gathered not because of some special anointing or feeling that they gave off, but because they had some apostolic link. The only New Testament books known to be written by men who were not apostles are Mark, Luke, and Acts. But to the early churches, the content in Mark's Gospel had been provided by Peter, and Luke's writings— he wrote Acts as well—were rendered apostolic because he was a companion of Paul. All the other writings of the New Testament were collected because at least some churches believed they came from apostles.[186]

---

[186] For this purpose Jude and James, the Lord's brothers, were considered apostles.

Thus, any tradition, such as not kneeling on the Lord's Day, that could be shown to be at least possibly from the apostles carried authority in the early churches.

Knowing this, but also knowing it had been more than two centuries since the apostles died, the council specifies with its last canon that this tradition of not kneeling should be observed in all the churches, not as an apostolic injunction, but in order to provide uniformity in the churches.

Chapter 8:
The Aftermath of Nicea

A thin bead of sweat ran down Philip's forehead, paused for a moment to hang precariously from his eyebrow, then dripped onto the emperor's edict. His hands trembled as he read it.[187]

The year was 343. Philip was the Praetorian Prefect, the most powerful man in the Roman empire after the emperors themselves, and he was being ordered to remove Paul, bishop of the "New Rome," the imperial city of Constantinople.

In any different year, there would have been no problem, but things had changed in the empire. Times were different. The battle between the Niceans and the Arians was heating up. Constantius, unlike his father, had sided with the Arians, ending the unsteady peace that had existed since the Council of Nicea 18 years earlier.

Emperor Constantius had already removed Paul once, just the previous year. He had been forced to do so in person because the people of Constantinople had murdered his general, Hermogenes, setting his house on fire and beating him to death in the streets.[188]

---

[187] The following story comes from *The Ecclesiastical History of Socrates Scholasticus*. II:16.

[188] *ibid.* II:13. The story is told in full in Chapter 10.

Now, Paul had returned—without Constantius' permission but armed with letters from Julius, bishop of Rome, and with the probable backing of Constans, Constantius' brother and co-emperor in the west. Constantius was furious, and he had ordered Philip to remove him ... a second time.

If the good Christians of Constantinople had resisted the army and beaten a general to death in the night, what would they do to a civil servant, no matter how high his rank?

But if politicians are good at nothing else, they are good at intrigue. Philip hatched a simple plan.

Paul was a powerful and important bishop. Philip was a powerful and important politician. He would arrange a simple meeting—alone—at the public baths.

History records that Paul arrived at the baths unsuspecting of the plot hatched against him.

But the people were not so naive.

When Paul arrived at the bath, Philip handed him the emperor's order. He took it quietly. Unlike the crowds, Paul was a Christian in more than name only. He did not resist. Guards led him quietly out the back door of the baths to the imperial palace. Within a short time, he would arrive in Thessalonica, Greece, where the emperor had decreed his banishment.

The people, however, unable to trust in the providence of God as Paul did daily, were reliant on their suspicion. They had an idea that the prefect's intentions were less than honorable. They gathered outside the baths, waiting to see what would happen.

When the prefect emerged alone, with a guard, their suspicions were confirmed. They followed Philip's chariot through the streets, trying to determine what had become of Paul. When the emperor's chariot stopped to pick up Macedonius, the Arian bishop tapped to replace Paul, they were enraged. As the chariot made its way to the church, they shouted to passersby and called people from their houses. Such a crowd gathered that the prefect's chariot crawled through the street at a painfully slow pace.

Philip's heart raced. He licked his lips and glanced nervously and repeatedly at the growing crowd.

His guards were no less nervous, but they were also becoming angry as they had to force their way through the streets, shoving people aside and waving naked swords to make a route for the chariot.

At the churchyard, room ran out. The road narrowed, the walls of the yard pressed in, the crowd wedged in on itself. Citizens, guards, horses, and chariot became one wriggling mass, and progress stopped.

Then something happened. Whether one of the citizens actually struck a guard or whether a frightened, angry soldier simply misinterpreted contact in the stuffed churchyard, we will never know. Either way, first one guard and then another turned his sword on the populace.

Citizens fled in terror. Or they tried to.

In the packed churchyard, there was little room to flee, and those that managed it did so over those who fell in front of them. Between the trampling and the swords over 3,000 people died that day.

Philip was safe, but his plan to avoid violence had failed.

No surprise. Violence was the order of the day.

Two *gladii* (plural of *gladius*), the type of sword
most likely used by the Roman guards

Wikimedia Commons. Public Domain.[189]

Marked by Violence

Unfortunately, the Council of Nicea was more the beginning than the end of the Arian Controversy. The battle over Nicea and the Nicene Creed would continue for almost 60 years.

> The Council of Nicaea did not bring the Arian controversy to an end. The orthodox party was victorious, it is true, but the Arians were still determined, and could not give up their enmity against the opponents of Arius, and their hope that they might in the end turn the tables on their antagonists.[190]

It is a horribly disappointing saga. It is, quite literally, gruesome. The behavior of the Christians and their clergy during those six decades is shocking to anyone familiar with Christian history before Nicea.

---

[189] Flanker. Wikimedia Commons. Accessed 24 Mar. 2011.
<http://commons.wikimedia.org/wiki/File:Crossed_gladii.png>.
[190] Schaff, Philip. "Prolegomena: Continuance of the Arian Controversy." *The Nicene and Post-Nicene Fathers*. Series II. Vol. 1.

In the second and third centuries, Christians boasted, as primary proof of the power of their faith, that even their weaker members did not return evil for evil or blow for blow.

> Among us you will find uneducated persons, craftsmen, and old women, who, if they are unable in words to prove the benefit of our doctrine, yet by their deeds exhibit the benefit arising from their persuasion of its truth. They do not rehearse speeches, but exhibit good works; when struck, they do not strike again; when robbed, they do not go to law; they give to those that ask of them, and love their neighbors as themselves.[191]

In the fourth century, however, Christians would burn down churches, assassinate Roman officials, persecute pagans, and beat each other to death in bloody riots over who would be bishop in major cities of the empire.

The situation was so bad that historians of that time period make loose comments about the extent of the violence. For example:

In many cities:

> Ursacius and Valens ... warmly supported the Arian error, and were instigators of the most violent conflicts in the churches, one of which was connected with Macedonius [*the Arian bishop mentioned above*] at Constantinople. By this internal war among the Christians, continuous seditions arose in that city, and **many lives were sacrificed in consequence of these occurrences.**[192]

In Constantinople:

> When [General] Hermogenes persisted in his efforts to drive out Paul [bishop of Constantinople] by means of his military force, the people became exasperated **as is usual**

---

[191] Athenagoras. *A Plea for the Christians* 11, AD 177
[192] *The Ecclesiastical History of Socrates Scholasticus.* II:12.

in such cases; and making a desperate attack upon him, they set his house on fire, and after dragging through the city, they at last put him to death.[193]

In Rome:

Dissension arose among the people [of Rome]; their disagreement being not about any article of faith or heresy, but simply as to who should be bishop. Hence frequent conflicts arose, **insomuch that many lives were sacrificed in this contention.**[194]

In Antioch:

And when Paulinus declared that it was contrary to the canons to take one who had been ordained by the Arians as coadjutor,[195] **the people had recourse to violence**, and caused him to be consecrated in one of the churches outside the city. When this was done, a great disturbance arose.[196]

These incidents were typical of a change in bishops in any major city in the fourth century, especially the eastern cities of Constantinople, Alexandria, and Antioch.

It is perhaps worth telling one more story to give you some idea of the kind of violence that could be perpetrated by "Christians" of the fourth century.

Dispute Over the Body of Constantine

Sometime after Macedonius became bishop in 343,[197] there was a dispute over the remains of Constantine. His coffin was kept in a church that was falling down, and the Christians of Con-

---

[193] *ibid.* II:13.
[194] *ibid.* IV:29.
[195] assistant bishop
[196] *ibid.* V:5.
[197] Described above in this chapter.

stantinople were in a quandary over whether it was appropriate to move his "relics" from where they lay.

In this case the Christians did not need the Arian Controversy to divide into separate parties. They divided simply over whether it was appropriate to move Constantine's remains.

Eventually, Macedonius became fed up with the indecision, and he took it upon himself to have the coffin moved to the church where the martyr Acacius[198] was interred. When the people heard this, they rushed to the church. The melee that ensued is awful enough that I will let Socrates Scholasticus describe it for you:

> Two hostile divisions ... attacked each other with great fury, and great loss of life was occasioned. The church-yard was covered with gore, and the well which was in it overflowed with blood, which ran into the adjacent portico, and from there even into the street.[199]

In this sort of atmosphere, it is amazing that the Arian Controversy was ended at all.

But it was. The process took almost 60 years, but we will try to tell the story in one chapter. Afterward, we will cover some of the interesting side roads the controversy took, and then finish Part I by telling the story of Athanasius, bishop of Alexandria and the most central figure of the Arian Controversy.

Settling the Arian Controversy

We should first point out that *there was no Arian Controversy in the west.* Arianism was exclusively an eastern phenomenon even prior to Nicea.

> The agitation ... was confined to the cities of the east. Those of Illyricum and the western parts of the empire ...

---

[198] Likely the Thracian Christian Acacius, who was tortured in Pyrrinthus, then brought to Byzantium—before it became Constantinople—in 303 at the beginning of the Great Persecution.

[199] *ibid.* II:38.

were perfectly tranquil because they would not annul the decisions of the Council of Nicea.[200]

It's not exactly true to say that the western Roman empire did not have a controversy over Arianism. In the 350's Constantius II, Constantine's son, was emperor over both halves of the empire, ruling alone. He replaced as many Nicene bishops as he could during that decade, and he even managed to get Liberius, bishop of Rome, to sign an Arian creed in 358 after a two-year exile.

However, as soon as Constantius died in 361 and Julian the Apostate became emperor, the western churches restored their Nicene bishops.

In the east, the situation became complicated rapidly.

Eusebius of Nicomedia and Theognis of Nicea, who had probably been exiled shortly after the Council of Nicea for refusing to support the condemnation of Arius, repented and were returned to their respective sees[201] in 328, just three years after the council.

Their letter of recantation mentions that Arius, too, had been recalled from exile already. History records nothing of what he did for the next seven years. We know only that Athanasius, who became bishop of Alexandria upon the death of Alexander the same year, refused to allow Arius to return to Alexandria despite threats from the emperor.

> Since you have been apprised of my will, afford unhindered access into the church to all those who are desirous of entering it. For if it shall be intimated to me that you have prohibited any of those claiming to be reunited to the church or have hindered their admission, I will imme-

---

[200] *ibid.* II:2.

[201] The area of a bishop's oversight.

diately send someone who at my command shall depose you and drive you into exile.[202]

This terse letter was sent to Athanasius by the emperor some time between 328 and 335. The time frames of the dealings between Constantine, Arius, and Athanasius are very difficult to determine.

What is clear is that Athanasius managed to avert the issue of Arius' reinstatement to the church until 335, but even then Arian issues were not settled.

Matters were made worse by Eusebius of Caesarea, whose love for peace made him recommend to the emperor that further talks ensue between Eusebius of Nicomedia, Arius, and the church at Alexandria. This sounds like a wonderfully kind thing to do, but by all accounts Eusebius of Nicomedia and Arius were less than honest in their dealings with the emperor.[203] They were willing to give lip service to the Nicene Creed in order to obtain reinstatement, but once their punishment was removed, they labored tirelessly to overthrow the Nicene Creed and, specifically, that confining term, *homoousios*.[204]

With Eusebius of Nicomedia back in power in the imperial city—Constantinople was still in the process of being built—things were not much different than before the Council of Nicea. Eusebius had to tread much more carefully because Constantine supported the Nicene Creed until his death, but the Arian bishops were simply biding their time, building their case and waiting for their opportunity.

---

[202] *Ecclesiastical History of Socrates Scholasticus.* I:27.

[203] The vacillation of the Arian bishops is discussed in Chapter 9.

[204] "One in substance." Chapter 9 discusses the problem that Arian bishops had with *homoousios*. Chapter 15 is devoted entirely to explaining the term and its history.

Athanasius

Perhaps an even larger difficulty than Constantine was Athanasius, the new bishop of Alexandria. Athanasius was sharp of mind and strong of will. Further, his see, Alexandria, was the most important diocese in the east. His authority was great, and his heart was wholly with the Council of Nicea.

Thus, much of the time period between the restoration of Eusebius to Nicomedia and 335 was spent trying to remove Athanasius from office. Eusebius and his cohorts were helped by the fact that Constantine was irritated with Athanasius for refusing even to talk to Arius.

> The partisans of Eusebius ... welcomed the emperor's displeasure as an auxiliary to their own purpose ... They raised a great disturbance, endeavoring to eject him from his bishopric,[205] for they entertained the hope that the Arian doctrine would prevail only upon the removal of Athanasius.[206]

There was no accusation too extreme. One such is a claim that Athanasius severed the hand of an Egyptian elder named Arsenius in order to use it in magic rites. The story, with a fabulous twist at its end, is told in Chapter 10, but there were many other accusations. These included using his position to extort money from citizens and even treason against the emperor.

Eusebius and his faction were so avid in their pursuit of Athanasius' condemnation that they aroused the ire of Constantine himself. After a synod in Tyre failed to convict him of several false allegations, the emperor wrote to the bishops assembled there:

> I am indeed ignorant of the decisions which have been made by your council with so much turbulence and storm, but the truth seems to have been perverted by

---

[205] The office of bishop.
[206] *The Ecclesiastical History of Socrates Scholasticus.* I:27.

some tumultuous and disorderly proceedings. ... In your mutual love of contention, which you seem desirous of perpetuating, you disregard the consideration of those things which are acceptable to God. It will, however, I trust, be the work of Divine Providence to dissipate the mischief resulting from this jealous rivalry.[207]

Interestingly enough, Constantine's letter was prompted by a very unusual appeal made directly to the emperor. Constantine's letter mentions that Athanasius and several others actually darted into a caravan returning to Constantinople. When Constantine was told who the intruders were, he did not order any punishment, but Athanasius was so much in Constantine's bad graces that Constantine refused to see him!

Later, in Constantinople, enough friends appealed to the emperor that Athanasius was finally granted audience. Obviously, Constantine believed enough of Athanasius' story to decide to intervene and send the letter to the bishops at Tyre.

Constantine called the bishops to appear before him in Constantinople, but the majority of the frightened bishops hurried back to their respective cities. Eusebius and Theognis, however, were mentioned by name along with several others, and they were forced to make the frightening trek.

Things were more favorable for Eusebius and his comrades than it might appear. Constantine was ready to have the Arian Controversy done with, and as far as he was concerned it was Athanasius who was standing in the way of peace. He had ordered the church in Alexandria to restore Arius, who had given promises to submit to the decisions of the Council of Nicea, but Athanasius wouldn't talk to him, despite the emperor's threats.

When the bishops realized that they were only being questioned, not reprimanded, they framed new charges against Athanasius, saying he had stopped the regular shipment of corn from

---

[207] *ibid.* I:34.

Alexandria to Constantinople.[208] Upon hearing this, Constantine decided that the simplest route to peace was to remove Athanasius, and he banished him to Treves in Gaul without a trial.[209]

Most historians, both modern and ancient, believe that the real reason Athanasius was banished was because he refused to see Arius.

With Athanasius out of the way, the bishops called a council in Jerusalem and reinstated Arius. Unfortunately for Arius, as he was being led to his first communion after his exile, he suffered a hemorrhage and died. His opponents called it the judgment of God, while his supporters said he was poisoned.[210]

Not long after, in 336, Constantine died.[211] He was replaced in the east by his son, Constantius II, while Constantius' two brothers, Constantine II and Constans, became Augustus and Caesar in the west.[212]

The Triumph of the Arians in the East

Constantius was soon won over to Arianism, and until his death in 361 he was the benefactor of Arian bishops. He brought Eusebius from Nicomedia to Constantinople in 341, giving Eusebius the prime see next to Alexandria in the east.

Meanwhile, Constantine II and Constans continued to support Nicene bishops in the west.

---

[208] A form of group welfare for the citizens of Constantinople. Rome enjoyed similar privileges.

[209] Modern Trier, Germany.

[210] In Athanasius' favor, he graciously wrote, specifically in reference to Arius' death, that Christians should not be too quick to attribute a death to divine judgment.

[211] Constantine was baptized by Eusebius of Nicomedia a few days before his death. More on whether Constantine was a Christian in Chapter 14.

[212] An Augustus outranked a Caesar. When possible in the fourth century, each half of the empire had both an Augustus and a Caesar. For the purposes of this book, I have simply referred to whichever emperor was making the decisions as "emperor."

Eusebius, now of Constantinople, wasted no time in giving the Arians control of the east. He called a council in Antioch in 341 and affirmed a creed that did not include the offensive term *homoousios*.[213] The council also removed Athanasius from Alexandria and installed an Arian bishop in his place.

All in all, Athanasius would be removed from his bishopric[214] five times, the council of Antioch's decree being his second removal.[215]

The creeds of the Council of Antioch were ignored by the western church, but for the most part, with the support of Constantius, Arian bishops would hold sway in the east until Julian the Apostate rose to power in 361.

Constantine II was killed by Constans' soldiers in 341. Not long after Constans demanded that his brother Constantius deal with the division in the empire over the conflicting creeds of Nicea and Antioch. An attempt was made to accomplish this at the Council of Sardica[216] in 343.

The Church Splits

The Council of Sardica, however, was one of the biggest disasters in the history of the church, creating a complete, though temporary, rift between east and west.

The western bishops brought both Athanasius and Paul—the deposed bishops of Alexandria and Constantinople, respectively—and the eastern bishops refused to meet with them. They then held their own council in Philippopolis,[217] a hundred miles southeast of Sardica. The Council of Sardica affirmed the Nicene Creed and emphasized the term *homoousios*, while the Council of Philippop-

---

[213] The two creeds of Antioch, along with a more thorough description of the proceedings, are given in Chapter 9.

[214] Office of bishop.

[215] Athanasius' story is told in the next chapter.

[216] Modern Sofia, Bulgaria

[217] Modern Plovdiv, Bulgaria

olis rejected the use of *homoousios* as divisive. They affirmed the creed of the Council of Antioch.

It was at this point that the divide between east and west became complete.

> From that time, therefore, the western church was severed from the eastern; and the boundary of communion between them was the mountain called Soucis, which divides the Illyrians from the Thracians. As far as this mountain there was indiscriminate communion, although there was a difference of faith; but beyond it they did not commune with one another. Such was the perturbed condition of the churches at that period.[218]

> Oddly enough, the split put Nicea itself in the Arian section of the empire. It is just as ironic that Theognis, bishop of Nicea, had been exiled for refusing to subscribe the council's condemnation of Arius.

Constantius seemed happy enough with the division. Constans, on the other hand, continued to plead with his brother to deal with the cases of Athanasius and Paul, finally threatening Constantius with civil war if he did not reinstate the two bishops in 346.

With the consent and counsel of prominent eastern bishops—Eusebius, bishop of Constantinople, had died shortly after the Council of Antioch[219]—Constantius received both Paul and Athanasius back from exile.

Arianism Makes Headway in the West

When Constans was killed in a coup in 350, Constantius went to the west to remove the usurper. On the way he ordered both Paul and Athanasius removed from office. Paul was removed and

---

[218] *ibid.* II:22.

[219] In AD 339, the other Eusebius, bishop of Caesarea, had also died.

put to death, while Athanasius managed to dodge the emperor's orders for a number of years while Constantius was busy settling things in the west.

It was then that Constantius began installing Arian bishops in the west. He even secured the imprisonment of Liberius, bishop of Rome, for two years and finally coerced him into signing an Arian statement of faith.

In 359, there were a number of Arian councils held, the most famous being the dual councils in Ariminum in the west and Seleucia in the East. I've read in modern histories that these councils, both of which affirmed creeds declaring that the Son was "similar" (*homoian*) to the Father, were a worldwide triumph for the Arians. In fact, even St. Jerome, in the early fifth century remarked about these councils:

> The whole world groaned and was astonished to find itself Arian.[220]

It is clear, however, that the Council of Ariminum's creed was rejected in the west by many bishops and that most of those bishops still held their sees.[221] Theodoret writes of the Council of Ariminum:

> The motives of the propounders of these views were seen through by the council, and they were consequently repudiated.[222]

Socrates adds:

> The emperor's object in these arrangements was to effect a general unity of opinion, but the issue was contrary to his expectation. For neither of the synods was in harmony with itself, but each was divided into opposing factions. For those convened at Ariminum could not agree with

---

[220] *The Dialogue Against the Luciferians.* 19.
[221] The area of a bishop's supervision.
[222] *The Ecclesiastical History of Theodoret.* II:15.

one another, and the eastern bishops assembled at Seleucia in Isauria made another schism.[223]

Thus, Constantius was able to cause much trouble in the west, to secure the agreement of the bishop of Rome to an Arian creed, and to install numerous Arian bishops. But Jerome was wrong. The world did not find itself Arian. It only found itself against the ropes, in need of a champion.

Who could have guessed in what form that champion would arrive!

Julian the Apostate

Constantius died in 361, within two years of the councils of Ariminum and Seleucia. He was replaced by his cousin, Julian, who would become known as Julian the Apostate.

Julian, apparently bitter over some occurrence in his younger years, turned against every form of Christianity. Thinking that the controversy over Nicea would cause Christians to destroy themselves, he ordered all the bishops banished by Constantius to be restored to their sees in both the eastern and western halves of the empire.

In the good will of God, Julius' plan didn't work. The churches enjoyed comparative peace under the Nicene bishops, and Julian, filled with delusions of grandeur and possibly considering himself a reincarnation of Alexander the Great, perished in much the same way that Alexander did. He led an incursion far into Persia and was killed by an unknown archer in battle.

Jovian

Julian was replaced by Jovian, a supporter of the Nicene Creed. Jovian's reign was brilliant and his demands that the bishops live in peace with one another were surprisingly effective.

---

[223] *The Ecclesiastical History of Socrates Scholasticus.* II:37.

When the various Arian sects came to appeal to him, each side trying to draw him to themselves, he answered:

> I abominate contentiousness, but I love and honor those who exert themselves to preserve unanimity.[224]

He promised not to persecute anyone because of their beliefs, but to "love and highly esteem such as would zealously promote the unity of the Church."[225]

The emperor's attitude was such that he won over an entire sect of Arians. These were the Acacians, named after Acacius, who succeeded Eusebius as bishop of Caesarea. It was their creeds that had been affirmed at Ariminum and Seleucia—by only some bishops, as pointed out above. They had wanted to replace the term *homoousios* with *homoian*, making the Son merely similar to the Father, not of one substance.

Under Jovian, though, the Acacians acknowledged the Nicene Creed and even the term *homoousios*.

> Therefore, lest we should be included in the number of those who adulterate the doctrine of the truth, we hereby declare to your piety that we embrace and steadfastly hold the faith of the holy synod formerly convened at Nicea. Especially since the term *homoousios*, which to some seems novel and inappropriate, has been judiciously explained by the fathers to denote that the Son was only begotten of the Father's substance and that he is like the Father as to substance.[226]

Just as it was an emperor, Constantius II, who stirred the Arian Controversy back to a fever pitch, so it was emperors who were able to lay matters to rest ... temporarily.

---

[224] *ibid.* III:25.
[225] *ibid.*
[226] *ibid.*

It is worth mentioning here that this recantation by the Acacians is an example of why it was said that the Arian bishops ...

> ... worship the purple and not God and resemble the changeful Euripus,[227] which sometimes rolls its waves in one direction and at others the very opposite way.[228]

It is highly probable that peace among the churches was delayed 20 years by the untimely death of Jovian, who reigned only seven months before dying of illness. He was replaced by another Arian emperor, Valens, who reigned for 14 years until 378. He reigned only in the east—his brother Valentinian I reigning in the west—but he once again installed Arian bishops in the sees of the major eastern cities.

The exception to this was Alexandria, where Athanasius' immense popularity ensured that, except for a brief respite of a few months, he would stay in power until his death in 373.

When Valens died, Gratian, Valentinian's successor in the west, took the opportunity to remove Arian bishops from the eastern churches. He then appointed Theodosius, a nobleman and soldier, as his co-emperor in the east.

The Council of Constantinople

Theodosius approved of the Nicene party, but he was not primarily a religious man. He simply wanted peace. In 381, he called a council of Nicene bishops at Constantinople, all from the east, and had them issue a decree in favor of the Nicene Creed. One-hundred fifty Nicene bishops were present along with 36 of the sect of the Macedonians, an Arian sect that promoted the creed of Antioch. The Macedonians refused to confirm the Nicene Creed and left the council.

The Council of Constantinople is usually credited with putting an end to the Arian Controversy, but this isn't true.[229] We are told

---

[227] A narrow strait in Greece between the mainland and the island of Euboea.

[228] *ibid.* Quoting Themistius. *Oration.* V. A contemporary Greek author.

that even after the council there was such unrest over the appointment of Nicene bishops that Theodosius found it necessary to call the bishops together again.

> Great disturbances occurred in other cities also as the Arians were ejected from the churches. I cannot sufficiently admire the emperor's prudence in this matter. He was unwilling to fill the cities with disturbance ... and so after a very short time he called together a general conference of the sects.[230]

I was astonished to find out that the famed Council of Constantinople, the "Second Great Ecumenical Council of the Church,"[231] was a mere regional council of 150 bishops! It is possible that the western bishops did not even know it took place!

I have been making use of *The Ecclesiastical History of Socrates Scholasticus* for this chapter, but Sozomen and Theodoret, the other two comprehensive histories of fourth-century Christianity make no bigger a deal of this minor council than Socrates does. All three mention that the council occurred, and then they move on, never mentioning it again.

The fame of this council is probably attributable to the Council of Chalcedon in 451, a much larger council, that confirmed an enlarged version of the Nicene Creed and attributed it to "the 150 bishops."

---

[229] *The Catholic Encyclopedia* even lists the Eunomians, an extreme Arian sect, as existing only from 350 to 381, as though they are unaware that the emperor Theodosius called them to a conference in 383. (Myers, Edward. "Eunomianism." Accessed 24 Mar. 2011.
<http://www.newadvent.org/cathen/05605a.htm>. Conference of 383 described below.)

[230] *The Ecclesiastical History of Socrates Scholasticus.* V:10

[231] Both the Roman Catholic and Orthodox churches recognize the Council of Constantinople as an authoritative, ecumenical council. The Orthodox recognize seven in total, and the Roman Catholics twenty. (Wilhelm, Joseph. "General Councils." *Catholic Encyclopedia.*)

Even that famous "Nicaeano-Constantinopolitanum Creed"[232] is not from the Council of Constantinople, and was probably never even addressed by it:

> There is no authentic evidence of an œcumenical recognition of this enlarged Creed till the Council at Chalcedon, 451, where it was read ... as the 'Creed of the 150 fathers,' and accepted as orthodox ... But the additional clauses existed in 374, seven years before the Constantinopolitan Council, in the two creeds of Epiphanius ... and most of them as early as 350, in the creed of Cyril of Jerusalem.[233]

Neither Socrates Scholasticus, Sozomen, nor Theodoret—our only reliable sources for the event—say anything at all about the Council of Constantinople creating or adjusting a creed. They simply expressed their agreement with *homoousios* and the creed as given at Nicea.

The "Conference" at Constantinople

For some reason—perhaps because both heretical and orthodox bishops were gathered together or because no decisions were made except by Theodosius afterward—when Theodosius gathered the various sects in 383, it is not referred to as a synod or council, but a "conference."

Because there was still unrest over the Nicene bishops that he was still in the process of appointing, Theodosius felt compelled to get the major sects together. These were:

- The Macedonians, who espoused the term *homoiousios*, or "similar substance" in the place of *homoousios*. (It is thought that they embraced the term primarily for its simi-

---

[232] Appendix G; The Nicaeano-Constantinopolitanum Creed is the official creed of the Roman Catholic Church, except that they have added "and the son" to the section concerning the Holy Spirit.
[233] Schaff, Philip. *Creeds of Christendom*. Sec. 8.

larity to *homoousios* in order to garner support from the public.)[234]

- The Eunomians, an extreme sect of Arians who taught that the son was "unlike" (*animoios*) the Father
- The Nicene bishops
- The mainstream Arian bishops, still trying to promote the creed from Antioch[235]

Theodosius, like many Christians today, naively hoped that if he got these bishops together to debate the Scriptures then they would come to an agreement.

> [Theodosius] called together a general conference of the sects, thinking that by a discussion among their bishops their mutual differences might be adjusted and unanimity established.[236]

It is apparent from fourth-century history that there was nothing reasonable about the Arian Controversy after Nicea. The controversy was both a political and religious quagmire, and no self-respecting bishop was going to let himself be defeated in an argument about the Scriptures just because his opponent's argument was reasonable, accurate, or even scriptural.

When Theodosius suggested his idea to Nectarius, bishop of Constantinople, it was not well received. Perhaps Nectarius had more experience with the biases of bishops than the emperor. Whatever the reason, Nectarius knew a debate would not work, and he went to get some more advice.

---

[234] Because of the similarity of *homoiousios* and *homoousios*, it is said that there was only one iota of difference between the competing sects, a reference to the Greek letter that is the only difference between the two words.
[235] The creeds of Antioch are given in full in Chapter 9.
[236] *ibid.*

Interestingly enough, knowing that the Novatians[237] concurred with the Nicene Creed, he sought that advice from Agelius, bishop of the Novatian church in Constantinople.

Agelius considered himself a shepherd, not a theologian, so he, too, sought advice. He went to Sisinnius, a mere reader—not even officially clergy—in the Novatian church.

Sisinnius, because of the advice he gave, is one of the most important unremembered men in the history of Christianity. He may have changed the course of the entire Christian world!

Sisinnius knew that "disputations, far from healing divisions usually create heresies of a more inveterate character." He also knew that "the ancients have nowhere attributed a beginning of existence to the Son of God."[238]

In other words, he knew that while scriptural arguments would just engender more arguments, the testimony of the churches before Nicea was universally in favor of the rule of faith expounded at Nicea. So he said:

> Let the emperor demand of the heads of each sect whether they will pay any deference to the ancients who flourished before schism distracted the church or whether they would repudiate them as alienated from the Christian faith. If they reject their authority, then let them also anathematize them. If they presumed to take such a step, they would be instantly thrust out by the people. In that case, the truth would be clearly victorious. If, on the other hand, they are not willing to set aside the fathers, it will then be our business to produce their books, by which our views will be fully attested.[239]

The advice was brilliant and remarkably effective.

---

[237] The Novatians are mentioned in Chapter 3 and described in the glossary. (Appendix A.) They began in Rome in the 250's, leaving the church over the readmission of lapsed Christians after persecution ended.

[238] *ibid.*

[239] *ibid.*

When Theodosius brought the heads of the sects together, they had no idea what was coming. As though he were just making conversation, he asked them, "Would you accept the teachings of those teachers who lived previous to the dissension in the church?"[240]

Even the Arians claimed to be holding to the faith of the fathers. Their most famous creeds stated this explicitly. For example, the creed formulated at Antioch under Eusebius of Nicomedia in 341 begins:

> We have neither become followers of Arius ... nor have we embraced any other faith than that which was set forth from the beginning. ... We have learned from the beginning to believe in one God ... [241]

At the same council, they developed another creed that began:

> In conformity with evangelic and apostolic tradition, we believe in one God ... [242]

In the famous—or possibly infamous—"Lengthy Creed," drawn up 3 years after Antioch in an effort "to clear ourselves from all strange suspicion regarding our faith which may exist among those who are ignorant of our real sentiments," the eastern Arian bishops had written:

> Nor **are we taught** that he had his being from any other pre-existing substance besides the Father.[243]

There simply was no room for any of the bishops to say anything except that they would—indeed, must—accept the teachings of those teachers who lived previous to the schism in the church.

So Theodosius, following the advice of Sisinnius the Novatian that had come through Nectarius, bishop of Constantinople,

---

[240] *ibid.*

[241] *ibid.* II:10.

[242] *ibid.*

[243] *ibid.* II:19.

pressed his point: "Would you defer to them as accredited witnesses of Christian doctrine?"[244]

Now, it would seem to any of us that the only possible answer to that question, after having already said that they would accept their teachings, is yes. But like the Pharisees and Sadducees, when our Lord caught them in their words, those who opposed the Council of Nicea dissimulated on their answer, conscious that a positive answer to Theodosius' question was "by no means favorable to their interests."[245]

The sects fell apart, not only arguing with each other, but arguing among themselves until Theodosius could take it no longer. He sent them off and told them to present their arguments to him in writing, and he would decide how to proceed from there.

Each sect went away to allow its most skillful writers to draw up a defense of its position.

The Emperor Theodosius Ends the Arian Controversy

On a given day, Theodosius received representative bishops from each sect. In a significant and interesting development, the representatives for the Nicene party were Nectarius of Constantinople and Agelius, the Novatian bishop.

Theodosius took the writings from each, one from the Nicene representatives, one from the Arians, one from the Macedonians, and one from the Eunomians. He then shut himself up alone, laid the writings before God, and prayed for guidance.

It was a foregone conclusion. Theodosius was already Nicene in his sentiments, and the other sects had, by their collapse under questioning, virtually acknowledged that they knew they were not holding to the ancient faith of the church. The embarrassment had been public, and the Macedonians at least had lost many of their members to the Nicene churches as a result.

---

[244] *ibid.* V:10.
[245] *ibid.*

Theodosius announced what all surely knew he would announce, that the Nicene faith was the only acceptable one.

Novatian churches thrived as a result. Arian churches, humiliated by their inability to submit to the ancient faith, lost their members or moved outside the cities.

Although Arianism continued to thrive for more than a century among the barbarians, the Arian Controversy was over. The catholic churches remained Nicene from then on.

What ended the Arian Controversy—and, in the case of Constantius, fanned it to flames—was the intervention of the emperors. Although the motivation of Constantine and Theodosius was almost certainly primarily political, they were nonetheless the real producers of peace and usually among the only cool heads of their time. Except for the intervention of the emperor the church was headed for an eventual permanent split over the origin of the Son of God.

Perhaps the most credit for the ending of the Arian Controversy should be given to Sisinnius, the Novatian reader! It was his idea that led to the public humiliation of the Arian position.

Of course, even Sisinnius' brilliant suggestion would never have succeeded without the support of Emperor Theodosius I.

Arianism and the Barbarians

It has always fascinated me that the majority of the barbarian hordes that conquered the western Roman empire were Arian. Eventually, they all acknowledged the leadership of the Roman bishop and embraced the Nicene faith, but originally they were Arian.

Why?

During the reign of Valens, possibly the most avid Arian of all the emperors, the Goths north of the Danube river had a civil war. The losing side, headed by a man named Fritigernes, appealed to Rome for help. Valens was delighted to help, and Fritigernes crushed his opponent, Athanaric, with the help of the Roman army. In gratefulness, Fritigernes embraced Christianity under Valens. In this way the Goths became Arian.

As it turned out, the split between east and west was only delayed.

The Great Schism

The western half of the empire was overthrown by barbarians in the 5th century. Romulus Augustus, the last Roman emperor in the west, was deposed by the barbarian leader, Odoacer, in AD 476.

The barbarians remained in control of the west until Charlemagne, a Frankish and thus a barbarian king, was crowned Roman emperor by the bishop of Rome in 800. The Holy Roman Empire and the eastern Roman empire remained separate. The eastern Roman empire did not fall until Constantinople, the eastern capitol, was finally defeated by the Ottoman Empire in 1453.[246]

During the political separation, the western and eastern bishops grew far enough apart that in 1054 the bishops of Rome and Constantinople finally excommunicated one another. It is known to history as "The Great Schism."

That split has never been healed.

Today there are two "catholic" churches, the Roman Catholic Church and the Eastern Orthodox Churches. With no emperor to intervene in their post-5th-century disputes, they found a new word to split over. In the fourth century, it was *homoousios*; today it is *filioque*, a Latin word meaning "and the Son." The Roman Catholic Church has declared that the Holy Spirit proceeds from the Father and the Son, while the ancient creed approved at Chalcedon and accredited to Constantinople allows the Orthodox to declare only that he proceeds from the Father.[247]

---

[246] The history of the eastern Roman empire, which has become known as the Byzantine empire, is more complicated than I describe, particularly in its later years.

[247] Significantly, Pope John Paul II once recited the Apostles Creed without the offending term *filioque*.

Only a very small percentage of Christians understand what it means for the Holy Spirit to proceed at all, much less the difference between procession from the Father and procession from the Son, but the organized catholic churches have nonetheless been divided over it for nearly a millennium.[248]

Of Emperors and Catholic Churches

The word "catholic" means something akin to "universal," and Christians have used the term to refer to the united, catholic churches since the earliest times. Even Ignatius, whose life belongs primarily to the first century and whose letters only barely belong to the second, used it, saying, "Where Jesus Christ is, there is the catholic church."[249]

Protestants will love that terminology: *Where Jesus Christ is, there is the catholic church.* But it should be noted that Ignatius did not believe Jesus Christ was present where Christians were not under the authority of the bishop and elders. Such separation he would term heresy or schism, not catholicity.

The catholic churches were also called apostolic churches because they were founded by the apostles or, if founded later, were in communion and agreement with the apostolic churches.

Unity was important to those churches. It is almost impossible to overstate the emphasis that the New Testament and the early Christian writings put on the unity of the church. Jesus begins that emphasis in his prayer in John 17:

> Nor do I pray for these alone [*i.e., the apostles*], but also for those who will believe on me through their word, that they may all be one as you, Father, are in me and I in you. [I pray] that they may all be one in us so that the world may believe that you sent me. The glory which you have

---

[248] The idea of the procession of the Spirit is very similar to the meaning of the term *homoousios*. Once you have read through Chapter 15, you will have a good idea of what it means to proceed from the Father.

[249] *Letter to the Smyrneans.* 8.

given me, I have given them so that they may be one just as we are one. I in them and you in me, so that they may be perfectly one, so that the world may believe that you sent me and have loved them as you have loved me. (Jn. 17:20-23)

The unity of Jesus' disciples, according to Jesus, is critical to the world being able to believe that he came from the Father.

While we modern Christians do not generally understand this, early Christians did. Early apologists regularly appealed to the unity of the catholic churches as proof that they held to the truth. Tertullian states the case the most clearly:

Is it likely that so many churches, and they so great, should have gone astray into one and the same faith? No casualty distributed among many men issues in one and the same result. Error of doctrine in the churches must necessarily have produced various issues. When, however, that which is deposited among many is found to be one and the same, it is not the result of error, but of tradition.[250]

Fourth-century bishops appear to have forgotten this.

Over and over, it was emperors who preserved the unity of the catholic churches in the fourth century. After Constantine embraced Christianity—whether he was really a Christian or not is irrelevant to this discussion[251]—the unity of the catholic churches was tied to the unity of the empire. If the church split, the empire was likely to split with it.

So it was Constantine who called the Council of Nicea in an urgent demand for unity. It was Constantine who arrived at the council willing to be diplomatic, kind, humble, and reassuring in order to gain that unity.

---

[250] *Prescription Against Heretics.* 28. Tertullian's argument is one more piece of evidence that there was no pope in the early churches. His argument would have had no validity if there had been a pope to decree universal beliefs. This is explained more fully in Chapter 15.

[251] Whether Constantine was a Christian is discussed in Chapter 14.

As long as Constantine was alive, that unity remained. When he died, the churches were unable to preserve that unity.

We can blame Constantine's son, the emperor Constantius II, for destroying the church's unity by embracing Arianism and ejecting Nicene bishops from their office, but Constantius did not come to his ideas on his own. He was evangelized.

> How this was done shall now be described. [An unnamed Christian elder] presented the will and the request of the deceased king to his son Constantius. [Constantius] found the dispositions in it much to his liking, for the empire of the East was apportioned to him by his father's will. So he treated the elder with great consideration, loaded him with favors, and ordered that free access should be given to him both to the palace and to [the emperor] himself.
>
> This license soon permitted him regular conversations with the empress, as well as with her eunuchs. ... The presbyter persuaded [Eusebius, the chief eunuch] to adopt Arius' views, after which the rest of the eunuchs were also prevailed on to adopt the same sentiments.
>
> Not only this but the empress also, under the influence of the eunuchs and the elder, became favorable to the tenets of Arius. Not long after the subject was introduced to the emperor himself.
>
> Thus it became gradually diffused throughout the court, and among the officers of the imperial household and guards, until at length it spread itself over the whole population of the city.
>
> The chamberlains in the palace discussed this doctrine with the women, and in the family of every citizen there was a logical contest. On top of this, the mischief quickly extended to other provinces and cities.
>
> The controversy, like a spark, insignificant at first, excited a spirit of contention in those who heard. For everyone who inquired into the cause of the tumult immediate-

ly found an opportunity to dispute and decided to take part in the strife the moment they asked about it.

By general altercation of this kind all order was subverted.[252]

Keep in mind that the churches were already in an uproar when Constantine got involved. Tertullian's argument, that the general unity of the churches was proof that they had held to apostolic truth, would have been meaningless in the few years before Nicea, at least in the eastern half of the empire. The churches were not in unity, and they could not be induced, even by the intervention of the emperor and a respected bishop from the west, to seek unity.

So Constantine forced it upon them. Contrary to many popular myths, he did not give them any new beliefs. As we have seen above, it was the Nicene party that was unafraid to defer to the teachings of their forefathers in the subjects discussed.[253]

Once Constantine died, the unity he engendered was gone. The uproar that existed before Nicea returned, but to a greater degree because more Romans were Christians.

There's a fascinating description of the controversy by the Roman historian Ammianus:

> Instead of reconciling the parties by the weight of his authority, [Constantius] cherished and promulgated, by verbal disputes, the differences which his vain curiosity had excited. The highways were covered with troops of bishops galloping from every side to the assemblies, which they call synods; and while they labored to reduce the whole sect to their own particular opinions, the public establishment of the posts was almost ruined by their hasty and repeated journeys.[254]

---

[252] *Ecclesiastical History of Socrates Scholasticus.* II:2.

[253] Those teachings and citations for them are covered in Part III of this book.

[254] Ammianus XXI:16 as cited by Gibbon, Edward. *Decline and Fall of the Roman Empire.* Vol. 2, ch. 21.

After the reigns of Constantius and Julian, it took an emperor to restore peace again. Unfortunately, the emperor Jovian died after just seven months at the helm of the eastern empire, and he was succeeded by another Arian emperor.

Arian emperors could never secure peace because the entire western church had rejected Arianism and embraced the Council of Nicea, the only truly universal council of the fourth century. There was simply no way, no matter how many bishops were deposed and replaced, that all eastern churches were going to stand against all western churches on a permanent basis.

> I would personally add that Jesus Christ is the Truth, and he is always going to intervene on behalf of the truth.
>
> Our Lord was not going to let Arius and Eusebius of Nicomedia—whose greatest faults were their self-reliant, divisive attitudes, not their false ideas—be a new foundation of truth for the catholic churches, who were still, for all intents and purposes, the only Christian churches in existence.[255]

Finally, the Nicea-embracing emperors Gratian and Theodosius were able to drive out the Arians with a sufficiently tolerant spirit to ensure that the people did not revolt.

Thus it was that the Emperors were more concerned about the unity of the church than bishops.

But we must go one step further here. In Chapter 15 we will discuss the theology of *homoousios*. Now, as we discuss the unity of the churches and the bishops' loss of respect for unity, we must discuss the word itself and the feelings associated with it.

---

[255] See Chapter 17.

Chapter 9:

Homoousios and the Creeds of the Arians

It has been said that there was only one iota of difference between the post-Nicene Arians and the Nicene party—literally the Greek letter ι (iota). It was the difference between the words *homoousios*, same substance, and *homoiousios*, similar substance. This was the term applied to the creed drawn up at Antioch by Eusebius of Nicomedia and his followers.[256]

That's cute, and it can be defended historically, but it was not the issue.

The issue was only *homoousios*, and it was an issue in and of itself. *Homoiousios* was convenient for the Arians because it approached *homoousios* but didn't touch it, and touching it would mean defeat.

There was pride at stake, not doctrine.

And neither side was going to bend.

---

[256] The Creed of Antioch doesn't actually contain the word *homoiousios*. The Arian sect of the Macedonians began referring to that creed, always popular among the Arians, as the *homoiousian* creed due to its similarity to *homoousios*, probably to gain support in the general population.

Arius' Creed of Recantation

Arianism, after Nicea, was much more of a movement *against* Nicea than *for* the teachings of Arius.

The Arians of the fourth century, at one point or another, denied every tenet that Arius held. Nicea anathematized those who say, "There was a time when he was not"; so did the post-Nicene Arians. Nicea anathematized those who say, "He was made from that which did not exist"; so did the post-Nicene Arians. Nicea anathematized those who assert, "He is of other substance or essence than the Father"; so did the post-Nicene Arians.

But they absolutely refused to embrace the word *homoousios*.

Arius had died in 336, while Constantine was still alive and thus before Arianism could gain any traction. Before he died, he verbally assured Constantine that he agreed with the creed and, indeed, always had. The emperor asked him for a written recantation. Arius provided it, but there is nothing in the creed he presented that revokes any of his old views:

> We believe in one God the Father Almighty; and in the Lord Jesus Christ his Son, who was begotten of him before all ages; God the Word through whom all things were made, both those which are in the heavens and those upon the earth; who descended, became incarnate, suffered and rose again, ascended into the heavens, and will again come to judge the living and the dead; also in the Holy Spirit, in the resurrection of the flesh, in the life of the coming age, in the kingdom of the heavens, and in one catholic[257] Church of God, extending from one end of the earth to the other.[258]

None of this contradicts anything Arius said even before the Council of Nicea. At the heart of his dispute with Alexander, he had written:

---

[257] Catholic is discussed in Chapter 15.

[258] *The Ecclesiastical History of Socrates Scholasticus.* I:26.

> We acknowledge one God ... who begat an only-begotten Son before eternal times.[259]

At Nicea, Arius was not censured for what he did *not* say, but for what he did say. And what he did say, in the same letter to Alexander, was:

> The Son ... did not exist before his generation.[260]

The statement of faith he submitted to Constantine did not in any way deny this.

After he died, however, and Constantius, Constantine's son, embraced Arianism, Eusebius of Nicomedia and his cohorts would eventually deny everything Arius said, even the statements anathematized by the Council of Nicea.

The Creeds of Antioch in 341

Eusebius of Nicomedia had always been the driving force behind Arianism. Arius, as a mere elder[261]—and an excommunicated one at that—could never have gathered a following of bishops. Eusebius, however, was the bishop of Nicomedia. Prior to the building of Constantinople, Nicomedia was the imperial city of the east. This made Eusebius, with the exception of the bishop of Alexandria, the most influential bishop in the east.

For a short time after Constantinople was built and became the "New Rome," the bishop of Alexandria carried more authority than Eusebius. Once Constantius II became emperor, however, Eusebius received a welcome boost.

Shortly after Constantius embraced Arianism, the bishop of Constantinople died. He left no successor, and the people had to choose between Macedonius—who would later embrace Arianism

---

[259] Athanasius. *On the Councils of Ariminum and Seleucia.* 16. The letter is given in full in Appendix D.

[260] *ibid.*

[261] There was one bishop per city and multiple elders. The offices of bishop and elder and their development are covered in Appendix C.

and found the sect of the Macedonians[262]—and Paul, who was eventually martyred for his defense of the Nicene faith.

The people chose Paul, but Constantius did not want a Nicene bishop in his capitol city. He immediately overrode the people's decision, and he called for Eusebius to move from Nicomedia to Constantinople.

Eusebius, whose own writings were condemned and destroyed at Nicea, was back on top.

Eusebius' first act was to call a council at Antioch of Arian bishops. This took place in AD 341. There, they first composed a creed as equivocal as the one Arius had submitted to Constantine:

> We have neither become followers of Arius—for how should we who are bishops be guided by an elder?—nor have we embraced any other faith than that which was set forth from the beginning. But being constituted examiners and judges of his sentiments, we admit their soundness rather than adopt them from him. You will recognize this from what we are about to state.
>
> We have learned from the beginning to believe in one God of the Universe, the Creator and Preserver of all things, both those thought of and those perceived by the senses; and in one only-begotten Son of God, subsisting before all ages and co-existing with the Father who begat him, through whom also all things visible and invisible were made; who in the last days according to the Father's good pleasure, descended and assumed flesh from the holy virgin, having fully accomplished his Father's will: that he should suffer, rise again, ascend into the heavens, sit at the right hand of the Father, and is coming to judge the living and the dead, continuing King and God for ever. We believe also in the Holy Spirit. And if it is necessary to

---

[262] It was the Macedonians who would refer to the Creed of Antioch as the *homoiousian* creed.

add this, we believe in the resurrection of the flesh, and the life everlasting.[263]

It was an attempt to make peace without conceding anything. The question was not whether the Son of God subsisted before all ages nor whether he existed with the Father before the ages began. As we saw above, even Arius admitted that.

The question is, was there a time, before the generation of the Son, when he did not exist, or had he instead, as pre-Nicene churches taught, always existed inside of the Father?

This creed does not answer the question, but dodges it; which was certainly purposeful.

They wrote this creed in a letter, and they sent it to churches all over the empire.

But Eusebius had overestimated his position. Even as bishop of Constantinople, with every right to call such a council, he was ignored. Neither western bishops, nor eastern bishops of the Nicene persuasion, were interested in this kind of ambiguous creed.

Underwhelmed by the response, the bishops decided to try again. This time, they would yield a little more to their Nicea-supporting brothers.

They prepared a more wordy creed, though it was every bit as obscure as the previous one. To this one, however, they added some anathemas, which conceded just a bit more.

> If any one shall teach contrary to the sound and right faith of the Scriptures, affirming that there is or was a period or an age before the Son of God existed, let him be accursed. And if any one shall say that the Son is a creature as one of the creatures, or that he is offspring as one of the offspring ... let him be accursed. [264]

This is a bit closer, but it still concedes nothing. From the beginning, Arius, in the same letter quoted above, had said, "[God]

---

[263] *The Ecclesiastical History of Socrates Scholasticus.* II:10.
[264] *ibid.*

made [the Son] subsist at his own will, ... perfect Creature of God, *but not as one of the creatures.*"

Further, we have seen that Arius had always said that the Son was generated before eternal times. He even adds that the Son was created "before times and before ages."

It would have been common in Alexandria since the time of Origen (the first half of the third century) to point out that God made time. In eternity past, there was no time. Arius agreed that God created all things through the Son, and thus times and ages were created by the Son as well. If times and ages were created by the Son, then his generation must have occurred before times, periods, or ages. [265]

Again, the real question, whether the Son existed prior to his generation, is not even addressed.

We have to remember that Athanasius warned of the goal of the Arians: concede terminology, but reinterpret it to defend their views.

> Eusebius [of Nicomedia] and his fellows endured [the discussion at Nicea] indeed because they did not dare to contradict. They were put to shame by the arguments which were urged against them. Nonetheless, they were caught whispering to each other and winking with their eyes that "like" and "always" and "power" and "in him" were ... common to us and to the Son, so that it was no difficulty to agree to those.[266]

Apparently, Eusebius was still using the same tactics.

---

[265] The idea of no time in eternity past is a rather "cosmic" thought, perhaps difficult to grasp. The Arian bishops needed it, though, in order to declare that there was no age in which the Son did not exist while still claiming that he did not exist before being generated by the Father. This is all explained more fully in Chapter 15.

[266] Athanasius. *Defense of the Nicene Definition.* V:20-21.

Eusebius and Eusebius

I mentioned earlier that there were two Eusebiuses, one of Nicomedia and one of Caesarea. Only Eusebius of Nicomedia, of whom we're speaking here, was an Arian. Eusebius of Caesarea had died, passing away in 339, two years before the Council of Antioch. Eusebius of Nicomedia died shortly after the council.

This second creed received no better a reception than the first. The Arians gave up and went home, but not before appointing a new bishop for Alexandria. That new bishop, Gregory, arrived with a military escort, and Athanasius was forced to flee his home town. It was not the first time, nor would it be the last.[267]

The Creed Presented to Constans

A third Arian creed was drawn up around 342 when Constans, emperor in the west, demanded of his brother Constantius an explanation of why Paul of Constantinople and Athanasius had been exiled.

Constantius complied and sent four bishops to Italy to offer an explanation.

For some reason, these bishops drew up yet one more creed and presented it to Constans. If there was any honesty to it, then it clearly denied everything Arius stood for and agreed with the Nicene Creed. The main part of the creed has nothing more substantial than any previous creeds, but the anathema at the end is decisive:

> Those who assert that the Son was made of things which are not, or of another substance, and not of God, or that there was a time when he did not exist, the catholic Church accounts as aliens.[268]

---

[267] Athanasius' story is told in Chapter 10.

[268] *The Ecclesiastical History of Socrates Scholasticus.* II:18.

Never mind that they avoided using the word "anathema." To be counted as an alien from the catholic church was to be condemned in the minds of all Christians of that time period. Perhaps that is the reason why the Arians were trying so hard to find a compromise—though short of using the word *homoousios* and thus conceding to the Nicene Creed—that would be acceptable to their western brethren.

There was no way for Arians to get around this statement. These bishops affirmed that anyone who asserts that the Son was made from what did not exist, or that he is of any other substance than that of God, is an alien to the church.

This covered all the anathemas of the Nicene Creed. What more was there to concede?

Even Athanasius, the strongest defender of the Nicene Creed in the east in the fourth century, acknowledges that anyone who acknowledges that the Son is "of the substance" of God has "destroyed the catchwords of irreligion."[269] This anathema by these eastern bishops is a complete concession to the ideas of Nicea.

Nonetheless, this creed again carefully avoids using the word *homoousios*, even though it concedes the very ideas that *homoousios* suggests.

And, once more, this concession did nothing at all to heal the rift between east and west. As far as western bishops were concerned, the Nicene definition was sufficient, and it had been confirmed by a council of bishops from east and west alike. Why were the eastern bishops even putting forth another creed?

The answer, of course, is that they were still trying to get rid of the word *homoousios*.

At this point, by the way, Socrates Scholasticus begins referring to the defenders of Nicea as "the *homoousians*."

---

[269] *Defense of the Nicene Definition.* V:20.

The Lengthy Creed

In 344, the eastern bishops made one more attempt at a creed that would unite the churches without having to consent to the Nicene Creed.

The creed is truly lengthy, more than 4 times as long as any other of that era. It contains the same concessions made by the bishops who appeared before the emperor Constans, and more:

- But those who assert that the Son was made of things not in being, or of another substance and not of God, or that there was a time or age when he did not exist, the holy catholic Church accounts as aliens.

- Neither is it safe to affirm that the Son had his existence from things that were not.

- Nor are we taught that he had his being from any other pre-existing substance besides the Father, but that he was truly begotten of God alone; for the Divine word teaches that there is one unbegotten principle without beginning, the Father of Christ. But those who unauthorized by Scripture rashly assert that there was a time when he was not, ought not to preconceive any antecedent interval of time, but God only who without time begat him; for both times and ages were made through him.

- [He] did, not by presence only, co-exist and was conversant with his Father before the ages, and ministered to him at the creation of all things, whether visible or invisible, but was the substantial Word of the Father, and God of God.[270]

The eastern bishops not only stated all these things, but they also explained why they were saying them:

---

[270] *ibid.* II:19.

We have been compelled ... to give this more ample exposition of the creed ... to clear ourselves from all strange suspicion respecting our faith which may exist among those who are ignorant of our real sentiments. And that the inhabitants of the West may both be aware of the shameless misrepresentations of the heterodox party ... and also know the ecclesiastical opinion of the eastern bishops concerning Christ.[271]

Surely this was a complete concession; right?

It was not. The western bishops refused even to read this creed, which was not written in Latin. They explained that it was not worth the effort because they already had a creed, agreed upon by all the bishops at Nicea.

I should point out that had they read it, they may not have approved of all that was in it:

The Son was begotten before the ages, but is not unbegotten like the Father, **but has a beginning**, viz. the Father who begat him, for "the head of Christ is God" [*1 Cor. 11:3*].[272]

Once more, despite all wording to the contrary, the Arian bishops seem to want to hold on to the idea that the Son in some way had a beginning. This statement, that his beginning is the Fatherwho begat him, may allow for the meaning of *homoousios*—that the Son existed inside the Father prior to his generation. But it may also have been an attempt to hold onto something of original Arianism.

Considering the Issues

What was it that the eastern bishops could not submit to? Why did they stand so strongly against *homoousios*?

---

[271] *ibid.*
[272] *ibid.* Emphasis mine.

You will note in the foregoing creeds that the eastern bishops conceded every tenet of Nicea except the wording. What was it in the wording that was so dangerous in their eyes, and why did the western bishops consider it so important?

The Nicene Bishops

I'm sure that to Athanasius and the western bishops, the issue was simple enough. There had been a creed advanced at Nicea with the agreement of all the bishops of the empire. Except for the addition of one word, *homoousios*, it was like all creeds before it, and even with that word, it corresponded with what had been handed down to the church.

Thus, in their eyes, the eastern bishops were simply in rebellion against a decision of the church.

The arguments didn't matter, and the wording didn't matter. The leaders of the church in AD 325 had decided upon *homoousios,* and there was no reason for there to be an issue with it. Surely the only reason these eastern bishops were not submitting is because they wanted to cling to the heresy of Arius in some way. Worse, by not submitting they were dividing the church!

Their logic is understandable. If you're really agreeing with Nicea and repudiating what Nicea repudiated, then why not just agree to the whole creed!

The "Arian" Bishops

I put Arian in quotes because the bishops hardly seemed Arian by this point.

When I first began reading the creeds of the fourth-century Arians in preparation for this book, I couldn't figure out the Arian objection to *homoousios*. By acknowledging that it was wrong to say that the Son was of any other substance but that of God, were they not already acknowledging *homoousios*? After all, *homoousios* merely means "same substance." Where's the rub?

I have come up with two possible reasons:

- Athanasius regularly accuses his opponents of hypocrisy. Their creeds, he said, were drawn up for no other reason than to overthrow Nicea. Thus, they constantly changed what they believed, attempting to get any creed whatsoever accepted if it would displace the Nicene.

• That eastern bishops had a real and legitimate concern that modalism,[273] the teaching that God is one person filling three roles—thus denying even the existence of the Son—would edge its way into the church through the doctrine of *homoousios*, a word that is nowhere found in Scripture.

The Hypocrisy and Vacillation of the Arian Bishops

Athanasius has a strong case for the first of those reasons. Even with the few creeds that we have looked at, we can see the eastern bishops conceding more and more without going so far as to give assent to the Nicene Creed itself. Even when they have conceded that the Son could be of no other substance but that of the father, they still refused to use or mention the word *homoousios* or to accept the Nicene Creed.

Nor is it just Athanasius who accused them of hypocrisy and capriciousness.

At one of the many fourth-century councils, this one occurring late in Constantius' reign, at Ariminum in Italy, several eastern bishops showed up with a creed that asked that the term substance (Gr. *ousia*) should never be brought up again. Two of these bishops were Ursacius and Valens. A decade earlier, when it appeared that Constans, Constantius' brother, had cowed Constantius into submission on the subject of the Nicene Creed, they had recanted their Arian opinions, embraced the term *homoousios*, and presented their recantation in person and in writing to Julius, bishop of Rome.

Since then Constans had died in a coup, and Constantius had again expelled the leading Nicene bishops. In fact, he had Paul of Constantinople killed and tried to do the same with Athanasius,

---

[273] Modalism is the same as Sabellianism, mentioned in Chapter 4.

who managed to escape. Now Ursacius and Valens, appearing every bit as fickle as Athanasius accused them of being, were asking the council in Ariminum to reject not only *homoousios* but *ousios* as well!

The council, of course, was not fooled. Fed up with the multiple new creeds of the Arians, they excommunicated Ursacius, Valens, and their coconspirators. They then wrote Constantius explaining their decision. Though this was of no effect because Ursacius and Valens got to Constantius before the council's letter did, one portion of the council's decree is relevant to the topic at hand.

> Ursacius and Valens, Gaius, Germinius, and Auxentius ... by so often changing what they had believed, have troubled all the Churches, and still are endeavoring to foist their heretical spirit upon the faith of the orthodox. For they wish to annul the formulary passed at Nicea, which was framed against the Arian heresy.[274]

The western bishops at Ariminum entirely concurred with Athanasius concerning the Arians. If they were rejecting the Arian heresy, why didn't they just quit troubling the church and agree to the Nicene Creed?

But there is a flip side to the issue, which I think is important to point out.

The Concerns of the Eastern Arian Bishops

The lengthy creed, mentioned above, mentions some concerns that are germane both to historical and modern Christianity.

> Those who say that the Father, Son, and Holy Spirit are the same person, impiously supposing the three names to refer to one and the same thing and person, we deservedly expel from the church because by the incarnation they render the Father, who is incomprehensible and insuscep-

---

[274] Athanasius. *On the Councils of Ariminum and Seleucia.* 11.

tible to suffering, subject to comprehension and suffering. Such are those denominated *Patripassians*[275] among the Romans, and by us Sabellians.[276]

Modalism, termed Sabellianism in the Lengthy Creed—after Sabellius, who was excommunicated for teaching it in the early third century—was a much more persistent heresy than Arianism. Arianism was new to the Christian scene.

Some version of Arianism may have been taught by Lucius in the late third century, but it was unknown before that. Today, it exists as a doctrine only among the Jehovah's Witnesses, a relatively recent heresy, only a century old.

Modalism, however, was around from at least the second century. Tertullian writes against the doctrine in *Against Praxeas* around AD 210 and says that it was a common belief among "the simple" in the church, who could not well understand the Trinity.[277] It has never disappeared, and there are a number of Christian sects, such as the United Pentecostals, who still fiercely hold to it as a cardinal doctrine.

It seems apparent that at least some bishops—such as Eusebius of Nicomedia, Ursacius, and Valens—were more concerned for their own position and reputation than for the truth of God. However, is it at least possible that many Arians were genuinely concerned that *homoousios* would lead either to modalism or to some modified version of it?

I don't know if that question can be answered except by speculating, but whether those bishops were afraid of it or not, it happened.

Homoousios, a true and accurate teaching from the pre-Nicene era, did bring in changes to the faith. Almost no Christian knows

---

[275] The name *Patripassians* suggests that they believe the Father suffered, attributed to them because they believe the Father and Son to be only one person, God acting out both roles like an actor in a play.
[276] *The Ecclesiastical History of Socrates Scholasticus.* II:19.
[277] *Against Praxeas.* 3.

it; even scholars seem convinced we've simply 'solved a problem.'[278] Nonetheless, the term *homoousios* and the theological battles of the fourth century did produce a doctrine of the Trinity that seems to be a merger of modalism and the Nicene faith.

Changes Prompted by the Council of Nicea and *Homoousios*

We'll go into this more thoroughly in Chapter 16, but there have been some changes in mainstream Christian belief since Nicea.

Here's a brief overview:

- The Nicene Creed refers to the Father as the one God. Mainstream Christians today never use such terminology, carefully stating that the One God is the Father, Son, and Holy Spirit together.

- At Nicea all Christians, Arian and catholic alike, understood Proverbs 8:22, "The Lord created me the beginning of his ways for his works,"[279] to refer to the birth of the Son in eternity past. Today, most churches would consider such a view heretical.

- Any bishops at Nicea that had been well-trained in theology would have held what is now known as a "subordinationist" view of the Trinity. Today, even scholars treat subordinationism as though it were a minority or borderline heretical viewpoint.

The first of those points does not need to be established. Anyone can read the Nicene Creed for themselves and see that it's

---

[278] Philip Schaff uses that terminology—'solving a problem'—in his "Prolegomena" to Eusebius' *Ecclesiastical History* in *The Nicene and Post-Nicene Fathers*. The full quote is given in the discussion below.

[279] This reading is from the Septuagint, the Greek translation of the Hebrew Scriptures, used by all the Greek-speaking churches of the pre-Nicene and Nicene time periods. There are dozens of references to this passage in the writings of the second, third, and fourth centuries. I cite many in Chapters 16 and 17, where we will address the pre-Nicene view of both *homoousios* and the Trinity.

true.[280] It does amaze me, however, that the Apostles Creed, a slightly longer version of the Nicene Creed, is repeated in thousands, or perhaps millions, of Christian churches on a weekly basis, yet almost no one pays attention to the fact that it calls only the Father the one God.[281]

The second point would be acknowledged by all scholars, and it will be fully discussed in Chapter 16, so we can forego it here.

The third point is not acknowledged by any historians that I know of except David Bercot, a former Jehovah's Witness and author of *Will the Real Heretics Please Stand Up*, an excellent treatise on early Christian theology.

Philip Schaff, for example, the great 19th-century historian, writes in his introduction to Eusebius of Caesarea's *Ecclesiastical History*:

> That Eusebius [of Caesarea] was a decided subordinationist must be plain to every one that reads his works with care, especially his earlier ones. ... The same subordinationism may be clearly seen in the writings of Dionysius of Alexandria and of Gregory Thaumaturgus, two of Origen's greatest disciples. ... Eusebius in his earlier writings shows that he holds both [the divinity of Christ and his subordination to the Father] ... but that he is as far from a solution of the problem, and is just as uncertain in regard to the exact relation of Father and Son, as Tertullian, Hippolytus, Origen, Dionysius, and Gregory Thaumaturgus were.[282]

These are important names that Schaff is throwing around. A limited number of writers wrote extensively on the subject of the Trinity prior to Nicea. Schaff has mentioned Tertullian, Hippolytus, Origen, Dionysius, and Gregory Thaumaturgus, and he has

---

[280] Appendix G.
[281] The reason for this is explained in Chapter 15.
[282] *The Nicene and Post-Nicene Fathers*. Series II, Vol. 1.

suggested that they are "uncertain in regard to the exact relation of the Father and Son."

That's five writers, plus Origen. There are not many left to choose from that purposely addressed the Trinity!

In fact, in Chapter 15, we'll see that *every* pre-Nicene writer who wrote extensively on the Trinity is accused of being subordinationist.

That accusation is accurate!

The reason that every pre-Nicene writer who wrote extensively about the Trinity seems subordinationist is because the pre-Nicene churches were subordinationist.

And if the pre-Nicene churches were subordinationist, so were the Nicene churches ... and so was the Council of Nicea.

Even Alexander, who excommunicated Arius and therefore had to be very careful in what he said about the Father and the Son, wrote:

> The apostolic church believes in one Father unbegotten ... who is unchangeable and immutable, who is always the same ... and in one Lord, Jesus Christ, the only-begotten Son of God... . That he is equally with the Father unchangeable and immutable, lacking in nothing, the perfect Son, and like to the Father, we have learned. In this alone is he inferior to the Father, that he is not unbegotten ... as the Lord himself has taught us when he says, "My Father is greater than I" [*Jn. 14:28*].[283]

This is a more acceptable subordinationism than some of the things found in earlier writers, but it is subordinationism nonetheless.

It is certain that at least some Arian bishops were unsubmissive, divisive, and prone to changing their opinions for their own benefit. It is also certain that divisiveness was rightly considered a terrible crime against God and his Church. Nonetheless, whatever fears that less-divisive bishops might have had concerning the Ni-

[283] *The Ecclesiastical History of Theodoret.* I:4.

cene Creed and the adoption of the word *homoousios* have been proven by history to be well founded.

Modern Christians are capable of listing every pre-Nicene Christian that wrote on the subject of the Trinity and rejecting their unanimous consensus as borderline heresy and as "uncertainty" concerning the relation of the Father and Son.

We have lost something.

A Respect for Tradition

Christian doctrine does not develop; it is to be preserved unchanged, as it was handed down from the apostles. The Nicene bishops believed this, and they sought not to develop the faith of their fathers, but to preserve and expound it.

When the Arian Controversy was finally resolved, it was resolved by an emperor who heeded the sage advice of Sisinnius, the Novatian reader. That advice was to find out who would submit to the opinions of the fathers from before the schism.

Personally, I believe we would be wise to do the same.

Chapter 10:
Athanasius, Champion of Nicea

It's a common saying among historians that the history of the fourth century *is* the history of Athanasius. No name stands out like Athanasius' in the overthrow of Arianism.

> Athanasius is the theological and ecclesiastical centre ... about which the Nicene age resolves. ... The personal fortunes of Athanasius are so inseparably interwoven with the history of the Arian controversy that Nicene and Athanasian are equivalent terms.[284]

It is very true that "the personal fortunes of Athanasius are ... inseparably interwoven with the history of the Arian controversy." The fortunes of Athanasius, however, were dependent on the whims of the various Roman emperors. Thus, we must acknowledge that the history of the Arian controversy is the history of the theological preferences of the Roman emperors, and particularly the emperors ruling in the east ... not of Athanasius.

In the end, it was the wisdom and steadfastness of one emperor—Theodosius I, who reigned just 4 years—and the sage advice

---

[284] Schaff, Philip. *History of the Christian Church.* Vol. III, sec. 163.

of a Novatian layman, that would put the Arian controversy to rest for good.

Athanasius' Biography

The year of Athanasius' birth is not known, but it can be reasonably supposed to be around AD 298. He wrote his first books by 319, when he was appointed deacon by Alexander, bishop of Alexandria. Yet, in 328, when he became bishop, his opponents argued that he had not yet attained the priestly age of 30. While the charge may not have been true, it must have been at least plausible.

Further, his parents were still alive in 358. With all these things combined, if we place his birth in 298, we won't be far off.

The story is told that some Christian boys were playing a game, pretending to be clergy, on the day when the martyrdom of Peter, former bishop of Alexandria, was being celebrated. Alexander, the current bishop, happened to be passing by and noticed them. He called for them and asked which office each had filled in their game, wondering if perhaps there might be some sign for the future in their game.

Alexander then had each of them assigned to be taught at the church, focusing especially on the one who had played the bishop. The boy turned out to be a masterful study, and Alexander ordained him deacon as soon as he was of age.

That boy was Athanasius.

That story, not told by Alexander nor anyone else contemporaneous to him, can carry no weight. But however it happened, it is true that Athanasius became secretary and understudy to Alexander and accompanied him to Nicea.

The bishopric of Alexandria was the most powerful in the east at the time. While the bishops of Constantinople and Rome, being imperial capitols—and in Rome's case, an apostolic church—could claim higher authority, no others could. Tradition held that Mark was the founder of Alexandria, and the powerful intellects of Clement and Origen added great prestige to their school. In addition, the bishop of Alexandria had officially been given authority over all of Egypt and Libya—which meant most north African Christians in the fourth century—at Nicea.[285]

Thus, Athanasius was not simply an upstart fighting for orthodoxy. He was in one of the most powerful Christian positions in the world.

Despite that power, Athanasius would have great difficulty holding office.

Athanasius at the Council of Nicea

Athanasius did not play a significant role at the Council of Nicea itself.

Eusebius tells us Athanasius was still a deacon at the Council of Nicea. Socrates Scholasticus gives a list of names that were present, but he does not list Athanasius despite providing reference to a list of attendees compiled by Athanasius (EHSS I:13). Only later does he tell us that Alexander brought him to Nicea "to assist him in the disputation there" (ibid. I:15).

In the first days of the council, as the bishops' companions disputed before the crowds, Socrates tells us that Arians like Eusebius of Nicomedia and Theognis of Nicea were "powerfully opposed by Athanasius" (ibid. I:8), though how he would know this we cannot determine. Eusebius the historian doesn't mention him at the council, and Athanasius leaves us no record of such a dispute. even in his account of the Arians plotting together, he does not call himself an eyewitness, but says simply that they "were caught whispering":

> When the bishops said that the Word must be described as the true Power and Image of the Father, in all things exact and like the Father ... Eusebius [of Nicomedia] and his fellows ... were caught whispering to each other and winking with their eyes, that [these terms] were ... com-

---

[285] Canon 6. Chapter 7.

mon to us and the Son, and that it was no difficulty to agree to these.[286]

What seems most likely is that only bishops were allowed into the council for discussions concerning Arius, the Paschal Controversy, and the various canons. So Athanasius merely heard a report of the Arians' whisperings. Beforehand, however, when the various attendees were disputing in the courtyard, he may well have been involved.

The Trials and Exiles of Athanasius

As noted, Athanasius became bishop of Alexandria in AD 328. His problems began immediately.

About the same time Eusebius of Nicomedia and Theognis of Nicea, who were banished shortly after Nicea, recanted and were restored to their respective sees.[287]

Arius' ideas seemed to be quashed at the Council of Nicea, but there were alternate forces at work. None of the Arian bishops really recanted their views. Almost all of them would devote the rest of their lives to opposing the Nicene Creed and the authority of the council.

Nor did Constantine stand in their way. Constantine's real interest was unity in the churches because their unity affected the unity of the empire. His closest advisors among the bishops were Eusebius of Nicomedia, Eusebius of Caesarea, and Hosius, who was officially bishop of Cordova in Spain. Hosius had delivered the letter from Constantine to Alexander and Arius telling them just to drop the whole controversy because it was not worth discussing. Eusebius of Nicomedia was, and would become again, the strongest proponent of Arian doctrines. And Eusebius of Caesarea had many influences working on him.

---

[286] *Defense of the Nicene Definition.* 20.
[287] The area of a bishop's oversight.

Eusebius of Caesarea was a historian and a well-informed one. He could never support the belief that there was a time when the Son did not exist. He knew, probably better than anyone, the historic doctrine of the church that the Son, as the *Logos* of God, had always existed inside the Father.

He also knew, though, that several of the great pre-Nicene writers had said that before the generation of the Son of God in the beginning, God was alone. The Son was not yet the Son, and the Father not yet the Father, for the *Logos* was inside of God, not yet begotten.[288] Thus, it is possible that Arius' views, while in error, did not seem as great a heresy to Eusebius as they did to others.

Eusebius was also a very conciliatory man. He wanted peace, and he did not want to maintain it by simply banishing all those who disagreed. If anyone was pushing for the reconciliation of all parties, it was Eusebius of Caesarea.

We call men like this peacemakers. Jesus, the only-begotten Son of God, said that such men would be known as sons of God. However, peacemakers are often overly trusting souls, and Eusebius underestimated the dishonesty and divisive spirit of his namesake, Eusebius of Nicomedia.

The Roman historian Ammianus Marcellinus tells us that Eusebius of Nicomedia was related to Julian, who was Constantine's nephew and later became the Emperor Julian "the Apostate." It is certain that he had the favor of the wife of the emperor Licinius, who was Constantine's sister. It was probably these relationships that enabled him to surreptitiously move from Berytus[289] to Nicomedia, Constantine's imperial home.

Eusebius of Nicomedia was no promoter of peace. Between his political connections and the encouragement of Eusebius of

---

[288] e.g., Tertullian. *Against Praxeas*. 5. Many more references are given in Chapters 16 and 17.

[289] Modern day Beirut, Lebanon

Caesarea and Hosius to let all parties reconcile, he saw an opportunity to reinstate his Arian ideas.

The one thing standing in the way was Athanasius, the powerful and insightful bishop of Alexandria, who saw right through him.

The years between Athanasius' appointment as bishop and his first exile in 336 were filled with attempts by Arian bishops to have him removed from office for various invented crimes. One of the most interesting and famous is the story of the magic hand of Arsenius.

The Magic Hand of Arsenius

Somehow, Athanasius' opponents obtained a human hand. They reported to the authorities that Athanasius had tortured an elder by the name of Arsenius, from a minor town in Egypt, then cut off his hand to use for magic rites.

Constantine heard about this charge while he was preparing to consecrate a church at Constantinople for the 30th anniversary of his reign. He was already frustrated with the constant bickering between the parties, for this was not the first charge against the bishop of Alexandria. He ordered Athanasius, Eusebius of Nicomedia, and Theognis of Nicea to Tyre, along with several other bishops and elders, to resolve their difficulties with one another before appearing at Constantinople for the dedication of a new church.

> By the Nicene era, buildings were regularly being called churches, a habit that appears to have developed slowly in the late third century.

Athanasius, hearing of the accusation, had friends make a diligent search for Arsenius, but they couldn't find him. Fortunately for him, however, curiosity forced Arsenius to Tyre to see the outcome of the trial. There, someone spotted him at a tavern and informed the governor.

The governor had Arsenius arrested and delivered to Athanasius. Thus, on the day that he appeared before the bishops, Arsenius was with him.

There were many bishops present. Most of them did not oppose Athanasius in principle, but many had believed the charges against them. They were surprised to see Arsenius brought in, his hands covered in a blanket. Athanasius spoke to the bishops, then exposed one of Arsenius' hands, and then the other. He then asked the stunned bishops whether Arsenius originally had a third hand that could have been removed.

Thus ended that particular synod at Tyre.

The First Exile of Athanasius

Amazingly, the failed accusation concerning Athanasius did not deter Eusebius of Nicomedia and his compatriots. They remained at Tyre devising new accusations against Athanasius.

Athanasius, frustrated, made his way to Constantinople and disrupted a convoy with Constantine in it. Constantine refused to see him, but after he appealed to imperial officers to be heard in front of the emperor himself, Constantine fired off an angry letter to the bishops at Tyre, accusing them of "a mutual love of contention." He ordered them all to appear before him.

The frightened bishops quickly dropped their accusations, disbanded their conference and except for those ordered by name to appear in Constantinople, returned to their respective cities.

Eusebius and Theognis arrived in Constantinople with a new charge against Athanasius. The city of Constantinople was provided with grain by the empire as a sort of welfare system and some of that grain came from Alexandria. They asserted that Athanasius was trying to prevent that grain from being shipped, and they provided several bishops of good reputation to back their assertion.

Constantine was prepared to blame Athanasius for all the contention because he had refused to see Arius, even when the emperor had ordered him to. Rather than deal with all the trouble while preparing for his 30th anniversary celebration, he condemned Athanasius without even seeing him. He banished him to Treves in Gaul.[290]

The Reinstatement and Death of Arius

If Constantine hoped by this to create peace among the churches in the east, he failed miserably. Arius returned to Alexandria once Athanasius had left, and the whole city was thrown into an uproar.

So Constantine, who must have been ready to pull his hair out by now, called Arius back to Constantinople to report to him directly. There Arius swore with an oath that he agreed with the council at Nicea and submitted a recantation which really didn't recant anything.[291] Constantine then ordered the church at Constantinople to receive him to communion.

Constantinople's bishop, Alexander, did not want to admit Arius to communion, but the emperor's command left him no choice. Unable to prevent it, Alexander spent the day and night before Arius' arrival praying and fasting in the church building.

When the day arrived, Arius was paraded through the streets to the church building, ironically named *Irene*—in English, peace. On the way, however, he was struck by a call from nature. Rapidly excusing himself, he found a private place behind "Constantine's Forum," where ...

> ... a faintness came over him, and together with the evacuations his bowels protruded, followed by a copious hemorrhage, and the descent of the smaller intestines: moreover portions of his spleen and liver were brought off in the effusion of blood, so that he almost immediately died. The scene of this catastrophe still is shown at Constantinople, as I have said, behind the shambles in the colonnade.[292]

---

[290] Modern Trier, Germany
[291] Chapter 9
[292] *The Ecclesiastical History of Socrates Scholasticus.* I:38.

I apologize for how graphic that description is. Athanasius, on hearing about it, reports simply that Arius "bent forward and burst in the middle."[293]

Those of the Nicene faith proclaimed this as the judgment of God, of course. The Arians insisted he was poisoned.

Was Arius Poisoned?

When I read that Socrates' disgusting description of the death of Arius to my wife, her immediate reaction was to ask, "Was he poisoned?"

Considering the state of things in the fourth century, after Nicea, it is very likely he was poisoned. As regards his judgment, even Athanasius, the strongest of Arius' opponents, writes: "With all men the common end of life is death. We must not blame a man, even if he be an enemy, merely because he died, for it is uncertain whether we shall live to the evening." Such a statement is an indication that Athanasius was perhaps as gracious a man as his proponents made him out to be.

The Timeline of Arius' Reinstatement

The dates for the recall of Arius are horribly confusing. The date given for the reinstatement of Eusebius and Theognis is 328. This must have been true, for they were actively opposing Athanasius from the beginning of his reign as bishop.

Their letter to Constantine mentions that Arius had already been recalled. Yet all the accounts of death of Arius (given below) place his letter of recantation to the emperor somewhere around the time of the council of Jerusalem that reinstated him, in 335.

Further, Athanasius was first banished in 336 after being condemned at the Council of Tyre in 335. At some point before this Constantine tried to send Arius to Alexandria, but Athanasius refused to allow him to come. This infuriated Constantine, of

---

[293] *The Ecclesiastical History of Sozomen.* II:30.

course, and all historians assume that was the real reason that he was banished to Gaul.

Where was Arius between 328 and the time Athanasius refused to receive him? It is difficult to believe that Athanasius was able to keep Arius out of Alexandria for seven years against the emperor's wishes. Socrates preserves a brief, terse letter in which Constantine threatens Athanasius with exile if he does not give Arius "unhindered access into the church."[294]

Theodoret says that Arius and his adherents lived at Alexandria "a long time" before he tried to gain readmission to the assemblies. It was only then, Theodoret says, that Athanasius refused him and Arius returned to Constantinople.[295]

Theodoret's story is the only one that makes any sense, but it seems hard to believe that Arius lived quietly in Alexandria for five years or more.

The Death of Constantine

In 337, Constantine resigned his office, turned the empire over to his 3 sons, and was baptized. Ironically enough, Eusebius of Nicomedia performed the baptism.

Constantine died only a few days after his baptism in 337, and his sons Constantius, Constans, and Constantine II began their reign, with Constantius reigning in the eastern empire and his brothers reigning together in the west.

The Return of Athanasius from His First Exile

Two conflicting things happened immediately:

- Constantine II sent Athanasius back to Alexandria as bishop. He attached a letter saying that the only reason his father had banished Athanasius was to spare him the persecution of his opponents.

---

[294] *The Ecclesiastical History of Socrates Scholasticus.* I:27.
[295] *The Ecclesiastical History of Theodoret.* I:13.

- Eusebius of Nicomedia and his followers gained the ear of the imperial court, including the emperor's eunuchs and the empress, who soon won Constantius II to the side of Arius.

Athanasius was back as bishop of Alexandria, but the emperor was against him. Things would only get worse.

Alexander, the aged bishop of Constantinople died without leaving a replacement. Though the results of the decades-long battle between the two suggested replacements, Paul and Macedonius, would be tragic, Socrates Scholasticus records a humorous anecdote about how it started.

> Alexander ... departed this life, having been bishop for 23 years and lived 98 years in all, without having ordained anyone to succeed him. But he had told to proper persons to choose between two people he had named. If they wanted someone who was competent to teach and very godly, they should elect Paul, whom Alexander had personally ordained an elder, though he was young in years. On the other hand, if they wanted someone who appeared dignified, but had only an outward appearance of holiness, they could appoint Macedonius, who had been a deacon for a long time and was older.[296]

I wonder who Socrates thought should have been chosen!

I'm relatively certain this story cannot be true.

Paul was elected, but Constantius didn't approve. He removed Paul and brought Eusebius from Nicomedia to be bishop of Constantinople. The year was 341.

The Second Exile of Athanasius

With the emperor on his side, and now bishop of Constantinople, Eusebius was ready to devote himself to restoring Arian opinions. He called the Council of Antioch to form a new creed, care-

---

[296] *The Ecclesiastical History of Socrates Scholasticus.* II:6.

fully avoiding the more objectionable wording condemned by Nicea, but also avoiding any reference to the substance of God.[297]

The council also had Athanasius deposed and Gregory installed in his place.

Athanasius fled to Rome, and once again, Alexandria was in an uproar. In the conflict one of the churches, called the Church of Dionysius after a third-century bishop of Alexandria, was burned down. Later the Arians would blame Gregory for the arson and replace him with a bishop named George from Cappadocia.

Paul of Constantinople

Not long after the Council of Antioch, Eusebius died. The bishop's seat was empty once again.

There was a tense battle between Paul, supported by the Nicene party, and Macedonius, who would later found the Macedonians and promote the *homoiousian* creed.

The battle was not merely theological:

> Continuous seditions arose in the city, and many lives were sacrificed in consequence of these occurrences.[298]

Constantius, who was staying in Antioch at the time, heard about these problems and sent his general, Hermogenes, to get rid of Paul whom he had already removed once.

It did no good. When the general went to sleep that night, the Nicene Christians surrounded his house, set it on fire, then dragged Hermogenes through the streets before beating him to death with their bare hands.

Constantius couldn't believe it. The citizens of Constantinople had assassinated a Roman general!

He mounted a horse and rode to Constantinople himself. There he expelled Paul and cut the empire's free supply of grain to Constantinople in half.

---

[297] See Chapter 9.
[298] *ibid.* II:12.

A Temporary Return to Alexandria

Socrates Scholasticus describes a return from Athanasius' exile in Rome that all historians I've consulted seem to ignore. It was certainly brief, so it is considered part of his second exile.

In 342, Athanasius and Paul arrived in Rome together, appealing to Julius, bishop of Rome, and thus the most powerful bishop in the empire. There, Julius, who like all western bishops, thought the east should just submit to the Council of Nicea, sent both back to their respective sees[299] with letters exhorting the people to receive them.

I'm not sure why they thought that Julius' letters would be sufficient, but they spent almost no time at all back in office.

Constantius reacted as soon as he heard Paul was back. He had removed this man from office twice!

He immediately sent an order to the praetorian prefect in Constantinople and ordered him removed. The prefect had to slip Paul away in secret, but the riot that occurred when the prefect tried to instate Macedonius resulted in over 3,000 deaths.[300]

Athanasius was removed just as rapidly. The Alexandrians were receiving a supply of grain for the care of the poor, and someone reported to Constantius that Athanasius was selling the grain and keeping the proceeds for himself. The emperor believed the charge, and Athanasius was forced to flee again.

Once again Athanasius and Paul arrived in Rome together. Paul had escaped his exile in Greece by telling authorities he was making a trip to Corinth, then slipping away.

Julius had been overridden by the emperor Constantius, but he had another card to play. He, Paul, and Athanasius appealed to Constans, the western emperor. Constans asked Constantius to

---

[299] The area of a bishop's oversight.

[300] The story is told to begin Chapter 8. There I state that the year was 343, which is a best guess. It could also have been 342.

send three bishops who could explain why Paul and Athanasius were removed from office.

Constantius complied, but the bishops who arrived simply submitted a creed and left.

At that point, Constans wrote his brother again, demanding that Paul and Athanasius be restored, but Constantius was able to delay this due to the danger of unrest in two major cities. So the two bishops asked that a council be convened to resolve their case.

The council would be earth-shaking.

The Council of Sardica

The council to decide the matter of Paul and Athanasius was to convene in Sardica, which is north of Greece and is now the city of Sofia in Bulgaria. It was held in AD 343 (probably).

When the eastern bishops arrived in Sardica, they objected to the presence of Athanasius and Paul, saying that both bishops had been legitimately deposed and the western bishops had no right to question their decision. The western bishops refused to give in, demanding that the two bishops be present.

When the two sides could not come to an agreement, the eastern bishops retired to the town of Philippopolis, about 100 miles southeast, and held their own council.

The Council of Sardica confirmed the Nicene Creed and restored Paul and Athanasius to their sees. The Council at Philippopolis condemned *homoousios* and confirmed the deposition of the two bishops. It completely split the church, right down the middle.

> From that time forward the western church was severed from the eastern and the boundary of communion was the mountain called Soucis ... As far as this mountain there was indiscriminate communion, although there was a dif-

ference of faith; but beyond it they did not commune with one another.[301]

The End of the Second Exile

The division was not satisfactory for Constans, who did not approve of anything his brother was doing.

Constans wrote again, demanding the reinstatement of the two bishops. When he got no response, Constans explained that if his brother would not reinstall the bishops, he would come with an army and do it himself.

Constantius did not simply give in. He actually called in Arian bishops to discuss what should be done. They told him that the church's controversy was not worth plunging the empire into civil war.

So Constantius wrote letters inviting Paul and Athanasius to return.

Athanasius had learned his lesson the last time. He feared for his life. It took three letters from Constantius before Athanasius would return, and even then he went only with the encouragement of Julius of Rome.

Athanasius appeared first before Constantius, who assured him of his goodwill and sent him to Alexandria with letters of support.

His next actions, however, made it clear that no matter how slow he had been to return, he had not become a coward.

Athanasius stopped in Jerusalem to hold a small synod with Maximus, who was bishop there. It was attended by two of the leading Arians, Ursacius and Valens. It's a testimony to the Athanasius' power of persuasion that these two bishops not only gave assent to the Nicene Creed and to the word *homoousios*, but they left Jerusalem and went all the way to Rome to present their recantation in writing!

---

[301] *ibid.* II:22

Athanasius' next step, however, would turn out to be a grave mistake.

On the way to Alexandria from Jerusalem, he passed through Pelusium and not only spoke on behalf of the Nicene Creed, but he also ordained elders who supported it, in violation of the canons of the very council he was seeking to support![302] The other bishops took notice, and a few years later this would help lead to his fourth exile.

One has to wonder if Athanasius didn't shoot himself in the foot by those ordinations. The universal testimony concerning Athanasius is that he was extremely persuasive and impossible to defeat in a debate. He won over Ursacius and Valens, though only temporarily. Eusebius of Nicomedia, his main opponent, had died a few years earlier. Had he not aroused enemies with his actions on the way to Alexandria, is it possible that he would have had opportunity to win over eastern bishops when he appeared before them face to face at synods?

We will never know.

Athanasius spent perhaps two years in Alexandria, about which nothing is recorded, before a most unfortunate event collapsed his political support.

The Third Exile of Athanasius

In AD 350, Magnentius, a commander of the imperial guard units, was declared king by the Roman army, which then killed Constans. This happened in the far west, in what is now modern France and Spain, but the uprising soon spread all the way to Italy.

Constantius immediately prepared an army to overthrow the usurper, but Athanasius' opponents took this opportunity to charge him fomenting unrest in Egypt and Libya. This was not hard to do because of the unlawful ordinations he'd undertaken on the way to Alexandria.

---

[302] Canons 6 and 16. Chapter 7.

Constantius had plenty on his mind due to the uprising, and in a fury he ordered Athanasius and several other Nicene bishops put to death. Athanasius managed to escape, but Paul was captured in Constantinople, removed from the city, and strangled.

Athanasius somehow managed to maintain his bishopric in Alexandria for six more years. It is likely that this happened because Constantius was busy in the west, calling church councils and deposing bishops. At that time, he even managed to remove Liberius, bishop of Rome, and have an Arian deacon by the name of Felix elected.[303]

In 356, Constantius finally had time to remove Athanasius. This time, he sent a military unit.

The soldiers arrived while Athanasius was holding evening vigils at the Church of St. Thomas. Realizing that the church was surrounded, Athanasius attempted to prevent his congregation from harm by sending them out. The soldiers pressed their way into the church, however, along with their general, Syrianus. The congregation and some of the clergy clamored for Athanasius to run, but he refused. He offered a prayer, and he asked for the people to leave.

Somehow, as the last of the congregation was leaving, some of the monks and clergy that were last to leave grabbed Athanasius and pulled him into their midst. They took him out with them right under the eyes of the Roman general.

This was surprising enough that Athanasius felt compelled to add to his story, "May the truth be my witness!"[304]

---

[303] There is dispute over whether Felix was really Arian. There are assumptions involved in declaring him Arian that we cannot be certain of. It is not central to our purpose to cover all the details here.

[304] Athanasius. *Defense of His Flight*. 24.

The Third Exile and the Writings of Athanasius

It is guessed that Athanasius hid among the hermits in Upper Egypt.[305] Most of Athanasius' more important writings were composed during those five years.

Many of those writings may have been composed in anguish. Stories of Arian persecution abound during those late years of Constantius' reign, and not only from Athanasius. George's persecution of the pagans led to his being torn to pieces by an angry mob in 361, the year Julian rose to power.

Emperor Julian himself wrote a letter to the Alexandrians against their vigilante justice, but George's behavior was so awful that the letter has an understanding tone to it:

> For what unjust deed were you so indignant at George? You will perhaps answer ... because he exasperated Constantius of blessed memory against you ... because he ... dared to send armed bands against you. ... It would have been better for his own safety had he not been guilty of this tyrannical conduct ... [306]

Julian, having adopted paganism, complains of what was done to pagans in Alexandria, but Theodoret adds some description of what George did to Nicene Christians.

> He ordered a fire to be kindled in the center of the city and placed the virgins, who were stripped naked, close to it, commanding them to deny the faith. Although they formed a most sorrowful and pitiful spectacle for believers as well as unbelievers, they themselves considered that all these dishonors conferred the highest honor upon them, and they joyfully received the blows inflicted on them on account of their faith.[307]

---

[305] Upper Egypt is actually southern Egypt. It is called Upper Egypt because the Nile flows north, so that southern Egypt is upriver from northern Egypt.

[306] *The Ecclesiastical History of Socrates Scholasticus.* III:3.

[307] *The Ecclesiastical History of Theodoret.* II:11.

Once George was murdered by the populace, Athanasius returned to Alexandria as bishop again. Julian had removed the banishment of all bishops, perhaps hoping that in the confusion Christianity would destroy itself and paganism would triumph.

The Fourth Exile

Athanasius, as has been said, was a persuasive man. Evidently, he was just as persuasive to the heathen as he was to other Christians. The emperor was told, "If Athanasius remains, not a heathen will remain, for he will get them all over to his side!"[308]

Julian had a simple remedy for this. He ordered Athanasius killed.

His escape is a beautiful story.

Athanasius heard about the sentence as the soldiers were approaching the city to arrest him. With friends, he hurried to the river to escape on a boat. The officer in charge of his execution was told where he had gone and headed to the river himself. When Athanasius was informed of the pursuit, the boat's captain suggested he hide in the desert, but Athanasius came up with a better plan.

They wheeled the boat around and as they approached the officer, who was racing down the river to catch him, Athanasius walked to the front of the boat. When he was near enough, the officer, thinking he was simply meeting a passing citizen, cried out, "How far away is Athanasius?"

With complete honesty, Athanasius replied, "Not far," then he continued back to Alexandria.

This exile can hardly be called an exile because Athanasius stayed hidden in Alexandria until Julian died in 363.

Jovian replaced Julius, and he embraced the Nicene faith. Athanasius was not only restored but enjoyed some correspondence

---

[308] *ibid.* III:5.

with the new emperor. That peace was as short-lived as the emperor, who died after a reign of only seven months.

The Fifth and Final Exile of Athanasius

Athanasius was banished a fifth time after Valens became emperor. In late 365, he banished all bishops that had been banished by Constantius, and Athanasius went into hiding again. Valens rescinded this order only four months later, however, and Athanasius spent the rest of his life writing in defense of the Nicene faith.

He died in 373, remembered as Nicea's most faithful and effective defender.

Part II:

The Myths

of

the Council of Nicea

Chapter 11:
Myths About the Council of Nicea

This book was originally prompted by all the myths circling the internet about the Council of Nicea.

Each day Google sends me an email with new sites they've found that fit the search term "council of nicea." Usually, these are blogs or someone commenting on a religious news item.

Today, as an example, there is a lengthy Facebook post that has the following bits of misinformation, presented as though the author actually knew something about history:

- "To understand the invention of Jesus Christ as a saviour you must go back to the Nicean Council of Bishops, most especially the second council I believe in 324 AD"[309]

- "First, they condemned Arius in 318 AD Then in 324 AD they took back what they said about Arius but also established the order of the trinity (The Father, Son and the Holy Ghost) as the true development of the saviour Jesus Christ."

---

[309] There was a Second Council of Nicea. It took place in AD 787, over 450 years after the first council, which took place in 325, not 324.

- "The Bishops renamed the god Serapis Christus to Jesus Christ as the way to disassociate from the corruption of the Serapis name. Then they eventually banned Arius and his teachings."

One has to wonder what the source is for this nonsense. Surely this lone internet person did not make up something this bizarre. He read it somewhere, and it was probably presented to him as breaking news, an outstanding insight into "true" history. After all, this Facebook person—posting on Glenn Beck's page, by the way!—declares:

> For all those who believe in Christ I am not here to try to defraud your beliefs. However, I do ask of anyone who is of the Christian faith to do the necessary research and not rely so much on mythology.

This is amazing, but not uncommon. Every day Google Alert sends me links to several blogs and comments full of this sort of imaginary history.

Serapis

It's interesting that this person mentioned the Greco-Egyptian god Serapis, as he is at the heart of one of my favorite bits of Christian history.

The book, *The Octavius*, written by Minucius Felix sometime between AD 160 and 230, is a debate between a Roman pagan and a Christian. It is one of the most fascinating discussions of early Christianity available.

That debate began when the Roman pagan found a small image of Serapis and kissed it. The Christian, far from acknowledging that Serapis and Jesus were the same person, rebuked a Christian friend for not having already spoken to the pagan about his ignorance and superstition.[310]

More amazing is the reason that there is a comment like that on Glenn Beck's page. Glenn Beck hosts the third highest rated talk show on the radio,[311] but he made a fool of himself on national media discussing the Council of Nicea. He said:

> The Council of Nicea, and what they did is brought all of the religious figures together, all the Christians, and then they said, "Okay, let's put together the Apostles' Creed, let's you know, you guys do it."
>
> So they brought all their religious scripture together, that's when the Bible was first bound and everything else. And then they said, "Anybody that disagrees with this is a heretic and off with their head!"
>
> Well, that's what the Dead Sea Scrolls are. The Dead Sea Scrolls are those scriptures that people had at the time that they said, "They are destroying all of this truth."

---

[310] The debate is abridged and put in a more modern format on my web site, *Christian History for Everyman*. <http://www.christian-history.org/christian-debate.html>.

[311] Among 25 to 54 year olds. Mercury Radio Arts. 2014. Accessed April 22, 2014. < http://www.glennbeck.com/content/radio/>

Whether it's truth or not is up to the individual, but at that time those people thought that this was something that needed to be preserved and so they rolled up the scrolls and put them in clay pots and they put them in the back of caves where no one could find them. They were hidden Scripture because everything was being destroyed that disagreed with the Council of Nicea and Constantine."[312]

Glenn Beck was excoriated across the internet for this historical blunder. The chances are he heard about the Nag Hammadi Scrolls, which were gnostic and found in clay pots, and he confused them with the more famous Dead Sea Scrolls, which are Jewish. That Constantine and the Council of Nicea destroyed gnostic writings is *the* most popular myth concerning the Council of Nicea, spread widely by Dan Brown's *The Da Vinci Code*.

The Dead Sea Scrolls

We have not addressed the Dead Sea Scrolls because they have nothing to do with the Council of Nicea.

The Dead Sea Scrolls date from between 300 B.C. and AD 70. A Jewish community—almost certainly Essene—abandoned them in AD 68 when the Roman army invaded to quash a Jewish rebellion.

The Dead Sea Scrolls, all Jewish writings, were lying in a cave, forgotten and unknown, when the Council of Nicea met in 325. They would not be found for another 1,622 years.

Nonetheless, even after we substitute the Nag Hammadi Scrolls in his story, it's still all invented.

I'm relatively certain that Glenn Beck did not get up that morning in May and say, "I think I'll say something historically

---

[312] This quote can be found on dozens of web sites. e.g., Shea, Mark P. "But I Learn So Much from Glenn Beck!" 8 June 2010. Free Republic. June 8, 2010. Accessed March 9, 2011. <http://www.freerepublic.com/focus/f-religion/2530437/posts>.

naive on the radio today so that I can be lampooned by thousands of blogs as well as the national news media."

No, Glenn Beck was caught unaware. He believed something he heard.

Addressing the Myths About the Council of Nicea

As I saw these myths being foisted on a mostly unaware internet readership, I wondered how to correct them. If I wrote comments or blogs disagreeing with the assertions of the internet rumor mill, why should anyone believe me? I have a large and popular web site on Christian history, but all that proves is that I know something about driving traffic on the internet.

I realized then that few who are involved in internet discussions know where to find accurate information about the Council of Nicea. I did, and I knew the sources were limited, so I thought, "I'll just let people know how they can know about Nicea."

With that in mind, I answered several Council of Nicea questions on Yahoo! Answers, and my answers were consistently picked as best answer. I knew I was on to something.

When I began this book, I was thinking, "List the sources; bash the myths." I was even intending to title the book, *The Council of Nicea: Dispelling the Myths.*

Then I began writing.

The book seemed to expand and grow under my fingers as I typed. It seemed for a while that there would be no end to telling stories, especially when I got to "The Aftermath of Nicea." There was approximately 60 years of controversial, rumbling, earth-shaking history to write, and it was so interesting to me that I wanted to include everything.

When I got done, I realized there was almost no point to addressing the myths. They were addressed. The story was told.

Did the Council of Nicea throw away 300 gnostic books and create the Bible for the first time?

If you read the Part I of this book, you know that didn't happen.

Did the Council of Nicea declare Jesus God for the first time, thus inventing the Trinity?

You know the answer to that. You even know the real story of the Trinity, which the Council of Nicea did not change, but approved.

Did Constantine preside at the Council of Nicea?

You know the answer to that, too; only in this case it's yes.

Was Constantine the pagan high priest at the time of the Council of Nicea, and did he have the title of Pontifex Maximus?

Okay, that one we haven't covered. We won't discuss that until Chapter 14.

It's always easier, they say, to spot a counterfeit if you know the real thing. If you study one counterfeit, you'll recognize that one counterfeit. If you study the real thing, you'll recognize anything that is not the original.

Myths That We Will Address

The idea that Constantine was the pagan high priest is not a myth, but it must be addressed. There are two other myths that must be addressed.

- Did the Council of Nicea put a purposeful end to the gnosticism and destroy gnostic writings?
- Did the Council of Nicea change the Sabbath day from the seventh day (Saturday) to the first day (Sunday), and did they do so because Constantine was the pagan priest of the sun?

The answer to both these questions is no, which is the reason we have not covered these issues yet. They do not come up when you read the historical sources. Gnosticism and the Sabbath day are simply not a part of the Nicea story.

One will never find quotes from primary sources[313] saying, "The Council of Nicea did not cover <such and such>." Because they did not cover gnosticism or the Sabbath, there are no quotes about gnosticism or the Sabbath in documents having to do with the Council of Nicea.

That does not mean there is nothing to say. Gnosticism does have a history, even if it is unrelated to Nicea. That history is interesting enough and important enough to be worth looking at briefly.

The Sabbath is a major Bible doctrine, and it was a controversy between Christians and Jews in the earliest days of the church. It is discussed often and—fortunately for our purposes—consistently in the pre-Nicene writings of the church.

Therefore, in the next three chapters we will discuss gnosticism, the Sabbath, and then address whether Constantine was really a Christian.

---

[313] Primary sources are eyewitness or at least contemporary sources. These were discussed in Chapter 2.

Chapter 12:
Gnosticism and the Council of Nicea

It is only because of misinformation that we are even discussing gnosticism in this book. Gnostic influence was long gone from the church by AD 325 when the Council of Nicea convened. It simply is not a part of Nicene history. It's never mentioned; it never comes up.

Gnosticism had its beginning, possibly even inside the Church, in the first century. Paul and John both had to write letters refuting their teachings (1 Cor. 15; 1 John 2:26).

Sometime in the early second century, gnostics were driven out of the church. Ignatius, the bishop of Antioch—Paul's home church—at the beginning of the second century, wrote seven letters on his way to martyrdom in Rome. In every one, he pleads with the churches to adhere to their leaders and to avoid heretical teachers who deny the flesh and blood of our Lord Jesus Christ, a clear reference to the gnostic teaching that all things material or physical are either evil or useless.

Apparently his efforts and those of other church leaders were successful.

By the time apologists like Irenaeus, Tertullian, and Hippolytus wrote in the late second and early third centuries, they addressed the gnostics as competing sects outside the church. They were concerned that Christians would be susceptible to gnostic teaching and argued against it, but the gnostic groups themselves had clearly been expelled from the catholic[314] churches.

By the time of the Council of Nicea, a century after Hippoly-tus' *Refutation of All Heresies*, gnostic heresies were barely mentioned. Driven out of the church, their system slowly died the death that is appropriate to such outlandish beliefs.[315]

Thus, the Council of Nicea did not have to do away with their influence, gnosticism was practically non-existent by the early fourth century.

Reviving Gnosticism in the twenty-first Century

In 1945, 12 codices[316] were found in Nag Hammadi, Egypt. In these books were numerous gnostic writings that had been lost for centuries.

As I pointed out, gnosticism had virtually died out by the time of Nicea. Groups like the Manichaeans are often said to be gnostic, but that was mostly just an accusatory term from the Christians. The Manichaeans and their later descendants were much more influenced by the ancient Ebionites, a Judaizing sect of early Christianity, and eastern religious thought, especially Zoroastrianism, a monotheistic religion emphasizing good works and the battle between good and evil.

The Nag Hammadi codices brought gnosticism back into modern thought, however.

There are several reasons that these ancient gnostic writings would be popular today:

- Gnostic writings tend to be very mystical, and they can be interpreted in a myriad of ways. There is no need to adopt the original, bizarre system of an unknowable God and ae-

---

[314] Catholic means "universal," and it was used from early in the second century to refer to the united, apostolic churches.

[315] Their system is explained below.

[316] Ancient books formed of paper or parchment. These were usually quite large. Codices is the plural of codex.

ons (or emanations) of the ancient gnostics in order to embrace modern gnosticism.

- Gnosticism was the earliest heresy and thus makes a great competitor for traditional Christianity.[317]

- A sensationalist account of a suppressed and hidden Christianity that has suddenly come to light is sure to be popular in a world where Jesus still has a good reputation but Christians do not.[318]

Carl Jung, the famous psychologist whose psychology is extremely mystical itself, picked up on the Nag Hammadi codices even though they were not discovered until he was 70. He claimed that they had truths in them corresponding to the discoveries of modern psychology.

But it is not Carl Jung who brought the Nag Hammadi Scrolls to popular attention. The two people most responsible for the popularity of Gnosticism today are Elaine Pagels and Bart Ehrman.

Elaine Pagels was fortunate enough to be put on the team that was studying the Nag Hammadi manuscripts while still a doctoral student at Harvard. She was only 24, and it would prove to be the break of a lifetime for her. She published her first book, *The Gnostic Paul* in 1975, and she has become a prolific and popular author since. She is currently the Harrington Spear Paine Professor of Religion at Princeton.

Ehrman is the James A. Gray Distinguished Professor of Religious Studies at the University of North Carolina, and he is even more prolific than Ms. Pagels. He has written over 20 books, three of which have been on the New York Times bestseller list.

---

[317] The earliest apologists say that it was Simon the magician, mentioned in Acts 8, who began gnosticism (e.g., Justin Martyr. *First Apology* 26.). Even if their testimony is inaccurate, gnosticism certainly dates back to apostolic times.
[318] Ronald Sider, in his book *The Scandal of the Evangelical Conscience* (Baker Books, 2005), does a thorough job of documenting why Christians, speaking in general, have a bad reputation in the developing world.

Gnostic Myths in the Second Century

Pagels and Ehrman have been responsible for making gnosticism popular in modern times, but they are not responsible for the myths about gnosticism that are circulating on the internet. I have my strong disagreements with both Pagels and Ehrman, and I believe their scholarship ignores the context of history, but they have confined themselves, for the most part, to first- and second-century arguments about gnosticism.

On the other hand, their arguments are just as much in error.

For example, in National Geographic's video special on the Gospel of Judas, Ehrman claims that it was Irenaeus, the great bishop from Lyons, who reduced the Gospels from thirty to four around AD 180:

> His argument is one that doesn't make sense to most people today. Irenaeus argued that since there were four corners of the earth, four winds of heaven, there had to be four Gospels. And they were Matthew, Mark, Luke, and John.[319]

The film had just quoted Irenaeus as saying:

> There are four Gospels and only four. Four like the points of the compass; four like the chief directions of the wind; The church, spread all over the world, has in the Gospels four pillars. Christ is at the center of them.[320]

Irenaeus really did say this. It's found in *Against Heresies* III:11:8. The wording's not very accurate, but the idea they are quoting is exactly what he said.

Ehrman's concern about this quote would be correct if Irenaeus was really distilling the Gospels down from 30 to four.

But he's not.

---

[319] "The Gospel of Judas, the Hidden Story of the Betrayal of Christ." YouTube. I watched this special online and carefully transcribed Professor Ehrman's words.
[320] ibid.

The Four Gospels

There are numerous Christian writings from before Irenaeus. They may not directly state that there are four Gospels, but it is easy to determine the accepted Gospels based on the quotations found in their writings.

Except for the early and anonymous *Letter to Diognetus*, every one of the second century writings is packed full of quotes from the Scriptures. These writers seem unwilling to say anything without copiously backing their statements from the holy writings.

In those writings, the four Gospels that are in our Bible are quoted early and often, especially the synoptic Gospels.[321] There are no quotes at all from known gnostic works, such as *The Gospel of Mary Magdalene* or *The Apocryphon of John*.[322]

Even more importantly, there is a list of the New Testament writings regarded as Scripture that dates from AD 170—more than 20 years before Irenaeus wrote the passage quoted by Bart Ehrman—called the Muratorian Canon.[323] It lists only the four Gospels we know, and its entire canon[324] is very close to what is accepted today.

---

[321] Matthew, Mark, and Luke.

[322] An apocryphal Gospel called *The Gospel of Thomas* is quoted as Scripture in *2 Clement*, an early-second-century anonymous sermon falsely attributed to Clement of Rome. (Ch. 12.) It's the only early Christian reference to a Gospel other than our four in the pre-Nicene Christian writings, and *The Gospel of Thomas* is not necessarily gnostic.

Nor is the sermon necessarily quoting *The Gospel of Thomas*. Clement of Alexandria, near the end of the second century, quotes the same passage and attributes it to a *Gospel of the Egyptians* that he treats as non-canonical. (*Miscellanies*, III:13.) It's possible that the passage came from somewhere else and made its way into both *2 Clement* and *The Gospel of Thomas*.

As an aside, it's important not to confuse *The Gospel of Thomas* with *The Infancy Gospel of Thomas*, which records an interesting but fantastic and unbelievable version of Jesus' childhood.

[323] The full text of the Muratorian Fragment is given in Appendix L.

[324] Canon is from a Latin word meaning "rule." Today, it is primarily used to refer to the set of books that are considered to be Scripture by a religion, but it

In addition, around the same time, Tatian, a disciple of Justin Martyr of Rome, had published a harmony of the four canonical Gospels called *The Diatessaron*. *The Diatessaron* also predates Irenaeus' letter by 20 years or more.

There was nothing new about Irenaeus' statement that there are only four Gospels.

Irenaeus was not a fool. He did not present the four directions of the compass as *proof* that there should be four Gospels, while throwing out twenty-six others. Such an argument makes no sense to us today, and it wouldn't have made any sense to second-century Christians, either.

His argument makes perfect sense, however, if the gnostics were trying to add gospels to the four that were accepted by the apostolic churches. He is not presenting proof; instead, he is saying, "Thank you, but we have enough. Our four is a perfect number."

Ehrman's assertion is based on nothing at all. There is simply no evidence on his side for me to refute. He can show that at least a couple of the gnostic gospels existed at that time, but there is no evidence to even hint that Irenaeus was sorting between the canonical[325] Gospels and the gnostic ones within the church.

Again, let me remind you, Ignatius, around AD 110, writes against gnostic beliefs infiltrating the church. There is no conspiracy. He says quite plainly that he is concerned about their errors, and he says quite plainly they are in the church. Irenaeus, 75 years later, writes against the gnostics as clearly outside the church. He admits that some Christians have been led astray by them, but he makes it clear that they left the church. To become gnostic in AD 185 was to leave the church, not be in it.

Finding some of their writings does not change that history. We know what happened to them. They were in the church, and in

---

also refers to ecclesiastical rules passed by a council, such as those passed by the Council of Nicea and given in Chapter 7.

[325] Those regarded as Scripture by the churches.

the early second century, they were finally driven out. In the late-second century they're always referred to as outside the church. By the late-third century they're not mentioned in Christian writings at all.

Why the Gnostics Were Driven Out of the Church

Modern gnostic scholars do not like to point out the nonsense taught in many of these gnostic writings.

For example, National Geographic's special shows Marvin Meyer, Griset Professor of Bible and Christian Studies at Chapman University, saying:

> Gnostics didn't need to have the advice and the control and the insight that came from the priests and the bishops. They had that insight in themselves. And that bothered the church leaders.[326]

That's what bothered the church leaders?

Not according to what we read in their writings!

What bothered the apostle Paul was that they taught that the resurrection wasn't going to occur (1 Cor. 15). What bothered the apostle John was that they denied that Jesus had come in the flesh (1 Jn. 4:3). What bothered Irenaeus was that they taught that the God of Israel was an ignorant deity, called the "Demiurge," accidentally produced by an emanation of the true God as she wailed in distress over the fact that the true God is unknowable.

> Sophia ... resigned herself to every sort of ... passion to which she was subject. ... This collection [of passions], they declare, was the substance of the matter from which this world was formed. For from returning, every soul belonging to this world, and that of the Demiurge himself, derived its origin.[327]

---

[326] Again, I watched National Geographic's special on the Gospel of Judas on YouTube and carefully recorded the professor's words.

[327] *Against Heresies.* I:4:2.

This, admittedly, bothered the church leaders.

> By means of specious and plausible words, they cunning-
> ly allure the simple-minded to inquire into their system.
> Nevertheless, they clumsily destroy them while they initi-
> ate them into their blasphemous and impious opinions
> regarding the Demiurge.[328]

True, the gnostics didn't want the "advice and the control and
the insight" of the elders—who were not yet called priests[329]—and
bishops. I would suggest, however, they desperately needed it!

As I said earlier, though, this has nothing to do with the Council of Nicea. Instead, the suggestion that the Council of Nicea
threw out the gnostic gospels came from Dan Brown's book and
movie, *The Da Vinci Code*.

The Da Vinci Code

Dan Brown claims in his book, *The Da Vinci Code*:

- "Until *that* moment in history, Jesus was viewed by his
  followers as a mortal prophet" (emphasis his).[330]

- "The Bible, as we know it today, was collated by the pagan Roman emperor Constantine the Great."[331]

- "More than *eighty* gospels were considered for the New
  Testament, and yet only a relative few were chosen for inclusion."[332]

Dan Brown's book is based almost completely on the research
of Michael Baigent, Richard Leigh, and Henry Lincoln, published
in a 1982 book called *Holy Blood, Holy Grail*.

---

[328] *ibid*. Preface.

[329] On bishops, elders, and priests, see Appendix C.

[330] Brown, Dan. *The Da Vinci Code*. 1st ed. New York: Anchor Books, 2003. p. 253. Emphasis his.

[331] *ibid*. p. 252

[332] *ibid*. Emphasis his.

Brown doesn't hide this. The British royal historian in *The Da Vinci Code* is named Leigh Teabing, which is the last name of two of the authors of *Holy Blood, Holy Grail* combined. Baigent's name is scrambled into Teabing.

We will not go into all the claims made in that book—that Jesus married Mary Magdalene, moved to Gaul, and went on to father children whose descendants eventually became the Merovingian dynasty of Frankish kings. There have been plenty of refutations of *Holy Blood, Holy Grail* (the book's U.S. title) published, and there will be many more as people refute *The Da Vinci Code*. All that concerns us is Brown's claim that the Council of Nicea threw hundreds of gnostic works out of the Bible, then devoted extensive efforts to purging their writings from the earth.

> Constantine did order one set of writings destroyed, which were those of Arius. After the council, he wrote:
>
> *If any treatise composed by Arius should be discovered, let it be consigned to the flames, in order that not only his depraved doctrine may be suppressed, but also that no memorial of him may be by any means left. This therefore I decree, that if any one shall be detected in concealing a book compiled by Arius, and shall not instantly bring it forward and burn it, the penalty for this offense shall be death; for immediately after conviction the criminal shall suffer capital punishment.*[333]
>
> Notice, though, that we have a record of the fact that Constantine ordered the destruction of Arius' writings and of the fact that he wished Arius' memory erased from the earth. Further, he did not succeed! Appendix D has four letters from Arius that were preserved; one by Sozomen, one by Theodoret, and two by Athanasius, the Arians' most stringent opponent, himself!
>
> If Constantine was unable to succeed in extinguishing the memory and writings of Arius, just one man, do we really believe that he destroyed all the gnostic writings and there's no record of his even trying?

---

[333] The Ecclesiastical History of Socrates Scholasticus I:9

The Council of Nicea and the gnostic Gospels

There is no evidence to refute in reference to gnostic writers at the Council of Nicea. The only historical sources available, which we have spent this book looking at, don't even mention gnosticism or their writings because they had almost completely died out by the early fourth century.

It is true that Constantine commissioned Eusebius to prepare 50 copies of the Scriptures. He records Constantine's letter to him in his *Life of Constantine*, ch. 36:

> I have thought it expedient to instruct your prudence to order fifty copies of the sacred Scriptures, the provision and use of which you know to be most needful for the instruction of the Church, to be written on prepared parchment in a legible manner, and in a convenient, portable form, by professional transcribers thoroughly practiced in their art.

This was a kind act of Constantine, but it hardly involved throwing out any accepted books. As pointed out above, the Muratorian Canon gives the first list of canonical books around AD 170, a list that is very similar to our New Testament today. Between 161 and the Council of Nicea numerous other Christians provided lists of the accepted books.[334]

Perhaps just as importantly to point out, Christians continued to provide lists of canonical books throughout the fourth century. Not only did Constantine not change the books that were already accepted, he never settled the canon at all. It was still *slightly* flexible even until the end of the fourth century.

One of the ways we know this is the direct statement of Augustine, the renowned theologian. In 397, more than 70 years after Nicea and more than a decade after the Arian Controversy was

---

[334] Appendix L provides all the lists of canonical books written before the Council of Nicea.

resolved, he gave the following advice to anyone who wished to be a "skillful interpreter" of Scripture:

> Now, in regard to the canonical Scriptures, [the skillful interpreter] must follow the judgment of the greater number of catholic churches. Among these, of course, a high place must be given to such as have been thought worthy to be the seat of an apostle and to receive epistles.
>
> Accordingly, among the canonical Scriptures he will judge according to the following standard: to prefer those that are received by all the catholic churches to those which some do not receive. Among those which are not received by all, he will prefer such as have the sanction of the greater number and those of greater authority to such as are held by the smaller number and those of less authority.
>
> If, however, he shall find that some books are held by the greater number of churches, and others by the churches of greater authority (though this is not a very likely thing to happen), I think that in such a case the authority on the two sides is to be looked upon as equal.[335]

All I can do here is tell you these pertinent parts of the true story of the development of the canon. I can't write a refutation of Dan Brown's claims because there's no evidence to refute. The idea that the Council of Nicea, or Constantine, threw out books of the Bible is just someone's imagination!

How Did the Canon Become Set?

Believe it or not, no council with any authority set the canon until the Council of Trent *in the 16th century*!

---

[335] *On Christian Doctrine*. II:8:12.

There's a rumor that the Synod of Hippo in 393 set the canon for good. It did dictate a list of accepted books, but it had no authority to enforce its decision. Augustine became the bishop of Hippo in 396 or 397, and he appears to know nothing of such a decision. He began *On Christian Doctrine* in 397, and there he states, as seen just above, that the churches still had varying canons.

Before we close this chapter, it seemed worth giving you a brief introduction to the weird and wild world of gnosticism. You will not wonder why it did not continue in the churches, nor why it simply died out once it did not have Christian converts off which to feed.

What Is Gnosticism?

Gnosticism was perhaps the major heresy that the early churches had to deal with, which includes even the apostles. Paul addresses gnostic ideas in 1 Corinthians 15, where he defends the resurrection against those who deny that there is or can be a resurrection. 1 John, as well, specifically addresses gnosticism, referring to gnostic teachers as "those that seduce you" (2:26).

The primary marker of what is gnostic is "docetism." This is the belief that everything material and physical is evil, or at best useless, and only what is spiritual matters.

By the second century, it would be common among the various gnostic sects to teach that the true God is distant and unknowable. He has "aeons" or "emanations" that dwell in a place called the *pleroma*, which is the Greek word for fullness.

These emanations, usually due to the influence of one specific aeon by the name of *Sophia* (Wisdom), either accidentally or in bad judgment, depending on the sect, produced a being called the Demiurge. Being abandoned outside of the *pleroma* by his mother, Sophia, the Demiurge created the physical universe.

Gnostic Quotes

Something imperfect came out of her, different in appearance from her. ... She gave rise to a misshapen being unlike herself. Sophia saw what her desire produced. It changed into the form of a dragon with a lion's head and [its] eyes flashed thunderbolts.[336]

The Demiurge, either in arrogance or in ignorance of the *pleroma*, considered himself to be the only god. He ruled the world he had created, but, according to the gnostics, there was nothing good about it.

Gnostic Quotes

Yaldabaoth[337] modeled his creation on the pattern of the original realms above him so that it might be just like the indestructible realms. Not that he had ever seen the indestructible ones. Rather, the power in him, deriving from his mother, made him aware of the pattern of the cosmos above.

When he gazed upon his creation surrounding him, he said to his host of demons, the ones that had come forth out of him: "I am a jealous God and there is no God but me!"[338]

It appears that all gnostic sects identified the Demiurge with Yahweh, the God of Israel. While some regarded him as ignorant rather than evil, they did all reject his teachings as being separate from the true God and the *pleroma*. They taught that the aeons from the *pleroma* sent an emissary to the earth to turn men away from the physical creation of the Demiurge and back to the spiritual world created by the unknowable God.

The aeons had various names depending on the particular gnostic sect. The names, however, always included important

---

[336] *The Apocryphon of John*

[337] The name of the Demiurge in *The Apocryphon of John*

[338] *ibid.*

Christian terms like church, *logos*, light, life, wisdom, Christ, mind, and thought.

Usually, the aeon that was sent to earth was Christ. Christ came to earth in spiritual form—for only what is spirit matters—and descended on the man Jesus. He guided Jesus in his teachings, but gnostics generally rejected or wildly and figuratively reinterpreted the four Gospels that we know. They had other gospels that were popular among them, such as the Gospel of Mary Magdalene, the Gospel of Thomas, the Gospel of Judas, the Gospel of the Egyptians, and the Gospel of the Hebrews which they used as sources for the teachings of Jesus.

Of those, only *The Gospel of Thomas* even possibly enjoyed any readership at all in the apostolic churches, and it's cited only in *2 Clement*, an anonymous second-century sermon, and Clement of Alexandria's *Miscellanies*, where it is not treated as Scripture. It is short, containing 114 sayings.

None of the gnostic churches believed that Jesus died for sin. Jesus simply died. The Christ spirit then moved on, continuing to teach through gnostic teachers.

Simon the Magician

Most catholic writers accused Simon the Magician, mentioned in Acts 8, of being the source of gnosticism. After being rejected by the apostles for trying to purchase the power to dispense the Holy Spirit, he returned to his magical ways. He claimed that Jesus had failed, but when he died the Christ spirit departed and came to Simon himself.

There is no way of knowing if Simon really did this. It will have to remain an interesting historical curiosity.

The route to salvation varied among the gnostics. The goal of salvation in the next life was to arrive in the *pleroma*, which I suppose makes the *pleroma* the gnostic heaven. The goal of salvation in this life was to partake of spiritual life from the *pleroma*.

One particular gnostic teacher, Valentinus,[339] taught that there were three kinds of people.[340]

- Some were innately spiritual. These were those who were ordained to believe the gnostic gospel. What they did with their bodies did not matter. They simply needed to know that they were spiritual and partake of spiritual life. The deeds of the body were neither good nor bad; they were insignificant.[341]

- The Christians, however, represented those who were part physical and part spiritual. These had to do deny their physical desires in order to let their spiritual side triumph. They would be saved in this way.

- Finally, there were the completely physical people who were just animals and could not be saved.

Not all gnostic teachers taught like Valentinus. Some taught that since everything physical was bad, then a complete denial of all physical indulgence was necessary for everyone to be saved.

The Motley World of Gnosticism

It will never be possible to distill all gnostic teachings down to one set. Innovation was prized among gnostic teachers. The only possible result of this is that there was no agreement among them except on major points.

> Let us now look at the inconsistent opinions of these here-tics ... how they do not agree in treating the same points,

---

[339] Irenaeus, in preparation for his book, *Against Heresies*, read the works of Valentinus and spent some time with his disciples, so he emphasizes their teachings. (*Against Heresies*. Preface by Irenaeus.)

[340] Irenaeus. *Against Heresies*. I:5:6 – I:6:3.

[341] Irenaeus says that they argued, "Even as gold, when submersed in filth, does not lose its beauty because of it, so they affirm that they cannot suffer any amount of harm or lose their spiritual substance, whatever the material actions in which they may be involved." (*ibid.* I:6:3.)

but they all, in things and names, set out opinions that are mutually discordant.[342]

There is a reason that gnostics end up with such varied opinions. Recently, I received an email from someone claiming to be a gnostic who had read my web page on gnosticism at *Christian History for Everyman.*

He explained to me:

> When someone achieves Gnosis, they receive information which enables them to understand those meanings within the apocryphal texts that confuse you.

There really is something delightful about the mystical, otherworldly feeling that you get when you feel that you're receiving revelation. Revelation, however, must always be tested. Christians do not just assume that every guidance they feel is good. We are taught to "test the spirits, whether they come from God" (1 Jn. 4:1)

Gnosticism, however, was a wide open field for those that wanted to feel particularly spiritual.

> Every one of them generates something new every day according to his ability, for no one is deemed perfect who does not develop among them some mighty fictions.[343]

The Mystical World of Gnosticism

I had a chance to review some of the gnostic writings for my web site, *Christian History for Everyman.*[344] I was amazed. It's no wonder that gnostics, always seeking some new revelation, would love interpreting these "sacred" texts.

I remember looking at eastern writings as a teenager, and the eastern writings were similar. Along with some excellent bits of wisdom were sayings that really didn't mean anything at all, but

[342] *ibid.* I:11:1.
[343] Irenaeus. *Against Heresies.* I:18:1.
[344] <http://www.christian-history.org>

they *sounded* profound. They could be interpreted any way you want.

The gnostic writings are like that. Here's one from the *Pistis Sophia*:

> Jesus said to his disciples, "I am come forth out of that first mystery, which is the last mystery, that is the four-and-twentieth mystery." And his disciples ... thought of that mystery, that it is the head of the universe and head of all existence; and they thought it is the completion of all completions ... that it surroundeth the First Commandment and the five Impressions and the Great Light and the Five Helpers and the whole Treasury of the Light.[345]

This next one is from *The Gospel of Thomas*. It happens to be the saying quoted in *2 Clement*, an orthodox and excellent early Christian sermon. The author of that sermon is not Clement, but whoever he is, he provides an excellent Christian interpretation of it. Nonetheless, anyone could interpret this any way they want because it's simply meaningless:

> The dead are not alive, and the living will not die. In the days when you consumed what was dead, you made it what is alive. ... On the day when you were one, you became two. But when you become two, what will you do?[346]

I'm not the only one who thinks this. Elaine Pagels herself, in her book *Gnostic Gospels*, quoted Professor Gilles Quispel as saying that Jesus, in the Gospel of Thomas, "speaks in sayings as cryptic and compelling as Zen koans."[347]

That is gnosticism, and it was a serious threat to the church at the end of the first century and beginning of the second. By the fourth century, however, when the Council of Nicea convened, it was a light so dim and so removed that no one even noticed it.

---

[345] *Pistis Sophia.*

[346] *Gospel of Thomas*

[347] Pagels, Elaine. *Gnostic Gospels.* Introduction, p. XV.

Why Gnosticism?

The appeal of gnosticism seems to have been special revelation and knowledge that made the hearer feel superior to those not "in the know." Gnostics could not trace their teachings back to the apostles, so they claimed to have received their knowledge in back rooms where the public was not invited.

These secret teachings, they said, were given by Jesus to one or to very few disciples and then transmitted to chosen teachers because not all Christians could receive them.

And of course, these teachers did not begin with their more bizarre teachings. They began with wording that was very similar to Christians, but they put very figurative, fanciful twists on the words of Jesus and the apostles. Irenaeus said, "Their language resembles ours, while their sentiments are very different."[348] He writes:

Their manner of acting is like someone who found a beautiful image of a king made with precious jewels by a skilled artist ... then rearranged the gems ... into the form of a dog or fox, and even that poorly executed. ... Thus exhibiting the jewels, they deceive the ignorant.[349]

---

[348] *Against Heresies*. Preface.
[349] *ibid*. I:8:1

Chapter 13:
From Sabbath to Sunday?

One more myth that found its way into *The Da Vinci Code* is that at the Council of Nicea, Constantine changed the Sabbath to Sunday.

> Originally ... Christianity honored the Jewish Sabbath of Saturday, but Constantine shifted it to coincide with the pagan's veneration day of the sun. ... To this day, most churchgoers attend services on Sunday morning with no idea that they are there on account of the pagan sun god's weekly tribute — *Sun*day.[350]

This idea is not in any way new to Dan Brown. The Seventh Day Adventist denomination, begun in the 19th century, charged Constantine, the Council of Nicea, and the Roman Catholic Church with changing the Sabbath to Sunday until Samuele Bacchiocchi wrote *From Sabbath to Sunday* in 1977. There Bacchiocchi made the claim that the change was made gradually beginning in the second century due to pagan influences on the church.

Bacchiocchi's claim is an improvement. We have already told the story of the Council of Nicea. You already know that what the

---

[350] Brown. *The Da Vinci Code*. Emphasis his. p. 225-26.

bishops really addressed was the Paschal Controversy, determining that the Passover should be kept on a Sunday—the Lord's Day—each year, rather than on Nisan 14 itself. What Christians did on a weekly basis was not a controversy, and so it was not addressed at all.

The Early Christian View of the Sabbath

Did the early Christians keep the Sabbath?

Yes and no.

It is impossible to answer that question without explaining the early Christian view of the Law of Moses.

The Early Churches and the Law of Moses

It would be easy to argue that the pre-Nicene churches did not keep the Law of Moses at all. One of the earliest Christian writings outside the New Testament is the anonymous *Letter to Diognetus*. What makes the *Letter to Diognetus* so fascinating is that it is the only early Christian writing that quotes no Scripture at all. And this, for modern Christians, is a very good thing.

The *Letter to Diognetus* is written to explain Christianity to a seeker. Because there is no Scripture quoted in the letter, it is clear that the author is a layman. He is not arguing for a position. Instead, he is careful to describe what Christians in general are doing.

He begins his description of Christianity by telling Diognetus that Christians "neither esteem those to be gods that are reckoned such by Greeks, nor hold to the superstition of the Jews."[351] Further down, he says:

> As to their scruples about meats, their superstition in regard to the Sabbaths, their boasting about circumcision,

---

[351] *Letter to Diognetus*. 1.

and their fancies about fasting and new moons, which are utterly ridiculous and unworthy of notice ...[352]

The *Letter to Diognetus* was written at the end of the first century or start of the second. Already, this early, there was a layman giving a general description of Christianity and rejecting circumcision, the Sabbath, new moons, and food laws.

He begins a pattern that doesn't change at all no matter how far you read into the writings of the pre-Nicene churches.

Around the same time, one of the leading clergymen[353] of their day would write something very similar:

It is absurd to profess Christ and to Judaize, for Christianity did not believe in Judaism, but Judaism Christianity.[354]

The clergyman was Ignatius, and he makes it clear that he's including the Sabbath in the Judaizing that he rejects.

If, therefore, those who have been brought up in the ancient order of things [*i.e., Jews*] have come to the possession of a new hope, no longer observing the Sabbath but living in observance of the Lord's Day, on which also our life has sprung up again by him and by his death ... how shall we be able to live apart from him?[355]

Somewhere in the vicinity of a half a century later, a Christian from Rome ran into a Jew from Palestine. This happened in Corinth, far from both their homes. They engaged in a debate, and the Jew, Trypho, said this to the Christian, Justin:

This is what we are most at a loss about: that you, professing to be pious and supposing yourselves better than others, are not separated from them in any particular way. You do not alter your way of living from the nations. You

---

[352] *ibid.* 4.

[353] The word "clergy" would not have been used in the early second century; I am using the term anachronistically.

[354] Ignatius. *Letter to the Magnesians.* 10.

[355] *ibid.* 9.

observe no festivals or Sabbaths and do not have the rite of circumcision. Further, resting your hopes on a man that was crucified, you still expect to receive something good from God, while you do not obey his commandments![356]

This discussion occurred in Corinth between a Jew from Palestine and a Christian from Rome. There could be no more widespread testimony that Christians across the Roman empire had rejected the keeping of the Law by the middle of the second century. Combined with the testimony of Ignatius and the anonymous *Letter to Diognetus*, we have powerful, seemingly conclusive, evidence that the early Christians had rejected the Law of Moses.

It would be easy to leave it there. This chapter would be a lot shorter and a lot less complicated.

But it wouldn't be honest.

The Early Christians and *The Fullness* of the Law of Moses

Trypho the Jew really did tell Justin Martyr that he knew that Christians did not keep the Sabbath. Justin really agreed with him, saying:

> Is there any matter, my friends, in which we are blamed than this, that we do not live according to the Law?[357]

But that's not all that Justin said. He also said:

> The new law requires you to keep perpetual Sabbath, and you, because you are idle for one day, suppose you are pious. You don't understand why this has been enjoined upon you.[358]

He also told them:

---

[356] Justin. *Dialogue with Trypho, a Jew*. 10.
[357] *ibid.*
[358] *ibid.* 12.

You have need of a second circumcision, though you take great pride in your flesh.[359]

What is he talking about? What is the new law? What is a perpetual Sabbath? And how can someone be circumcised a second time? (That sounds excruciatingly painful!)

The new law is only mentioned once in the New Testament. The writer of Hebrews tells us that "where the priesthood is changed, of necessity a change is made in the law also" (Heb. 7:12).

The new law is also hinted at by Jesus, when he was asked why the disciples of John and the Pharisees fasted, but his did not. Jesus told them:

> No one puts a piece of new cloth on an old garment, for the patch will pull away from the garment, and the tear is made worse. Nor do men put new wine in old wineskins. If they do, the wine runs out and the wineskins burst. Instead, they put new wine into new wineskins, and both are preserved. (Matt. 9:16-17)

The point of that illustration is that the new law—the teachings and commands of Christ—could only be followed by new creatures, by those born again and empowered by God to live under the new covenant.

Jesus had another description of the new law, which he stated plainly, without any illustrations. He said:

> Do not think that I came to destroy the Law or the Prophets; I did not come to destroy, but to fill up. (Matt. 5:17)

You've probably read that verse as saying that Jesus came to "fulfill" the Law, but that's really not a very good translation of the Greek word *pleroo*, at least not in this context. You'll see that in just a moment.

The King James Version actually has the word "fulfill" in both verses 17 and 18 of Matthew 5:

---

[359] *ibid.*

Think not that I am come to destroy the law, or the prophets: I am not come to destroy, but to fulfil [*sic*]. For verily I say unto you, Till heaven and earth pass, one jot or one tittle shall in no wise pass from the law, till all be fulfilled.

The two fulfills in this passage translate two different Greek words. The second one is the Greek word *genoito*, which simply means "happens."

Jesus is saying two different things in this verse. In verse 17, he is telling us that he didn't come to get rid of the Law (*kataluo*, to destroy, dissolve, or bring to an end), but to fill it up or bring it to fullness. In verse 18, he is telling us that every bit of the Law will happen. *Genoito* is a prophecy word. Everything the Law has predicted will come to pass.

So what does it mean that Jesus came to bring the law to fullness or to fill it up?

We are not left wondering. Jesus spends the rest of Matthew 5 telling us exactly what he means.

- You have heard that it was said by those of old, "You shall not murder," and whoever murders shall be in danger of the judgment. But I tell you that whoever is angry with his brother without a cause will be in danger of the judgment. (vv. 21-22)

- You have heard that it was said by those of old, "You shall not commit adultery," but I tell you that whoever looks at a woman to lust after her has already committed adultery with her in his heart. (vv. 27-28)

- You have heard that it was said by those of old, "You shall not break your oaths, but you shall fulfill your oaths to the Lord." But I tell you, do not swear at all. … But let your yes be yes and your no be no, for anything more than this comes from the evil one. (vv. 33-34)

- You have heard that it was said, "An eye for an eye, and a tooth for a tooth," but I tell you, don't resist an evil man. (vv. 38-39)

I have not included all of Jesus' statements in Matthew 5, but these will suffice to make our point.

This is the new law. These commands are Jesus bringing the Law to fullness.

The early Christians loved the Law of Moses. It was the basis for the new law of Christ.

But they did not take any Old Testament command in its earthly, fleshly form. The earthly form of the commandments was for the Israelites, the Lord's earthly kingdom. They were a fleshly people because they were supposed to be a fleshy people. They fought with fleshly weapons, and they had a kingdom that belonged to this earth.

Jesus' kingdom, however, is a spiritual kingdom. His people fight with spiritual weapons. They are also new wineskins, made fresh by the Holy Spirit, ready to receive the new wine of the *fullness* of the Law of Moses.

This is why Justin could say that the Christians didn't keep the Sabbath, but also say that the new law requires Christians to keep perpetual Sabbath.

Evidence for the "New Law"

While Paul doesn't spend any time describing the new law, he does give examples proving he understood and taught it.

In 1 Corinthians 9, Paul tells the Corinthian church that it's appropriate for the Lord's workers to ask for financial support from the church. Then—oddly considering what we know about Paul—he appeals to the Law to back himself up!

> Do I say these things as a man, or does the Law not say the same as well? (v. 8)

Even more oddly, he then quotes a verse that says that oxen should not be muzzled while they grind corn. Then he explains:

> Does God care about oxen? Or does he say this completely for our sake? For our sake, no doubt, it is written, so that he that plows should plow in hope. (vv. 9-10)

Here Paul puts the fullness of the Law, brought by Jesus, into effect. There was an old meaning and a new meaning to every law of the old covenant. Jesus did not come to abolish those laws; he came to breathe the fullness of life into those laws, making them the new and life-giving law, with himself as the priest of that new law.

Jesus applied that principle throughout his ministry on earth, not just in Matthew 5.

In Mark 7:15, Jesus tells that people that nothing that enters into a man from outside can defile him. Only what comes out of him can defile him.

Certain laws of the Jews were of great importance to them. The food laws were one of them. To this day, orthodox Jews go to great lengths to ensure that their food is "kosher." They are not allowed to eat pork, but many will not even eat from a pot that once had pork cooked in it.

That is why the Pharisees were complaining that Jesus' disciples were eating without washing their hands. They didn't know that they were killing germs when they washed their hands. Science had not advanced that far. Instead, they were being very careful that no invisible specks of some unclean substance wound up on their bread and thus in their mouths, defiling them.

Any one of us today might tell those Jews that they were being too fastidious. God is not and has never been that picky.

But Jesus told them something far more. He told them that nothing they put in their mouth could defile them.

This statement was so shocking to them that even his disciples didn't believe it. They thought he was giving them a parable, a mystery that they had to figure out.

> When he entered into the house away from the people, the disciples asked him about the parable. (Mk. 7:17)

Jesus quickly informed them that it was no parable. What goes into a person doesn't enter his heart, but his stomach, and it is soon purged back into the earth. There can be no defilement from such things because it's what's in the heart that matters.

Paul got it. Decades later he would say:

> Foods for the belly, and the belly for foods, but God shall destroy both it and them. (1 Cor. 6:13)

Food was the old Law! Food laws were for a fleshly nation that had to keep itself pure in the physical realm. Jesus' spiritual kingdom is concerned with the heart. Those under the new covenant keep their hearts pure, and they give no importance to their bellies.

But that doesn't mean that the food laws were worthless. Remember, Jesus did not come to abolish those laws, but to bring them to fullness!

> The Law has figuratively predicted all these [types of people], delineating men by the various animals. Whichever of these, it says, have a double hoof and ruminate, it proclaims as clean [*Lev. 11:2-3; Deut. 14:6*). ... Who then are the clean? Those who make their way by faith steadily toward the Father and the Son, for this is denoted by the steadiness of those which divide the hoof. They also meditate day and night on the words of God so that they may be adorned with good works, for this is the meaning of the ruminants.[360]

How much we've lost by forgetting these valuable truths!

Early Christians on the Filling Up of the Law

> The Lord did not abrogate the natural [precepts] of the Law, by which man is justified, which also those who were justified by faith and who pleased God observed before the giving of the Law ... he extended and fulfilled them.

That quote is from Irenaeus, one of the most important of the early Christian writers because he is only two links from the apostles. Polycarp had the words of the apostles ringing in his ears, and Irenaeus had sat under his teaching.[361]

Irenaeus goes on to explain what Jesus means by 'extending and fulfilling' the Law:

---

[360] Irenaeus, *Against Heresies*. V:8:4.
[361] "Fragments from the Lost Writings of Irenaeus." Fragment 2. *The Ante-Nicene Fathers*. Vol. I.

What does the excess referred to mean? In the first place, we must believe not only in the Father, but also in the Son now revealed. ... In the next place, we must not only say, but do, for they [*i.e., the Jews*] said but did not do. And [we must] not only refrain from evil deeds but even from desiring after them. Now he did not teach us those things as opposing the Law, but as bringing the Law to fullness and implanting in us the varied righteousness of the Law.

Does God really want to fulfill the righteousness of the Law in us?

For what the Law could not do because it was weak through the flesh, God did. By sending his own Son in the likeness of sinful flesh, because of sin, he condemned sin in the flesh so that the righteousness of the Law might be fulfilled in us who do not walk according to the flesh but according to the Spirit. (Rom. 8:3-4)

Paul believed that God wanted to fulfill the righteousness of the Law in us. But he was not talking about the Law in the original, unexpanded state in which God gave it to Moses.

That Law, when brought to fullness by Christ, does not concern itself with things like food and drink. God, after all, doesn't care about foods or the belly, as both Jesus and Paul have told us. Nothing that enters into us can defile us.

No, he wants us to part the hoof and chew the cud. Those represent separating from the world—or 'making our way by faith steadily' as Irenaeus puts it—and meditating on the words of God.

Tertullian also discusses the Law, which he describes as "augmented" by Christ:

Did Christ rescind the aforementioned commandments: "Do not kill; do not commit adultery; do not steal; do not bear false witness; honor your father and mother"? Or did he both keep them and add what was lacking to them? ...

[God's] commandments he both maintained and augmented with his own supplementary precepts.[362]

If it is now clear that Christ came to bring the Law to fullness, how does this apply to the Sabbath? Why would Christians stop resting on Saturday if Jesus "augmented" the commandment?

The Early Christians and the Sabbath

We have already mentioned above that Justin said that Christians keep perpetual Sabbath.

What would happen if Christians refused to work on every day of the week rather than on just the seventh day? We would all starve, or we would all become dependent on the world for our food. Neither of those things is something God wants.

So how did Christ augment the Sabbath command?

Justin has an explanation, but first let's give an explanation that comes from Scripture:

> Let us fear, therefore, since a promise is left of entering into his rest, that any of us would seem to come short of it. ... For we who have believed enter into rest, as he said, "As I have sworn in my wrath, they shall not enter into my rest" [Ps. 95:11], although the works have been finished since the foundation of the world. For he spoke of the seventh day in a certain place in this way, "And God rested the seventh day from all his works" [Gen. 2:2]. And in this place, he said again, "They shall not enter into my rest." Since we see that it remains that some must enter into it, and those to whom it was first preached did not enter in because of unbelief ... There remains therefore a rest to the people of God. For he that has entered into his rest, he has also ceased from his own works, as God did from his. Let us labor, therefore, to enter into that rest.

---

[362] Against Marcion. V:36.

This isn't the clearest passage I've ever read in the Scriptures. The point, however, is pretty simple. In Psalm 95:11, God says that he swore to the Israelites in the wilderness that they would never enter into his rest. But, the writer of Hebrews points out, God's Sabbath rest belongs to the beginning, at the foundation of the world. This must be some other rest to which God is referring.

There's another rest that the people of God must enter into.

What is that rest?

> The new law requires you to keep perpetual Sabbath, and you, because you are idle for one day, suppose you are pious ... The Lord our God does not take pleasure in such observances. If there is any perjured person or thief among you, let him cease to be so; in any adulterer, let him repent; then he has kept the sweet and true Sabbaths of God.[363]

That's Justin again, but he's far from being the only person to say such things.

The *Letter of Barnabas* is an early second century writing that would probably not carry a lot of weight on its own except that it was apparently treated as Scripture in Alexandria and Carthage, two important churches. Both Clement of Alexandria and Tertullian (from Carthage) mention it and treat it as Scripture.

Keep in mind that early Christians feared innovation. Their job was to preserve the apostolic faith intact and without change. No church and no individual Christian would simply find a writing and add it to the accepted books of the church. Nor would they allow any accepted book to change the rule of faith that had been handed down to them.

Thus, the *Letter of Barnabas* carries great weight today, not because of its own testimony, but because anything it clearly teaches has to represent what the churches of Alexandria and Carthage already believed. They would never have treated this letter as Scripture had they not already held to its major tenets.

---

[363] Justin, *Dialogue with Trypho, a Jew*. 12.

And the *Letter of Barnabas* has a lot to say about the Law of Moses and the Sabbath:

> [God] says, "You shall sanctify [the Sabbath] with pure hands and a pure heart" [*Ex. 20:8*]. Therefore, if anyone can sanctify the day God has sanctified except by being pure in heart in everything, then we are deceived.
>
> Behold, therefore: the one who properly rests sanctifies it. When we are able to perform righteousness—wickedness no longer existing and all things having been made new by the Lord—then we shall be able to sanctify it, when we have first sanctified ourselves.
>
> Further, he says to them, "Your new moons and your Sabbath I cannot endure" [*Is. 1:13*]. You understand what he is saying. Your present Sabbaths are not acceptable to me, but instead, that which I have made when, giving rest to all things, I shall make a beginning of the eighth day— the beginning of another world. Therefore, also, we keep the eighth day with joyfulness, the day on which Jesus rose from the dead.[364]

Justin and pseudo-Barnabas (no scholar today believes Barnabas, the companion of Paul, wrote the epistle) give thorough explanations of the early Christian understanding of the Sabbath day, but many writers mention it in passing.

We've already looked at the *Letter to Diognetus* and Ignatius. With Justin and Pseudo-Barnabas, that's four already. Let's add some more.

Irenaeus, c. AD 185:

> These things ... were given for a sign, but these signs were not without symbolism. ... **the Sabbaths taught that we should continue daily in God's service.** ... Moreover, the Sabbath of God, that is, the kingdom, was ... indicated by created things, in which the man who shall have per-

---

[364] *Letter of Barnabas.* 15.

severed in serving God shall, in a state of rest, partake of God's table.[365]

Clement of Alexandria, c. AD 190:

> To restrain oneself from doing good is the work of vice, but to keep from wrongdoing is the beginning of salvation. **So the Sabbath, by abstinence from evil, seems to indicate self-restraint.**[366]

Tertullian, c. AD 210:

> We understand that we still more ought to observe a Sabbath from all servile work **always, and not only every seventh day, but through all time**. And through this arises the question for us, what Sabbath God willed us to keep? For the Scriptures point to an eternal Sabbath and to a temporary Sabbath. For Isaiah the prophet says, "Your Sabbaths my soul hates" [*Is. 1:13*]. And in another place he says, "My Sabbaths you have profaned" [*Ezek. 22:8*]. From this we determine that the temporary Sabbath is human and the eternal Sabbath is accounted divine.

Origen, c. AD 230:

> With regard to those things which were written in the Prophets or in the Law of Moses, it was only a few persons at that time ... who were able to look beyond the mere corporeal meaning and discover something greater, something spiritual ... but now there are countless multitudes of believers who ... are ... most firmly persuaded that **neither circumcision, nor the Sabbath rest, ... ought to be understood literally**. This method of apprehension is undoubtedly suggested to the minds of everyone by the power of the Holy Spirit.[367]

Archelaus, c. AD 277-78:

---

[365] *Against Heresies.* IV:16:1.
[366] *Miscellanies.* IV:3.
[367] *De Principiis.* II:7:2.

After God had made the world ... in the space of six days, he rested on the seventh day from all his works. ... And yet in the sequel, the new law, it says, "My Father works up to now, and I work" [*Jn. 5:17*]. Does that mean, then, that he is still making sky, sun, man, animals, trees, or any such thing? No, but the meaning is that when these visible objects were perfectly finished, he rested from that kind of work, while, however, he still continues to work at invisible objects with an inward mode of action and saves men.

In the same way, the Legislator wants every individual among us to be devoted unceasingly to this kind of work, even as God himself is. **He enjoins us to rest continually from secular things and to engage in no worldly sort of work whatsoever, and this is called our Sabbath.**[368]

I could continue, but these should suffice to show that this understanding of the Sabbath was universal in the early churches.

I want to point out here, once more, that it is not individual arguments that matter. Each quotation builds an ongoing case. What we want to know is whether Christians in general held to a practice, and if so, whether it was universal.

For the keeping of a "fulfilled" Sabbath we have abundant testimony. Justin and Trypho provide a witness that stretches from Rome to Palestine. The *Letter of Barnabas* provides a witness across north Africa due to its use by Clement of Alexandria and Tertullian. Ignatius was from Asia Minor (modern Turkey). Irenaeus was in Gaul in modern France.

The testimony is universal. There is no contradictory testimony.

The Council of Nicea had nothing to change. The Sabbath of the Christians was a perpetual Sabbath made holy by repentance and a godly life. The Lord's Day was their day of rejoicing. It was not just the first day, but the eighth day, the creating of not just a new life, but a new world by the resurrection of Christ.

---

[368] *The Acts of the Disputation with the Heresiarch Manes.* 31.

The Lord's Day was not a new Sabbath. Until Constantine declared it an official day of rest for the empire a few years before the Council of Nicea, no Christian considered resting on the Lord's Day.

Constantine's New Sabbath

The charge that Constantine turned Sunday into a Sabbath could accurately be levied. What he could not be charged with is moving the seventh-day Sabbath to Sunday. This he could not do because the Christians were not keeping a seventh-day Sabbath. They were keeping a perpetual Sabbath.

Objections to the Early Christian "Fulfilled" Sabbath

It should come as no surprise that I have heard numerous objections to the Sabbath as taught by the early Christians.

My response to those objections is that the view of the Sabbath I am describing is the tradition held by all apostolic churches from earliest times. There is little doubt this tradition is from the apostles.

Further, almost every objection I have heard is answered in some way in some early Christian writing. Recently someone pointed out to me that the Scriptures say that in the new earth, "all flesh" will come worship the Lord "from one Sabbath to another" (Isa. 66:23). The early Christians address even this.

The problem is, explaining their answer would involve discussing their understanding of "the last days," something else that most modern Christians have forgotten. To lay the background for their answers would require far more room than we can devote in this book.

Oh, that the Lord's people could feast once more on the tradition of the apostles!

There is a small revival of interest in the early church fathers even among Protestants. Perhaps soon we shall reap some of the benefits of apostolic teachings received and preserved by those early and blessed stewards of the mysteries of God.

As it turned out, Constantine's order to make Sunday a holiday would be much of the reason that the things I am saying in this chapter are not familiar to you.

Over the centuries, much that was once symbolic became literal. The threefold leadership in the early churches found a symbol in the high priest, the priests, and the Levites of the old covenant. By the Middle Ages, it was no longer symbolic. The elders had really become priests, standing between God and men, replacing the one Mediator of 1 Timothy 2:5. So, too, when the Lord's Day became a replacement Sabbath, the true Christian Sabbath—described throughout this chapter—was forgotten. In its place was a pitiful, half-hearted replacement for the earthly, one-day rest that had been appropriate for God's earthly kingdom under the old covenant.

Colossians 2:16-17

Colossians 2:16-17 is a very rough verse for those that want to keep the Sabbath the Jewish way.

> Let no man judge you in food, in drink, in regard to a feast, new moon, or Sabbaths, which are a shadow of things to come, but the body [which casts the shadow] is Christ's.

The standard argument presented by Christians who want to keep the Jewish version of the Sabbath is that this passage is referring only to those Sabbaths that are part of feasts. The weekly Sabbaths, they say, are attached to the creation, not to the Law, so those are not shadows fulfilled by Christ; they are eternal.

Many years ago, when I first heard this, I wondered about it. I still did not know what the early Christians taught at that time, and I was curious why Christians didn't keep the Sabbath. I was certain that there was no Scriptural reason to believe that Jesus changed it to Sunday!

So I looked up the phrase "feasts, new moons, and Sabbaths." I was very surprised at what I found.

Feasts are yearly occurrences; new moons are monthly; and the Sabbaths occur every week. Each of those has special sacrifices attached to them in the Law.

As a result, the Hebrew Scriptures refer the special yearly, monthly, and weekly sacrifices repeatedly, using the phrase "feasts, new moons, and Sabbaths" or some version of it.

That wording occurs in 1 Chronicles 23:31; 2 Chronicles 2:4; 2 Chronicles 8:13; 2 Chronicles 31:3; Nehemiah 10:33; Ezekiel 45:17; and Hosea 2:11. The Hebrew Scriptures refer to those special sacrifices together seven times, each time indicating the yearly, monthly, and weekly sacrifices in their due course.

We'll use 2 Chronicles 31:3 as an example. The others are very similar:

> [Hezekiah] appointed the king's portion of his substance for the burnt offerings, for the morning and evening burnt offerings, the burnt offerings for the Sabbaths, for the new moons, and for the set feasts, as it is written in the Law of the Lord.

Knowing that this phrase is used in the Hebrew Scriptures *seven* times, is it really possible that a scholar like Paul didn't know that?

I believe it's undeniable that he did, and it is apparent that Colossians 2:16, like every other similar passage of Scripture, is talking about the yearly, monthly, and weekly holy days. They are a shadow of Christ, and that includes the weekly Sabbath as well.

Some Additional Thoughts on the Law of Moses

The early Christian use of the Law is a beautiful thing. I would encourage all of you, if I have piqued your interest at all, to read especially Justin's *Dialogue with Trypho, a Jew*. By now, you should know that you can read it for free or download it for a nominal fee on the web at <http://www.ccel.org/fathers/>.

Here, however, is an overview on some major issues from the Law as briefly and quickly as I can cover them, solely because it's so interesting and important to us as Christians.

Circumcision:

This one modern Christians still remember. The true circumcision is of the heart and by the Spirit (Rom. 2:28-29; Php. 3:3).

What the early Christians added to this issue is the argument that circumcision has nothing whatsoever to do with righteousness. If circumcision is really necessary to righteousness, then all women are unrighteous, for circumcision is only commanded of males. Further, Abraham and all who came before him were chosen before they were circumcised. Enoch, for example, was so righteous, apart from circumcision, that God took him up to heaven.

Animal Sacrifices:

Surprisingly, the early Christian reason for not offering sacrifices was not that Jesus was the ultimate sacrifice, making all other sacrifices unnecessary.

No, they argued that God *never* wanted animal sacrifices.

> Those who imagine that by means of blood and the smoke of sacrifices and burnt offerings they offer sacrifices to [God] ... these, by supposing that they can give anything to him who stands in need of nothing, appear to me to be no different, not in any way, than those who studiously confer the same honor on [idols].[369]

> For he has revealed to us by all the prophets that he needs neither sacrifices, nor burnt offerings, nor oblations, saying thus: "'What is the multitude of your sacrifices to me?' says the Lord. 'I am full of burnt offerings and do not desire the fat of lambs. ... For who has required these things at your hands?'" [*Is. 1:11-14, LXX*]. He has therefore abolished these things, that the new law of our Lord Jesus Christ, which is without the yoke of necessity, might have a human oblation. And again he says to them, "Did I command your fathers, when they went out from the land of Egypt, to offer me burnt offerings and sacrifices? I rather commanded them this, 'Let no one of you cherish evil in his heart against his neighbor ... '" [*Jer. 7:22; Zech. 8:17*].

---

[369] Anonymous. *Letter to Diognetus*. 3.

First, as to our not sacrificing: The Framer and Father of this universe does not need blood, nor the odor of burnt offerings, nor the fragrance of flowers and incense, since he himself is the perfect fragrance, needing nothing within or without. ... What have I to do with conflagrations, which God does not stand in need of?[370]

Again, I could produce many more passages than this; this is a universal teaching of the early churches.

Why would they say such things? In fact, why would Jeremiah, who's quoted in one of these passages, speak for God and tell the Israelites that God never commanded their fathers, when he took them out of Egypt, about burnt offerings? The Law is full of commands and explanations about animal sacrifices.

The argument of the early Christians was that these were added for the sake of keeping the eyes of the Israelites on the Lord their God. The sacrifices were not for God, but for the Israelites.

This is borne out by what we know of the mercy of God. The Scriptures teach that the righteous shall live by faith, not by sacrifices (Hab. 2:4). When David had sinned, he said:

You do not want sacrifice, or I would have given it. You do not delight in burnt offerings. The sacrifices of God are a broken spirit. A broken and a contrite heart, oh God, you will not despise. (Ps. 51:16-17)

And of course we all know the famous statement that the prophet Samuel made to Saul: "To obey is better than sacrifice, and to listen than the fat of rams" (1 Sam. 15:22).

Justin told Trypho, the Jew:

God, accommodating himself to that nation, commanded them to offer sacrifices, as if to his name, in order that you might not serve idols.[371]

---

[370] Athenagoras. *A Plea for the Christians*. 13.
[371] *Dialogue with Trypho, a Jew*. 19.

There are some important ramifications of this. For example, today we tend to believe that Jesus' death was a payment to God for our sins, as though his death replaced all punishment for sin. Of course, we know this can't be true because there is still a judgment according to works, and that is true for Christians as well as non-Christians.[372] On top of this, Jesus threatens all sorts of punishments, including having one's name blotted from the Book of Life, if we don't overcome (Rev. 2-3).

Sins are not simply paid for.

The theory that sins are simply paid for would never have flown in early Christianity because they believed that God was not looking for sacrifice, but for obedience. Jesus did not die to change God by making him more merciful. God was already merciful. God sent Jesus to die for us so that we could be obedient and thus obtain the mercy of God.

It is we who needed Jesus' death. It is we who needed to change. That is why there are so many verses that say Jesus died so that he could be our Lord (Rom. 14:9; 2 Cor. 5:15), so that we would be zealous for good works (Tit. 2:13-14), and so that the righteousness of the Law could be fulfilled in us (if we walk in the Spirit—Rom. 8:3-4).

The need, according to the Scriptures was not just that we were facing a judgment, but that we could not find the power to do what is right, even when we knew to do it (Rom. 7:18). Romans 8:3-4 tells us that Jesus' death resolved that need. Romans 6:14 tells us that the grace that is the product of his death delivers us from the power of sin.

The point is that Jesus' death was for us, not God. It changed us; it didn't change the judgment. It set us free so that we, with the mercy and grace and God, could face the judgment.

> And now, little children, remain in him, so that when he appears, we may have confidence, and not be ashamed

---

[372] Matthew 25:31-46. John 5:28-30. Romans 2:5-8. 2 Corinthians 5:10. 1 Peter 1:17. Revelation 20:11-15.

before him at his coming. If you know that he is righteous, then you know that everyone who practices righteousness is born of him. (1 Jn. 2:28-29)

Yes, Jesus' death also allowed our sins to be forgiven. Yes, it was an incredible and precious price paid for our salvation. But it was not a payment to buy God's mercy. God was always willing to forgive sin without sacrifice. It is impossible to read the Hebrew Scriptures without learning that our God is abundant to pardon and always has been.[373]

The early Christians knew nothing of an angry God that had to be appeased by Jesus' death. How can that make sense? God sent his Son because he already loved us even while we were sinners! (Jn. 3:16; Rom. 5:8).

It may help you to know that the doctrine that Jesus' death was a payment to God to absolve our punishment was originated by St. Anselm in the eleventh century and completed by Thomas Aquinas in the thirteenth. It stuck, but it really shouldn't have. Innovation is never a good thing when it comes to Christian doctrine.

The Case of Cain

Another interesting ramification of the truth that God does not desire sacrifice but obedience is the case of Cain, Abel's brother.

Modern Christians are keenly aware that Abel offered a sacrifice from his flock, and that Cain offered a sacrifice of grain from his field. We believe that God likes to be appeased with blood, so we teach that Cain was rejected because his sacrifice was bloodless.

This is not what the early Christians taught.

---

[373] The phrase "abundant to pardon" is found in Isaiah 55:7. Other verses that give a comprehensive picture of God's mercy apart from sacrifice are Exodus 34:6-7; Psalm 51:16-17; Psalm 103: 12; Ezekiel 18:21-22. Of course, there are dozens more like those.

In fact, it's not what the Scriptures teach.

> We should love one another, not like Cain, who was of the wicked one and slew his brother. And why did he slay him? Because his own works were evil and his brother's righteous. (1 Jn. 3:11-12)

This passage is from John's first epistle, and John says that Cain killed his brother because his works were evil. How did John know this? Did he just have revelation because he is an apostle?

Actually, he learned this from the account of Cain in Genesis. Cain offered his sacrifice, and, as we know, it was rejected. As a result, "Cain was very angry, and his countenance fell" (Gen. 4:6)

So what did God tell Cain?

> If you do good, will you not be accepted? If you do not do good, then sin lies at your door. It wants to rule over you, but you must rule over it. (Gen. 4:7)

God seems to think the problem was Cain's behavior, not his sacrifice.

Something I picked up from reading the writings of the pre-Nicene church is that the sacrifice does not purify the heart. Instead, the heart purifies the sacrifice.

That is why in Psalm 51, David can say God doesn't want a sacrifice, but later, after he repents and offers God what he does want, a broken and contrite heart, "then shall you be pleased with the sacrifices of righteousness, with burnt offering and whole burnt offering" (v. 9).

We have wandered far afield. I hope the importance of the subject will drive you to further study and prove my efforts to have been worth the time. For now, though, we must return to the issues surrounding the Council of Nicea; in particular, whether Emperor Constantine the Great was a Christian.

Chapter 14:
Was Constantinc a Christian?

Was Constantine a Christian?

The answer to that question probably depends on what we mean by that. I will attempt, then, to address two questions:

- Was Constantine *trying* to be a Christian? Was he rejecting paganism, clearly portraying himself as a Christian, and choosing at least the semblance of a Christian lifestyle?

- Was Constantine *really* a Christian? Did he devote himself to Christ and give evidence of being born again?

It would be wonderful if we could simply appeal to the church of his day and ask them. Unfortunately, the only contemporary Christian source to which we can appeal is Eusebius' *Life of Constantine*, and it is entirely suspect:

> He was far from being so pure and so venerable as Eusebius, blinded by his favor to the church, depicts him, in his bombastic and almost dishonestly eulogistic biog-

raphy, with the evident intention of setting him up as a model for all future Christian princes.[374]

Was Constantine Trying to Be a Christian?

There can be no doubt that Constantine considered himself a Christian, despite the fact that he was not baptized until he was on his deathbed. Oddly—a comment I will explain below—there is also no doubt that the Christians who wrote about him thought he was a Christian, none more so than Eusebius of Caesarea, who was an advisor to the emperor and wrote *The Life of Constantine*.

Constantine's picture of himself as one of the Christians is evident in every one of his letters addressed to churches or bishops. For example:

> I will not deny what I especially rejoice in, that I am your fellow-servant.[375]

And:

> For our Savior left **us** but one day to be observed in commemoration of **our deliverance**, that is the day of his most holy Passion.[376]

In reading through Eusebius' description of Constantine, we find that Eusebius has the highest opinion of the emperor's character. In fact, he had a high opinion even of Constantine's father, Constantius I.[377]

> Accordingly, during the whole course of his quiet and peaceful reign, [Constantius I] dedicated his entire household, his children, his wife, and domestic attendants, to the One Supreme God; so that the company assembled within the walls of his palace did not differ in any way

---

[374] *History of the Christian Church.* Vol. III, Sec. 1.

[375] *The Ecclesiastical History of Socrates Scholasticus.* I:9.

[376] *ibid.* Emphasis mine.

[377] Not to be confused with Constantius II, of whom we wrote so much in Chapter 8.

from a church of God, in which also were to be found his ministers, who offered continual supplications on behalf of their prince.[378]

It's no wonder that Philip Schaff found Eusebius' descriptions of Constantine so overblown.

Schaff mitigates Eusebius' description, but he does grant the emperor some credit for his efforts in a virtuous life:

> His moral character was not without noble traits, among which a chastity rare for the time, and a liberality and beneficence bordering on wastefulness were prominent. Many of his laws and regulations breathed the spirit of Christian justice and humanity, promoted the elevation of the female sex, improved the condition of slaves and of unfortunates, and gave free play to the efficiency of the church throughout the whole empire. Altogether he was one of the best, the most fortunate, and the most influential of the Roman emperors, Christian and pagan.[379]

But Schaff expresses concerns that Eusebius does not express.

Here is what Schaff adds to Eusebius' description:

> It must, with all regret, be conceded, that his progress in the knowledge of Christianity was not a progress in the practice of its virtues. His love of display and his prodigality, his suspiciousness and his despotism, increased with his power.[380]

What does Schaff mean by this?

The year before the Council of Nicea, Constantine won a civil war with Licinius, his co-emperor in the east. At the end of it, he ordered Licinius executed, despite having promised him mercy.

Schaff also tells us that Constantine had his 11-year-old nephew, also named Licinius, put to death out of political suspicion,

---

[378] Eusebius. *Life of Constantine.* 17.
[379] Schaff. *History of the Christian Church.* Vol. III, Sec.1.
[380] *ibid.*

and finally, put even his eldest son Crispus to death for both political suspicion and alleged advances toward his step-mother Fausta.

And then there are religious matters. In 321, only four years before Nicea and long after he had supposedly become a Christian, he commanded that soothsayers be consulted whenever there were public misfortunes. These soothsayers used the pagan sacrifices to read fortunes.[381]

His favoritism toward Christianity did grow as time passed, but there is indication even in Christian historians that his faith in the Christian God was highly superstitious. His mother Helen was obsessed with finding artifacts of Christ, and she had Jerusalem, which was still in ruins at the time, thoroughly excavated. She became convinced that she had found Jesus' tomb, his cross, and his birthplace.

Despite all this, when Constantine dedicated his new residence in Byzantium (later Constantinople), he put it under the protection of "the God of the martyrs and the heathen goddess of Fortune."[382]

Even where he was being only Christian, the description of the emperor's devotion to Christianity shows his superstitious leanings.

> So great indeed was the emperor's devotion to Christianity, that when he was about to enter on a war with Persia, he prepared a tabernacle formed of embroidered linen on the model of a church, just as Moses had done in the wilderness; and this so constructed as to be adapted to conveyance from place to place, in order that he might have a house of prayer even in the most desert regions.[383]

Of course, this house of prayer was being carried into Persia to take the kingdom of the Persians away from them for no other reason than an emperor's desire to expand his empire. While this

---

[381] ibid.
[382] ibid.
[383] The Ecclesiastical History of Socrates Scholasticus. I:18.

may have been typical of the spirit of Israel, God's earthly kingdom, when fighting and conquering was a matter of survival, God's heavenly kingdom is not based on fighting, conquering, or killing. In fact, Jesus doesn't seem to think that defending ourselves is necessary, either:

> My kingdom is not of this world. If my kingdom were of this world, then my servants would fight so that I would not be delivered to the Jews. But now my kingdom is not from here. (Jn. 18:36)

This was the Christianity of Constantine. It seemed to affect his life in some ways, but in others he remained an emperor and politician.

Constantine and Persecution

Constantine actually wrote a letter to "the people of the eastern provinces" in which he explains why he has ended the persecution of Christians. In it he includes a prayer to the God of the Christians which acknowledges that he is the only way:

> Only let men of sound judgment be assured of this, that those only can live a life of holiness and purity, whom you call to a reliance on your holy laws.[384]

The letter even includes a statement that the prophets of Apollos were unable to prophesy while Christians were around:

> It is said that Apollos spoke from a deep and gloomy cavern and through the medium of no human voice declared that the righteous men of the earth were a bar to his speaking the truth ... Hence it was that he suffered his tresses to droop in token of grief and mourned the evils which the loss of the oracular spirit would entail on mankind.[385]

---

[384] *Life of Constantine*. II:56.
[385] *ibid.* II:50.

He then concludes by saying there should be no persecution over religious belief:

> Let everyone, if possible, apply what he has known and understood to the benefit of his neighbor; if otherwise, let him relinquish the attempt. It is one thing voluntarily to undertake the battle for immortality, another to compel others to do so from the fear of punishment.[386]

Constantine as *Pontifex Maximus*

Socrates gives another interesting picture of the conflict between Constantine's multiple roles as emperor, as *Pontifex Maximus* of the pagan religion, and as attempting to play a similar role in the Christian religion:

> After this [*i.e., the Council of Nicea*] the emperor became increasingly attentive to the interests of the Christians and abandoned the heathen superstitions. He abolished the combats of the gladiators, and set up his own statues in the temples.[387]

He "abandoned the heathen superstitions," but he was putting his own statues in pagan temples? That is not the way a Christian abandons heathen superstitions.

Perhaps we can say that Constantine saw himself, like his predecessors, as the head of not just the state but of the state religion as well. He clearly was trying to bring his subjects to Christianity as the state religion, for he was eminently successful at that, but as long as he had pagans and Christians under him, he saw himself as both a pagan and a Christian leader; even if he preferred one over the other.

Schaff reports that Constantine knew of the conflict between these choices for himself. Once it was apparent that he was going

---

[386] *ibid.* II:60.
[387] *The Ecclesiastical History of Socrates Scholasticus.* I:18.

to die, he resigned his office and entered his deathbed with the statement, "Now let us cast off all duplicity."[388]

On that deathbed he was finally baptized a Christian, oddly enough, by Eusebius of Nicomedia.

Was Constantine Really a Christian?

By this question I am asking whether Constantine sincerely devoted himself to Christ and showed evidence of being born again.

It is now apparent that unless we are discussing the last six days of life on his deathbed, the answer is no. Nonetheless, to my astonishment, the bishops of his time write about him as though he were a Christian.

Not having been baptized, there is no way that Constantine would have been admitted to the communion table. He would have had to be considered a catechumen, one being trained in the doctrines of the faith, and such did not receive the Eucharist.

Further, Constantine's duties as emperor would have forbad his being a Christian, certainly in the third century and most likely during his reign as well. In the early third century, Tertullian wrote:

> The Caesars, too, would have believed on Christ, if either the Caesars had not been necessary, or if Christians could have been Caesars.[389]

Not only in the third century, but in the early fourth as well, Christians did not fight in wars. Eventually, this would have to changes as almost everyone in the Roman empire became officially Christian, but even the Council of Nicea itself, in AD 325, it was forbidden for Christians to be in the military.[390]

---

[388] *History of the Christian Church.* Vol. III, Sec. 1.

[389] *Apology* 21. c. AD 210.

[390] Canon 12. Chapter 7.

Constantine himself fought in many wars. That was unavoidable as emperor of a large empire surrounded by barbarian tribes and bordered on by Persia. Constantine, however, was a particularly bloody emperor:

> Thus, like a faithful and good servant, did he act and testify, openly declaring and confessing himself the obedient minister of the supreme King. And God immediately rewarded him by making him ruler and sovereign and victorious to such a degree that he alone of all rulers pursued a continual course of conquest, unsubdued and invincible, and through his trophies a greater ruler than tradition records ever to have been before. So dear was he to God, and so blessed; so pious and so fortunate in all that he undertook, that with the greatest facility he obtained the authority over more nations than any who had preceded him, and yet retained his power, undisturbed, to the very close of his life.[391]

Ouch! Eusebius obviously thinks Constantine's life of conquest was a wonderful thing.

I confess that to my modern ears, this sounds awful. Nor do I understand why this wasn't awful to the ears of Eusebius as well, who had to know the reason that Christians were forbidden to be in the military. He was, after all, at the Council of Nicea and played a leading role there. As a historian, he was also more familiar with the writings of his predecessors than any man of his time.

And on the subject of war, they wrote things like this regularly:

> "For out of Zion shall go forth the law, and the word of the Lord from Jerusalem. And he shall judge among the nations and shall rebuke many people. They shall beat their swords into ploughshares, and their spears into pruning hooks. Nation shall not lift up sword against na-

---

[391] Eusebius. *Life of Constantine*. I:7.

tion, neither shall they learn war any more" [*Is. 2:3-4*]. And that it did so come to pass, we can convince you. For from Jerusalem there went out into the world men, twelve in number ... by the power of God they proclaimed to every race of men that they were sent by Christ to teach to all the word of God. And we who formerly used to murder one another do not only now refrain from making war upon our enemies, but also, that we may not lie nor deceive our examiners, willingly die confessing Christ.[392]

Tertullian, a few decades later, shows the same attitude towards war.

But how will a Christian man war? Nay, how will he serve even in peace without a sword, which the Lord has taken away? For although soldiers had come to John and had received the formula of their rule; although, likewise, a centurion had believed; still the Lord afterward, in disarming Peter, undressed every soldier. No dress is lawful among us if assigned to any unlawful action.[393]

Remember that it is not the individual arguments of these early Christians that is important. Each reference slowly builds a case that there was a universal opinion in pre-Nicene Christianity. In this case, many references could be found, and they all would show the same belief: Christians do not participate in war.

Constantine, however, did.

If joining the military was crime enough for a Christian to be banned from the communion table for up to 13 years,[394] then surely leading the military should be enough for Constantine not to have been considered a Christian by bishops like Eusebius. Whatever Constantine thought of himself was one thing, but that bishops would join him in that appraisal is quite another.

---

[392] Justin Martyr. *Dialogue with Trypho, a Jew*. 39. c. AD 155.
[393] Tertullian. *On Idolatry*. 19.
[394] Canon 12. Chapter 7.

Conclusion

Constantine's love for Christianity and his superstitious trust in the God of the Christians is, I think, undeniable. That he lived his life in a real knowledge of Jesus Christ, following him as taught by the apostles and by the churches up to his time seems impossible. The best we can conclude is that perhaps there was enough sincerity that his deathbed baptism was a real conversion to a real but temporary Christianity.

Each one will make his own decision, but in the end only one decision will matter, for we must all stand before the judgment seat of Christ, to receive the deeds done in the body, whether good or bad (2 Cor. 5:10).

Part III

The Trinity before Nicea

Chapter 15:
The Trinity: *Homoousios*

We have already looked at the Nicene and pre-Nicene view of the Trinity, but we need to take a much deeper look at it for two reasons.

- Since Nicea the Trinity has become a touchy subject, and the words "heresy" and "heretic" are quickly thrown around.

- Trained theologians think that we understand the Trinity better today than Christians did before Nicea.

The comments of historians on the matter of the Trinity make it clear that modern Christians believe that it took some time to really understand the doctrine of the Trinity. For example, in his comments on the Arian Controversy in the "Prolegomena" to Eusebius' *Ecclesiastical History*, Philip Schaff writes:

> It must not be forgotten that at the beginning of the fourth century the problem of how to preserve the Godhood of Christ and at the same time his subordination to the Father ... had not been solved.[395]

---

[395] Schaff, Philip. Prolegomena: "The Outbreak of the Arian Controversy. The Attitude of Eusebius." *The Nicene and Post-Nicene Fathers*. Series II. Vol. I.

In his eight-volume series, *History of the Christian Church*, he writes:

> The Nicene fathers still teach, like their predecessors, a certain subordinationism, which seems to conflict with the doctrine of consubstantiality. But we must distinguish between a subordination of essence (*ousia*) and a subordination of hypostasis ... In this point, as in the doctrine of the Holy Ghost, **the Nicene system yet needed further development**. The logical consistency of the doctrine of the consubstantiality of the Son ... **must in time overcome this decaying remnant of the ante-Nicene subordinationism**.[396]

The International Standard Bible Encyclopedia, still the standard in Bible Encyclopedias for Protestant pastors, in its section on the Trinity, written by famed Evangelical theologian B.B. Warfield, says:

> The formulated doctrine [*of the Trinity*] was of slow attainment. ... In the 2nd century the dominant neo-Stoic and neo-Platonic ideas deflected Christian thought into subordinationist channels, and produced what is known as the Logos-Christology ... meanwhile, to a great extent, the Spirit was neglected altogether.[397]

Is this true? Was "Logos-Christology" the product of Stoic and Platonic influence on second-century Christians? Have we improved our understanding of the Trinity by throwing off the "Logos-Christology"?

---

[396] Schaff, Philip. *History of the Christian Church*. Vol. III. Section 130. Emphasis mine, parentheses his.
[397] Warfield, Benjamin B. "Trinity, 2." *International Standard Bible Encyclopedia*.

Pre-Nicene Christianity and the Apostles

We have already seen that the pre-Nicene Christians believed they were carefully preserving the teachings of the apostles, not teaching "neo-Stoic and neo-Platonic" ideas.

> And this is what the holy writings teach us, as well as all the Spirit-bearing men.[398]

Theophilus, the writer of that passage, was the seventh bishop of Antioch, the apostle Paul's home church. He was writing just over 50 years after Ignatius was martyred. Ignatius was the first bishop of Antioch, and tradition holds that he had been chosen by apostles. Theophilus' claim to have the backing of the Scriptures and "all the Spirit-bearing men," is no frivolous assertion!

How likely is it that Theophilus really got his teaching from the apostles? We must remember that it was the apostle John who wrote:

> In the beginning was the *Logos*, and the *Logos* was with God, and the *Logos* was God. ... The *Logos* became flesh and lived among us. (Jn. 1:1,14)

Should we now accuse the apostle John of being infected with "neo-Stoic and neo-Platonic" ideas?

We have further seen that the bishops at Nicea believed themselves to be simply outlining the teaching of the fathers who came before them. Their goal was to preserve apostolic teaching, not invent a new definition of the Trinity.

The in-depth and perhaps overwhelming look at the early Christian view of the Trinity in this chapter and the next are, I believe, necessary to establish that the Nicene view of the Trinity was both orthodox and apostolic. It does not need to be improved, but to be received as the early Christians received it.

---

[398] Theophilus, *To Autolycus*. II:22.

The Simplicity of the Nicene View of the Trinity

I am not going to bore you in these two chapters any more than I have bored you in previous ones. I am going to spare you the difficult details of *homoousios*, *homoiousios*, and *homoian*. I am also going to spare you a discussion of the role of *hypostases* in explaining the Trinity.

We can complicate things so much that we miss the forest for the trees.

It is hard for me to conceive of books being written to explain why *hypostasis* is a necessary term to distinguish the persons of God when in fact we modern Christians have completely missed the fact that the Nicene Creed says the one God is the Father, something we would never say! We are careful always to include the Father, Son, and Holy Spirit when mention the one God.

Why should we linger on the difference between *homo-ousios* and *homoi-ousios* when we haven't even discussed the fact that the Nicene Creed—and the Bible!—says that the Son is begotten in the beginning, while most Christians have no concept of the Son being begotten except at Bethlehem. To modern Christians, the Son is eternal in exactly the same sense that God is.

In fact, most modern Christians wouldn't say that sentence the way I just did. They would say "eternal in exactly the same sense that *the Father* is." Distinguishing God and his Son is not something we do, even though it's something the Scriptures always do.

Give yourself a thought experiment here:

- Can you picture the Scriptures saying, "The Son is sitting at the right hand of God"?
- Can you picture the Scriptures saying, "The Father is sitting at the left hand of God"?
- Can you picture an apostle greeting the church with "grace to you from God our Father and Jesus Christ his Son"?
- Can you picture an apostle greeting the church with "grace to you from God, Jesus Christ, and the Father his Father"?

Tertullian tells us that there's a reason that the answer to questions one and three are yes and the answers to questions two and four are no.

> I shall follow the apostle [Paul], so that if the Father and the Son are alike to be invoked, I shall call the Father "God" and invoke Jesus Christ as "Lord."

> But when Christ alone [is invoked], I shall be able to call him "God." As the same apostle says, "Of whom is Christ, who is over all, God blessed forever" [*Rom. 9:5*].

> For I should give the name of "sun" even to a sunbeam, considered by itself. But if I were mentioning the sun from which the ray emanates, I would certainly withdraw the name of sun from the mere beam. For although I do not make two suns, still I shall reckon both the sun and its ray to be as much two things—and two forms of one undivided substance—as God and his Word, as the Father and the Son.[399]

The places where we have wandered away from the apostolic understanding of the Trinity are not huge, but we have wandered. And we have wandered far enough to have our own difficulties with the Scriptures. Many new Christians blanche when they read that there is "One God and one Mediator between man and God, the Man Christ Jesus" (1 Tim. 2:5).

No one has told those Christians, nor is it likely that they've told you, dear reader, that it was the practice of the apostle Paul that "if the Father and Son are alike to be invoked, I shall call the Father 'God' and invoke Jesus Christ as 'Lord.'" Yet it only takes a cursory familiarity with the Scriptures to realize that it's true.

How can we move on to *homoousios* and *hypostasis* when we haven't even mastered the basics of the faith, the things that the apostolic churches say were handed down to them?

In fact, why move on to *homoousios* and *hypostasis* at all? What good has it done us? We find even a great historian like

---

[399] *Against Praxeas.* 13.

Philip Schaff referring to the pre-Nicene Christians as "uncertain in regard to the exact relation of Father and Son"?

Not uncertain, my worthy Mr. Schaff; nothing about their quotes indicate uncertainty. They haven't defined the Trinity to the satisfaction of later generations because we ask for too fine a definition. We ignore their broader one because it does not suit our tastes.

Origen tried to check our curiosity some 1800 years ago.

> If, then, it is once rightly understood that the only-begotten Son of God is his Wisdom existing in **substance**, I do not know whether our curiosity ought to advance beyond this.[400]

We have strained at gnats, but we have swallowed camels.

The Eastern Orthodox Churches and the Trinity

I am writing this chapter as a westerner because I believe the vast majority of my readers are westerners influenced by Roman Catholic or Protestant Christianity.

One further proof of my point in this chapter is that Eastern Orthodox Christians, who represent at least half of Christian tradition after Nicea, would agree that the western churches have greatly over-defined the Trinity.

On a web page created by Orthodox monks from the Decani monastery in Kosovo, I found:

> An important element of the Eastern Christian understanding of God is the notion that God, in his essence, is totally transcendent and unknowable and that, strictly speaking, God can only be designated by negative attrib-

---

[400] Origen. *De Principiis.* I:2:1-2. c. AD 230.

utes: it is possible to say what God is not, but it is impossible to say what he is.[401]

In other words, there are some aspects of the relationship between the persons of the Trinity that are best left undefined.

The Orthodox view of the Trinity was pointed out to me by a reader of my web site, *Christian History for Everyman*, who wrote:

> It is good to see someone else defend the Nicene view of the Trinity. But remember, you are not alone!

He then gave me a list of podcasts by Orthodox priests on *Ancient Faith Radio*[402] espousing the kinds of ideas you will be reading in the next two chapters. As it turns out, half of the world's Christian tradition does not believe that pre-Nicene and Nicene Christians were confused on the subject of the Trinity.

The Faith Once for All Delivered to the Saints

I make regular reference in this book to Jude 3, where we are commanded to "contend earnestly" for "the faith once for all delivered to the saints."

God is far greater than we can understand. It would be demeaning to think that the God who created at least a hundred billion galaxies with at least a hundred billion stars each would be fathomable to the tiny human mind!

But there are things that God has revealed to us. He has revealed himself to us as the Father, Son, and Holy Spirit, and—as we shall see in this chapter—there are aspects of that relationship that he has revealed to us as well.

I find it objectionable that we think that our precise definitions and our sophisticated—and perhaps ostentatious—theological

---

[401] "The Doctrine of the Orthodox Church: The Basic Doctrines." Orthodox Christian Information Center. Accessed 2 Apr. 2011. <http://orthodoxinfo.com/general/doctrine1.aspx>.

[402] e.g., <http://ancientfaith.com/podcasts/podup/hopko/the_holy_trinity>.

terms are an improvement on the faith that was so carefully pre-served in the early churches and outlined at the Council of Nicea.

It is true that the pre-Nicene Christians didn't have the precise definitions that we now have. But perhaps that is because some aspects of the relationship between the persons of the Trinity were *supposed to be* a mystery.

Homoousios and Proverbs 8:22

In AD 325, all Christians believed that Proverbs 8:22 was a statement about the generation, begetting, or even "creation" of the Son of God in the beginning. Since pre-Nicene Christians, and fourth-century Christians in the east, used the Septuagint (LXX for short), a Greek translation of the Hebrew Scriptures, I will quote from it:

> The Lord created me the beginning of his ways, with an eye to his works.

The Septuagint uses the word "created" (*ektisen* in Greek) in this passage that all pre-Nicene and Nicene Christians understood to refer to the generation of the Son in eternity past. Therefore, pre-Nicene Christian writers were not afraid to refer to the Son as "created" in the beginning.

Then Arius came along.

Arius applied the word "created" in a way that no pre-Nicene writer understood it. When pre-Nicene Christians used the word "created," they meant that inexplicable, incomprehensible, and mysterious birth of the Son of God before time began. They gen-erally preferred to use the word "beget," as that's the word used almost exclusively in the New Testament.

They also understood, and clearly explained, that the Son of God was not created from nothing like all other creatures, but he came out of God. He was always the *Logos*—the "Word" or "Rea-son" of God—even before his generation before the creation.

Thus, to hear Arius declare that he was created from nothing, as all other creatures were, would have horrified earlier Christians every bit as much as it horrified the bishops of Alexandria in the fourth century. They would also have had the same objection that the bishops at Nicea had. If the Son was created from nothing, then he was of some other substance than God's. If he was the *Logos* of God, birthed from inside of God, only then did he shared God's divine substance.

And they would have used the same terminology as the bishops at Nicea: *ousios* and *homoousios*.

Homoousios and the Substance of God

"Substance," in the context of *homoousios*, means the "stuff" God is made of, if you'll excuse the expression. When we talk about God, we are talking about something far above ourselves. We will never be able to explain God.

On the other hand, pre-Nicene Christians argued that their conception of God and their understanding of the Trinity was passed down to them by the apostles. We may not be able to thoroughly describe God with any accuracy, but we can say the things that have been handed down to us as part of "the faith once for all delivered to the saints" (Jude 3)

Athenagoras, a second-century apologist, provides a definition of the substance, or "essence," of God some 150 years before Nicea:

> Because the multitude [of Roman pagans], who cannot distinguish between matter and God, or see how great is the interval which lies between them, pray to idols made of matter, are we therefore, who do distinguish and separate the uncreated and the created ... and who give the fitting name to each of them—are we to come and worship images? ... But if they are at the greatest possible distance from one another, as far apart as the artist and the materials of his art, why are we called to account?[403]

Athenagoras says here that there is a divine substance, which is uncreated, and there is matter, which is created. By "matter," he

---

[403] *A Plea for the Christians.* 15.

does not mean only material things, but everything that is not divine. Thus angels, humans, animals, trees, and rocks are all summed up in the word "matter." Everything that is created, living or not, is meant by "matter."

On the other hand, there is God, whose "substance" is uncreated.

Keep in mind here that Athenagoras is writing to the emperor of Rome. He is trying to describe Christianity in general; he is not trying to win a theological argument.

Notice also his use of "we." He says that "we" distinguish and separate the created and uncreated.

Throughout the pre-Nicene writings, you will find this sort of terminology. They cared about what "we," the churches in general, believed. It is no wonder that Arius aroused the ire of his contemporaries. Not only was he failing to distinguish between the uncreated and the created, between God and matter, but he also refused to be corrected. His divisive, unsubmissive attitude, so willing to split the church of God, was far worse than his misunderstanding of this somewhat technical issue.

Clement of Rome, possibly the earliest of the early Christian writers, writing around AD 96, describes the importance of the unity of the church and the attitude that Arius should have had:

> Who, then, is noble-minded among you? Who compassionate? Who full of love? Let him declare, "If on my account sedition, disagreements, and schism have arisen, I will depart. I will go away wherever you desire, and I will do what the many command. Only let the flock of God live on terms of peace with the elders set over it."[404]

How different things would have been—and how much less reliant upon emperors—if this had been the attitude of the fourth-century bishops!

---

[404] *1 Clement.* 44.

Athenagoras goes on to say that distinguishing between God and matter, between uncreated substance and created substance was important enough to Christians that ...

> We employ language which makes a distinction between God and matter ... For we acknowledge a God and a Son, his *Logos,* and a Holy Spirit, **united in essence**.[405]

As of this writing, I am unable to find the Greek original of Athenagoras' phrase, "united in essence." So perhaps here is the best place to discuss the importance of words.

The "Idea" of *Homoousios*

Did Athenagoras use the same wording that the Nicene Creed uses? Is "essence" a translation of the Greek word *ousios*? Is "united in essence" possibly *homoousios* in the original Greek?

I don't have and don't know how to get the Greek original of *A Plea for the Christians,* so I can't answer that. I do know that it's very unlikely that Athenagoras actually used the word *homoousios* or, in all the research I've done, I would have found someone, or more likely many someones, who mentioned it. That he used *ousios* is very likely.

However, it is not words that matter, but ideas. Athenagoras explains what he means, and he does so thoroughly enough that it is easy to understand his point no matter what words he used. With or without *homoousios,* he is clearly conveying the same idea that the bishops at Nicea meant to convey.

That idea is this: What was the state of the Son of God prior to his generation?

It doesn't matter what term you apply to that generation. You can call it creation, birth, or begetting. The point is, what was the state of the Son of God prior to that creation, birth, begetting, or generation?

---

[405] *A Plea for the Christians.* 24. Emphasis mine.

Arius' answer was that "he was not"; he didn't exist. The early Christian answer is that he was the *Logos* of God, inside of God.

> For those that don't remember, *Logos* is the Greek word that we usually render "Word" in English. It has a wider meaning than "word." Early Christians suggest it is related to reason, mind, thought, and even wisdom, and, of course, we regularly translate it "message" in our English Bibles.

This is the main and most important meaning of *homoousios*.

Eusebius of Caesarea, after discussing *homoousios* with the council, wrote back to his church in Caesarea to explain what it meant:

> That he is *homoousios* with the Father then simply implies that the Son of God has no resemblance to created things but is in every respect like the Father only who begat him; that he is of no other substance or essence but of the Father. To this doctrine, explained in this way, it seemed right to assent.[406]

This is what the council itself said that it meant by the term.

It corresponds exactly with what earlier Christians said about the relationship between the Father and the Son.

I apologize in advance for inundating you with all the quotes which follow, but I want you to see that the idea that the Son is "begotten, not made, *homoousios* with the Father," was not a novel concept dreamed up by the bishops of Nicea. It is brought up in the pre-Nicene writings over and over again.

Justin Martyr, c. AD 155:

> For I have already proven that he was the only-begotten of the Father in everything, being begotten, in a unique way, *Logos* and Power by him, and afterwards become

---

[406] *The Ecclesiastical History of Socrates Scholasticus* I:8

man through the virgin, as we have learned from the memoirs.[407]

> The following quote by Tatian is a little complicated. His last point is simply that just because God begat his *Logos* doesn't mean that he was left without *Logos*. God still had the ability to reason and speak as much as he did before the generation of his *Logos* as a person second to himself.
>
> Hard to visualize? That's why the early Christians used such illustrations as the lighting of a torch or the procession of a stream from its source in a spring. We're not meant to fully understand God; the procession of the Son from the Father is supposed to be a mystery. We can understand only what he's revealed to us, and as we can see on these pages, that is mind-bending enough!

Tatian, c. AD 165:

> God was in the beginning, but the beginning, we have been taught, is the power of the *Logos*. For the Lord of the universe ... was alone, but ... with him, by *Logos* power, the *Logos* himself also, who was in him, subsists. By his simple will, the *Logos* springs forth, and the *Logos*, not coming forth in vain, becomes the first-begotten work of the Father. ... But he came into being by participation, not by abscission [*i.e., cutting off*], for what is cut off is separated from the original substance. ...
>
> For just as from one torch many fires are lit, but the light of the first torch is not lessened by the kindling of many torches, so the *Logos*, coming forth from the *Logos* power of the Father, has not divested him ... of the *Logos* power.[408]

---

[407] *Dialogue with Trypho, a Jew.* 105. Justin uses the term "memoirs" or "memoirs of the apostles" to refer to the four Gospels, which he quotes frequently.
[408] *Address to the Greeks.* 5.

Theophilus, c. AD 168:

> God, then, having his own *Logos* internal, within his own bowels, begat him, emitting him along with his own Wisdom before all things. He had this *Logos* as a helper in the things that were created by him, and by him he made all things. ... Therefore he speaks in this way by the prophet Solomon: "When he prepared the heavens I was there, and when he appointed the foundations of the earth I was by him as one brought up brought up with him" [*Prov. 8:27*].[409]

> But when God wished to make all that he determined, he begot this *Logos*, uttered, the firstborn of all creation, not himself being emptied of the Word, but having begotten Reason, and always conversing with his Reason.

> And this is what the holy writings teach us, as well as all the Spirit-bearing men, one of whom, John, says, "In the beginning was the *Logos*, and the *Logos* was with God" [*Jn. 1:1*], showing that at first God was alone, and the *Logos* in him. Then he says, "The *Logos* was God; all things came into existence through him, and apart from him not one thing came into existence" [*Jn. 1:2*].[410]

Athenagoras, AD 177:

> We acknowledge ... a Son of God. Don't let anyone think it ridiculous that God should have a Son. ... The Son of God is the *Logos* of the Father ... He is the first product of the Father, not as though he was being brought into existence, for from the beginning God, who is the eternal Mind, had the *Logos* in himself.[411]

Irenaeus, c. AD 185:

> [The Gospel] according to John relates [Jesus Christ's] original, effectual, and glorious generation from the Fa-

---

[409] *To Autolycus*. II:10.

[410] *ibid*. II:22.

[411] *A Plea for the Christians*. 10.

ther, thus declaring, "In the beginning was the *Logos*, and the *Logos* was with God, and the *Logos* was God" [*John 1:1*].[412]

Clement of Alexandria, c. AD 190:

> Though despised as to appearance, [Jesus] was in reality adored, the expiator of sin, the Savior, the merciful, the Divine Word; he that is truly most apparently Deity. He is made equal to the Lord of the universe because he was his Son, and the Word was in God.[413]

Tertullian, c. AD 210:

> I am led to other arguments derived from God's own dispensation, in which he existed before the creation of the world, up to the generation of the Son. For before all things God was alone ... He was alone because there was nothing external to himself except himself. Yet even then he was not alone, for he had with him that which he possessed in himself, that is to say, his own Reason. This Reason is his own Thought, which the Greeks call *Logos* ... Therefore, it is now usual with our people, owing to the mere simple interpretation of the term, to say that the Word[414] was in the beginning with God. ...
>
> For although God had not yet sent his Word, he still had him within himself ... I may therefore without rashness first lay this down: that even before the creation of the universe God was not alone, since he had within himself ... his Word, which he made second to himself by agitating it within him.[415]

---

[412] *Against Heresies*. III:11:8.

[413] *Exhortation to the Heathen*. 10. "Word" is not rendered *Logos* here because Clement of Alexandria wrote in Latin, not Greek.

[414] Latin, *sermonem*. Clement and Tertullian's writings are in Latin, so they didn't generally use *Logos*, a Greek word. In *Against Praxeas*, Tertullian did use *Logos* regularly, despite the fact that the work is in Latin, because he was addressing the Trinity.

[415] *Against Praxeas*. 5.

In Origen's quote that follows, note his statement that this "Power" from God was "never at any time non-existent." It almost seems that he foresaw the appearance of such a man as Arius (or perhaps Lucian). But that is not the case; he died long before Lucian began his school. Arius was simply treading all over apostolic tradition, and that is why he was condemned.

Origen, c. AD 230:

> Another Power ... is produced, which exists with properties of its own, a kind of breath, as Scripture says, of the primal and unbegotten power of God, deriving from him its being and never at any time non-existent.[416]

> Therefore we have always held that God is the Father of his only-begotten Son, who was born of him in truth and derives from him what he is, but without any beginning.[417]

Eusebius, c. AD 325:

> Whoever then defines the Son as made of things that are not, and as a creature produced from nothing pre-existing, forgets that while he concedes the name of Son, he denies him to be a Son in reality. For he that is made of nothing cannot truly be the Son of God, any more than the other things which have been made. The true Son of God, forasmuch as he is begotten of the Father, is properly denominated the only-begotten and beloved of the Father. For this reason also, he himself is God; for what can the offspring of God be but the perfect resemblance of him who begot him?[418]

---

[416] *De Principiis.* I:2:9.

[417] *ibid.* I:2:2.

[418] *Against Marcellus.* As cited by *The Ecclesiastical History of Socrates Scholasticus.* II:21.

And finally, even Athanasius, the recognized "father of ortho-doxy," explains the Son in the same way, c. AD 350:

> As the Savior says, "I in the Father and the Father in Me," so that it follows that the Word is in the One that begot him and that the One that is begotten lives eternally with the Father.[419]

As we read through these quotes, it almost seems as though they knew there would be an Arius and a Council of Nicea, and they prepared their defense against Arianism in advance!

The truth is that they did not prepare a defense against Arianism in advance. Instead, the bishops at Nicea achieved their goal. They based their response to Arius on the teachings of their fore-fathers, making the Nicene Creed a powerful, concise, and accurate summation of the apostolic faith that had been handed down since the earliest days of the church.

Note that I have only given you quotes that directly address the issue of the existence of the Son inside of God as the *Logos* of God prior to his generation before the creation of all things. There are many more passages that *imply* the eternal existence of the Son as the divine *Logos*. Nor have I given you a comprehensive list of quotes that directly address this subject.

That long list of quotes could have been much longer!

To complete our look at the Nicene term *homoousios*, we really need only address the pre-Nicene use of the terms "essence" and "substance" so that we can show that these, too were not novel at Nicea.

Pre-Nicene Reference to the Shared *Ousios* of the Father and the Son

I mentioned above that *ousios* is a reference to the "stuff" God is made of. Again, I must apologize for using such terminology. We are mere humans, and God is beyond our comprehension.

---

[419] *Against the Heathen.* III:47.

Nonetheless, the pre-Nicene Christians believed that *homoousios*, the same or shared substance of divinity, was a teaching handed down to them as part of the apostolic faith. They talked about it, and they believed that the apostles wanted us to know it.

What is handed down to us from the apostles, Jesus' chosen messengers, is something that we can and should talk about.

> Therefore, brothers, stand fast and hold onto the traditions which you have received from us, whether by word or by our letter. (2 Thess. 2:15)

Irenaeus speaks marvelously of what God has given us to understand:

> Through his love and infinite kindness, [God] has come within reach of human knowledge; knowledge, however, not with regard to his greatness or with regard to his essence—for that no man has measured or handled—but after this sort: that we should know that he who made, formed, and breathed in them the breath of life, and nourishes us by means of the creation, establishing all things by his *Logos* and binding them together by His Wisdom, this is he who is the only true God.[420]

While we may not understand his essence, and while speaking of the "stuff" of which God is made is crude and beyond us; nonetheless, we can know that he established all things by his preexistent *Logos*, and we can know that the essence of God, which is so far beyond our comprehension, is shared by the Father and the Son.

Therefore, the pre-Nicene Christians wrote these sorts of things:

---

[420] *Against Heresies*. III:24:2.

Justin Martyr, c. AD 155:

> This Power was begotten from the Father, by his power and will, but not by abscission [*i.e., cutting off*], as if the **essence** of the Father were divided.[421]

Athenagoras, AD 177:

> We employ language which makes a distinction between God and matter ... For we acknowledge a God and a Son, his *Logos*, and a Holy Spirit, **united in essence**.[422]

Irenaeus, c. AD 185:

> Carefully, then, has the Holy Spirit pointed out, by what has been said, [Jesus'] birth from a virgin, and his **essence**, that he is God—for the name Emmanuel indicates this.[423]

Tertullian, c. AD 210:

> [I] derive the Son from no other source but from the **substance** of the Father.[424]

Clement of Alexandria, c. AD 190

> [When First John] says, "That which was from the beginning," he touches upon the generation without beginning of the Son, who is co-existent with the Father: ... The Word itself, that is, the Son of God, who being by equality of **substance** one with the Father, is eternal and uncreated.[425]

---

[421] *Dialogue with Trypho.* 128.
[422] *A Plea for the Christians.* 24.
[423] *Against Heresies.* III:21:4.
[424] *Against Praxeas.* 4.
[425] "Fragments of Clemens Alexandrius." Fragment III. *The Ante-Nicene Fathers.* Vol. II.

> Notice Clement's use of "uncreated" here. Clement is among those who applies Proverbs 8:22-31 to the Son,[426] but he nonetheless calls the Son uncreated. His generation in the beginning can be called a creation, but his substance, because he has eternally existed as the *Logos* of God inside of God, is uncreated.

Origen, c. AD 230:

> If, then, it is once rightly understood that the only-begotten Son of God is his Wisdom existing in **substance**, I do not know whether our curiosity ought to advance beyond this.[427]

Dionysius, c. AD 245:

> The plant that springs from the root is something distinct from that from which it grows up. Yet it is of one nature with it. The river which flows from the spring is something distinct from the spring. For we cannot call either the river a spring, or the spring a river. Nevertheless we allow that they are both one according to nature, and also **one in substance**; and we admit that the spring may be conceived of as father, and that the river is what is begotten of the spring.[428]

Again, these quotes are so relevant to *homoousios* that it seems that these pre-Nicene Christians foresaw the Arian Controversy and prepared for it. Of course, they did not; instead, the framers of the Nicene Creed were careful to frame their case in the wording that was handed down to them by the fathers of their faith.

The wording there, "handed down to them," is key. These bishops were not dependent on a man like Eusebius of Caesarea, a scholar and historian, to sift through the ancient writings and find

---

[426] *Miscellanies.* VII:2.

[427] *De Principiis.* I:2:1-2.

[428] "Of the One Substance." *The Ante-Nicene Fathers.* vol. VI.

quotes such as these. *These quotes exist because the teaching that the Son as the pre-existent Logos of the Father was passed down from bishop to bishop, elder to elder, and generation to generation in the catholic churches.*

Thus, the bishops at Nicea already understood these things before scholars like Eusebius of Caesarea or Sisinnius[429] had to pull out the ancient scrolls. In AD 325, apostolic tradition[430] still had a somewhat firm hold upon the church.

This is what made Arius' crime so great. The handing down of apostolic truth had been a foundation of Christian unity for three centuries. The church was built upon the foundation of the apostles and prophets (Eph. 2:20), and it was the job of the elders in the church to preserve the faith unchanged, not manufacture new doctrines based on personal interpretations of Scripture.

> It is unlawful to assert that [the apostles] preached before they had perfect knowledge, as some venture to say, boasting of themselves as improvers of the apostles. ... When we refer them [i.e., the gnostics] to that tradition which originates from the apostles and which is preserved by means of the succession of elders in the churches, they object to tradition, saying that they are wiser not only than the elders, but even than the apostles.[431]

> The Church, having received this preaching and this faith ... carefully preserves it. ... For the faith being ever one and the same, one who is able to discourse regarding it will not make any addition to it, nor does one who can say but little diminish it.[432]

---

[429] The Novatian scholar whose advice helped put an end to the Arian Controversy in AD 383. See Chapter 8.
[430] References to apostolic tradition are found in Scripture in passages like 1 Corinthians 11:2 and 2 Thessalonians 2:15 and 3:6.
[431] Irenaeus. *Against Heresies.* III:1:1, III:2:2. c. 185.
[432] *ibid.* 1:10:2.

> Oh Timothy, guard what is committed to your trust, avoiding profane things and unimportant issues and the opposition of *gnosis*, falsely named. (I Tim. 6:20)[433]

> Hold the pattern of healthy words which you heard from me in faith and love, which is in Christ Jesus. Guard the good deposited with you by the Holy Spirit who dwells in us. (2 Tim. 1:13-14)

Apostolic Tradition and Apostolic Succession

Apostolic succession will be discussed directly in Chapter 18, but we should touch on it here.

Apostolic succession, in the pre-Nicene writers, was simply a means to preserve apostolic tradition. If the bishops and elders lost the apostolic tradition, then succession became meaningless. Succession was never said by the earliest Christians to convey authority. Yes, bishops and elders had authority, but that was given to them by the election of the people and the approval of the rest of the elders.

Succession was never a **teaching** addressed to the church; it was an **argument** addressed to heretics. The question was, do the catholic churches teach the truth as it was sent from heaven? Their answer was, yes, we have a succession from God to Jesus to the apostles to the elders they appointed and, finally, to the elders who succeeded them and are around today. These have faithfully preserved the truth as it was given by the apostles.

> We refer [the gnostics] to that tradition which originates from the apostles, which is preserved by means of the succession of elders in the churches.[434]

---

[433] Paul was specifically referring to gnosticism in that verse, which he calls *pseudonymos*, a pseudonym.

[434] Irenaeus. *Against Heresies*. III:2:2.

A Different Foundation

It is of note that all the major players of the early Arian Controversy were trained in the school of Lucian. As Tertullian pointed out, "No casualty distributed among men results in one and the same result." Eusebius of Nicomedia, Theognis of Nicea, and Arius were in agreement against the tradition of the apostles because of a common source, the late third-century school of Lucian in Antioch.

Lucian may or may not have been a great teacher, but, as Irenaeus put it a century before Lucian's time:

> Nor will any one of the rulers in the churches, however gifted he may be in point of eloquence, teach doctrines different from these, for no one is greater than his Master. ... Because the faith is ever one and the same ... one who is able at great length to discourse regarding it does not make any addition to it.[435]

To drive the point home even further, he adds:

> It does not follow that because men are endowed with greater and less degrees of intelligence that they should therefore change the subject matter of the faith itself.[436]

The Arian Controversy found its wellspring in Lucian's teaching, not in the apostles' teaching, and it found its power in the divisive, self-confident attitude of Arius and of Eusebius of Nicomedia.

---

[435] *Against Heresies.* I:10:2.
[436] *ibid.* I:10:3.

Saint(?) Lucian

Believe it or not, despite the fact that Lucian and his school were excommunicated for between 16 and 35 years, he is honored as a martyr by the Roman Catholic Church and canonized by the Orthodox Churches. He had been reinstated at the beginning of the Great Persecution and was martyred a year after it was supposed to end.

There is no record of what Lucian taught or why he was out of fellowship with the church of Antioch for so long a time. He is only mentioned in passing by those who were taught by him, though his writings on the interpretation of Scripture and his work on the text of the Septuagint left him held in the highest regard by men like Eusebius of Caesarea and Jerome.

Even good men can produce bad things if they divide and do not hold firmly to the source, which would explain why Paul emphasized to Timothy that he must guard what was committed to him.[437]

Scriptural Sources for *Homoousios*

Everything the apostles taught the church was based in the Hebrew Scriptures and the teaching of Christ. The letters of the apostles are laced with scriptural quotations to justify their position.

However, though *apostolic teaching could be proven from Scripture; its source was not Scripture, but Jesus Christ himself* (Jn. 5:39-40; Matt. 5:17-48).

---

[437] I have been asked repeatedly by Roman Catholics why, if I believe in holding firmly to "the source," I have not returned to "mother church." The reason is that the Roman church is not "mother church." The independent apostolic churches maintained a unity that was based on apostolic tradition and obedience to the teachings of Christ. (Chapter 15.) I live in Selmer, Tennessee. If the church in Rome will hold to apostolic tradition, then the church in Selmer will be in fellowship and mutual submission with them. But submitting to a bishop in another country has nothing to do with anything the apostles taught.

More on Roman Catholicism in Chapter 18.

No apostle or any other man properly predicted the coming of Christ before our Lord came. There were those who recognized and believed in him, but there were none who properly understood the prophecies before he came.

Just as no one was ever able to come up with an accurate picture of the coming Messiah from the Scriptures, so no one was going to come up with an accurate picture of the generation of the Son in the beginning until he came. After he came, John would provide us the clearest description of the Son as *homoousios* with the Father.

John 1:1

The following exposition of John 1:1 could easily be a highly emotional issue. Thank God for the internet! At *Resources for Learning New Testament Greek* on the web[438] is a scholarly exposition of John 1:1 saying exactly what I'm saying here, and he is kind enough to give numerous mainstream Protestant sources for it.

These include, and I'm quoting with copy and paste: "Daniel Wallace ('Greek Grammar Beyond the Basics'), A.T. Robertson (both his 'Grammar' and 'Word Pictures'), R.C.H. Lenski (in his commentary on the Gospel of John), Henry Alford ('Greek Testament'), J.A. Bengel ('Word Studies'), Albert Barnes ('Barnes' Notes'), B.F. Westcott, and F.L. Godet, (and many others)."

The point is that what I'm saying here about John 1:1 may not be widely known, but it is not controversial, neither to Protestant nor to Roman Catholic scholars.

John 1:1 reads:

> In the beginning was the *Logos*, and the *Logos* was with God, and the *Logos* was divine. This one was in the beginning with God. All things were made by him, and without him nothing was made that was made. (Jn. 1:1-3)

---

[438] *Learning New Testament Greek.* <http://www.ntgreek.org/answers/answer-frame-john1_1.htm>.

I have written "the *Logos* was divine" here rather than "the *Logos* was God," for a reason.

In a sentence like the last part of John 1:1, "Θεοσ ην ο Λογοσ" ("God is the Word") both nouns, "God" and "Word," can be considered subjects of the sentence. English teachers would call the verb "reflexive." The verb makes both words equivalent, so they are both subjects.

It is not the same in Greek. Greek speakers can indicate the subject of the sentence by putting the word "the" in front of it. That noun becomes the subject, and the other word is an adjective.

In this sentence, it is "*Logos*" that is preceded by "the." It is the noun, and the word "God" is the adjective.

Because of this, my first year Greek teacher[439] explained that John 1:1 could best be translated, "The Word has the character and nature of God," or, "The Word is exactly like God." I have since read several other scholarly discussions on John 1:1, all of them, without exception, agreeing that the sense of the sentence is that the Word is exactly similar to God.

My thought is, why bother with all those words when we have a word that exactly suits the purpose? God, used as an adjective, is "divine."

The web site I reference in the text box above suggests an even more interesting word to use in that sentence, one with which we are already familiar. He explains that this verse says that the Word has the same "essence" and "nature" as God.

---

[439] I've only had one year of Greek, which I took from a college professor at a large Assembly of God church. My claim to fame in Greek is that I read the excellent book *Do It Yourself Hebrew and Greek* by Professor Ed Goodrick. Thus, I learned that I should never trust my limited Greek and always lean on those who know more than me, a practice I've been careful to follow throughout this book.

This is exactly how the pre-Nicene Christians understood John 1:1:

> When God wished to make all that he determined, he begot this *Logos* ... Hence the holy Scriptures teach us, as well as all the Spirit-bearing men, one of whom, John, says, "In the beginning was the *Logos*, and the *Logos* was with God," showing that at the first God was alone and the *Logos* in him. Then he says, "The *Logos* was God."[440]

Proverbs 8:22-31

Since almost all pre-Nicene Christians read the Septuagint, the Greek translation of the Hebrew Scriptures, I am going to cite Proverbs 8:22-31 from an English translation of the Septuagint.

> The Lord made me the beginning of his ways for his works. He established me before time was in the beginning, before he made the earth: even before he made the depths; before the fountains of water came forth: before the mountains were settled, and before all hills, he begets me. The Lord made countries and uninhabited tracks, and the highest inhabited parts of the world. When he prepared the heaven, I was present with him; and when he prepared his throne upon the winds: and when he strengthened the clouds above; and when he secured the fountains of the earth: and when he strengthened the foundations of the earth: I was by him, suiting myself to him, I was that wherein he took delight; and daily I rejoiced in his presence continually. For he rejoiced when he had completed the world, and rejoiced among the children of men.[441]

It's easy to see that if you were a pre-Nicene Christian, taught that the Son of God was the pre-existent *Logos*, birthed by the Fa-

---

[440] Theophilus. *To Autolycus.* II:22. c. AD 168. That last sentence could be translated "The *Logos* was divine" because Theophilus is directly quoting John 1:1 in Greek.

[441] Brenton. *English Translation of the Greek Septuagint Bible.*

ther before time began, that this passage of Scripture would leap out at you as clearly indicative of the eternal generation of the Son of God and the subsequent creation of the world.

It leaps out at us today, too, but we're not really allowed to believe it's a prophecy of Christ—because Arius used it.

We have overreacted to Arius. We have thrown out the baby with the bathwater.

Even Alexander, the bishop of Alexandria who excommunicated Arius, applies Proverbs 8 to the Son of God, though we find him quoting from a little further down in the passage in a letter to the bishop of Constantinople, also named Alexander:

> Since the Son is always with him, the Father is always perfect ... who ... has begotten his only-begotten Son. How, then, is it not impious to say that the Wisdom of God once did not exist, when it speaks in this way concerning itself: "I was with him forming all things; I was his delight" [*Prov. 8:30*].[442]

Justin Martyr is the earliest known writer to use Proverbs 8:22, writing between AD 150 and 160. He applies it to convince some Jews, with whom he is debating, that the one God has an only-begotten Son:

> It is written in the book of Wisdom: " ... The Lord created me the beginning of his ways for his works. From everlasting he established me in the beginning, before he formed the earth, before he made the depths, before the springs of waters came forth, and before the mountains were settled. He begets me before all the hills." When I repeated these words, I added: "You perceive, my hearers, if you pay attention, that the Scripture has declared that this Offspring was begotten by the Father before all things created."[443]

---

[442] Alexander of Alexandria. "Epistles on the Arian Heresy and on the Deposition of Arius." *The Ante-Nicene Fathers*. vol. VI.
[443] *Dialogue with Trypho, a Jew*. 129.

A Little More Foreign Grammar

Nowadays we struggle with identifying Jesus with Wisdom of Proverbs, despite the obvious similarities, because Wisdom is identified as a she.

Struggle no more!

In English, he and she indicate sex. I'm a male, and you call me "him." My wife's a female, and you call her "her." My house is an object, so I call it "it."

It's not so simple in Hebrew, Greek, German, Spanish, or most other languages. In German, for example, my coffee cup is a she. The coffee in it is a he. My car is an it, but only if I call it "*Auto*." If I call it "*Wagen*," another German word for car, then it's he. Worse yet, that *Fräulein* you see in the movies is also an it! (Or, at least, until the last few decades she was.)

Most languages are like that. Their pronouns indicate gender, not sex. Why that is, I don't know. As an American, it seems pointless to me. But it's real.

Thus, Wisdom in Proverbs is only called "she" because the Hebrew word *chokmah* is feminine. So is the Greek word *Sophia*. The use of "she" in Proverbs has nothing whatsoever to do with Wisdom actually being a woman. It's simply the nature of the language.

Some 30 years later, Irenaeus uses Proverbs 8:22 in his refutation of the gnostics, although he applies the passage to the Holy Spirit:

> I have ... demonstrated that the *Logos*, namely the Son, was always with the Father, and that Wisdom also, which is the Spirit, was present with him before all creation. He declares by Solomon: ... "The Lord created me the beginning of his ways in his work. He set me up from everlasting, in the beginning, before he made the earth." ... There

is therefore one God, who by the *Logos* and Wisdom created and arranged all things.[444]

The editors of *The Ante-Nicene Fathers* add a note that says, "This is one of the favourite Messianic quotations of the Fathers, and is considered the base of the first chapter of St. John's Gospel."[445]

They're right. Early Christians consistently applied Proverbs 8 to the birth of the *Logos* in the beginning:

Theophilus, seventh bishop of Antioch, c. AD 168:

> For the prophets did not exist when the world came into existence, but the wisdom of God which was in him and his holy *Logos*, which was always present with Him. Therefore he speaks in this way by the prophet Solomon: "When he prepared the heavens I was there, and when he appointed the foundations of the earth I was with him, putting things in order" [*Prov. 8:27*].[446]

Athenagoras, AD 177:

> The Son of God is the *Logos* of the Father ... But if ... it occurs to you to inquire what is meant by the Son, I will state briefly that he is the first product of the Father, not as having been brought into existence, for from the beginning God, who is the eternal mind, had the *Logos* in himself, being from eternity instinct with *Logos* ... The prophetic Spirit also agrees with our statements: "The Lord," it says, "made me the beginning of his ways to his works" [*Prov. 8:22*].[447]

Clement of Alexandria, c. AD 190:

> Ignorance does not apply to the God who before the foundation of the world was the Counselor of the Father. For he was the Wisdom in which the sovereign God "de-

---

[444] *Against Heresies.* IV:20:3I acI .

[445] Note 4074.

[446] *To Autolycus.* II:10.

[447] *A Plea for the Christians.* 10.

lighted" [*Prov. 8:30*]. For the Son is the Power of God, as being the Father's most ancient Word before the production of all things, and his Wisdom.[448]

Cyprian, c. AD 255:

> This passage from Cyprian uses an interesting convention. Cyprian provides headings, and then he simply lines up Scripture under the headings.

"That Christ is the firstborn and that he is the Wisdom of God by whom all things were made:"

Solomon in the Proverbs: "The Lord established me in the beginning of His ways, into His works: before the world He founded me ... " [*Cyprian gives all of Prov. 8:22-31, then lists other Scriptures*].[449]

Dionysius of Alexandria, c. AD 260:

Being the brightness of the eternal Light, [the Son] himself also is absolutely eternal. ...He is that Wisdom which says, "I was the one in whom he delighted, and I was daily his delight before his face at all times" [*Prov. 8:30*].[450]

Athanasius, c. AD 350:

> Athanasius changed his position as the battle over Nicea progressed because of the Arian use of Proverbs 8:22 to say that the Son was created. From about AD 350 on, Athanasius takes the position that Proverbs 8:22 applies to the Son only in reference to the incarnation. On the other hand, he uses Proverbs 8:25 and 8:27 to apply to the generation of the Son before the beginning.

Who was with him when he made all created existence, except his Wisdom, who says, "When he was making the

---

[448] *Miscellanies*. VII:2.

[449] *Three Books of Testimonies Against the Jews*. II:1.

[450] "Letter to Dionysius, Bishop of Rome." *The Ante-Nicene Fathers*. Vol. VI.

heaven and the earth, I was present with him"? [*Prov. 8:27*]. ... Being present with him as his Wisdom and his Word, looking at the Father, he fashioned the universe ... being the good Offspring of him who is good and true Son, he is the Father's Power and Wisdom and Word ... To sum all up, he is the wholly perfect fruit of the Father and is alone the Son.[451]

Of the Son [divine Scripture] introduces not another, but the Father himself, saying, "I have begotten you from the womb before the morning star" [*Ps. 110:3, LXX*[452]], and again, "You are my Son, this day have I begotten you" [*Ps. 2:7*]; and the Lord says of himself in Proverbs, "Before all the hills, he begets me" [*Prov. 8:25*].[453]

Is it really acceptable that we have not had these things explained to us? It has taken me many pages to explain, but that is only because I have had to justify it with many quotes. The description of the generation of the Son in the beginning could be done in a paragraph or two.

Instead, we have replaced it with assertions that the doctrine of the Trinity had to be carefully developed after Nicea by bishops whose congregations were the entire population of a city, and whose positions were as political as they were ecclesiastical. They were almost as reliant on the writings of the fathers before them as we are.

Worse, the "developed" doctrine of the Trinity is confined to theological seminaries, requiring an exact knowledge of persons, natures, and the one essence of God expressed in terms like *hypostasis* and *ousios*. How much simpler—and more Scriptural!—to simply say that God was able to beget his Wisdom in the beginning, before the creation, and through that Son, who is his Wisdom and Word, he created all things?

---

[451] *Against the Heathen.* III:47.

[452] LXX is short for Septuagint. Both terms suggest the number 70, which was believed to be the number of Jewish scholars who translated the Septuagint.

[453] *Defense of the Nicene Definition.* 13.

What's the Septuagint?

The text most commonly used for the Old Testament of our English Bibles is called the *Masoretic* text. It was carefully preserved by Jewish scribes, known as *Masoretes*, for centuries.

It might seem that the Masoretic text would be more reliable because it is Hebrew, the original language of the Old Testament, whereas the Septuagint is a translation. That is not necessarily so.

The Septuagint ... is a version of a Hebrew text earlier by about a millennium than the earliest dated Hebrew manuscript extant ... a version, in particular, prior to the formal rabbinical revision of the Hebrew that took place early in the 2nd century AD [454]

Thus, the Septuagint, though a translation, represents a more ancient textual tradition.

It was hoped that the Dead Sea Scrolls would solve the debate between which is preferable, but they raised as many questions as they answered. [455]

Psalm 45:1

Psalm 45 was another favorite of the early Christians. In the LXX[456] it read:

> My heart has brought forth a good Word. [457]

Again, this passage leaped out at the early Christians. Psalm 45 is a Messianic Psalm anyway; verses six and seven are quoted in Hebrews. (If you don't know, understand, and practice verses 10 and 11, then you're missing out on a great blessing.)

---

[454] Thackeray, H. St. J. "Septuagint." *International Standard Bible Encyclopedia.*

[455] Sussman, Ayala & Peled, Ruth. "The Dead Sea Scrolls." *Jewish Virtual Library.* Sussman and Peled are the authors of *Scrolls from the Dead Sea.* Library of Congress, 1993.

[456] Short for Septuagint.

[457] Brenton. *English Translation of the Greek Septuagint Bible.*

Psalm 45:1 is quoted extensively in the early Christian writings. Both Justin Martyr and Cyprian used it to convince Jews, as though they had some confidence that this verse would mean something to them. Jews of that day would have interpreted the Scriptures somewhat symbolically, just as Christians of that day did, so it's likely that this verse was effective with them.

Psalm 110:3

Psalm 110:3 is another that only applies in the Septuagint.

> I have begotten you from the womb before the morning star.[458]

This passage was employed by Alexander, bishop of Alexandria in his letter explaining the excommunication of Arius:

> How can [the Son] be made of things which do not exist, when the Father says, "My heart has dictated a good Word" [Ps. 45:1] and, "From the womb, before the morning, I have begotten you"? [Ps. 110:3].[459]

Athanasius, too, the "father of orthodoxy," was still using Psalm 110:3 in AD 350:

> Of the Son [divine Scripture] introduces not another, but the Father himself, saying, "I have begotten you from the womb before the morning star" [Ps. 110:3, LXX], and again, "You are my Son, this day have I begotten you" [Ps. 2:7]; and the Lord says of himself in Proverbs, "Before all the hills, he begets me" [Prov. 8:25].[460]

Miscellaneous Verses

Pre-Nicene Christians were masters at putting the Scriptures to good use. They found passages we never consider. For example,

---

[458] ibid.
[459] "Epistle Catholic." *The Ante-Nicene Fathers.* vol. VI.
[460] *Defense of the Nicene Definition.* 13.

this one, having to do with his being born as man rather than his generation before the beginning, is in our Hebrew Bibles as well as the Septuagint:

> Binding his foal to the vine, and his donkey's colt to the choice vine, he washed his garments in wine and his clothes in the blood of grapes. (Gen. 49:11)

What a terrific prophecy of Jesus' work on earth! Who washes their garments in wine? Who washes their clothes in grape juice?

This passage is a bizarre description of laundering, but it is an excellent picture of the cleansing blood of Christ which washes us and makes our robes, representative of our righteousness (Rev. 19:8), white.

Perhaps because they lived so close to the time that Jesus expounded the Scriptures concerning himself on the road to Emmaus (Luk. 24:27), their repertoire of prophecies from the Old Testament Scriptures were much greater than ours today. (Everyone should avail themselves of Justin's *Dialogue with Trypho, a Jew*[461] for the most extensive collection of old covenant verses about Christ ever put together.)

Alexander's letter explaining the excommunication of Arius by over 100 Egyptian and Libyan bishops provides a taste of the many verses that provide a picture of the generation of the *Logos* before the beginning:

> Who that hears John saying, "In the beginning was the Word" [*Jn. 1:1*], does not condemn those that say, "There was a period when the Word was not"? Or who, hearing in the Gospel of "the only-begotten Son" and that "all things were made by him," [*Jn. 3:16; Jn. 1:3*] will not abhor those that pronounce the Son to be one of the things made?
>
> How can he be one of the things which were made by himself? Or how can he be the only-begotten, if he is reck-

---

461 *Ante-Nicene Fathers.* vol. I. Available for free to read or a nominal price to download on the web at <http://www.ccel.org/fathers/>.

oned among created things? And how could he have derived his existence from nonentities when the Father has said, "My heart has dictated a good Word," and, "I begat thee out of my bosom before the dawn"? [*Ps. 45:1; 110:3, LXX*]. Or how is he unlike the Father's essence, who is "his perfect image" and "the brightness of his glory" and says, "He that has seen me has seen the Father"? [*Col. 1:15; Heb. 1:3; Jn. 14:9*].

Again how, if the Son is the Word and Wisdom of God, was there a period when he did not exist? For that is equivalent to their saying that God was once destitute both of Word and Wisdom.

How can he be mutable and susceptible to change when he says of himself, "I am in the Father, and the Father in me," and, "I and the Father are one"? [*Jn. 14:10; Jn. 10:30*]. And again by the prophet, [he says], "Behold me because I am, and have not changed" [*Mal. 3:6*]. But if any one may also apply the expression to the Father himself, yet would it now be even more fitly said of the Word because he was not changed by having become man, but as the apostle says, "Jesus Christ, the same yesterday, today, and forever" [*Heb. 13:8*].

But what could persuade them to say that he was made on our account, when Paul has expressly declared that "all things are for him, and by him"? [*Heb. 2:10*]. One need not wonder indeed at their blasphemous assertion that the Son does not perfectly know the Father; for ... they reject even the words of the Lord himself, when he says, "As the Father knows me, even so I know the Father" [*Jn. 10:15*].[462]

We have thoroughly covered the idea of *homoousios* an its relation to the "Logos-doctrine" in early Christianity. We've also looked at some of the verses they used. Let us turn now to the one God and the "heresy" of subordinationism.

---

[462] *The Ecclesiastical History of Socrates Scholasticus.* I:6.

Chapter 16:
The Trinity at Nicca

We have already had an in-depth introduction to the Trinity in early Christian thought in the last chapter. That will save us a lot of time in this chapter!

I commend you for making it this far. If you skipped here to see what I have to say on the Trinity, you skipped one chapter too far. The chapter on *homoousios* contains the most important information on the pre-Nicene and Nicene view of the Trinity.

One God, the Scriptures, and the Jehovah's Witnesses

The Jehovah's Witnesses have at least one unique accomplishment. They are the only significant sect to revive and perpetuate the Arian heresy in the history of the church.

They appear to have adopted the Arian heresy exactly as it came from the mouth of Arius. Their main headquarters, the Watchtower, writes:

> Thus, Jesus had an existence in heaven before coming to the earth. But was it as one of the persons in an almighty, eternal triune Godhead? No, for the Bible plainly states

that in his prehuman existence, Jesus was a created spirit being, just as angels were spirit beings created by God. Neither the angels nor Jesus had existed before their creation.[463]

So we see that like Arius, the Jehovah's Witnesses teach that before he was created by the Father, the Son did not exist. In fact, they may go further than Arius because "created" is their preferred term for the generation of the Son in the beginning. They don't appear even to have heard of the idea that the Son was "generated" or "begotten" in the beginning.

They defend their view by appealing to the same Scriptures that we looked at in the last chapter, verses that modern Christians no longer understand because we no longer understand the faith that was promulgated and triumphed at the Council of Nicea.

If you have read this entire book to this point—or even if you have only read this chapter—you understand the true meaning of the verses that Jehovah's Witnesses throw at mainstream Christians. Since almost no one else does, however, the Watchtower uses those verses, combined with quotes—and misquotes—from the early church fathers, to produce a plausible and confusing defense of their monotheism.

I have obtained the following quotes from *Watchtower: Official Website of the Jehovah's Witnesses* at watchtower.org. Because I want you to see how comfortably Scriptural the faith of the Nicene Christians is, I ask you to read these slowly and consider how easily the Council of Nicea would have addressed the following Scriptures, but what anguish they might cause to modern Christians.

---

[463] "What Does the Bible Say About God and Jesus." *Watchtower*. Accessed Feb. 15, 2011 <http://www.watchtower.org/e/ti/article_05.htm>.

From "Who Is 'the Only True God'":[464]

> Jesus petitioned: "Father, the hour has come; glorify your son, that your son may glorify you. This means everlasting life, their taking in knowledge of you, the only true God, and of the one whom you sent forth, Jesus Christ." — John 17:1, 3.[465]

> Notice that Jesus prays to One whom he calls "the only true God." He points to God's superior position when he continues: "So now you, Father, glorify me alongside yourself with the glory that I had alongside you before the world was." (John 17:5) Since Jesus prayed to God requesting to be alongside God, how could Jesus at the same time be "the only true God"?

> "This Jesus God resurrected," the apostle Peter reports, "of which fact we are all witnesses." (Acts 2:31, 32) Could Jesus have resurrected himself?

> For example, Jehovah is "from everlasting to everlasting." But the Bible says that Jesus is "the firstborn of every creature." That Jehovah is greater than Jesus, Jesus himself taught when he said: "My Father is greater than I." (Matthew 6:9; Psalm 90:1, 2; Colossians 1:15; John 14:28, King James Version) Yet, the Trinity doctrine holds that the Father and the Son are "equally God."

From "Those Who Are Called 'Gods'":[466]

> Consider how John identified "the Word" in the first chapter of his Gospel. "The Word became flesh and resided among us," he wrote, "and we had a view of his glory, a glory such as belongs [not to God but] to an only-begotten son from a father." So "the Word," who became flesh, lived

[464] "Who is 'the Only True God.'" *Watchtower*. Accessed Feb. 15, 2011 <http://www.watchtower.org/e/20050422/article_02.htm>. Parentheses theirs.

[465] Unless otherwise referenced, their Scripture quotes are from *The New World Translation*, their own translation of the Bible.

[466] "Those Who Are Called 'Gods.'" *Watchtower*. Accessed Feb. 15, 2011 <http://www.watchtower.org/e/20050422/article_03.htm>.

on the earth as the man Jesus and was seen by people. Therefore, he could not have been Almighty God, regarding whom John says: "No man has seen God at any time."—John 1:14, 18.

From "Is Jesus Almighty God?":[467]

> "If you loved me, you would rejoice that I am going my way to the Father, because the Father is greater than I am." (John 14:28) Jesus acknowledged that he and his Father are not equals.

> Even after his death and resurrection, Jesus is described in the Bible as being subordinate to God. The apostle Paul reminds us that "God is supreme over Christ." (1 Corinthians 11:3, Today's English Version)

The Jehovah's Witnesses have naturally tailored their arguments to what they know will be most effective among Christians. Of course, they have to ignore many passages of Scripture to hold the Arian view, but they are keenly aware of the passages that modern Christians have to ignore as well. John 17:3 does not fit well into modern Trinitarian doctrine!

> This is eternal life, that they may know you, the only true God, and Jesus Christ, whom you have sent.

Of course, neither does the Nicene Creed ...

The Nicene Creed and One God

At the heart of the Nicene Creed[468] is the threefold statement of belief:

> We believe in one God, the Father ... and in one Lord, Jesus Christ, the Son of God ... also in the Holy Spirit.

That is the basic outline. The rest is explanatory.

---

[467] "Is Jesus Almighty God." *Watchtower*. Accessed Feb. 15, 2011 <http://www.watchtower.org/e/20090201/article_04.htm>. Parentheses theirs.
[468] Appendix G.

Notice that the one God, according to the Nicene Creed, is the Father. Jesus is the one Lord and the Son of God, and nothing at all is said about the Holy Spirit except that he exists. (Sorting out early Christian opinion on the Holy Spirit is very hard work, and I am glad that nothing about the Council of Nicea obligates me to do that in this book!)

Of course, the fact that the Nicene Creed says that the one God is the Father does not shoot down the modern understanding of the Trinity. It doesn't even prove that the modern understanding of the Trinity is different than the Nicene understanding. All educated modern Christians know, for example, that most of Paul's letters begin with a blessing "from God our Father and the Lord Jesus Christ."

So we all know that the Bible occasionally applies the title "God" to the Father only. In fact, 1 Corinthians 8:6 uses almost exactly the same words as the Nicene Creed:

> But for us there is but one God, the Father, from whom are all things, and we for him; and one Lord, Jesus Christ, through whom are all things, and we through him.

Modern Christians know this kind of Biblical terminology, and we accept it. That is not the issue. The issue is whether we would dare use the same terminology.

Would we dare say in our churches (for which churches I'm referencing, see the text box above) that the Father is the one true God? Jesus said it. Would we dare teach that we have only one God and that that God is the Father? Paul taught it.

I believe that if we're honest with ourselves, we have to admit that we have adopted a view of the Trinity that is different from Nicea. We would never write a creed that says, "We believe in one God, the Father, and in one Lord, Jesus Christ, and in the Holy Spirit." That simply is not the terminology we would use.

My Intended Audience

I need to point out here that I am addressing my words to those that hold the same belief as the early Christians concerning the Scriptures and the apostles. To the early Christians the Scriptures were fully inspired and fully authoritative. You did not disagree with the Scriptures, you learned from them.

It is true that the Nicene, and even the pre-Nicene, Christians honored apostolic tradition, but they never believed apostolic tradition to contradict the Scriptures. The apostles were taught the Old Covenant Scriptures by Jesus, then they wrote the New Covenant Scriptures. Therefore, it is impossible that tradition that is truly apostolic would contradict the Bible.

For those that freely disagree with the Bible, the words in this chapter are not addressed to you. You may perhaps benefit from them as a historical curiosity, but I am writing as though I am addressing those who consider the Scriptures inspired and the apostles sent from God.

Instead, we would use something closer to what is known as the Athanasian Creed, which Athanasius did not write, but dates to somewhere around the end of his life in AD 360 or later. I am quoting just portions of it here because it is quite long.[469]

> We worship one God in Trinity and Trinity in Unity ... The Father is Almighty, the Son Almighty, and the Holy Spirit Almighty. Yet there are not three Almighties, but one Almighty. So the Father is God, the Son is God, and the Holy Spirit is God. Yet there are not three Gods, but one God

No wonder the Trinity is so confusing to people! Is this anything like the wonderfully clear explanations of the pre-Nicene Christians that we've been reading about?

---

[469] You can read the entire creed at my web site, *Christian History for Everyman*. <http://www.christian-history.org/athanasian-creed.html>.

Is there anything in Scripture resembling the terminology we see here in the Athanasian Creed?

The Nicene Creed and the doctrine of the pre-Nicene churches—with its one God the Father and one Lord Jesus Christ—find their match in every greeting of Paul's letters, in 1 Corinthians 8:6, in John 17:3, and in dozens of other places.

Our terminology, on the other hand—that there is one God, the Father, Son, and Spirit—finds no corresponding terminology in the Bible at all.

But is my description true? Do modern churches really say something closer to the Athanasian Creed than the Nicene Creed?

The Roman Catholic Church

The Roman Catholic Church is the largest Christian denomination in the United States, with 68 million members, according to the National Council of Churches.[470] The Nicene Creed in the version known as the Nicaeano-Constantinopolitanum Creed[471] is still the official creed of the Roman Catholics. Nonetheless, the *Catholic Encyclopedia* article on "The Dogma of the Trinity" appeals first to the Athanasian Creed:

> The Trinity is the term employed to signify the central doctrine of the Christian religion — the truth that in the unity of the Godhead there are Three Persons, the Father, the Son, and the Holy Spirit, these Three Persons being truly distinct one from another.

---

[470] Jenks, Philip E. "Catholics, Mormons, Assemblies of God growing; Mainline churches report a continuing decline." 12 Feb. 2010. *National Council of Churches*. Accessed 4 Apr. 2011.
<http://www.ncccusa.org/news/100204yearbook2010.html>.
[471] Appendix G.

Thus, in the words of the Athanasian Creed: "the Father is God, the Son is God, and the Holy Spirit is God, and yet there are not three Gods but one God."[472]

Southern Baptist Convention:

The Southern Baptist Convention is the largest non-Catholic denomination in the U.S. with more than 16 million members. Its official website says:

> The eternal triune God reveals Himself to us as Father, Son, and Holy Spirit, with distinct personal attributes, but without division of nature, essence, or being.[473]

United Methodist Church:

The United Methodist Church is third largest denomination. It's official website says:

> We describe God in three persons. Father, Son, and Holy Spirit are commonly used to refer to the threefold nature of God. Sometimes we use other terms, such as Creator, Redeemer, and Sustainer.[474]

---

[472] Joyce, George. "The Blessed Trinity." *The Catholic Encyclopedia.* Accessed 15 Feb. 2011. <http://www.newadvent.org/cathen/15047a.htm>.
[473] "The Baptist Faith and Message." *sbc*net. Southern Baptist Convention. 1999-2011. Accessed 15 Feb., 2011 <http://www.sbc.net/bfm/bfm2000.asp>.
[474] "Our Christian Roots." *The People of the United Methodist Church.* United Methodist Communications. 2006-11. Accessed 15 Feb. 2011 <http://www.umc.org/site/c.lwL4KnN1LtH/b.2299859/k.13B7/Our_Christian_ Roots.htm>.

Church of God in Christ:

The Church of God in Christ is the fourth-largest denomination.[475] Their main web site says:

> We believe that there is only One God, eternally existent in three persons: God the Father, God the Son, and God the Holy Spirit.[476]

The Evangelical Lutheran Church in America:

The Evangelical Lutheran Church in America, the sixth-largest denomination,[477] begins their "Statements of Belief" with:

> Lutherans believe in the Triune God.[478]

The Assemblies of God:

The Assemblies of God, The USA's eighth-largest denomination,[479] lists 16 "nonnegotiable tenets of faith" on their official website. Number two is:

> There is only One True God-revealed in three persons...Father, Son, and Holy Spirit.

The explanation following is:

> We therefore may speak with propriety of the Lord our God who is One Lord, as a trinity or as one Being of three persons.[480]

---

[475] I ignored the Latter Day Saints (Mormons) on the National Council of Church's list because they openly reject the faith embraced by Nicea.

[476] "Statement of Faith." *Church of God in Christ* . Church of God in Christ, Inc. 2001-09. Accessed 15 Feb., 2011 <http://cogic.net/cogiccms/default/cogic-history/statement-of-faith/>.

[477] I skipped the fifth and seventh-largest because they were both Baptist, and we've already addressed Baptists in the second-largest denomination.

[478] "Statements of Belief." *Evangelical Lutheran Church in America.* Accessed 4 Apr. 2011. < http://www.elca.org/What-We-Believe/Statements-of-Belief.aspx>.

[479] I skipped the fifth and seventh-largest because they were both Baptist, and we've already addressed Baptists in the second-largest denomination.

If we have not changed the faith confirmed at Nicea, then why have we changed the terminology?

It's not that I have a great problem with the idea behind these statements of faith, but ...

- if the Council of Nicea confirmed the faith of their forefathers;

- and, if their forefathers received that faith from the apostles;

- and, if their terminology is much closer to Scripture than ours ...

then shouldn't we be saying what they say?

The One God in Scripture and Pre-Nicene Christianity

What exactly did the early Christians say? Was the Nicene Creed's terminology really normative? Do the verses quoted above by the Jehovah's Witnesses really represent the way early Christians—and, more importantly, the apostles—spoke on a regular basis?

To begin with, let's look at Tertullian's *Against Praxeas*, written around AD 210. Tertullian found Nicene terminology typical enough to offer an explanation for it! (He is, of course, not referring to the Nicene Creed itself, since it would not be written for more than a century.)

> I shall follow the apostle [Paul], so that if the Father and the Son are alike to be invoked, I shall call the Father "God" and invoke Jesus Christ as "Lord."
>
> But when Christ alone [is invoked], I shall be able to call him "God." As the same apostle says, "Of whom is Christ, who is over all, God blessed forever" [*Rom. 9:5*].

---

[480] "Fundamental Truths (Condensed Statement)." *Assemblies of God USA*. General Council of the Assembly of God. 2010. Accessed Feb. 15, 2011 <http://www.ag.org/top/beliefs/statement_of_fundamental_truths/sft_short.cfm>.

> For I should give the name of "sun" even to a sunbeam, considered by itself. But if I were mentioning the sun from which the ray emanates, I would certainly withdraw the name of sun from the mere beam. For although I do not make two suns, still I shall reckon both the sun and its ray to be as much two things—and two forms of one undivided substance—as God and his Word, as the Father and the Son.[481]

Tertullian seems to think that the apostles, or at least the apostle Paul, only called Jesus God when the Father is not being discussed along with him. Is this true?

If you're familiar with the Scriptures, you probably don't need me to tell you it's true. You already know. But let's give you some statistics:

For the following chart, I am using only the books from Acts to the Revelation. It seemed irrelevant to reference the Gospels because Jesus, the Son, was doing so much of the speaking.

- The Father is referred to as God in a verse where Jesus is also mentioned—and not called God—42 times.

- Jesus is referred to as God in a verse where the Father is also mentioned—and also called God—1 time: Heb. 1:8-9.

- God is used in such a way as to clearly indicate a reference to all three persons of the Trinity 0 times.

- Jesus is called God in a verse where the Father is *not* mentioned at least 7 times: Matt. 1:23; Jn. 1:1; 10:33; 20:28; Rom. 9:5; Tit. 2:13; Heb. 1:8.

I'm not sure how accurate that last number is. I couldn't figure out how to do a search that would ensure that I didn't miss a place where Jesus is called God. The exact number won't matter, because seven is enough to establish that it's not unusual to call Jesus God *as long as the Father isn't being mentioned with him.*

---

[481] *Against Praxeas.* 13.

These numbers make it abundantly clear that Tertullian is correct. When the Father and Son are named together, the Father is *usually* referred to as God, whereas the Son is only once referred to as God when the Father is mentioned as well (Heb. 1:8-9). Even then, the Father is called Jesus' God in that verse.

Which leads me to ask: In all the studies of the Trinity that have been published since the printing press has been invented, is it really true that no one has noticed these things? While scholars and historians were publishing careful definitions of *hypostasis*, *ousios*, and *homoios* did they really not notice that the Nicene Creed calls the Father the one God and we don't? Did they really never run across Tertullian's explanation for that?

I can't help but feel that it's dishonest to point out that Tertullian was the first early Christian writer to use the term Trinity, but then never to tell us what he meant by the term!

Worse, it's larceny! We have been robbed of a closer, easier relationship with the Scriptures and a better understanding of God, within the context he's been revealed to us! We're not overstepping our bounds in understanding God more fully this way; instead, we are holding more closely to "the faith once delivered to the saints" (Jude 3).

The One God and the Son in the Pre-Nicene Churches

We have already thoroughly covered the generation of the Son in eternity past.[482] We do not need to go over the early Christian quotes one more time.

It would be good, however, to review their explanation of the relationship between the Father and the Son because it will help nail down the reason that the Father is called the one God in the Nicene Creed and in pre-Nicene terminology.

This is a review. The quotations supporting what I am about to describe were given in Chapter 15. We will look at a number of

---

[482] Chapter 15

other references further in this chapter. There will be no shortage of evidence and elaboration for what follows.

The Pre-Nicene Explanation of the Trinity

In the beginning, God was alone in the sense that there was nothing outside of him. Inside of him, however, was the *Logos*— his Reason, Thought, or Word. When he was ready to create all things, he birthed his *Logos* in some manner that we cannot comprehend.

There is not a separation between the two, for the divine substance fills all things. Instead, the *Logos* became distinct from God, his Father, in the way that a stream issues from a spring or a beam of light from the Son. The substance is not divided. There is only one divine substance, and the Son of God shares that substance with the Father.

Just because the one God has a Son, produced from his divine essence, does not mean that he ceased being the one God. The Son does the will of the Father. There is only one divine rule, and the rule comes from the Father. God sends his Son; the Son does not send the Father.

Thus, when we speak of the Father and the Son together, we refer to the Father as God and the Son as Lord. When the Son is referred to alone, then it is permissible and proper to speak of him as God because he is not one of the creatures. He is the only-begotten Son of God. He has always existed, though at one time he existed inside of the Father. Thus, he is intrinsically eternal. Unlike us, who must be given eternal life by the Son, the Son has eternal life in himself. He had no beginning, and he not only will not, but cannot, have an end.

Subordinationism

Subordinationism is the teaching that the Son is subordinate to the Father. Today, it is always seen as an error, for the Son is believed to be equal to the Father in every way. Taken far enough, subordinationism is seen as heresy.

However, some sort of subordinationism is unavoidable. The Father sent the Son, not vice versa. The Father loved the world and gave his Son for it, not vice versa. The Son always does the will of the Father, not vice versa.

Everyone agrees with subordinationism when it is simply a matter of rank. As long as the Son only submits to the Father, but is not less than him in any other way, then modern Christians will not complain.

But we have seen that the doctrine of the Trinity espoused by the early church and by the Council of Nicea teaches that the Son is the *Logos* of the one God. When they are mentioned together, the Father is called the one God, and the Son is called Lord.

You can probably deduce on your own that the early Christians believed God is greater than his Son in some way other than just rank.

And you would be right.

In John 14:28, Jesus said:

> If you loved me, you would rejoice because I said, "I go to the Father," for my Father is greater than I.

Modern Christians, holding to a co-equal Trinity, generally believe that the Father was only greater than the Son while the Son was on earth. On the other hand, every pre-Nicene or Nicene writer who addresses John 14:28 believes that the Father is *eternally* greater than the Son because God is greater than his own *Logos*. Such a belief is called *subordinationism*.

The following is, as far as I know, an exhaustive list of Pre-Nicene references to John 14:28.

Irenaeus, c. AD 185:

> For if any one should ask the reason that the Father, who has fellowship with the Son in all things, has been declared by the Lord to alone to know the hour and the day, he will find at present no more suitable, becoming, or safe reason than this ... that the Father is above all things. For "the Father," he says, "is greater than I" [*Jn. 14:28*].[483]

---

[483] *Against Heresies*. II:28:8.

Tertullian, c. AD 210:

> For the Father is the entire substance, but the Son is a der-
> ivation and portion of the whole, as [the Son] himself
> acknowledges: "My Father is greater than I" [*Jn. 14:28*].[484]

Origen, c. AD 230

> Grant that there may be some individuals among the mul-
> titudes of believers who are not in entire agreement with
> us and who incautiously assert that the Savior is the Most
> High God; however, we do not hold with them, but rather
> believe him when he says, "The Father who sent Me is
> greater than I" [*Jn. 14:28*].[485]

Novatian, c. AD 255[486]

> Who does not acknowledge that the person of the Son is
> second after the Father, when he reads that it was said by
> the Father, consequently to the Son, "Let us make man in
> our image and our likeness"? [*Gen. 1:26*]. ... Or when he
> finds it written: "Because he who sent me is greater than
> I"? [*Jn. 14:28*]. Or when he considers the passage. "I go to
> my Father, and your Father; to my God, and your God"?
> [*Jn. 20:17*].[487]

Methodius, c. AD 300

> And so the prophets and apostles—who spoke more fully
> concerning the Son of God, and assigned to him a divinity
> above other men—did not refer their praises of him to the
> teaching of angels, but to him upon whom all authority
> and power depend. For it was fitting that he who was

---

[484] *Against Praxeas*. 9.

[485] *Against Celsus*. VIII:14.

[486] Novatian was the founder of the Novatianist sect; however, we saw in Chapter 8 that the catholics and Novatians were in agreement on the Nicene Creed
and thus on the Trinity. Novatian split from the church at Rome only over the
readmission of Christians who lapsed during persecution. On other matters,
they were orthodox.

[487] *Concerning the Trinity*. 26.

greater than all things after the Father, should have the Father, who alone is greater than himself, as his witness.[488]

Alexander, bishop of Alexandria, c. AD 320

But we must say that to the Father alone belongs the property of being unbegotten, for the Savior himself said, "My Father is greater than I" [*Jn. 14:28*].[489]

Comments on Subordinationism

Today subordinationism is seen as a borderline heresy. What amazes me is that *the early Christians themselves are seen as borderline heretics* for embracing subordinationism.

Somewhere we have forgotten that the faith was handed down *in full* by the apostles and meant to be preserved by the church. Paul asked the Thessalonians to hold fast to his traditions, not to improve on them! (2 Thess. 2:15)

Our view of the Trinity has changed since Nicea, which I hope is obvious to you by now, and the scholars who know and admit it somehow believe that we have improved it! We have better words to use, they think. Because we have embraced *homoousios*, and because we apply it to the shared divinity of the triune God while applying *hypostasis* to the individual persons, then we are better able to explain the Trinity than they were.

Not true! We do not differ on mere wording. We differ on our understanding of what happened in the beginning, who the Son is in relation to the Father, and in the titles we apply to them. Getting *homoousios* and *hypostasis* correct will not resolve our differences with them!

What's worse is that in our blind assumption that we cannot be wrong, we assume that every early Christian writer who does not

---

[488] *The Banquet of the Ten Virgins*. Discourse VII. Chapter 1.
[489] "To Alexander, Bishop of Constantinople." *The Ante-Nicene Fathers*. Vol. VI.

explicitly disagree with us must agree with us. For, after all, we naively assume, we are the standard for what is true.

Scholars are aware that "some" pre-Nicene Christians were subordinationist. They believe that this is forgivable to pre-Nicene Christians who were not "enlightened" by later councils as we have been. But let's examine just whom they charge with this forgivable error.

Let's begin with a man for whom I have great respect, Philip Schaff, the great 19th-century historian. He writes in his introduction to Eusebius of Caesarea in *The Nicene and Post-Nicene Fathers*, series II, vol. I:

> That Eusebius [of Caesarea] was a decided subordinationist must be plain to every one that reads his works with care, especially his earlier ones. ... The same subordinationism may be clearly seen in the writings of Dionysius of Alexandria and of Gregory Thaumaturgus, two of Origen's greatest disciples. ... Eusebius in his earlier writings shows that he holds both [the divinity of Christ and his subordination to the Father] ... but that he is as far from a solution of the problem, and is just as uncertain in regard to the exact relation of Father and Son, as Tertullian, Hippolytus, Origen, Dionysius, and Gregory Thaumaturgus were.

These are important and many names that Schaff is throwing around! A limited number of writers wrote extensively on the subject of the Trinity prior to Nicea. Schaff has mentioned Tertullian, Hippolytus, Origen, Dionysius, and Gregory Thaumaturgus, and he has suggested that they are "uncertain in regard to the exact relation of the Father and Son."

Those are five writers, plus Origen. There are not many left to choose from!

And other sources get them all!

- An article at *Theopedia* refers to subordinationism as a "heretical view." It then quotes the *Ellwell Evangelical*

Dictionary as stating **Justin Martyr**, **Origen**, and **Tertullian** show a certain amount of subordinationism.[490]

- *The Concise Oxford Dictionary of the Christian Church* says, "[Subordinationism] was a characteristic tendency in **much teaching of the first three cents.** (*sic*), but by the standards of orthodoxy established in the fourth cent. it came to be regarded as heretical."[491]

- *Oxford Encyclopedia of the Early Church* tells us, "Subordinationist tendencies are evident esp. in theologians like **Justin**, **Tertullian**, **Origen** and **Novatian**; but even in **Irenaeus**, to whom trinitarian speculations are alien, commenting on Jn 14, 28, [*sic*] has no difficulty in considering Christ inferior to the Father" (II:797).[492]

- The *Catholic Encyclopedia*: "Philosophic speculation is responsible ... for the subordinationism of **Justin**'s theology."[493]

- The *Catholic Encyclopedia* again: "As to the Divine Nature of the Word, all apologists are agreed but to some of them, at least to **St. Justin** and **Tertullian**, there seemed to be in this Divinity a certain subordination."[494]

[490] "Subordinationism." *Theopedia*. Accessed 19 Mar. 2011 <http://www.theopedia.com/Subordinationism>.
[491] Livingstone, E. A. "Subordinationism." *The Concise Oxford Dictionary of the Christian Church*. 2000. Encyclopedia.com. Accessed 19 Mar. 2011 < http://www.encyclopedia.com/topic/subordinationism.aspx>.
[492] Simmonetti, M. *Oxford Encyclopedia of the Early Church*. II.797. As cited by "Subordinationism." Wikipedia. Wikimedia Foundation, Inc. Accessed 19 Mar. 2011 <http://en.wikipedia.org/wiki/Subordinationism>.
[493] Lebreton, Jules. "St. Justin Martyr." *The Catholic Encyclopedia*. Accessed 19 Mar. 2011 <http://www.newadvent.org/cathen/08580c.htm>.
[494] Lebreton, Jules. "The Logos." *The Catholic Encyclopedia*. Accessed 19 Mar. 2011 <http://www.newadvent.org/cathen/09328a.htm>.

- The same page in the *Catholic Encyclopedia* has: "In **Clement [of Alexandria]**, it is true, we find only a few traces of subordinationism ... **Origen**, on the other hand, frequently and formally defended subordinationist ideas."

- The *Catholic Encyclopedia* one last time: "**Hippolytus** ... stood uncompromisingly for a real difference between the Son (Logos) and the Father, but so as to represent the Former as a Divine Person almost completely separate from God (Ditheism) and at the same time altogether subordinate to the Father (Subordinationism).[495]

What are we to do with these statements? Justin Martyr, Clement of Alexandria, Tertullian, Hippolytus, Origen, Novatian, Dionysius, Gregory Thaumaturgus, and Eusebius the historian; with these, they've managed to list every writer that wrote a treatise specifically devoted to the doctrine of the Trinity prior to Nicea and some that didn't!

Subordinationism was the doctrine of all pre-Nicene writers familiar with the faith once handed down to the saints because it follows naturally from what we know about the Son as the *Logos* of God.

But what about Jesus being the *Logos* of God? Is that really from the apostles? Is it really the tradition of the church?

Some say that the idea of the *Logos* comes from Greek philosophy, not the apostles.

The *Logos* of God and Greek Philosophy

The idea that the *Logos* doctrine came from Greek philosophy is another case of missing the forest for the trees. Here, we could go into a long history of the Greek philosophers, and we could

---

[495] Kirsch, Johann Peter. "St. Hippolytus of Rome." *The Catholic Encyclopedia*. Accessed 19 Mar. 2011 <http://www.newadvent.org/cathen/07360c.htm>. Parentheses original.

analyze the use of Greek philosophers by men like Justin, Athenagoras, Clement of Alexandria, Origen, and even the historian Socrates Scholasticus.

Such an analysis would be pointless.

For those of us who classify ourselves as Bible believers, we have no choice but to see the *Logos* doctrine as apostolic because *it is in the Bible.* There is no more clear exposition of Jesus as the *Logos* of God than the John 1:1-3. It is short, but it is unmistakable.

> In the beginning was the *Logos*, and the *Logos* was with God, and the *Logos* was divine.[496] This one was in the beginning with God. All things were made by him, and without him nothing was made that was made. ... And the *Logos* became flesh and lived among us. ... No one has seen God at any time; the only-begotten Son, who is in the bosom of the Father, he has revealed him. (Jn. 1:1-3, 14, 18)

> As an aside, it is fascinating to me that the word I've rendered "reveal" from John 1:18, and which the King James Version translates as "declare," is the same Greek word from which we get "exegesis." We strive to be exegetes of the Bible, but Jesus was an exegete of God himself!

All the major tenets of the *Logos* doctrine of the pre-Nicene and Nicene Christians—for the Nicene Creed espouses the *Logos* doctrine as well—are right here in John chapter one.

I provided a long list of early Christian quotes concerning the *Logos* in the last chapter. If you look at them, you will see some central issues that are in John 1:

- The *Logos* was in the beginning.
- The *Logos* made all things, hearkening back to Proverbs 8:22-31.

---

[496] The explanation for this rendering of John 1:1 is given in Chapter 15. As pointed out there, it is not controversial even among Protestant scholars.

- The *Logos* had the character, nature, and essence of God.[497]

- The *Logos* comes from "the bosom" of the Father, hearkening back to Ps. 45:1 and 110:3 in the Septuagint.[498]

So the *Logos* doctrine did not come into the church through Greek philosophy. It came into the church through the apostle John.

In fact, it would be more fair to say that it came into the church through Proverbs 8:22-31.

How are we to explain Proverbs 8, and its consistent and constant use by the church, if not by the teaching of the *Logos*? It is a glorious picture, and one that I believe should thrill the heart of believers. I'm quoting it again from the Septuagint:

> The Lord made me the beginning of his ways for his works. He established me before time was in the beginning, before he made the earth: even before he made the depths; before the fountains of water came forth: before the mountains were settled, and before all hills, he begets me. The Lord made countries and uninhabited tracks, and the highest inhabited parts of the world. When he prepared the heaven, I was present with him; and when he prepared his throne upon the winds: and when he strengthened the clouds above; and when he secured the fountains of the earth: and when he strengthened the foundations of the earth: I was by him, suiting myself to him, I was that wherein he took delight; and daily I rejoiced in his presence continually. For he rejoiced when he had completed the world, and rejoiced among the children of men.[499]

---

[497] See the explanation of the translation of John 1:1 in Chapter 15.

[498] The Greek translation of the Hebrew Scriptures that was the Old Testament of the Greek-speaking early churches and is still used by the Easter Orthodox Churches today.

[499] Brenton. *English Translation of the Greek Septuagint Bible.*

Here it would be good to address one more issue concerning John chapter one that is talked about often in the pre-Nicene writings of the church.

No One Has Seen God at Any Time

> No one has seen God at any time; the only-begotten Son, who is in the bosom of the Father, he has revealed him. (Jn. 1:18)

If Jesus is God, then how could John have said that no one has seen God at any time?

We addressed this above, but this is easy to resolve for anyone familiar with the Nicene doctrine of the Trinity, which, admittedly, is not very many people. That group now includes you!

John 1:18 clearly distinguishes between God the Father and his Son, the *Logos*. People have seen the *Logos*, the one who reveals the Father, but no one has seen the Father ... not at any time.

Obviously, this means that all the appearances of God in the ancient Israel were not *theophanies*, but *Christophanies*. The Israelites were seeing their Messiah, the *Logos*, before he was born among men.

This is the obvious conclusion from John 1:18 if we are reading it from the perspective of our fathers in the faith, and they all read it that way.

We'll cite only a few examples.

Justin Martyr, c. AD 155:

> You must not imagine that the unbegotten God himself came down or went up from any place. The ineffable [*i.e., unnamable*] Father and Lord of all neither has come to any place, nor walks, nor sleeps, nor rises up, but remains in his own place, wherever that is, quick to behold and quick to hear, having neither eyes nor ears, but being of indescribable might. He is not moved or confined to a spot in the whole world, for he existed before the world was

made. How, then, could he talk with anyone, be seen by anyone, or appear on the smallest portion of the earth when the people at Sinai were not even able to look upon the glory of the one who was sent by him?[500] ... Therefore, neither Abraham, nor Isaac, nor Jacob, nor any other man saw the Father and ineffable Lord of all ... but saw him who was according to his will his Son, being God, and the Angel,[501] of whom also it pleased [God] that he would be born man by the virgin.[502]

Theophilus, c. AD 168:

It is true that the God and Father of all cannot be contained and is not found in a place ... but his *Logos*, through whom he made all things, ... assuming the person of the Father and Lord of all, went to the garden in the person of God, and conversed with Adam. For the divine writing itself teaches us that Adam said that he had heard the voice. But what else is this voice but the *Logos* of God, who is also His Son? ... The *Logos*, then, being God, and being naturally produced from God, whenever the Father of the universe wills, he sends him to any place; and he, coming, is both heard and seen, being sent by him, and is found in a place.[503]

Eusebius of Caesarea, AD 323:

For if it is unreasonable to suppose that the unbegotten and immutable essence of the almighty God was changed into the form of man ... [then] when the God and Lord who judges all the earth and executes judgment is seen in

---

[500] Exodus 34:29-30. Moses' face shone so brightly that the Israelites could not keep looking at him.

[501] Justin explains elsewhere that he is called "Angel" because he is God's Messenger. The word translated "angel" in our Bibles, from both Hebrew and Greek, means "messenger." It does not specifically mean a species of heavenly being, and it is used a number of times of men in the New Testament. (e.g. Luke 7:24; 9:52.)

[502] *Dialogue with Trypho, a Jew*. 127.

[503] *To Autolycus*. II:22.

the form of a man, who else can be called [God], if it be not lawful to call him the first cause of all things, than his only pre-existent *Logos*? Concerning whom it is said in the Psalms, "He sent his Word and healed them and delivered them from their destructions" [*Ps. 107:20*].[504]

Rather than inundate you with even more quotes, I think it is more profitable to discuss the note that the editors of *The Nicene and Post-Nicene Fathers* attach to the quote from Eusebius above. They write:

Eusebius accepts the common view of the early Church, that the theophanies of the Old Testament were Christophanies; that is, appearances of the second person of the Trinity. Augustine seems to have been the first of the Fathers to take a different view, maintaining that such Christophanies were not consistent with the identity of essence between Father and Son, and that the Scriptures themselves teach that it was not the Logos, but an angel, that appeared to the Old Testament worthies on various occasions (cf. De Trin. III. 11).[505]

Why would Augustine, who became bishop of Hippo in north Africa in AD 395 or 396, some 70 years after Nicea, deny what was "the common view of the early Church"?

The editors answer that for us. He maintained that Christophanies were "not consistent with identity of essence between the Father and Son."

I mentioned in Chapter 9 that some eastern bishops may not have been Arian, but merely concerned about adding a non-scriptural word, *homoousios*, even if it were not *un*scriptural, to the creed of the Church. The concern would be that later Christians would take the word and run with it, producing doctrines in-

[504] *Ecclesiastical History*. I:2:8.
[505] *The Nicene and Post Nicene Fathers*. Series II. Vol. 1. Note 31. Parentheses theirs.

consistent with Scripture and the faith handed down from the beginning.

Here we have an example of it in Augustine.

Augustine argues:

> Therefore the substance, or, if it is better to say, the essence of God, wherein we understand ... the Father, Son, and Holy Spirit, since it is in no way changeable, can in no way in its proper self be visible.[506]

I have said repeatedly that we must beware of the dangers of over-analyzing the faith. Today, we have become such excellent expositors of the doctrine of the Trinity that we have changed what was delivered to us from the fathers. In Augustine, we have an example of this already at the turn of the fifth century, less than a century after Nicea.

The fact is, it is not just the fathers who tell us that the appearances of God in Old Testament times were Christophanies. Jesus tells us himself!

> Your father Abraham rejoiced to see my day; he saw it, and was glad. (Jn. 8:56)

The apostle John adds his own comment to Jesus' quote:

> They could not believe because Isaiah said again, "He has blinded their eyes and hardened their heart ..." [Is. 6:10]. Isaiah said these things when he saw his glory and spoke of him. (Jn. 12:39-41)

When did Isaiah see these things? He saw them when he saw "the Lord sitting on a throne, high and lifted up" (Isa. 6:1-10).

Even this incredible appearance of Isaiah in the throne room of God finds the pre-incarnate *Logos* sitting on the throne!

The Father cannot be seen with human eyes. Both our Christian forefathers and God himself tell us so, for God once told Mo-

---

[506] *On the Trinity.* III:11.

ses, "You cannot see my face, for no one can see me and live" (Ex. 33:20).

If the Israelites could not bear to see the face of Moses shining with God's glory, how could they possible behold God himself? But the *Logos*, say the early Christians and the apostle John, can reveal the glory of the Father.

Augustine, one of the greatest theologians who ever lived, was just wrong.

And he was wrong because he ignored the faith that had been handed down to him since the beginning.

Two Lord Yahwehs

In my early days as a Christian I read a lot of books answering the "cults." Today, because I am familiar with the faith once delivered to the saints, I no longer need to read such books. The Scriptures are easy for me to read, and almost nothing in them is difficult. I have learned the faith from men who learned it from the apostles, and I have been careful to learn from those that have borne good fruit (Matt. 7:15-20). I can recognize counterfeits because I have learned to handle the real thing.

I should add that by the incredible grace, mercy, and kindness of God I am in a church that cares only about pleasing our Lord Jesus Christ. I have a lot of freedom to pursue the faith of our fathers because our church has respect for holiness and for the church through the ages, willing to learn from all those who have named the name of Christ and departed from iniquity (2 Tim. 2:19). The church is, after all, the pillar and support of the truth (1 Tim. 3:15).

One of the passages that those anti-cult books liked to use against the Jehovah's Witnesses was Genesis 19:24. They claimed that it showed two persons called Yahweh (or Jehovah), something the Jehovah's Witnesses could never agree with.

> Then Yahweh rained brimstone and fire on Sodom and on Gomorrah from Yahweh out of heaven.

One Yahweh in heaven, and one on earth: two Yahwehs. [507]

The early churches agreed.

> When Scripture says, "The Lord rained fire from the Lord out of heaven," the prophetic word indicates that there were two in number: One upon the earth, who, it says, descended to behold the cry of Sodom; another in heaven, who also is Lord of the Lord on earth, as he is Father and God.[508]

> Since, therefore, the Father is truly Lord and the Son truly Lord, the Holy Spirit has fitly designated them by the title of Lord. ... referring to the destruction of the Sodomites, the Scripture says, "Then the Lord rained upon Sodom and upon Gomorrah fire and brimstone from the Lord out of heaven." For it here points out that the Son, who had also been talking with Abraham, had received power to judge the Sodomites for their wickedness.[509]

Irenaeus, author of the second of those quotes, adds that Genesis 19:24 isn't the only place this truth is shown:

> This declares the same truth: "Your throne, O God, is for ever and ever; the scepter of your kingdom is a right scepter. You have loved righteousness and hated iniquity:

---

[507] Most English Bibles render LORD or GOD in all caps when they are a translation of YHWH, which most scholars write as "Yahweh" and which the Jehovah's Witnesses render "Jehovah." The vowels and pronunciation of YHWH have been lost because the Jews refused to pronounce the name of God for centuries.

[508] Justin. *Dialogue with Trypho, a Jew*. 129. c. AD 155.

[509] Irenaeus. *Against Heresies*. III:6:1. c. AD 185.

therefore God, your God, has anointed you" [*Ps. 45:6-7*]. For the Spirit designates both by the name of God—both him who is anointed as Son and him who anoints, that is, the Father.[510]

Another such passage, and a very interesting one is Zechariah 2:8-11. This passage is quoted often by the early Christians to talk about Jerusalem as the apple of God's eye, but for some reason they don't seem to point out that there are two Yahwehs mentioned in this passage as well, one sending the other:

For this is what Yahweh of Armies says, "After the glory he has sent me to the nations which spoiled you, for he that touches you touches the apple of his eye. For, behold, I will shake my hand upon them, and they shall be a spoil to their servants. Then you will know that Yahweh of Armies has sent me.

"Sing and rejoice, O daughter of Zion; for, lo, I come, and I will dwell in your midst," says Yahweh, "And many nations shall be joined to Yahweh in that day and shall be my people. And I will dwell in the midst of you, and you shall know that Yahweh of Armies has sent me to you."

Again here you have Yahweh sending Yahweh. While there was no way for anyone to pick up on it before the *Logos* came to the earth and revealed the Father to us, the eternal and divine Son of God is talked about often in the Hebrew Scriptures.

Early Christian Illustrations of the Trinity

Today we have lost the idea of the similar substance of the Father and the Son. We have lost the idea of the Father being the source of the Son, though that is what the name "Father" implies.

As a result we don't use the same illustrations that the early churches used.

---

[510] *ibid.*

Because we dare not make the persons of the Trinity unequal, our illustrations often use parts of a whole: The skin, pulp, and core of an apple, for example, or the shell, white, and yolk of an egg.

The early Christians didn't use such illustrations. They preferred to use substances that flowed from a source, like a stream from a spring or the light from the sun.

> The plant that springs from the root is something distinct from that from which it grows up. Yet it is of one nature with it. The river which flows from the spring is something distinct from the spring, for we cannot call either the river a spring or the spring a river. Nevertheless we allow that they are both one according to nature and also one in substance; and we admit that the spring may be conceived of as father, and that the river is what is begotten of the spring.[511]

> When we give out some word, we beget ; yet not by abscission [i.e., *cutting off*], so as to lessen the word in us. Just as we also see happening in the case of a fire, which is not lessened when it has kindled [another], but remains the same; and that which has been kindled by it likewise appears to exist by itself, not diminishing that from which it was kindled.[512]

Tertullian even gives us an illustration that includes the Holy Spirit.[513] I include this long passage in its entirety in hope that illustrations like this may help you in fully grasping the early Christian—and Nicene—concept of the Trinity:

> I would not hesitate ... to call the tree the son or offspring of the root, and the river of the spring, and the ray of the sun. Every original source is a parent, and everything

---

[511] Dionysius. "Exegetical Fragments V: Of the One Substance." *Ante-Nicene Fathers*. Vol. VI.

[512] Justin. *Dialogue with Trypho, a Jew*. 61. c. AD 155.

[513] The reason the Holy Spirit is not addressed in this chapter or in this book is explained below.

which issues from the origin is an offspring. Much more is the Word of God, who has actually received as his own peculiar designation the name of Son.

But still the tree is not severed from the root, nor the river from the spring, nor the ray from the sun. Nor, indeed, is the Word separated from God.

Following, therefore, the form of these analogies, I confess that I call God and his Word, the Father and his Son, two. For the root and the tree are distinctly two things, but correlatively joined. The spring and the river are also two forms, but indivisible. So likewise the sun and the ray are two forms, but coherent ones. Everything which proceeds from something else must needs be second to that from which it proceeds, without being on that account separated. Where, however, there is a second, there must be two; and where there is a third, there must be three.

Now the Spirit indeed is third from God and the Son; just as the fruit of the tree is third from the root, or as the stream out of the river is third from the spring, or as the apex of the ray is third from the sun. Nothing, however, is alien from that original source whence it derives its own properties.[514]

Such illustrations help us to picture things that are infinitely beyond us. It is important, though, to remember that they really are infinitely beyond us. These are just illustrations that the church, our mother, has provided to help us grasp what is by nature unable to be fully comprehended by man.

Therefore, let us limit ourselves to what has been handed down, but let us not limit ourselves beyond what has been handed down. These things have been recorded in Scripture and handed down to us by the church to assist us in the knowledge, praise, and worship of our Almighty God and his eternal, only-begotten Son.

---

[514] *Against Praxeas.* 8.

That said, Tertullian offers us one other illustration that is unique to him. It does not carry any authority, being only his own, but I have yet to find anyone who didn't enjoy hearing it.

An Early Christian Definition of *Logos*

Tertullian is the only author that explains the *Logos* this thoroughly, though no other author says anything to contradict it. I present this for your interest, not as apostolic tradition.

> Observe, then, that when you are silently conversing with yourself, this very process is carried on within you by your reason, which meets you with a word at every movement of your thought ... Whatever you think, there is a word ... You must speak it in your mind ...
>
> Thus, in a certain sense, the word is a second person within you, through which in thinking you utter speech ... The word is itself a different thing from yourself. Now how much more fully is all this transacted in God, whose image and likeness you are?[515]

Tertullian is also responsible for another fascinating piece of conjecture. Once again, Tertullian is alone on this, and it is presented merely for your interest:

> Then, therefore, does the Word also himself assume his own form, glorious garb, and sound and vocal utterance when God says, "Let there be light." This is the perfect nativity of the Word, when he proceeds forth from God, formed by him first to devise and think out all things by the name of Wisdom.[516]

Here, Tertullian suggests that the *Logos* was begotten at the time God said, "Let there be light."

This speculation of his has a lot to do with his translation of *Logos* into Latin. He prefers "Reason" to "Word" as a translation,

---

[515] *ibid.* 5.
[516] *ibid.* 7.

but "Word" is more common among his Latin contemporaries. So he suggests the idea that the *Logos* was Reason while he was inside of God, and he did not become Word until God first spoke.

Interesting. Not apostolic tradition, and not something you'd want to put into a creed, but interesting.

In Tertullian's defense, Irenaeus has something to say about Christians speculating. He suggests it's a gift of God if it does not interfere with the faith as it has been handed down:

> It does not follow that because men are endowed with greater and lesser degrees of intelligence they should change the subject matter of the faith itself ... [It] simply implies this: that one may bring out the meaning of those things which are spoken of in parables ... explain the operation and dispensation of God connected with human salvation ... set forth why it is that one and the same God has made some things temporary and some eternal, some heavenly and some earthy ... show why it was that more covenants than one were given to mankind ... search out for what reason God has included everyone in unbelief so that he may have mercy on all [etc.] ... For in reference to these points and others of a like nature, the apostle exclaims, "Oh! The depths of the riches both of the wisdom and knowledge of God; how unsearchable are his judgments, and his ways past finding out!"[517]

And since we're talking about speculation, for historical purposes, it is probably important to discuss a speculation of Origen's that became popular in Alexandria.

Eternal Generation

Alexandrians seemed to be a highly mystical bunch. Origen especially loved to talk about the "time" before time was created.

---

[517] *Against Heresies.* I:10:3. Brackets in original translation from *The Nicene and Post-Nicene Fathers.*

To him, there was no such time. What was before time, always was.

Is your head spinning yet?

I'm sorry for the necessity of writing about such an otherworldly, fantastical subject. It's not a talent of mine, but I'm afraid it's unavoidable.

> Who that is capable of entertaining reverential thoughts or feelings regarding God can suppose or believe that God the Father ever existed, even for a moment of time, without having generated this Wisdom?[518]

To Origen, if God generated the Son before time was created, then the Son was always generated. Unlike Tertullian and others who say that before the beginning God was alone except that he had his *Logos* already inside of him, Origen says that the *Logos*, whom he here terms Wisdom, was always generated. Never, not even "for a moment of time," was God not the Father.

> For in that case [*i.e. if God existed at any time without having generated Wisdom*] he must say either that God was unable to generate Wisdom before he produced her ... or that he possessed the power indeed, but—what cannot be said of God without impiety—was unwilling to use it. Both of which suppositions, it is patent to all, are alike absurd and impious, for they amount to this: Either God advanced from a condition of inability to one of ability or, although possessed of the power, he concealed it and delayed the generation of Wisdom.[519]

That may be brilliant thinking—and I am a huge fan of Origen, who tried to be martyred with his father as a young man and was tortured for the faith as an old man—but it is not apostolic, and it is not traditional. Origen breaks new ground with his version of the eternal generation of the Son.

---

[518] Origen, *De Principiis*. I:2:2.
[519] *ibid.*

His argument is not very convincing to me, but his idea caught on in Alexandria, where Christians were prone to being mystical anyway. Clement of Alexandria has some of the most unusual comments in all the Christian writings, and he loved philosophy. Origen was similar.

Dionysius, who became bishop of Alexandria near the time of Origen's death, had obviously picked up on Origen's idea of eternal generation.

> There certainly was not a time when God was not the Father. Nor, indeed, as though he had not brought forth these things, did God afterwards beget the Son ... Being the brightness of the eternal Light, he himself also is absolutely eternal. For since light is always in existence, it is manifest that its brightness also exists, because light is perceived to exist from the fact that it shines ... But God is the eternal Light, which has neither had a beginning nor shall ever end. Therefore the eternal brightness shines out from him, and coexists with him, in that, existing without a beginning and always begotten, he always shines before him.[520]

Its funny that Origen, who makes the begetting of the Son of God eternal, and thus is a bit closer to our modern version of the Trinity, is usually the first to be maligned for being a subordinationist!

Why Doesn't This Book Talk About the Holy Spirit

This book does not address the Holy Spirit because the Council of Nicea didn't address the Holy Spirit. The extent of their creed's reference to the Spirit is, "[We believe] also in the Holy Spirit."

That's it!

---

[520] "Letter to Dionysius, Bishop of Rome." *The Nicene and Post-Nicene Fathers*. Vol. VI.

I'm glad that I don't have to address the subject of the Holy Spirit in early Christianity because it would require an entire book on its own!

Part IV

The Church Before Nicea

Chapter 17:
Holy, Catholic, and Apostolic?

The original Nicene Creed doesn't actually mention the one holy, catholic, and apostolic church, but the later version, approved at the Council of Chalcedon in 451 and attributed to the Council of Constantinople in 381, does.[521]

I will only touch on the word "holy." That word, I am sure, is familiar to my readers, who can define it as well as I can. Modern churches have done an excellent job of keeping us informed that "holy" conveys the idea of "separated." A holy man will also choose to live a righteous life, but it is being set aside for God's disposal that the word "holy" fixes upon, not that man's righteous life.

So a holy church is one that is set aside for the use of God, and thus is under the control of God. As such, it is a fitting sister to the words "catholic" and "apostolic."

Catholic

Catholic means "universal," and it was used from the earliest times to refer to the united churches formed by the apostles.

---

[521] The Nicaeano-Constantinopolitanum Creed. Appendix G.

While the earliest churches were independent and had no hierarchy to report to,[522] they nonetheless felt an obligation to one another from the very beginning. The word "catholic" portrayed that obligation for there to be one church and one faith. While each congregation was to be independent, they were also each to maintain the one faith handed down from the apostles and to stay in communion with one another.

This was understood from the earliest times.

Thus, when the church at Smyrna sent out an encyclical letter to inform other churches of the martyrdom of the great and aged bishop, Polycarp (c. AD 165), they address it to "all the congregations of the holy and catholic church in every place."

One of the evidences I present in Chapter 18 to show that there was no pope in the early churches is the attempt by Victor, bishop of Rome, to excommunicate all the churches of Asia Minor over the Paschal Controversy[523] around AD 190. His attempt failed miserably. He was severely admonished by everyone, even those who supported his position on the date of Passover.

Nonetheless, right or wrong, Victor felt free to play a role in the decisions of the churches in Asia Minor.

During the reign of his predecessor, the bishop Eleutherus, the shoe was on the other foot. The church in Lyons, Gaul wrote a letter to Eleutherus and several others giving their advice on how to deal with the Montanist heresy.

Irenaeus speaks of the interactive nature of the churches long before Nicea:

> Suppose there arise a dispute relative to some important question among us. Should we not have recourse to the most ancient churches with which the apostles held con-

---

[522] Personally, I believe this is obvious from history, but tradition blinds people to it. The evidence against an early Christian hierarchy above the local church is addressed in Chapter 18.

[523] The controversy over the day on which to celebrate Passover, which is now called Easter. Covered in Chapter 6.

stant interaction and learn from them what is certain and clear in regard to the present question?[524]

This was not an appeal to one church that had final authority to tell all churches what to believe. This was, however, an appeal to the most ancient churches, in trust that all of them together were after one thing: to maintain the faith that was given to them by apostles, and to maintain it unchanged.

This unity between the churches was what made them "catholic."

And they were eminently successful at it!

> The church, though dispersed through the whole world, even to the ends of the earth, has received from the apostles and their disciples this faith in one God, the Father Almighty, maker of heaven, earth, and the sea, and all that are in them; and in one Christ Jesus, the Son of God, who became incarnate for our salvation; and in the Holy Spirit, who proclaimed through the prophets the dispensations of God ... [525]
>
> The church, having received this preaching and this faith, although scattered through the whole world, yet, as if occupying but one house, carefully preserves it. She also believes these points just as if she had but one soul and one and the same heart, and she proclaims them, teaches them, and hands them down with perfect harmony, as if she possessed only one mouth.[526]

The Council of Nicea was called in order to preserve that "catholic" faith. It was entirely unacceptable for Arius to have a small congregation in Alexandria that held opinions different from

---

[524] *Against Heresies* III:4:1

[525] Notice the resemblance between these statements and the Nicene Creed. Before Nicea each church had its own creed, called a "rule of faith," that was learned at baptism. The Nicene Creed was based on the rule of faith of the church in Caesarea.

[526] *ibid.* I:10:1,2

the rest of the church on a matter that concerned the truth that was handed down to the church.

The one divinity of the Father and the Son was an integral part of the church's faith, and it had been talked about by numerous early Christian writers in the two centuries between the apostles and Nicea.[527] Thus, the Arian Controversy was a threat to the catholicity of the church.

This is also why the important point was not what the Scriptures say. To the early Christians it was acceptable for teachers to interpret Scripture, but not when it touched on the subject matter of the faith itself. The apostles had "like a rich man in a bank, deposited in [the church's] hands, in abundance, all things pertaining to the truth."[528] Therefore, "It is not necessary to seek the truth among others which it is easy to obtain from the church."[529]

Anyone can dispute Scripture. Look around. We can call those who disagree with us dishonest, but it seems much more fair to say that people genuinely disagree. And of course they do! If the Scriptures are foolishness to the natural man (1 Cor. 2:14), then they are certainly going to be misunderstood by men wherever they are motivated by what is not spiritual—and the most common unspiritual motivation is defense of one's personal Christian denomination or tradition.

God has promised to lead us—the church—into the truth, but only together (1 Jn. 2:27[530]). Allowing individuals like Arius or Eusebius of Nicomedia to determine their own interpretation of Scripture against the faith that the apostles delivered to the church was not something the church could allow.

So Catholic does mean universal, but it carries all the connotations described above. Catholic means above all that the churches of Jesus Christ have chosen to maintain union and communion

---

[527] See Chapters 15-16.

[528] *ibid.* III:4:1

[529] *ibid.*

[530] All the yous in 1 John 2:27 are plural. For more on this, see Chapter 19.

with one another, and that they are holding to the faith delivered once for all to the saints (Jude 3).

Which brings us to the subject of exactly who was responsible for delivering that faith to the saints.

Apostolic

Bit by bit, we have already covered the import of the term apostolic both above and in previous chapters. The catholic churches were apostolic churches. The reason they could appeal to each other in case of dispute is not because the opinion of any particular church mattered. *It is because the opinion of the apostles mattered.* Consulting an ancient church was for no other reason than to find the teaching of the apostles.

It is impossible to overstate the early churches' reliance on the apostles. Everything they wrote emphasized apostolic authority.

I'm going to show you a relatively long list of quotes here, but it is just a minor sampling. To the early churches, the faith had come in lineage from God to Jesus to the apostles and then to the churches. They emphasized tradition, but the only tradition that mattered to them was apostolic tradition.

Apostle Paul, c. AD 62:

> You are ... fellow-citizens with the saints ... and are built upon the foundation of the apostles and prophets, Jesus Christ himself being the chief cornerstone. (Eph. 2:20)

Clement of Rome, AD 96:

> The apostles have preached the Gospel to us from the Lord Jesus Christ; Jesus Christ from God. Christ, therefore, was sent forth by God and the apostles by Christ. ... And preaching in this way through countries and cities, they appointed the first-fruits, having first proven them by the Spirit, to be bishops and deacons of those who would afterward believe.[531]

---

[531] *1 Clement.* 42.

Anonymous, c. AD 100:

> Then the fear of the law is chanted, the grace of the
> prophets is known, the faith of the Gospels is established,
> the tradition of the apostles is preserved, and the grace of
> the church exults. If you do not grieve this grace, you will
> know those things which the Word[532] teaches, by whom
> he wills and when he pleases.[533]

Ignatius, c. AD 110:

> Apart from [Christ Jesus] let nothing attract you, for
> whom I carry these shackles, these spiritual jewels ... that I
> may be found in the lot of the Christians at Ephesus, who
> have always been of the same mind with the apostles
> through the power of Jesus Christ.[534]

> Study ... to be established in the doctrines of the Lord and
> the apostles so that everything, whatever you do, may
> prosper both in flesh and in spirit; in faith and in love; in
> the Son, in the Father, and in the Spirit.[535]

Polycarp, c. AD 120:

> Forsake the vanity of many and their false doctrines, and
> let us return to the word which was handed down to us
> from the beginning.[536]

Justin Martyr, c. AD 150:

> Our Jesus Christ was crucified and died, rose again, as-
> cended to heaven, and reigned. By those things which
> were published in his name among all nations by the

---

[532] This reference to "the Word" is a reference to the *Logos*, Jesus Christ. When the early churches used the phrase "the Word" or "the Word of God," it was almost always a reference to Christ, not the Scriptures. Hebrews 4:12-13 is an example of a place where the Scriptures do the same, but we modern Christians usually miss it.

[533] *Letter to Diognetus.* 11.

[534] *Letter to the Ephesians.* 11.

[535] *Letter to the Magnesians.* 13.

[536] *Letter to the Philippians.* 7.

apostles there is joy afforded to those who expect the immortality promised by him.[537]

Irenaeus, c. AD 185

We have learned from no others the plan of our salvation than from those through whom the Gospel has come down to us, which at one time they proclaimed in public, and at a later period, by the will of God, handed down to us in the Scriptures to be the ground and pillar of our faith. For it is unlawful to assert that they preached before they had perfect knowledge, as some venture to say, boasting of themselves as improvers of the apostles. ...

Matthew ... issued a written Gospel among the Hebrews in their own language, while Peter and Paul were preaching at Rome, laying the foundations of the church. After their departure, Mark, the disciple and interpreter of Peter, handed down to us what was preached by Peter. Luke also, the companion of Paul, recorded in a book the Gospel preached by him. Afterwards John, the disciple of the Lord ... published a Gospel during his residence at Ephesus in Asia [Minor].

If anyone does not agree to these truths, he despises the companions of the Lord. No, worse, he despises Christ himself the Lord. Yes, he despises the Father also and stands self-condemned, resisting and opposing his own salvation.[538]

Clement of Alexandria, c. AD 190

Well did they preserve the tradition of the blessed teaching derived directly from the holy apostles Peter, James, John, and Paul, the sons receiving it from the fathers (though few were like the fathers). They came by God's will to deposit those ancestral and apostolic seeds.[539]

---

[537] *First Apology*. 42.

[538] *Against Heresies*. III:1:1.

[539] *Miscellanies*. I:1.

Tertullian, c. AD 210

The churches, although they are so many and so great, comprise but the one primitive church, by the apostles from which they all spring. In this way all are primitive and all are apostolic.

All doctrine which agrees with the apostolic churches, those molds and original sources of the faith, must be considered truth as undoubtedly containing that which the churches received from the apostles, the apostles from Christ, and Christ from God. On the other hand, all doctrine must be prejudged as false which smells of disagreement to the truth of the churches and apostles of Christ and God.[540]

Hippolytus, c. AD 225

The apostles ... received power from God, set themselves to labor, and became farmers for the Lord, cultivating the earth ... with the preaching of our Lord.[541]

Origen, c. AD 230

Since the teaching of the church, transmitted in orderly succession from the apostles and remaining in the churches to the present day, is still preserved, that alone is to accepted as truth which does not differ in any way from ecclesiastic and apostolic tradition.[542]

Cyprian, c. AD 250

Since you have asked our advice, know that we do not depart from the traditions of the Gospel and of the apostles.[543]

---

[540] *Prescription Against Heretics.* 20,21.
[541] "The Extant Works and Fragments of Hippolytus." Part I: "On Genesis." Gen. xlix. 12-15. *The Ante-Nicene Fathers.* Vol. V.
[542] *De Principiis.* Preface.
[543] "Epistle 61: Letter to Pomponus." *The Ante-Nicene Fathers.* Vol. V.

This is what it means for the church to be apostolic. Every effort was made by the early churches to accurately preserve the tradition of the apostles, the faith that was once for all delivered to the saints, without change or addition. Those who count themselves "improvers of the apostles"[544] are to be rejected as divisive and opinionated men.

It's for this reason that I argue that the only standard that the church used to determine what books to include in the canon was apostolicity. Was the book or letter written by an apostle or approved by an apostle? If it was, it was Scripture. If it was not, then it didn't matter how excellent or even how inspired the book was; it didn't belong in the canon.

You will notice above that I included a quote from Irenaeus that expresses the universal early Christian belief that Mark's Gospel was approved by Peter and Luke's by Paul. Their Gospels became part of the church's canon because they were apostolic.

I don't have time in a book on the Council of Nicea to go into the arguments for a position on the canon, but one of the strongest arguments is the long list of quotes I have printed above.

The early church, if nothing else, was apostolic.

One

There is one more issue which we must touch on.

We have talked throughout this chapter about the unity of the catholic, apostolic churches. The question arises, at least for modern Protestants: Is that all there was?

We spoke in Chapter 3 about the argument of *The Pilgrim Church* and *The Trail of Blood* that there was a line of independent churches outside the catholic churches from a very early date. We have seen that this just isn't true. The only independent, separated churches to which they can appeal in the pre-Nicene and Nicene age are the Montanists and the Novatianists, neither of which

---

[544] Quote references the the Irenaeus passage above.

would provide any benefit for Protestants. On doctrinal issues, the Montanists and Novatianists did not differ from the catholic churches. They were simply harsher in their judgments, and in the case of the Montanists, wilder in their prophecies.

So what was a Christian to do when the churches went from being persecuted and holy to persecuting and nominal?[545] What was a Christian to do when his bishop was replaced by Constantius II with a bishop who embraced the heresy of Eusebius of Nicomedia? What was a Christian to do when his bishop *was* Eusebius of Nicomedia and his repentance after his banishment proved to be feigned?

Those of us who are used to western Christianity will probably be shocked by this answer, but there was *nothing* to do. Though division within a city would become habit-forming by the height of the Arian Controversy, it was unheard of at the beginning of it. You simply did not leave the church to form your own division. That's what gnostics did.

There were some who did find an alternative. The fourth century saw the beginning of monasticism, a movement which made perfect sense in the new way of things. Joining a monastery allowed one to remain in communion with the church at large, yet separate from its carnal membership and diligently pursue holiness.

To this day, membership in a monastery or society would still be the catholic churches' recommended method for separating oneself for the pursuit of holiness.

What a difficult situation we would face if we lived in the fourth century! It is commanded by the Scriptures that we put wicked men out of the church (1 Cor. 5:13). Even more pertinently, we are commanded to have no fellowship with and not even to eat with someone "named a brother" who is sexually immoral, greedy, or who drinks excessively (1 Cor. 5:11). How are we to do that if *everyone* is a "brother"?

---

[545] "Nominal" means "in name only."

> I read once in a *Reader's Digest* that a thief had broken into the home of a man while he was watching television. The thief pulled a gun on the man, then noticed that the TV was playing Billy Graham. He said to the homeowner, "Oh! Are you a Christian? So am I!"
>
> The problem with nominal Christianity has obviously not gone away.

In addition, Cyprian tells us that a congregation will not be held guiltless if it breaks bread with a "sinful prelate."

> Nor let the people flatter themselves that they can be free from the contagion of sin while communicating with a priest who is a sinner and yielding their consent to the unjust and unlawful episcopacy of their bishop. ... A people obedient to the Lord's precepts and fearing God ought to separate themselves from a sinful prelate and not to associate themselves with the sacrifices of a sacrilegious priest, especially since they have the power either of choosing worthy priests or of rejecting unworthy ones. [546]

So let's suppose you were living in Constantinople while Eusebius or Macedonius was bishop. Could you really separate from those bishops and the elders they appointed without creating your own division?

I don't pretend to have the answers, but these are the questions faced by committed fourth-century Christians. It seems apparent that most chose either to join a monastery or to continue in communion with their sinful prelates and nominal brothers and sisters.

It is hard to fault them. What a difficult choice they faced!

Having covered the catholic and apostolic church(es), let's now look at what it is those churches believed on the issues covered by Nicea. Was the Council of Nicea successful in preserving the faith of the apostles, or did they add to it?

---

[546] "Epistles of Cyprian 67: To the Clergy and People Abiding in Spain." *The Ante-Nicene Fathers*. Vol. V.

Chapter 18:

Was the Nicene Church Roman Catholic?

One of the popular misconceptions about the Council of Nicea is that the Roman Catholic Church was founded there. There is nothing true about this claim, but what is false depends on what is meant by "the Roman Catholic Church."

"Catholic" in early Christianity simply meant universal.[547] The churches that were founded by the apostles, or by those churches afterward, and who were in unity with one another, referred to themselves as catholic from the earliest times. Ignatius was the earliest writer known to use the term, in his letter to the church at Smyrna around AD 110.

We find the reference in chapter eight, where he writes, "Wherever Jesus Christ is, there is the catholic church."

Clearly, he was not referring only to the Roman church.

The Roman church was, however, most certainly catholic, as were all other churches that were founded by the apostles or that were founded by apostolic churches and their missionaries. Thus,

---

[547] See Chapter 15.

there was a Roman catholic church, with a small "c"; but it was only in Rome.

When we ask if the churches at the time of Nicea were Roman Catholic, however, what is being asked is: did all the churches submit to the pope—the bishop of Rome—as the authority over the Church universal?

The answer to that question is no. Neither before nor at the time of Nicea did any church regard the Roman bishop as supreme over all churches. The evidence for this is both abundant and one-sided.

Canon 6 of the Council of Nicea

This one detail, the 6th canon of Nicea, should have settled the issue long ago.

It reads:

> Let the ancient customs in Egypt, Libya and Pentapolis prevail, that the Bishop of Alexandria have jurisdiction in all these, since the like is customary for the Bishop of Rome also. Likewise in Antioch and the other provinces, let the Churches retain their privileges.

This canon tells us that the bishop of Rome has a similar authority to the bishop of Alexandria.

I have been told by Roman Catholics that this canon is to be understood to mean that it is customary for the bishop of Rome to give the bishop of Alexandria permission to have authority over Egypt, Libya and Pentapolis. Since it is clear from the wording that such an interpretation is far-fetched at best, I will not take time to further refute it.

Further, if that is what the canon means, then no one in the early churches seemed to know it.

Bishops Continually Rejected the Intrusion of the Bishop of Rome

There were several incidents in the pre-Nicene Christian history where the bishop of Rome tried to exercise something resembling papal authority. No bishops, however, ever submitted to it.

The first such incident concerned the Paschal Controversy.[548] Victor, who became bishop of Rome in AD 189, held a council which determined that Passover should always be held on a Sunday nearest Nisan 14 on the Jewish calendar rather than on the exact day on which Nisan 14 fell. The council wrote the churches outside their area to tell them of their decision.

Polycrates, one of the bishops of Asia Minor, wrote back explaining that their tradition of observing Nisan 14 had come from such great names as the apostle John and the evangelist Philip.

Polycrates then adds that he consulted other bishops "whose names ... would constitute a great multitude" before sending his letter back to Rome.

Finally, in wording that indicates that Victor's letter to the east must have included threats of excommunication, Polycrates says:

> I, therefore, brethren, who have lived sixty-five years in the Lord, have met with the brethren throughout the world, and have gone through every Holy Scripture, am not frightened by terrifying words. For those greater than I have said, "We ought to obey God rather than man."[549]

Victor was furious. He declared that all the churches of Asia Minor were "wholly excommunicate."[550]

Even the bishops at the Victor's council in the west could not agree with this action. Eusebius reports that "words of theirs are extant, sharply rebuking Victor." One of those letters, from Irenaeus, the highly respected bishop and missionary to the barbarian Gauls, is preserved in Eusebius' history.

Irenaeus' letter tells the story with which I began Chapter 6. In that story, an earlier bishop of Rome, Anicetus, yielded to the tradition of the churches of Asia Minor. Those churches never considered that they were obligated to follow the practice of the church of Rome when they themselves already knew that their

---

[548] Covered in Chapter 6.

[549] Eusebius. *Ecclesiastical History*. V:24.

[550] *ibid.*

own tradition was apostolic. Irenaeus appealed to the graciousness of Anicetus to persuade Victor.

The words of Irenaeus and the other bishops settled Victor, and he backed off from his position. No one had considered yielding to him anyway!

Some 60 years later, Stephen, bishop of Rome, tried to make a sweeping ecclesiastical decision on the rebaptism of heretics. The specific heretics in question were the Novatians, who had formed a separate church in Rome over the issue of the readmission of Christians who had lapsed during persecution. Stephen felt that Novatianists who returned to the catholic churches did not need to be rebaptized but that the laying on of hands would be sufficient.

But Stephen did not just decide for the church at Rome. Apparently, he argued that he was a "bishop of bishops," and he aroused the ire of the North African bishops who were closely affiliated with the church at Rome.[551]

The most prominent of these was Cyprian of Carthage, who wasted no time in calling a council, known as the Seventh Council of Carthage, to disagree with Stephen. Eighty-seven bishops met there and issued this declaration:

> It remains that upon this same matter each of us should bring forward what we think, judging no man, nor rejecting any one from the right of communion, if he should think differently from us. **For neither does any of us set himself up as a bishop of bishops, nor by tyrannical terror does any compel his colleague to the necessity of obedience;** since every bishop, according to the allowance of his liberty and power, has his own proper right of

---

[551] Carthage was only 374 miles from Rome. Even though it was in Africa, the short distance between southern Italy and modern Tunisia ensured that Carthage was colonized by Italians. This is why the earliest "Latin" fathers include men like Tertullian and Cyprian, both from Carthage.

judgment, and can no more be judged by another than he himself can judge another.[552]

This was as clear a rejection of papal authority as one can conceive, and it came from 87 bishops at one time.

An important facet of this event is that the Seventh Council of Carthage was led by Cyprian, bishop of Carthage. He is now considered a saint by the Roman Catholic Church. Ironically, no early Christian writer is quoted more often than Cyprian as proof that the bishop of Rome had papal authority in the pre-Nicene church.

We will address Cyprian later in this chapter.

First, we must address the council at Antioch in the early 340's, which also rejected a show of authority by a Roman bishop.[553] It was led by Eusebius of Nicomedia and attended by primarily Arian bishops. Eusebius was a divisive and unruly man, and his whole life was occupied with troubling and dividing the catholic churches. Nonetheless, insofar as the letter from that council correlates with other ancient testimonies, it provides one further bit of evidence that the bishop of Rome was not recognized as pope, not even in the fourth century.

In this case, the issue was the removal of Athanasius from his see[554] in Alexandria and his reinstatement by Julius, bishop of Rome. Eusebius and his fellow bishops complained.

> It was not [Julius'] province, they said, to take cognizance of their decisions in reference to any whom they might wish to expel from their churches; seeing that they had not opposed themselves to him when Novatus was ejected from the church.[555]

---

[552] "The Seventh Council of Carthage Under Cyprian." *The Ante-Nicene Fathers*. Vol. V. Emphasis mine.

[553] This is the same council discussed in Chapters 8 and 9, which produced the famous *homoiousian* creed.

[554] The area of a bishop's oversight.

[555] *Ecclesiastical History of Socrates Scholasticus*. II:15.

What we see in history is a unanimous rejection of the bishop of Rome's attempts to interfere in affairs outside Italy. While various bishops of Rome have considered themselves to have authority outside their jurisdiction, other bishops did not concur, not even in Carthage despite its close relationship with Rome.

This fact makes it certain that Canon 6 of Nicea did not mean that the bishop of Rome had universal authority; certainly not enough to circumscribe the authority of the bishop of Alexandria. No eastern bishop—and the Council of Nicea was still primarily eastern—would ever have agreed to such invasiveness by the bishop of Rome.

In fact, that would be true to this very day.

Eastern Bishops Reject Papal Authority to this Day

The Council of Nicea established three "patriarchates": in Rome, Alexandria, and Antioch. At the Council of Constantinople in 381, the bishop of Constantinople was added to the patriarchs and assigned a status even higher than the bishop of Alexandria. (Constantinople did not exist in AD 325.)

The overthrow of the western empire by barbarian hordes in the fifth century caused a political separation between the bishop of Rome and the other patriarchs. When communication was fully restored centuries later, the church at Rome had added the Latin word *filioque* to the updated version of the Nicene Creed that was supposedly approved at the Council of Constantinople but only certainly introduced at the Council of Chalcedon in 451.

Filioque means "and the son," and the creed of the Roman church now said that the Holy Spirit proceeds from the Father and the Son rather than from just the Father.

The bishops of the east objected that the bishop of Rome had no authority to change the official creed of the church, but the bishop of Rome insisted that he did. The bishop of Rome finally excommunicated the bishop of Constantinople in 1054, and the excommunication has been in force to this day.

So today, just as with Polycrates in the second century, Cyprian in the third century, and Eusebius of Nicomedia in the fourth century, the eastern bishops continue to reject the bishop of Rome's claim to be the representative of God on earth.

On the other hand, even at the Council of Constantinople, which the bishop of Rome did not attend and may not even have known about, the bishop of Rome was said to have first place among the patriarchs. The bishop of Constantinople was made second over even the bishop of Alexandria but nonetheless second to the bishop of Rome.[556]

To this day, should the Roman Catholic and Orthodox Churches be reconciled, the eastern bishops agree that the bishop of Rome is to have an authority that is "first among equals," just as the Council of Constantinople decided. The authority that he claims for himself, though—to be the representative of Christ on earth—has been universally rejected by eastern bishops since it was asserted for the first time sometime after AD 189.

Cyprian

Many Roman Catholic scholars quote Cyprian of Carthage in defense of papal primacy. It was hard to decide upon a source to reference.

I finally settled on a web site at realpresence.org. I chose this site both because it is on the internet so you can see it and because it was written by Father John A. Hardon, a Jesuit priest who authored *The Catholic Catechism* and *The Modern Catholic Dictionary*. Father Hardon died in 2000, and there are Catholics petitioning for him to be beatified.[557]

It seemed hard to beat those credentials.

---

[556] Schaff, *History* Bk. III, Sec. 46
[557] To be officially recognized as a Catholic saint.

Call No Man Father

In Matthew 23:9 Jesus instructed us to call no man father. So why am I referring to Father Hardon as "Father"?

I do not believe that Jesus was trying to get us to show disrespect. I believe Jesus was trying to set a standard in the church that is violated every bit as much by Protestants who give their leaders the title of "Pastor" or "Reverend" as by Roman Catholics who give their priests and bishops the title of "Father."

Father Hardon's page on Cyprian begins with:[558]

> St. Cyprian ... is one of the earliest and most outspoken defenders of papal primacy.

He is? St. Cyprian, who was only bishop for 10 years and who called a council during his eighth year to reject the "tyrannical terror" of the Roman bishop's claim to be "bishop of bishops" ... *that* St. Cyprian is an outspoken defender of papal primacy?

Why would Fr. Hardon say such a thing?

> In the seventeen centuries since Cyprian wrote these words, his name has been a stumbling block to those who quiver at his uncompromising faith. But Cyprian's witness is a tower of strength for those who, like him, believe in the papal primacy.[559]

To what words is Fr. Hardon referring?

They are from Cyprian's tract, "On the Unity of the Church," and I will give them to you in the translation Fr. Hardon used:

> [Jesus] says to [Peter] again after the resurrection, "Feed my sheep." It is on him that He builds His Church, and to him that He entrusts the sheep to feed. And although He

---

[558] Hardon, Fr. John A. "Cyprian Teaches Papal Primacy." *Challenge*. Vol. 16. Oct. 1989. *The Real Presence Association*. Inter Mirifica, 1998. Accessed 20 Mar. 2011
<http://www.therealpresence.org/archives/Papacy/Papacy_017.htm>.
[559] *ibid.*

assigns a similar power to all the Apostles, "Receive the Holy Spirit. If you forgive any man his sins, they shall be forgiven him; if you retain any man's sins, they shall be retained" [*Jn. 20:22-23*]. - yet, in order that the oneness might be unmistakable, He established by His own authority a source for that oneness having its origin in one man alone.[560]

A primacy is given to Peter, and it is thus made clear that there is but one Church and one Chair.

If a man does not hold to this oneness of Peter, does he imagine that he still holds the truth? If he deserts the Chair of Peter upon whom the Church was built, has he still confidence that he is in the Church?

Now this oneness we must hold firmly and insist on — especially we who are bishops and exercise authority in the Church—so as to demonstrate that the episcopal power is one and undivided too. Let none mislead the brethren with a lie, let none corrupt the true content of the faith by a faithless perversion of the truth.

Paradoxical, perhaps even bizarre, isn't it? Cyprian called a council in Carthage and rejected the authority of Stephen, bishop of Rome, but here we see that he wrote a tract on the unity of the church saying that bishops especially should promote the unity of the church by holding to the primacy of Peter.

Was Cyprian schizophrenic? Did he change his mind?

His statements and his action seem so contradictory that Dr. A. Cleveland Coxe, American editor of *The Ante-Nicene Fathers*, asserts that several of those statements are "beyond all question spurious."

Those are:

A primacy is given to Peter, and it is thus made clear that there is but one Church and one Chair.

---

[560] *ibid.* Reference for Scripture quotation added by me.

and:

> If he deserts the Chair of Peter upon whom the Church was built, has he still confidence that he is in the Church?

Dr. Coxe gives no reason for his assertion except his own incredulity, so let's proceed as though all these phrases were written by Cyprian.

The truth is, neither of these statements conflict with Cyprian's theology.

Cyprian most certainly taught, and taught repeatedly, that Peter had a primacy over the other apostles. He based that primacy on Matthew 16:18-19, a favorite passage of the modern Roman Catholic Church.

> I say to you, "You are Peter, and upon this rock I will build my church, and the gates of hell shall not prevail against it. And I will give you the keys of the kingdom of heaven, and whatever you shall bind on earth shall be bound in heaven and whatever you shall release on earth shall be released in heaven."

Do we really all need to hold to Peter in order to be in unity with the apostolic churches?

According to Cyprian, yes, we do.

But look through Cyprian's quote above. Do you see any mention of Rome in that passage?

You do not, and you will not find a mention of Rome in any similar passage by Cyprian because he did not believe that the Roman bishop had individually inherited Peter's primacy.

The explanation for Cyprian's words is found right in the passage Fr. Hardon quoted from "On the Unity of the Church." Most Catholic apologists choose other, similar statements from Cyprian. They do not normally quote the key passage here:

> Now this oneness we must hold firmly and insist on ... **so as to demonstrate that the episcopal power is one and undivided too.**[561]

To Cyprian, the "episcopal power," that is, the authority of the bishops, is "one and undivided." The bishops, together, have received the keys of the kingdom and the leadership of the church from Peter. *Every* bishop is a successor of Peter, at least in Cyprian's eyes.

This explains Cyprian's statement at the Council of Carthage:

> Nor does any of us set himself up as a bishop of bishops, nor by tyrannical terror does any compel his colleague to the necessity of obedience since every bishop ... has his own proper right of judgment and can no more be judged by another than he himself can judge another.[562]

That council was aimed directly at the bishop of Rome. Cyprian's other letters make that clear, but let me add the testimony of the Edinburgh translators of the *Ante-Nicene Fathers*, for they preface the text of the proceedings of the Council of Carthage with:

> When Stephen, Bishop of Rome, Had by His Letters Condemned the Decrees of the African Council on the Baptism of Heretics, Cyprian Lost No Time in Holding Another Council at Carthage with a Greater Number of Bishops.[563]

---

[561] *ibid.* Emphasis mine.

[562] "The Seventh Council of Carthage Under Cyprian." *The Ante-Nicene Fathers.* Vol. V.

[563] *ibid.*

Originally, I had to find an explanation for Cyprian's references to the primacy of Peter on my own. I knew that a man who called a council of 87 bishops to refute a claim by the bishop of Rome to be "bishop of bishops" could not possibly agree with papal primacy. I had to read and reread Cyprian's references to Peter until I realized that I was only assuming, based on what the Roman Catholics had put in my mind, that Cyprian was equating Peter and the bishop of Rome.

Since then, however, I have found out that I am not alone, even among the modern "catholic" churches, in drawing that conclusion. For example, Orthodox Answers, an Eastern Orthodox apologetic organization, addresses Cyprian's statements as well, drawing the same conclusion I have:

> "De Unitate (On the unity of the catholic church)" is often misunderstood.
>
> The "catholic church" is obviously (in context, but not so obviously to the modern reader) the local church (diocese). The unity of the catholic church is anchored in the office of the bishop who holds the chair of Peter and who is "Peter's successor" in the church. ...
>
> This treatise does not deal with the unity of the "Catholic Church" in the modern sense (a worldwide organism) but of the catholic church as then understood, the local church. For Cyprian, the churches are held together in communion by the unity of their bishops (called sacerdos or priests in context) who each hold in fullness the Chair of Peter.[564]

---

[564] Fr. Laurent. "Question Number 710." *Orthodox Answers*. St. Innocent Orthodox Church. 13 Dec. 2010. Accessed 20 Mar. 2011 < http://www.orthodoxanswers.org/answer/710/>. Parentheses in original.

Father Richard McBrien, Crowley-O'Brien Professor of Theology at Notre Dame and former president of the Catholic Theological Society of America, adds:

> Catholic tradition regards Peter (d. ca. 64) as the first pope, but the first succession lists identified Linus (ca. 66-ca. 78), not Peter, as the first pope. Peter was not regarded as the first bishop of Rome until the late second or early third century.[565]

And ...

> The correlation between Peter and the Bishop of Rome ... did not become fully explicit until the pontificate of Leo I in the mid-fifth century.[566]

No Monarchial Bishop in Rome at the Turn of the Second Century

This subject is addressed more fully in Appendix C. We will only touch on it briefly here.

A "monarchial" bishop is a bishop that rules alone. Paul and Peter's churches had multiple elders, all of whom were called bishops, though "overseer" or "supervisor" would be a better translation of the Greek word *episkopos*. Thus, bishop and elder are interchangeable terms in the New Testament (Acts 20:17,28; 1 Pet. 5:1-4).

By the late second century, however, all churches had only one bishop and the elders were no longer called bishops.

Two of the earliest pre-Nicene writings still show the New Testament form of church government, elders and deacons. Those are *1 Clement*, which is a letter from the church of Rome to the church at Corinth, and Polycarp's letter to the Philippians. *1 Clem-*

---

[565] McBrien, *The Church* p. 93
[566] *ibid.* p. 99

ent uses bishops and elders interchangeably, like the New Testament does.

> [The apostles] appointed the first fruits, having first proven them by the Spirit, to be bishops and deacons of those who would afterwards believe.[567]

> Our sin will not be small if we eject from the office of bishop those who have fulfilled its duties in blamelessness and holiness. Blessed are those elders who ... have obtained a fruitful and perfect departure [from this world], for they need not fear that someone will deprive them of the place now appointed to them.[568]

Polycarp's letter to the Philippians simply neglects to mention a bishop or bishops, even when he discusses the duties of deacons and elders in chapters five and six.

Not all the earliest writings show this multiple bishop system. History seems to clearly indicate that the churches that the apostle John led in the late first century had monarchial bishops. Both Ignatius and Polycarp are held by tradition to have been appointed by the apostles, and both were monarchial bishops.

[567] *1 Clement.* 42.
[568] *1 Clement.* 44.

"Tradition Holds ... "

You've probably been told before that there are things we know "by tradition." "Tradition holds," for example, that Peter was crucified upside down, saying he was unworthy to die in the same manner as our Lord.

There is not a book of tradition somewhere that teaches these things. "Tradition" is a way of saying that there are ancient rumors that something happened. Those rumors can be more or less reliable depending on where they came from.

In the case of Polycarp, it is Irenaeus, Clement of Alexandria, and Tertullian who say that he was appointed by apostles.

Since Irenaeus had been taught by Polycarp as a young man and claimed to be able to remember him well, his testimony is given some weight, though it cannot be conclusive. He did live at a time period and in a location where it is at least possible that the apostle John would have confirmed his appointment.

It is even more likely in the case of the older Ignatius, whom some sources say was appointed by Peter.

Both Ignatius and Polycarp wrote letters to churches that were founded by Peter or Paul. Ignatius wrote to the Romans, and Polycarp wrote to the Philippians. Neither letter mentions a monarchial bishop.

This is especially significant in the case of Ignatius. Ignatius wrote six other letters, five to churches that were overseen by the apostle John in Asia Minor, and one to Polycarp himself. All his letters to the five churches of Asia Minor not only mention a monarchial bishop but they extol the bishop and command obedience to him in such strong terms that Protestants cringe to read his letters.

Except the letter to the Romans.

The letter to the Romans never even mentions a bishop.

This, combined with what we saw in *1 Clement* and in the Scriptures themselves, is very strong evidence that Rome, founded by Paul and overseen by Peter, had no monarchial bishop.

And if Rome had no monarchial bishop, then there was no person to be the pope.

There is later testimony that Rome did have a monarchial bishop at that time. Irenaeus, writing about AD 185, gives a list of Roman bishops that goes all the way back to Linus. Clement himself is listed as the third after Linus and Anacletus.

What are we to conclude? I believe the impartial historian has to conclude that Irenaeus, writing 90 years after Clement and approximately 75 years after Ignatius, is much more likely to be mistaken. By Irenaeus' time, Tertullian tells us that it was normal among catholic churches to have a roll of bishops going back to the apostles.[569] It seems much more likely that somewhere along the line someone tried to complete Rome's list going backward than that Clement, who is on that list, was simply mistaken.

Father Richard McBrien, the Catholic theologian mentioned earlier, agrees:

> Indeed, it was not until the middle of the second century that Rome changed from a collegial form of leadership to a monepiscopal form.[570]

In all fairness, I do have to grant the possibility that Clement was doing what Polycarp did. Polycarp was a monarchial bishop who does not mention a bishop because he was writing to the Philippians, a Greek church founded by Paul, without a monarchial bishop. Perhaps Clement, who was writing to Corinth, uses bishop and elder interchangeably because of Corinthian practice, not Roman practice.

The problem is that there is no reason, other than wishful thinking, that Rome would have a monarchial bishop. Adding one more piece of evidence against it, 1 Peter, which uses bishop and elder interchangeably (5:1-4), was almost certainly written from Rome, which would explain the cryptic reference to Babylon in 1 Peter 5:13. That, combined with the Ignatius' letter to the Romans—an example of silence being deafening if ever there was one—seems to put the evidence strongly against a monarchial

---

[569] The reason for this is given in our section on apostolic succession below.
[570] McBrien, *The Church* p. 44

bishop in Rome until at least after Ignatius' martyrdom in 107 or 116.

Irenaeus

Another early writer quoted in defense of a pope during the pre-Nicene era is Irenaeus, who wrote a very large defense of the faith against gnosticism, titled *Against Heresies*, around AD 185.

Irenaeus is not like Cyprian. Cyprian has a context to explain his statements about the primacy of Peter. He said outright that no bishop could rule over or judge another, and he did so at a council whose proceedings are still extant.[571] To quote Cyprian in support of papal primacy without mentioning the Seventh Council of Carthage is dishonest.

Irenaeus has no such context within which to work. Nonetheless, It is not difficult to correctly interpret the one passage from Irenaeus that is quoted in defense of an early papacy.

Irenaeus makes the most stunning statement in all of early Christian literature in reference to the primacy of the church at Rome:

> Since it would be very tedious ... to reckon up the successions of all the churches, we confound all those who ... assemble in unauthorized meetings by indicating the tradition derived from the apostles of the very great, the very ancient, and universally known church founded and organized at Rome by the two most glorious apostles, Peter and Paul. ... For it is a matter of necessity that every church should agree with this church, because of its preeminent authority, that is, the faithful everywhere, inasmuch as the apostolic tradition has been preserved continually by those who exist everywhere.[572]

---

[571] "Extant" means still existing in our day.
[572] *Against Heresies*. III:3:2.

The last part of that quote, I'm told, is very difficult to translate, but I am going to show you that it is irrelevant to our discussion anyway. Catholic.com renders it:

> For with this church, because of its superior origin, all churches must agree, that is, all the faithful in the whole world. And it is in her that the faithful everywhere have maintained the apostolic tradition.[573]

They have added the "in her," but otherwise this translation is as good as any other. That translation is approved as "free from any doctrinal error" on the subscript of that page by "Bernadeane Carr, STL, Censor Liborum, August 10, 2004."

We don't need a special non-Catholic translation of this passage to argue that the Roman Catholic Church misinterprets this passage from Irenaeus. There is no doubt that all the early Christian writers would have agreed that "with this church ... all churches must agree."

In his own refutation of gnostics and other heretics, Tertullian, about 20 years later than Irenaeus, wrote:

> You have Rome, from which there comes into our hands the true authority. How happy is its church, on which the apostles poured forth all their doctrine along with their blood![574]

So both Irenaeus and Tertullian tell us of the importance of agreeing with the church of Rome.

The important question to ask is: why?

Modern Roman Catholics quote Irenaeus because they want us to agree with the church at Rome *today*. They quote Irenaeus because they want us to submit to the authority of the bishop of Rome—the pope—*today*.

---

[573] "Apostolic Succession." *Catholic Answers*. 10 Aug. 2004. Accessed 20 Mar. 2011. <http://www.catholic.com/library/Apostolic_Succession.asp>.
[574] *Prescription Against Heretics*. 36.

Both Irenaeus and Tertullian, however, give very thorough explanations of why all churches—in Tertullian's case, all Christians—should agree with the church of Rome *at the turn of the third century*. And their reasons have nothing whatsoever to do with the authority of the bishop of Rome, nor do they have any application to the twenty-first century.

Nor do either of them teach that the church at Rome is the only church with whom all Christians must agree.

Irenaeus' quote begins by saying that he could list a succession from many churches, but that would be too tedious. Therefore, he says, he is picking one, and he picks Rome because it was founded by the two most eminent apostles, Peter and Paul.

But why is he listing a succession of bishops at all?

Irenaeus explains. We must remember that his book is entitled *Against Heresies*. He is refuting gnostics, and he is doing so by arguing that the catholic churches hold to the truth *as taught by the apostles*. He complains that the heretics refuse to listen to Scripture or to the elders *who knew the teachings of the apostles*.

> When ... they are refuted from the Scriptures, they turn around and accuse these same Scriptures as if they were not correct, nor of authority, and that they are ambiguous and that the truth cannot be extracted from them by those who are ignorant of tradition. ... But again, when we refer them to **that tradition which originates from the apostles and which is preserved by means of the succession of elders in the churches**, they object to tradition, saying that they are wiser not merely than the elders, but even than the apostles.[575]

The issue to Irenaeus, then, was not authority, but truth. He was not saying that the heretics should listen to the church of Rome no matter what it said. He was saying that all churches should listen to the church of Rome because it had received truth from the two most eminent apostles, Peter and Paul, and had pre-

---

[575] *Against Heresies*. III:2:1,2. Emphasis added.

served it for just over a century by handing it down from one set of elders to the next, and from one bishop to the next, until Irenaeus' time.

In case this last passage from Irenaeus was not clear enough, he made the point that the issue was truth, not authority, several times in that section of *Against Heresies*. Before he lists the succession of bishops in the church at Rome, he says:

> If the apostles had known hidden mysteries, which they were in the habit of imparting to "the perfect" apart and privately from everyone else, they would have delivered them especially to those to whom they were also committing the churches themselves.[576]

After he is done listing Rome's bishops, he concludes by saying:

> In this order and by this succession the ecclesiastical tradition from the apostles and the preaching of the truth have come down to us. This is most abundant proof that there is one and the same life-giving faith which has been preserved in the church from the apostles until now and handed down in truth.[577]

Many years ago, I was part of a small church in Tyler, Texas that put heavy emphasis on the writings of the early Christians in an attempt to sort through the many Christian doctrines that abound in the United States. Our concern was knowing what the early churches taught so we could follow them in it.

Eventually, though, we had members who were causing problems in the church. Suddenly, we needed more than correct teachings. At least one of our leaders wanted a recognized authority so that we could get unruly members under control. He and several other members suggested that we join one of the catholic churches that had apostolic succession in order to have real authority in the church.

[576] *ibid.* III:3:1.
[577] *ibid.* III:3:3.

I presented the arguments to them that I am presenting to you now, and one member there told me, "Truth, truth, truth! Is that all you care about, the truth?"

Well, yes, it is. And that is what Irenaeus cared about, too.

Nor did Irenaeus think that it need only come from Rome:

> Polycarp also was not only instructed by the apostles, and conversed with many who had seen Christ, but was also, by apostles in Asia, appointed bishop of the church in Smyrna ... There is also a very powerful letter of Polycarp written to the Philippians, from which those who choose to do so and are anxious about their salvation, can learn the character of his faith and the preaching of the truth. Then again, the church in Ephesus, founded by Paul and having John remaining among them permanently until the times of Trajan,[578] is a true witness of the tradition of the apostles.[579]

Remember, though, it is not only Irenaeus who discussed this issue. Tertullian argued for the authority of the church in Rome, too. Did he do so for the same reasons as Irenaeus?

Tertullian was writing his own book against heretics, *Prescription Against Heretics*, when he mentioned the authority of Rome. The context of his quote is this:

> Come now, you who would indulge a better curiosity, if you would apply it to the business of your salvation, run to the apostolic churches, in which the very chairs of the apostles are still presiding in their places, in which their own authentic writings are read, uttering the voice and representing the face of each of them separately. Achaia is very near you, in which you find Corinth. Since you are not far from Macedonia, you have Philippi; you have the Thessalonians. Since you are able to cross to Asia [Minor], you get Ephesus. Since, in addition, you are close to Italy, you have Rome, from which comes into our own hands

---

[578] Trajan became emperor in AD 98.
[579] *ibid.* III:3:4.

357

true authority. How happy is its church, on which the apostles poured forth all their doctrines along with their blood! ... See what she has learned, what taught, what fellowship [she] has had with even churches in Africa.[580]

Again, the issue is learning truth from those churches that are apostolic in origin, whose job it was to preserve the faith once delivered to the saints (Jude 3).

And in case he wasn't clear enough in chapter 36, a few chapters earlier he had talked about a succession from the apostles as well. There he challenged the gnostics to ...

> ... produce the original records of their churches. Let them unfold the roll of their bishops, running down in due succession from the beginning in such a manner that bishop shall be able to show for his ordainer and predecessor one of the apostles or apostolic men—a man, moreover, who continued steadfast with the apostles.[581]

But what if they could? What if one of the gnostic churches had produced a roll of bishops going back to the apostles, so that they could show that some apostle or some companion of the apostles had appointed their first bishop? Does such a succession prove that a church has authority?

> Even if they managed to contrive this, they will not advance a step. For their very doctrine, after comparison with that of the apostles, will declare by its own diversity and contrariety that it had for its author neither an apostle nor an apostolic man.[582]

---

[580] *Prescription Against Heretics.* 36.
[581] *ibid.* 32.
[582] *ibid.*

And what if a church does not have a list of bishops going back to the apostles, but its doctrine is in agreement with the apostles? Should a church be rejected if it does not have apostolic succession?

> Those churches who, though they do not derive their founders from the apostles or apostolic men—since they are of a much later date, for they are in fact being founded daily—yet, since they agree in faith, they **are accounted as not less apostolic because they are akin in doctrine**.[583]

These quotes make my case so effectively that you might think I am inventing them, writing them down, and then ascribing them to Tertullian, but I'm not. Apostolic succession was never meant to defend anyone's authority to dictate doctrine or to rule over other Christians or other churches.

Apostolic succession is not a doctrine; it's an argument.

That is why apostolic succession is mentioned only in books against heretics. Apostolic succession is evidence that you possess apostolic truth unchanged from the beginning, not a license for promoting what you believe to be the truth.

As an argument for apostolic tradition, it has no effect once 2,000 years have passed. In AD 200, when only 100 years had passed since the last apostle died, and when succession could be shown to have produced the same truth in many independent churches, it was a powerful argument. When two millennium have passed, and when popes and patriarchs have had the power to disseminate error from non-apostolic sources into many churches, apostolic succession is no evidence at all that you possess apostolic truth.

Which brings us to our final piece of evidence against there being a pope in the pre-Nicene churches.

---

[583] *ibid.* Emphasis added.

The Natural Sense of Tertullian's Unity Argument

One of Tertullian's arguments against the heretics was the unity of the churches.

First, it is worth pointing out that Tertullian's opinion was that there was absolute unity among the catholic churches.

> Is it likely that so many churches, and they so great, should have gone astray into one and the same faith? No casualty distributed among men issues in one and the same result. Error of doctrine in the churches must necessarily have produced various issues. When, however, that which is deposited among many is found to be one and the same, it is not the result of error, but of tradition.[584]

It's often been asserted that the early churches fell away immediately after the time of the apostles. Evidence for this has been found in the Scriptures themselves. Paul had to rebuke the Corinthians for division (1 Cor. 1-3) and even for denying the resurrection (1 Cor. 15). John had to write concerning those that were seducing the church (1 Jn. 2:26), and one church had even cut off communication with him! (3 Jn. 9). Jesus' letters to the seven churches in the Revelation indicate problems in many of them (chs. 2-3).

But we cannot assume that because Ephesus left its first love (Rev. 2:4) or because the Laodiceans had grown lukewarm (Rev. 3:16) or because some Corinthians rejected faith in the resurrection or were dividing over teachers—we cannot assume that because these things *happened* that they also *continued*. Obviously, Jesus hadn't given up hope for the Laodiceans; he said he was standing at their door knocking (Rev. 3:20).

History indicates that the Ephesians and the Laodiceans repented. They stayed in fellowship with the apostolic churches. Jesus did not remove the candlestick from the church at Ephesus (Rev. 2:5) nor vomit the Laodiceans out of his mouth. (Rev. 3:16).

---

[584] *Prescription Against Heretics.* 28.

1 Clement, the letter from the church of Rome to the church at Corinth written in AD 96, says that Corinth repented fully when they received Paul's letter. In fact, *1 Clement* was written to rebuke them for falling back into a divisive attitude after such a sincere repentance.

Jesus' letters and the apostles' letters were so effective in producing repentance that apologists like Irenaeus and Tertullian were able to boast about the beautiful unity of the apostolic churches:

> The churches, although they are so many and so great, comprise but the one primitive church, [founded] by the apostles, from which they all [spring]. In this way all are primitive and all are apostolic, while they are all proven to be one in unity by their peaceful communion, title of brotherhood, and bond of hospitality; privileges which no other rule directs than the one tradition of the selfsame mystery.[585]

Note here that Tertullian not only describes the unity of the churches, but he gives a source for it: the one tradition of the mystery of the Gospel. The churches were not united by a unanimous submission to the church of Rome which dictated or approved their doctrines. They each maintained their own tradition, preserving it carefully so that they wound up united in the one and same faith that they had received from the apostles.

Irenaeus' description of the unity of the apostolic churches is far more poetic:

> The church, though dispersed through the whole world, even to the ends of the earth, has received from the apostles and their disciples this faith in one God, the Father Almighty, maker of heaven, earth, and the sea, and all that are in them; and in one Christ Jesus, the Son of God, who became incarnate for our salvation; and in the Holy

---

[585] *Prescription Against Heretics.* 20.

Spirit, who proclaimed through the prophets the dispensations of God ...

The church, having received this preaching and this faith, although scattered through the whole world, yet, as if occupying but one house, carefully preserves it. She also believes these points just as if she had but one soul and one and the same heart, and she proclaims them, teaches them, and hands them down with perfect harmony, as if she possessed only one mouth.[586]

The church handed down her preaching and her faith *as if* she had only one mouth. It is not that she did have only one mouth, the pope, but only *as if* she had only one mouth.

This is an important point because Tertullian would press it as an argument:

Is it likely that so many churches, and they so great, would have gone astray into one and the same faith?[587]

If there had been a pope in AD 200, then this argument of Tertullian's would have been invalid. Yes, it is very likely that so many churches, no matter how great they were, would go astray into one and the same faith ... *if* there were one authority to direct them into an erroneous faith.

There was not, however, one authority. Instead, Tertullian says that when something "deposited among many" proves to be one, then it is the result of tradition. This is why both he and Irenaeus argue that their readers should appeal not just to Rome, but to any of the apostolic churches.

Again, apostolic succession is an argument, not a doctrine. It was a *defense*, not a *decree*.

There was no pope in the Nicene and pre-Nicene churches. The Roman Catholic Church as an organization that rules all of western Christendom was not a product of apostolic teaching. The papacy was not a product of the blessing that Jesus conferred upon

---

[586] *Against Heresies.* 1:10:1,2.
[587] *Prescription Against Heretics.* 28.

Peter. The Roman Catholic Church is, instead, the product of the conquest of the western Roman empire by the barbarian hordes in the fifth century. Their conquest politically isolated the bishop of Rome from the other major bishops of the Roman empire and led to his having sole authority over all the churches west of the Byzantine empire.

It is that political isolation which would cause the bishops of Rome to begin to imagine that they had entitlement to such authority over all the churches of the world. No one concurred, and eventually the bishop of Rome simply excommunicated eastern Christianity, isolating his own private Christian world.

That separation from eastern Christianity and their rejection of papal primacy continues to this day.

Chapter 19:

Can Unity Be Holy
and Apostolic?

Are there any lessons to be learned from the story of the Council of Nicea?

There is one in particular that I want to address.

It is difficult to overemphasize the importance that Jesus and the apostles attached to unity.

> Nor do I pray for these alone [*i.e., the apostles*], but also for those who will believe in me through their word, that they may all be one as you, Father, are in me and I in you. [I pray] that they may all be one in us so that the world may believe that you sent me. The glory which you have given me, I have given them so that they may be one just as we are one. I in them and you in me, so that they may be perfectly one, so that the world may believe that you sent me and have loved them as you have loved me. (Jn. 17:20-23)

The unity of Jesus' disciples, according to Jesus, is critical to the world being able to believe that he came from the Father.

At the end of Chapter 15, we addressed the fact that fourth-century Christians faced incredibly difficult choices in the preservation of unity. While the Scriptures commanded them to separate from wicked men, their love of unity forced them into fellowship with *primarily* nominal[588] Christians.

> From the time of Constantine church discipline declines; the whole Roman world having become nominally Christian, and the host of hypocritical professors multiplying beyond all control.[589]

In the fourth century, the typical response of the average layman was simply to continue in the midst of a nominal church, or, in the case of the more radical, to join a monastery. Today, however, we face a situation where "heretics" cast out by the Roman Catholic Church—in particular Martin Luther and John Calvin—were supported by secular rulers. Divisions multiplied, the time of free churches has arisen, and the divisions in Christianity now number in the tens of thousands.

John 17:20-23, however, still says the same thing it always did.

Is unity even possible? If so, what is the standard? Is there any guidance given in the Scriptures for unity? Or will we forever be found dividing over how many angels can dance on the head of a pin?

The Source of Unity

Everything that I'm about to say in this chapter is based on the premise that unity comes from the Gospel and from the Spirit of God. This chapter is not about how to create unity. Those who have received the Gospel and thus received the Spirit already have a unity no matter how humans behave in this present world.

How, though, do we live out that unity.

> Be diligent to maintain the unity of the Spirit in the bonds of peace. (Eph. 4:3)

---

[588] "Nominal" means "in name only."
[589] *History of the Christian Church.* Vol. III, Section1.

Unity is divine. It is our job to *maintain* the unity that is forged in heaven by the love of God shed abroad in our spirits (Rom. 5:5), not to create it; something we cannot do even if we try.

We can, however, destroy the unity God has commanded us to maintain by building some other foundation for unity than what God has built.

Modern Foundations

Our whole modern Christian system is based on what we call doctrine.

It is not what the Scriptures call doctrine. The Scriptures refer to our doctrines with words like *zetesis*, topics of debate, and *logomachia*, word battles. Another word the Scripture would use is *paradiatribe*, which means, roughly, "a waste of time."

All three words are found in 1 Timothy 6:3-5, where Paul refers to those who argue about such things as having a "neurotic obsession" with disputes.

I make such an accusation because most of what modern Christians divide over is, for all practical purposes, worthless. I read a biography once of a man who started a missions organization, then later switched his eschatological view from a pre-tribulation rapture to a post-tribulation rapture. The missions organization then forced their founder to resign over a doctrine that has no practical application whatsoever.

Can you imagine those Christians trying to explain their purposeful choice to destroy the unity Jesus prayed for among his disciples to, for example, Blandina, a young barbarian of the Gauls who had tasted of the unity that comes from the one Spirit alone?

> We all trembled. [Blandina's] earthly mistress, who was also one of the martyrs, was afraid that [Blandina] would be unable to make a bold confession because her body was so weak.
>
> But Blandina was filled with so much power that she was not only delivered, but she was lifted far above the ones that were torturing her from morning until evening.

They tried every method of torture in turn until they acknowledged that they were conquered. They could do nothing more to her.

They were astonished at her endurance. Her entire body was mangled and broken. They testified that just one of these tortures was enough to destroy life, much more so many and so intense sufferings.[590]

The church in Lyons told of the torture of Blandina and the martyrdom of many others in a letter they composed around AD 180.

What would the church in Lyons say to a divisive discussion over the pre-tribulation rapture?

We all know what they would say. *"Tribulation? What tribulation are you speaking of? We are already in tribulation, my friend, and you had better prepare for it now, lest you deny the Lord of all in weakness and he deny you when you appear before his Father and ours."*

Ancient Foundations

To the apostles, doctrine was eminently practical.

Have you ever looked up "sound doctrine" in the Scriptures? It's a surprising study.

It's in the Bible four times, all of them in the pastoral epistles. Titus 2:1-10 is the clearest of the four references. It provides a fascinating list of sound doctrines. Perhaps as you peruse the list you can ask yourself whether they are on the statement of faith of any church you know.

- Older men should be temperate, honorable, and self-controlled. They should have a healthy faith, love, and patience.

---

[590] Eusebius. *Ecclesiastical History.* V:1.

- Older women should live like holy people. They should avoid slander and a lot of wine, and they should teach good things.
- Older women should train the younger women ...
  - to love their husbands
  - to love their children
  - to be self-controlled
  - to be pure
  - to keep house
  - to be good
  - to be submissive to their own husbands
- Titus, a young man himself, should train the younger men in self-control
- Titus should ...
  - be an example of good works
  - teach with integrity, respectably, and with sincerity
  - speak wholesomely, so that no one will have anything negative to say about his character
- Servants should submit to their own masters, please them in everything, and not talk back. They should not pilfer, but adorn the doctrine of God with good works.

Paul then adds a comment about salvation by grace. He says that the grace that brings salvation teaches us to deny irreverence and worldly desires. It also teaches to live self-controlled, just, and godly lives in this world. It teaches us to watch for the return of our great God and Savior Jesus Christ.[591]

Finally, Paul tells us that Jesus died to purify a people for himself who are zealous for good works.

That's Paul's idea of sound doctrine. Do we agree with him?

---

[591] Titus 2:13 is one of those passages that call Jesus God when the Father is not also being referred to. See Chapter 15.

Just in case you wonder if Titus 2 is some kind of aberration, let's do a quick review of the other three occurrences of "sound doctrine" in the New Testament.

- In 1 Timothy 1:10, Paul gives us examples of the opposite of sound doctrine. These include: disobeying laws, unruliness, irreverence, sinning in general, unholiness, crudeness, murdering your father, murdering your mother, murdering anyone else, sexual immorality (heterosexual), homosexuality, slave trading, lying, and perjury.

- In 2 Timothy 4:3, "sound doctrine" is not defined, but those who won't listen to sound doctrine are said to be people who pick teachers because they're driven by their lusts. The nearest context is a statement that the Scriptures are given to thoroughly equip the man of God for every good work.

- In Titus 1:9 Paul says bishops (or elders, which are the same thing to Paul[592]) are supposed to be able to use sound doctrine to silence those who speak against them. These opponents are said to be unruly and to talk about useless things. Paul describes them and those who listen to them as liars, dangerous animals, and lazy gluttons. He then makes a comment about those who "profess to know God, but in works they deny him."

It seems that Titus 2 is not an aberration. The content of sound doctrine is amazingly consistent.

In 1 Timothy 6:3-6, Paul talks about those who won't listen to "healthy words," which you now probably realize are words that would restrain us from bad behavior and cause us to live in such a way as to please God and cause the Gospel to be honored. People who won't listen to such words are described as having a neurotic obsession with arguing.

We might want to look at what we call sound doctrine and ask ourselves whether we have a neurotic obsession with arguing.

---

[592] See Appendix L.

AD 177:

> Among us you will find uneducated persons, craftsmen, and old women, who, if they are unable in words to prove the benefit of our doctrine, yet by their deeds exhibit the benefit arising from their persuasion of its truth. They do not rehearse speeches, but exhibit good works; when struck, they do not strike again; when robbed, they do not go to law; they give to those that ask of them, and love their neighbors as themselves.[593]

AD 160 – 230:

> We, on the other hand, who do not carry our wisdom in our clothes, but in our minds, don't speak great things; we live them.[594]

c. AD 210:

> It is mainly the deeds of a love so noble that lead many to label us. "See," they say, "How they love one another!" For they themselves are animated by mutual hatred. "How they are ready even to die for one another!" For they themselves will sooner put to death. ... The family possessions, which generally destroy brotherhood among you, create fraternal bonds among us. One in mind and soul, we do not hesitate to share our earthly goods with one another. All things are common among us but our wives.[595]

A Standard for Unity

It is true that unity cannot exist among *everyone* that names the name of Christ. Jesus warned repeatedly of counterfeits and false prophets. Paul warned that the church's own elders would draw disciples away to themselves (Acts 20:30). Wicked men

---

[593] Athenagoras. *A Plea for the Christians.* 11.

[594] Minucius Felix. *The Octavius.* 38.

[595] Tertullian. *Apology.* 39.

must be put out from among us (1 Cor. 5:13), and opinionated men must be rejected (Tit. 3:10) and avoided (Rom. 16:17-18).

Nonetheless, there is a standard that the Scriptures and the church have set, and unity can be maintained within the boundaries of that standard if we are willing. Today, however, few understand the critical importance of unity, and as a result little effort is devoted to providing a foundation for that unity.

Paul helps us understand that standard by declaring exactly what the foundation doctrines are:

> The foundation of God stands firm, having this inscription: "The Lord knows those that are his," and, "Let those who name the name of Christ depart from iniquity." (2 Tim. 2:19

Notice how simple the foundation of God is to the apostle Paul! Notice what is of primary importance to him.

Admittedly, there are theological issues that are declared in the Scriptures to be important. For example, those that deny that Jesus has come in the flesh are said to be antichrists (1 Jn. 4:3 with 2:22-23).

It is of note, however, that in the 300 years between the resurrection of Christ and the Council of Nicea, the church had found only a paragraph's worth of essential theology, summed up in the Nicene Creed.

I am prone to telling modern Christians that behavior is more important than belief. This is for three reasons:

- The validity of teaching, according to Jesus, is established by the fruit it produces. (Matt. 7:16-21)

- When Paul refers to sound doctrine, he is almost always referring to moral teachings, not theological ones.

- When good, godly Christians are united, they have repeated promises that God will teach them and keep them from error. (Eph. 4:13-16; 1 Tim. 3:15; 1 Jn. 2:26-27)

We have already addressed the first two points thoroughly enough in this chapter.

So let's look at the third.

The Unity of the Spirit Leads to the Unity of the Faith

Paul makes a couple of interesting, and I believe critically important, statements in Ephesians chapter four.

- Be diligent to maintain the unity of the Spirit.
- Until we all come to the unity of the faith.

Those two statements are separated by ten verses (Eph. 4:3,13), but I think it's legitimate to put them together.

The second of those statements is the result of a process. That process, described in Ephesians 4:11-12, goes like this:

Certain gifted Christians in the church—apostles, prophets, evangelists, shepherds, and teachers—train the saints, and the saints, once trained, do the work of service and build up the body of Christ.

They do that until we all *come to* the unity of the faith.

The words "come to" indicate a process. We don't begin at the unity of the faith. We begin at the unity of the Spirit, a unity based on a combined obedience to the Gospel.

The apostles were given a commission. We all know that commission, and we call it *The Great Commission*. That commission was to go into the whole world, disciple all nations, baptize those disciples, and teach them to obey everything Jesus commanded (Matt. 28:19-20).

Modern Christians are not without some knowledge. Many churches realize and teach that Jesus did not just tell the apostles to "teach" all nations. The Greek word is *matheteuo*, and it means "disciple." The apostles were to *disciple* all nations, and Jesus tells them exactly how to do it: Baptize them, the initiation rite of the church, and teach them to obey everything he commanded.

Simple. And very similar to Paul's description of the foundation of God.

Teaching them to obey is critical. Disobedience is foolish and destructive, while obedience will allow a Christian to weather every storm that comes his way.

Jesus made the issue of obedience clear over and over again. The first sermon recorded in Matthew is full of Jesus' commands. It is a short but remarkably comprehensive essay on how we are to live. At the end, he makes it very clear what he expects us to do with his sermon.

> Whoever listens to these sayings of mine and does them, I will compare him to a wise man who built his house on a rock. The rain came down, the floods came, and the winds blew and beat upon that house, but it did not fall because it was built on a rock. But everyone that hears these sayings of mine and does not do them shall be compared to a foolish man who built his house on the sand. The rain came down, the floods came, and the winds blew and beat upon that house, and it fell; and its fall was great. (Matt. 7:24-27)

Obedience was everything to Jesus. Shortly before he concluded with that challenge to *do* what he said and not just *hear* what he said, he told the people, "Not everyone who says 'Lord, Lord' to me will enter the kingdom of heaven, but only those who do the will of my father in heaven" (Matt. 7:21)

George MacDonald once said, "The one great heresy of the church is to teach something other than obedience as faith."

Paul once described his Gospel in this way:

> I was not disobedient to the heavenly vision, but announced first to those of Damascus, at Jerusalem, throughout all the coasts of Judea, and to the Gentiles that they should repent, turn to God, and do works suitable to repentance. (Acts 26:20)

Yes, Paul, the great apostle of faith, says that his Gospel could be summed up as announcement to repent, turn to God, and do works suitable to repentance.

Because my early days as a Christian were spent in "faith only" churches, I feel obliged to pause here and provide a little help for those who have been threatened with eternal damnation, not to mention an immediate cold shoulder, should they ever question the "don't-add-to-faith" theology that was developed and expanded over the last 500 years.

> [Jesus] became the author of eternal salvation to those that *obey* him. (Heb. 5:9. Emphasis mine.)

Faith Alone

Often when I start teaching the things I'm teaching in this chapter, someone will say, "Aren't you teaching works?"

Well, of course I am. Didn't James say, "A man is justified by works and not by faith only"? (Jam. 2:24). Didn't Paul say that Timothy should "affirm constantly" that those who believe in God should "be careful to maintain good works"? (Tit. 3:8).

There are two sorts of people that the Scriptures address. In Romans, Paul addresses people that are hoping that if they perform certain works, such as circumcision and Sabbath-keeping, then they would be justified by God. Paul tells such people that faith, not works, is the route to justification.

You may notice, if you are willing to take the time to look, that Paul never tells them that faith is the route to heaven. No, like his Master Jesus, Paul told his hearers that if they expected to go to heaven, they would actually have to obey the Gospel.

- God ... will recompense everyone according to his deeds. To those who, by patiently continuing to good, seek after glory, honor, and immortality, [he will repay] eternal life. But to those who honor themselves and disobey the truth but obey unrighteousness, [he will repay] indignation and wrath. (Rom. 2:5-7)

- Do you not know that the unrighteous will not inherit the kingdom of heaven? Do not be deceived. (1 Cor. 6:9)

- Do not be deceived; God is not mocked. Whatever one sows, that will he also reap. He that sows to his flesh will reap corruption from the flesh, but he that sows to the Spirit will reap everlasting life from the Spirit. Let us not grow weary in doing good, for in due season we will reap if we do not grow weary. (Gal. 6:7-9)

James addresses a different audience than Paul does in Romans. He is addressing people who are claiming to have faith but who have no interest in obedience. They are the very people Jesus spoke of, who say, "Lord, Lord," but who do not do the will of our Father in heaven.

To such people James said—and we, too, need to say—"A man will be justified by works and not by faith only."

Peter may put works in the clearest context of all:

> Giving all diligence, add to your faith, virtue; and to virtue, knowledge; and to knowledge, self-control; and to self-control, endurance; and to endurance, godliness; and to godliness, brotherly love; and to brotherly love, agape.[596] For if these things are in you and increasing, they will make you neither barren nor unfruitful in the knowledge of our Lord Jesus Christ.

> But he that lacks these things is blind, sees dimly, and has forgotten that he was purified of his former sins. Therefore, all the more, brothers, be diligent to make your calling and election certain because if you do these things you will never stumble. In this way an entrance shall be richly provided to you into the everlasting kingdom of our Lord and Savior Jesus Christ. (2 Pet. 1:5-11)

Faith *in What* Alone?

The majority of our "faith alone" confusion has its root in one problem:

In what are having faith alone?

The apostles consistently preached faith in a person: the only-begotten Son of God come to earth as a man, Jesus Christ. We, however, consistently preach faith in a fact: that Jesus, the God-man, died on a cross for our sins.

It is not enough to believe that Jesus died for your sins. That's just a fact. That happened whether you believe it or not, and it accomplishes nothing for God that you agree it's true. The demons agree it's true, and they tremble (Jam. 2:19).

---

[596] I have left *agape* untranslated here because there is more than one Greek word for love in this sentence and most Christians recognize *agape* as the love we are commanded to have in the New Testament. The other word is *philadelphia*, which most Americans recognize as the Greek word for "brotherly love."

The Gospel that the apostles preached calls you to believe in Jesus, not any particular thing he did.

Once we understand this, our confusion vanishes. Everyone, even in the United States with all our "faith alone" confusion, knows that you can't claim to believe a person if you don't at least try to do what he says. You can't say, "I believe in Jesus," but then say, when you're presented with some difficult thing that he taught, "I think that's too extreme" or "I don't think we have to do that." That would mean you didn't really believe in him!

Here's a key scriptural fact for you to wrestle with. All the New Testament letters are written to Christians. Acts, on the other hand, has passages where the apostles were talking to non-Christians.

And in the Acts of the Apostles, no apostle ever told a lost person that Jesus died for their sins.

The apostles do tell the lost that Jesus died. They had to, since they were appointed as witnesses of the resurrection. You can't very well testify to a resurrection of you don't testify to a death to be resurrected from.

But they never told a lost person why Jesus died. Never. Not once.

Feel free to go look and see if I'm telling you the truth.[597]

I want to suggest that there's a reason for that. The reason is, lost people don't need to know why Jesus died in order to be saved. They need to believe in Jesus, not the atonement. The apostles told their disciples about the atonement after they were saved.

Taught of God

It is written in the prophets, "They shall all be taught by God" [*Is. 54:13*]. Everyone, therefore, that has heard and has learned from the Father comes to me. —Jesus (Jn. 6:45)

---

[597] Also see my booklet *The Apostles' Gospel*, which is available on Amazon in paper or electronic form.

Jesus prayed for his disciples to be one (Jn. 17:20-23). His disciples are those who have been baptized and taught to obey everything he commanded (Matt. 28:19-20). Paul said the foundation of God is that the Lord knows those who are his and that those who name the name of Christ would depart from iniquity (2 Tim. 2:19).

We need to add only one verse to get to the point I have been hoping to make for several pages now. It is:

> [Jesus Christ] gave himself for us so that he might redeem us from all lawlessness and purify for himself his own special people, zealous for good works. (Tit. 2:13-14)

Jesus wants one united people, zealous for good works. When he has that, he can take care of everything from there.

The promises that are made to the people of God are absolutely incredible.

God has promised to teach his people. He has promised to lead them into everything that they need, and he has promised that his leading will be absolutely reliable: "true, and not a lie" (1 Jn. 2:27).

He says it first in Ephesians four:

> And he gave some to be apostles, some prophets, some evangelists, and some shepherds and teachers to equip the saints for the work of service for the building up of the body of Christ until we all come to the unity of the faith and the knowledge of the Son of God, to a perfect man, and measure up to the full stature of Christ.
>
> Then we will no longer be children, tossed here and there and driven by every wind of teaching, by the hustling of men skilled in crafty deception. Instead, speaking the truth in love, we can grow up into him who is the head, that is, Christ. The whole body—properly joined, and united by what every joint supplies, each part having its own proper role—causes the growth of the body, which builds itself up in love. (Eph. 4:11-16)

What an incredibly promise! If we will do what Jesus teaches—obey everything he teaches and do it together—then as we speak to each other in love and honesty, *we will be protected from deception, even from men who are as skilled at deceiving us as a street hustler.*

This is why Paul is telling us that if we will *be diligent* to maintain the unity of the Spirit, then, if we will give God the time to work in us together, he will bring us, eventually, to the unity of the faith.

The apostle John tells us almost exactly the same thing:

> I have written these things to you about those who are trying to seduce you. But the Anointing [Greek is *chrisma*, a word closely related to Christ] which you have received from him remains in you, and you do not need anyone to teach you. That anointing teaches you everything, and it is the truth and no lie. Just as it has taught you, you will remain in him. (1 Jn. 2:26-27)

The first thing to point out here is that all these yous are plural. There is not a singular you in the whole bunch. This is not a verse for mavericks who think they have special revelation from God. The Scriptures has a different promise for loners:

> Exhort one another every day ... so that none of you are hardened by the deceitfulness of sin. (Heb. 3:13)

Proverbs has something similar to say about mavericks:

> He who separates himself seeks his own desire, he quarrels against all sound wisdom. (Prov. 18:1, NASB)

But to us, together, *even when people are purposely trying to deceive us*, there is the promise that the Anointing that comes from God will be "truth and no lie."

No wonder Jesus promised, "They will all be taught of God."

For centuries the Roman Catholic Church used Paul's statement that "the church of the living God [is] the pillar and support of the truth" as justification for asking that all Christians agree to their doctrinal assertions and remain in communion with them. It doesn't take a church history professor to know the results of that. The centuries-long rule of the Roman Catholic Church is known to history as "The Dark Ages."

If you read the last chapter, then you know that the early churches, although they relied heavily upon and appealed to one another, were independent. 1 Timothy 3:15 cannot be a reference to the doctrines of some overarching hierarchy because no overarching hierarchy existed in Paul's day.

If there is any truth to the promises that Paul and John make in Ephesians 4 and 1 John 2, then we don't have to interpret 1 Timothy 3:15 at all. 1 Timothy 3:15 follows naturally from Ephesians 4 and 1 John 2. The church, together, speaking the truth in love to one another and relying upon the anointing, will be protected from deception, and they will be guided into everything by the Anointing, which will be true and not a lie.

Most Christians seem to hate it when I tell them these things. I cannot fathom why. I don't know if they simply don't believe it, or if believing it will cost them something that I don't understand.

If there's any truth to what I just said, then we ought to rejoice!

Can This Be Done?

But how will we know whether there's any truth to these things?

Jesus said, "You will know them by their fruit" (Matt. 7:20). The things the apostles taught were eminently practical. You could *see* whether there was truth in their teachings.

Paul, for example, said once:

> I am not ashamed of the Gospel because it is the power of God, for in it the righteousness of God is revealed from faith to faith. (Rom. 1:16-17)

Paul wasn't just claiming that his Gospel was the power of God. He was explaining that he was not ashamed of the Gospel because he could see that it is the power of God. He could see it because the righteousness of God was being "revealed" in those who had faith in Jesus. To the Galatians that power was manifested by the supply of the Spirit and by miracles (Gal. 3:3). To the Thessalonians it was manifested by turning them from idols to following the true and living God (1 Thess. 1:5-10).

Truly, when Paul preached and hearers believed, the world saw their good works and glorified God in heaven (Matt. 5:16[598]).

In the same way, the things I'm writing to you in this chapter are not theories I've dreamed up by reading the Bible.

Even this book is a product of living out what I've explained above. I did the historical study, and I chose the words, so this book is infused with my personality (for good or for bad).

But this book was written by a church ... or at least by a church's life.

I write this as part of a community of about 300 Christians. We started with nothing except a desire to experience what we read about in Acts:

> They devoted themselves to the apostles' teaching and fellowship, the breaking of bread, and prayers. Fear came upon every soul, and many miracles and signs were done by the apostles. All who believed were for each other and had all things in common. They sold their property and possessions and divided them among everyone as each had need.
>
> They devoted themselves every day with one purpose in the temple and breaking bread from house to house, and they ate their meals in gladness and oneness of heart. They praised God and had favor from all the people, and the Lord added to the church every day those who were being saved. (Acts 2:42-47)

We started with nothing and with hardly any people. We had only a firm conviction, based on years of experience, that we did not have the power to produce or offer what we were reading about in Acts. We were, however, willing to pursue it like we were desperate; whatever God wanted, wherever He led.

That was 20 years ago. By now, we have grown used to hearing the words, "This is how everyone ought to live!"

---

[598] Another verse in which all the yous are plural.

We have traveled all over the world. God has even been kind enough to let us plant a church in Kenya that is now beginning to help other churches learn the Way of our Savior: love in obedience to all he commanded us. We've been able to offer help to several missionaries, and we're finally getting a chance to travel around the United States preaching repentance toward God, faith toward our Lord Jesus Christ, and helping Christians learn how to quit destroying the unity God sends them.

It works. Our message and our life create both a desire for unity and unity itself—when Christians are willing to pay the cost for embracing it. If history has anything to say at all, it's that Jesus has never been popular in institutions.

One of the things we've learned above all is that the Anointing, which is just Christ himself by his Spirit in his (local, united) church, is never going to answer all the questions we want answered. When is he going to come? That's the Father's business, not Christ's. Pre-trib, mid-trib, or post-trib? Jesus told us to be ready no matter when he comes. We all have our own "trib," because Paul warned us that it is through many tribulations that we must enter the kingdom of God (Acts 14:22).

It is not just the apostles that are eminently practical in their theology; so is the Anointing of God. He has answers for the troubles the churches are facing. Are you in a home church that's not growing? The Anointing has answers for you. Are you in an institutional church that's boring? The Anointing has answers for you.

But if you're trying to resolve the latest doctrinal controversy, you'll probably find he's not going to help you much. After all, if he shows you the correct theological position on some controversial doctrinal issue, you're just going to use it to damage the unity of the Spirit that you've been commanded to preserve with that brother who is not as enlightened as you are.

To me, nothing stands out from the Council of Nicea and the Arian Controversy more than that while bishops held possibly hundreds of councils on *homoousios* in the fourth century, there was not even one held on how to prevent Christians from beating each other to death in the streets.

Behavior is better than belief.

You don't have to tell me what you believe. Live your life, and I will tell you what you believe.

APPENDICES

Appendix A:
Glossary

Acacian

A sect of Arians begun by Acacius, the bishop who replaced Eusebius the historian in Caesarea. They espoused the term *homoian*, "similar," until they embraced the Nicene Creed under the reign of Jovian in 363.

Acolyte

In general, this word means a "devoted follower or attendant,"[599] but it's usually used of someone who assists a clergyman with religious services. By the time of the Council of Nicea, Christian gatherings were quite formal,[600] and there would have been numerous minor religious offices, such as reader at church services.

Anathema

Anathema is a difficult word to define precisely but an easy one to define generally. It means accursed or destined for destruction. I read numerous definitions and possible derivations of the word in order to come to the conclusion that it does not have a specific meaning, such as an assurance of going to hell or some such thing. The general "accursed" or destined for some unspecified destruction is about as precise as we can get.

Anathematize

To pronounce an anathema upon a person or doctrine.

---

[599] TheFreeDictionary.com

[600] Descriptions of Christian meetings in *The Apostolic Tradition of Hippolytus* from the early third century and *Apostolic Constitutions* from the Nicene time period are significantly more formal and organized than the meetings described by Justin Martyr and Tertullian between about AD 150 and 210.

Apostolic

From the apostles. The word is applied to the catholic churches regularly in early Christian writings, and it is used by the Council of Nicea regularly in its canons. It is used to distinguish those churches that were started by apostles and held to *apostolic* doctrine from heretical groups owing their origin to other sources, such as gnostic, Novatian, and Paulianist churches. It had long been an argument of 2nd and 3rd century apologists that the *apostolic* churches had maintained their unity from the beginning, a claim that I personally believe to be evidently true to anyone who researches the period.[601]

Arian

Anything having to do with Arius, the elder who was excommunicated by the church in Alexandria and whose doctrine was condemned by the Council of Nicea. Thus, there was an *Arian* controversy, an *Arian* doctrine, and those who adhered to that doctrine are often called *Arians*.

Bishop

A *bishop*, by the mid-2nd century and later, was the highest ranking church leader in a city. Each *bishop* would have a group of elders under him who handled the shepherding of the congregation.

The *bishop* of a large city might be in charge of several cities or a whole province. He would be known as a metropolitan. The Council of Nicea made the role of patriarch official, assigning authority over what appears to be at least an entire country to the *bishops* of Alexandria, Antioch, and Rome.

The *bishop* is called an "overseer" in some Bible translations, which is the literal meaning of the Greek word *epis-*

---

[601] See Chapter 15.

kopos. "Supervisor" would also be a literal translation of *episkopos.*[602]

Canon

From a Latin word meaning "rule," *canon* is primarily used today concerning the authorized books in the Bible, which vary among churches, but not by much. Protestants, and even Jehovah's Witnesses and Mormons, use a Bible of 66 books. Roman Catholics add 7 to the Protestant 66, as well as additions to Esther and Daniel. Orthodox churches have closer to 80 books in their Bible, though the canon varies among the Orthodox.

Canon is also the term given to decisions by major church councils. Thus, the Council of Nicea issued 20 canons constituting their decisions on everything except the doctrines of Arius, which were covered and condemned by the Nicene Creed.

Catechumen

A person who is being "catechized," or trained in the basics of the faith prior to baptism. By the time of the Council of Nicea it was normal for a person to spend a year or more as a *catechumen* before being baptized in order to prove their commitment to continuing in the faith.

Cathari

Cathari means purists, and it was a designation of Novatianist churches, which descended from a church split caused by Novatian in Rome in AD 251.[603]

Catholic

Catholic, to the early churches, meant something similar to "universal." The term was interchangeable with "apostol-

---

[602] A history of the terms bishop, elder, and priest can be found in Appendix C.
[603] See Novatianist below.

ic" churches, and it was used to distinguish those churches that had remained in fellowship with each other from those that had deviated, divided, or been expelled. Today, when capitalized, it means those churches that recognize the bishop of Rome as the representative of Christ on the earth and the leader of the church universal. It had no such significance in the 4th century.

Chorepiscopus

A rural bishop that was subject to the bishop of a nearby city.

Confessor

A person who suffered during persecution without denying Christ. These were held in high honor in the early churches, as they are today.

Consubstantiality

"One in substance." Consubstantiality translates the term *homoousios*, the source of so much controversy during the 4th century.

Deacon

Deacon comes from the Greek word *diakonos*, which means servant. "Deacon" is *diakonos* untranslated. The word *diakonos* is used over 30 times in the New Testament, and the only place it is rendered *deacon* is in the list of qualifications given in 1 Timothy 3.

Dialectics

A method of argument developed by Greek philosophers, but popular in the east as well, that advocates a back and forth presentation of ideas working toward agreement, which makes it a little different than typical debate.

Edict of Milan

Edict issued in 313 by co-emperors Constantine and Lucinius restoring privileges and property to Christian churches and leaders that were taken during the Great Persecution. The Edict of Toleration ended the persecution two years earlier.

Edict of Toleration

Edict issued in 311 by Galerius along with co-emperors Constantine and Lucinius officially ending the Great Persecution.

Elder

When discussing fourth-century churches, it is common to refer to the *elder* as a presbyter, thus leaving the Greek word *presbuteros* untranslated. *Presbuteros* literally means *elder*, though, and it is translated that way in most Bibles. In the century before the Council of Nicea *elders* began to be called priests, though this terminology makes war on the Biblical understanding of the church as a kingdom of priests and gets in the way of Jesus Christ's role as the one Mediator between God and man. In the 4th century, each city or town would have multiple *elders*, and one bishop would be over them all.[604]

Eucharist

From a Greek word meaning "thanksgiving," *Eucharist* is the bread and wine of the communion meal or Lord's Supper.

Eunomian

A follower of Eunomius, an Arian theologian who was at one time bishop of Antioch. The *Eunomians*, with the Nicene party, the main Arian party, and the Macedonians were allowed to present arguments for their own opinion to Theodosius in 383 when he finally put the Arian Controversy to rest. The *Eunomians* were the most extreme Ar-

---

[604] A history of the terms bishop, elder, and priest can be found in Appendix C.

ian party, declaring that the Son was "unlike" (*anomoian*) the Father.

Extant

A writing is *extant* if it is still available today, even if all we have are much later copies. Many ancient writings are completely lost, and we don't know what they say except perhaps for quotes by other ancients. If the text, or most of the text, is known today, then the writing is *extant*.

Great Persecution

Empire-wide persecution from AD 303 to 311, instituted by the emperor Diocletian at the instigation of Galerius, then general of the Roman army. In 311, Galerius, who had become emperor, ended the persecution with the Edict of Toleration, which was additionally signed by his co-emperors Constantine and Licinius. Galerius died in 311, and Constantine and Licinius issued the Edict of Milan in 313, which legalized Christianity and restored privileges and property to Christian churches and their leaders.

Gnostics

A widely varying set of groups that believed that salvation came through the knowledge (Gr. *gnosis*) of certain mysteries. In general, they believed that all material things were created by an inferior god (the God of the Hebrews) and that the true God had sent certain spiritual beings, called aeons, to bring the truth of the spiritual world to man. Believing all of the physical creation to be outside the true God's will, they denied that Christ came in the flesh, died, or resurrected physically.

Hearers

Those who came to Christian worship services in order to determine whether they wanted to be Christians. In fourth-century churches, these would sit in an area by themselves, as would the catechumens (those being trained in the basics of the faith) and the prostrators (those temporarily banned from communion for some sin).

Heresy

In the Bible and in early Christian literature, a *heresy* is both a faction within a religion and a teaching that produces such a faction. Thus, the Pharisees, Sadducees, and the Christian "Way" are all referred to by the Greek word *hairesis* in the Book of Acts (Acts 5:17; 15:5; 24:5). The followers of Arius and of Eusebius of Nicomedia taught *heresy* because they said that the Son was created from nothing, and they were members of a *heresy* because their churches separated from the catholic churches.

Homoiousios

Homoiousios, "similar substance," is not to be confused with *homoousios*, "same substance." The difference in Greek is just one iota (ι), but the difference theologically is vast. Many battles, both verbal and physical, were fought over the two terms.

Homoousios

"Same substance" or "same essence." This word was added to the rule of faith of the church in Caesarea in order to produce the Nicene Creed. *Homoousios* proposed that the Son of God was composed of the same substance as God, thus making him truly divine and eternal, for the divine substance, being uncreated, has always existed and always will exist. *Homoousios* was a controversial term because it did not come from Scripture and thus was a questionable addition to an official creed of the Church.

Impious

Not pious.

Lector

Another name for a reader, an ordained position that existed at least as early as the third century and still exists today in Roman Catholic and Orthodox churches.

LXX

Short term for the Septuagint, the Greek translation of the Hebrew Scriptures that was the Old Testament of the early churches in the Roman empire. It was called the *LXX* because it was believed to have been translated by seventy Jewish scholars.

Macedonian

A sect begun by Macedonius, bishop of Constantinople. *Macedonians* opposed the Nicene Creed by promulgating the term *homoiousios*, just one iota different from *homoousios*. They sent 36 bishops to the Council of Constantinople in 381 but lost many of their members when they would not embrace the historic faith under Theodosius.

Melitians

Followers of Melitius, a pre-Nicene bishop of Lycopolis in Egypt. Melitius, like Novatian and the Novatianists, did not want to receive Christians who lapsed during persecution then repented later. He began appointing bishops who agreed with him without the approval of the bishop of Alexandria. Canon 6 of Nicea emphasized the authority of the bishop of Alexandria, and the council specifically condemned Melitius in a letter to the church at Alexandria.[605]

Metropolitan

The bishop of a large city who ruled over smaller cities and towns in the surrounding area.

Modalism

The belief that God acts in various "modes," so that the Father, Son, and Holy Spirit are not separate persons of the Godhead, but instead various roles filled by the one God,

---

[605] The letter to the church in Alexandria can be found in Appendix H.

much as one actor might play three roles in the same play. Modern modalists like to say God is "the Father in creation, the Son in redemption, and the Holy Spirit in the church."

Modalism was a persistent heresy in the Pre-Nicene church, and Tertullian even says, around AD 200, that it was the majority belief of "the simple" in the church.[606]

Monarchianism

Another name for modalism, the belief that God is just one person acting in three "modes." *Monarchianism* argues that God is only one person because there can be only one "monarchy" or rule of God. Tertullian answers this effectively in Against Praxeas, arguing that the unique, singular, and shared divinity of the Father and the Son does not in any way destroy the divine Monarchy.

Novatianist

Novatianist churches descended from a church split in Rome in AD 251. Novatian, a leading elder, was passed over for bishop and Cornelius was selected instead. Novatian engineered a separate ordination, which was not recognized by any surrounding churches, and formed his own congregation. They became known as *Cathari*, or "purists," because they refused to admit Christians who lapsed during persecution then repented afterwards. Once persecution ended in the 4th century, the *Novatianist* churches slowly merged back into the catholic churches. They are addressed in Canon 8 of Nicea.

Overseer

A bishop. *Overseer* (or "supervisor") is a more accurate way of translating the Greek *episkopos*.[607]

---

[606] *Against Praxeas.* 3.

[607] A history of the terms bishop, elder, and priest can be found in Appendix C.

Patriarch

A *patriarch* is a bishop given authority over extremely large areas, usually at least a country. Since the time of the Council of Nicea certain bishops have been specifically given this designation. The Roman Catholic Church does not use this term, but the Eastern Orthodox Churches and Orthodox churches that have split from them use it even of the bishop of Rome. The list of patriarchs has grown significantly longer since the 4th century, but the primary patriarchs are the bishops of Constantinople (now Istanbul), Antioch, and Moscow. The patriarchs in Alexandria and Rome are separated from the Eastern Orthodox Churches and are both known as popes to the churches under their rule.

Paulianist

Paulianists were people who held to the doctrines of Paul of Samosata, a bishop of Antioch from AD 260 (or so) to AD 268. He was deposed by the Council of Arles for denying the divinity of Christ. He claimed Jesus was just a man who received the power of the impersonal *Logos* at his birth, then grew in power with God throughout his life.

Pious

"Having or exhibiting religious reverence; earnestly compliant in the observance of religion; devout."[608] I have often replaced this word with "godly" when updating the vocabulary of the translators of the *Ante-Nicene Fathers* and *Nicene and Post-Nicene Fathers* series.

---

[608] TheFreeDictionary.com

Presbyter

A *presbyter* is an elder. *Presbyter* is just a way of leaving the Greek word for elder, *presbuteros*, untranslated. See elder above for more information.

Primary Sources

Testimony from an eyewitness or participant. A list of *primary sources* for the Council of Nicea is given in chapter two. Secondary sources are reports from someone who has read or seen the *primary sources*. Many modern history books are not even secondary sources, but tertiary or even further down the line, based on other histories rather than direct research.

Professor

A person who professes to be a Christian. In the Nicene era such a person would have to have been baptized, as no one was considered a Christian who was not baptized. Even those who had professed faith, but were awaiting baptism, were known as catechumens, not *professors*. No judgment is implied by the term *professor*, as though a person only professed but was not a Christian; nonetheless, the term is usually used in exhortation, that those who profess Christ ought to live as he lived.

Prostrators

Those who were under penance and banned from communion for some sin. In the larger churches of the fourth century, they would sit in a group, as would the catechumens (those being instructed in the faith prior to baptism) and hearers (those attending services to decide whether to become a Christian).

Reader

An office in liturgical churches. A *reader* must be ordained to the position, and today it is considered one step before deacon. The position existed as early as the third century for sure, and it's possible that the early Christian sermon known as *2 Clement* contains a reference to a *reader*.[609] The position is also known as "lector."

Rule of Faith

Before Nicea, each church had a *rule of faith* that was pronounced at baptism and required to be believed by all church members. The *rule of faith* of the church at Caesarea[610] became the basis for the Nicene Creed. Most early rules of faith—several are found in pre-Nicene writings—are quite similar to the Nicene Creed.[611]

Sabellianism

Another name for the persistent heresy of modalism, the belief that God is just one person acting in three "modes," the Father, Son, and Holy Spirit. Sabellianism is named after Sabellius, an early third-century modalist.

Secondary Source

A history or testimony given by someone referencing primary sources, which are the testimonies of eyewitnesses or participants. Tertiary sources are histories based on secondary sources.

See

The area of a bishop's jurisdiction. Note that the word is see and not "sea." *See* is related to overseer, the literal meaning of the Greek word *episkopos*.

Septuagint

The Greek translation of the Hebrew Scriptures that was the Old Testament of the early churches in the Roman

---

[609] *2 Clement*. 19.

[610] Appendix K.

[611] Some examples of early rules of faith can be found at my web site, *Christian History for Everyman*. <http://www.christian-history.org/rule-of-faith.html>.

empire. It was so named because it was believed to have been translated by 70 Jewish scholars in Alexandria. Legend had it that King Ptolemy II of Egypt had put the 70 scholars in 70 separate rooms, and each had produced a translation that corresponded word for word with all the others. There is no reason to suppose this legend is true.

Subordinationism

The belief that the Father is intrinsically greater than the Son, even prior to the incarnation. This was the orthodox Pre-Nicene position, as espoused by every Pre-Nicene writer who wrote extensively on the Trinity. To pre-Nicene writers, the Father is greater than the Son because God is greater than his *Logos*.[612]

Substance

Substance, of course, is capable of many meanings, but at the Council of Nicea the issue was the substance of God; the "material," if you will excuse the term, that God is made of. The question before the council as part of the Arian Controversy was whether the Son of God was of the same divine substance as the Father. If he was created from nothing, as Arius proposed, then he could not be of the Father's substance, but was composed of matter—even in his divine person—as all other creatures are. *Homoousios* is explained fully in Chapter 15.

Suffragan

An assistant bishop who would serve under an important bishop such as a metropolitan.

---

[612] Chapter 15 deals extensively with subordinationism.

Synod

1. A council or an assembly of church officials or churches; an ecclesiastical council. 2. A council or assembly.[613]

Viaticum

From a Latin word meaning "food for the journey," this is the Eucharist when it is given to a dying person as a last rite. Notes in *The Nicene and Post-Nicene Fathers*[614] concerning Canon 13 of the Council of Nicea say that viaticum can also refer to any other ecclesiastical service done as a last rite, but it normally concerns the Eucharist.

Zoroastrianism

A monotheistic, non-Christian religion emphasizing good works and the battle between good and evil.

---

[613] TheFreeDictionary.com
[614] Series II, Vol. XIV.

Appendix B:

The Timeline of the Council of Nicea

The Apostolic and Pre-Nicene Era

- AD 29-33: Jesus is crucified, rises again, and the church begins at Pentecost (see *Acts* in the Bible).
- AD 33-100: Apostolic era; independent churches spread throughout the Roman empire and even outside of it.
- c. AD 100: John is the last apostle to die.
- AD 100-303: The church expands throughout and outside the Roman empire, suffering intermittent persecution that only fuels even more growth. As churches grow, they become more organized, and clergy become more important and more powerful.

The Great Persecution and the Rise of Constantine to Power

- AD 303-311: Led primarily by Galerius, the two Augusti and two Caesars of the Roman empire conduct an empire-wide persecution known as the Great Persecution.
- AD 311: Galerius signs the Edict of Toleration, ending the persecution, and he admits it was a failure.
- AD 311: Galerius dies from a terrible disease that the Christians attribute to the judgment of God.
- AD 312: Constantine has a vision of a Christian symbol similar to a cross, inscribes the symbol on the shields of his soldiers, and defeats Maxentius to unite the western empire.
- AD 313: Constantine and Licinius issue the Edict of Milan, legalizing Christianity and restoring property to churches.

The Events Leading to the Council of Nicea

- AD 268 – AD 312: Lucian, an elder in Antioch, runs a theological school that trained all the early leaders of Arianism. He was out of fellowship for at least 16 years, and perhaps more, but he died a martyr in communion with the church in 312.

- AD 318: Arius, an elder of the church in Alexandria, tells Alexander, his bishop, that the Son did not exist before his generation by God in the beginning.

- AD 321: Arius is excommunicated by a council of over 100 bishops and moves to Nicomedia, where he is welcomed by the bishop, Eusebius.

- AD 321 – 325: Arius and Eusebius teach their doctrine to sailors, merchants, and children and write letters to other bishops trying to spread Arian doctrine.

- AD 324: Constantine defeats and then executes Licinius, uniting the entire Roman empire under his rule.

- AD 325: Constantine offers transportation to every bishop in the empire to come to the resort city of Nicea for a council to resolve the Arian controversy.

The Council of Nicea and Its Aftermath

- 325: The Council of Nicea. Arius is banished along with Theonas and Secundus.

- 325-326: Eusebius of Nicomedia and Theognis of Nicea are banished (probably).

- 328: Eusebius and Theognis write a letter of recantation, which states that Arius has been received back from exile as well. Constantine restores them to their sees.[615]

---

[615] Area of a bishop's oversight.

- 328-335: Constantine orders the church in Alexandria to talk with Arius; Athanasius refuses.

- 335: The Council of Tyre, led by Eusebius of Nicomedia and Theognis of Nicea, attempts to convict Athanasius of various crimes, but fails. Constantine calls the major bishops to Constantinople, then expels Athanasius for preventing the shipment of grain from Alexandria to Constantinople. Most historians, even ancient ones, agree that Athanasius is really being banished for refusing to receive Arius.

- 336: A council in Jerusalem restores Arius to communion, but he dies on the way to the church in Constantinople for his first communion after his banishment. Supporters say he was poisoned; opponents say he was judged by God.

- 337: Constantine is baptized by Eusebius of Nicomedia, dies several days later, and leaves the empire to his 3 sons: Constantine II, Constans, and Constantius. Constantine II sends Athanasius back to Alexandria.

- 337-361: Constantius, emperor in the east, embraces Arianism, installs Arian bishops in many cities of the east, and there is general pandemonium.

- 339: Eusebius of Caesarea, the historian, dies.

- 341: Constantius brings Eusebius from Nicomedia to Constantinople. Eusebius wastes no time in calling a council in Antioch to affirm a new creed and expel Athanasius from Alexandria. The creed is rejected by western bishops.

- 343: A council is called in Sardica to reconcile east and west. A controversy over Paul and Athanasius, who were ejected from their sees in Constantinople and Alexandria, causes the eastern bishops to hold their own council in Philippopolis. Sardica confirms *homoousios*, Philippopolis rejects it, and east and west are completely divided; Arian in the east, Nicene in the west.

- 347-348: Constans threatens Constantius with civil war if he does not reinstall Paul and Athanasius as bishops of Constantinople and Alexandria, respectively. At the gracious advice of important eastern bishops, Constantius agrees and orders those cities to support them.

- c. 348: Athanasius calls a council in Jerusalem, and two leading Arian bishops, Ursacius and Valens, temporarily embrace the Nicene Creed. Athanasius then alienates most eastern bishops and Constantius by appointing elders in other bishops' jurisdiction on his way back to Alexandria.

- 350: Magnentius, with very unfortunate timing, kills Constans in an uprising and gains control of Gaul and Italy. With Constans, a supporter of Nicea, dead, Arian bishops bring new charges against Athanasius. Constantius orders both Athanasius and Paul killed. Paul is strangled, but Athanasius escapes and remains bishop until 356.

- 350-361: Constantius overthrows Magnentius, then tries to spread Arianism in the west. He removes bishops in the west as well as in the east, replacing them with bishops espousing Arian opinions.

- 356: Liberius, bishop of Rome, is banished, and Athanasius is forced to flee Alexandria for his life.

- 358: Liberius is restored to his position after signing a creed with Arian sentiments under duress.

- 359: The Council of Ariminum is held in the west, and the Council of Seleucia in the east. Both councils approve an Arian creed, but numerous bishops, especially in the west, object. Jerome later mourns that at this point, "The world groaned and was astonished to find itself Arian."[616]

- 361: Constantius dies, and Julian the Apostate becomes emperor in the east. He embraces paganism and recalls all the bishops Constantius banished, perhaps hoping the Christians will battle each other into extinction. He also introduces some persecution against Christians.

---

[616] *The Dialogue Against the Luciferians.* 19.

- 363: Julian is killed in battle with the Persians, and Jovian becomes emperor. Jovian supports the Nicene Creed with wisdom and without violence, bringing rapidly growing peace to the east, but he dies of illness after only seven months. The Acacian sect of Arians embraces the Nicene Creed. They submit a letter to the bishop of Rome acknowledging their repentance and their condemnation of Arius.

- 364: Valens becomes emperor in the east, embraces Arianism, persecutes the Nicene churches, and attempts to install Arian bishops in every eastern church. Valentinian I becomes emperor in the west, and he holds to the Nicene Creed.

- 375: Barbarian Goths kill Valentinian, the emperor in the west.

- 375: Gratian, nephew of Valens, becomes emperor in the west; he is firmly Nicene.

- 375: Valens defeats the Goths, gives them mercy, and they embrace Christianity, becoming Arians. The barbarian tribes will remain Arians for at least a century.

- 378: Valens is slain in battle with the Goths.

- 378-381: Gratian recalls all banished Nicene bishops in the east, but he allows the various sects, which now include Macedonians as well as the Arians, to worship unmolested in their own churches.

- 379: Gratian appoints Theodosius as emperor in the east to replace Valens.

- 381: Theodosius calls a council in Constantinople to affirm the Nicene Creed. 150 bishops arrive, as well as 36 Macedonian bishops, whom the emperor wished to convert because they had their own large church in Antioch. The Macedonians refuse to accept the Nicene Creed and leave. The council assigned authority to the bishops of several important cities and disbanded. This insignificant council, attended by no western bishops, becomes remembered as "The Second Ecumenical Council of the Church."

- 383: Theodosius requests a defense of the faith from all four major sects proving that what they believe is the faith given by the apostles to the church. He retires alone, and after much prayer and consideration decides for the *homoousian* party. It was this event that ended the Arian Controversy and constituted the final victory for the Nicene Creed. Arianism does not disappear, but is permanently considered unorthodox and outside the catholic faith.

Appendix C:

Bishops, Elders, and Priests

Terminology in the early Christian writings can be difficult for those of us not familiar with Catholic and Orthodox ecclesiastic structure.

But perhaps it is even more difficult for those who are familiar with it! As the saying goes, there are none so blind as those who will not see. There is an emotional and doctrinal tie to the monarchial bishop among those that trace a succession of authority through that bishop. For Roman Catholics especially there is an unwillingness to see the obvious: Rome, like all of Paul and Peter's churches, was founded with no monarchial bishop.[617]

I'll explain "monarchial bishop" further down the page, though Catholics and Orthodox will already know what I mean.

We must begin with the terms "bishop" and "elder," for these are the only terms for church leaders that are found in Scripture or in the writings of the second century church. (Note that the word "pastor," used once in the New Testament of a church leader, will be addressed as part of the discussion on bishops and elders.)

"Priest," now in common use as a replacement for "elder," is discussed afterward.

Bishops and Elders

In the New Testament, bishop and elder are interchangeable terms:

> And from Miletus, [Paul] sent a message to Ephesus, calling for the **elders** of the church. When they had come to him, he said, " ... Pay attention, then, to yourselves and to the entire flock, over which the Holy Spirit has made you

---

[617] See Chapter 18.

bishops, to **shepherd** the church of God, which he has purchased with his own blood.[618]

Your translation of the New Testament may, and probably will, have "overseers" where I have inserted "bishops." Both are translations of the same Greek word, *episkopos*. "Overseer" is a much better translation, for *episkopos* comes from *epi*, meaning over, and *skopos*, meaning sight. "Supervisor" is an equivalent English word, though it descends to us from Latin, not Greek. "Bishop," however, has been in common use for so long that it is hard to imagine switching to the more accurate "overseer" or "supervisor."

Here in Acts 20, the apostle Paul tells the elders of Ephesus that they have been appointed overseers, or bishops, by the Holy Spirit and given the task of *shepherding* the church of God.

The position of elder is the only pastoral position in the New Testament. The elders are the bishops, and they are the pastors. As some have put it, the elder is the man, overseer or bishop is his office, and shepherding or pastoring is his duty.

Peter verifies Paul's usage of bishop and elder. Note the use of the word oversight here, for you now know that it is a reference to the office of bishop or *episkopos*.

> I exhort the **elders** among you, for I am also a fellow elder and a witness of the sufferings of Christ ... **Shepherd** the flock of God which is among you, **overseeing** it, not under obligation but willingly, not for selfish gain but cheerfully. Nor be lords over your area of responsibility, but be examples to the flock. And when the **Chief Shepherd** appears, you will receive a glorious crown of eternal flowers.[619]

Again, the elders are told that they have the oversight (Gr. *episkopeo*), and they are to shepherd the flock of God. Even Peter,

---

[618] Acts 20:17-18, 28
[619] 1 Peter 5:1-4

supposedly the first monarchial bishop of Rome, refers to himself as a fellow elder, not as a bishop.

A "monarchial bishop" is a bishop that rules alone (from *mo-non*, alone, and *archo*, to rule). In practice, what it means is that the elders had a head elder, and he alone held the title of bishop (or overseer). By the middle of the second century we never again find reference to multiple bishops. Each church had a monarchial bishop and elders with him, and every early Christian writer seems to assume it had always been so.

How did this happen?

It seems certain to me that what we read in the New Testament represents only the practice of Peter and Paul. The apostle John lived until AD 100, some 35 years after Peter and Paul, and he spent those decades in the area of Asia Minor overseeing the churches. Seven of those Asia Minor churches are mentioned in the Revelation of John in our Bible, chapters two and three.

Ignatius of Antioch

Ignatius' letters can be shocking to Protestants. Such a strong emphasis on the bishop, and at so early a date!

It must be remembered that Ignatius was combating a plague in the Asia Minor churches, the heresies of gnosticism.[620] Even the apostolic churches had to battle their insidious teachers, who were whisperers pulling Jesus' sheep to the side to expound their fantastic doctrines. 1 Corinthians 15 and the entire letter of 1 John are written to refute gnostic teachings.

Ignatius' answer is to exhort the churches under his care to adhere closely to their bishop and do nothing without him.

Thus, Ignatius is not propounding an extreme emphasis on the bishop; he is combating heresy. It is important not to pull his writings out of context.

There is every indication that the churches of Asia Minor all had one bishop and multiple elders even from the time of John.

---

[620] Described in Chapter 12.

Two of the most famous of early Christians, Ignatius and Polycarp, are believed to have been appointed by John, and their letters make it clear that they were monarchial bishops.

Nonetheless, outside of Asia Minor the terms bishop and elder were still used interchangeably. Polycarp's letter to the Philippians, for example, mentions only elders and deacons, despite the fact that Polycarp himself was a monarchial bishop. Philippi was in Greece, started by Paul and outside John's jurisdiction in Asia Minor. Apparently, in the first half of the second century, when Polycarp's letter was written, Philippi still had a group of elders, all of whom were overseers.

Similarly, Ignatius addressed letters to five Asia Minor churches around AD 110. In all of these, he offers profuse praise for each church's bishop, and he exhorts the churches to do nothing without the bishop's approval. It's a notably central emphasis of Ignatius' letters. Yet, in his only letter to a church outside Asia Minor, his epistle to Rome, a church formed by Paul and Peter, he makes no mention of a bishop.

The reason is not hard to determine.

Just ten years earlier, around AD 96, the church at Rome had written a letter to the church at Corinth which is attributed to Clement of Rome by tradition and is known as *1 Clement*. That letter, too, uses bishop and elder interchangeably and speaks of both in the plural.[621]

The Roman church was considered to be founded by Paul and Peter, and Peter, as his letter indicates, had remained there as an elder for many years.[622] It seems apparent that they were still using Peter and Paul's leadership system, with multiple elders who were all called bishops.

---

[621] *1 Clement*. 42,44.

[622] We saw that in 1 Peter 5:1-2, Peter refers to himself as one of the elders. In 5:13, he sends greetings from the church at Babylon, a city which did not exist at the time. Most scholars agree that this was a coded reference to Rome.

So how did John's practice become the prevailing one throughout the catholic churches?

We can only speculate. My own guess is that individual leadership is natural. Even in churches with supposedly co-equal elders, there is normally one who takes the lead and is looked to by all the others. This is not a bad thing. Such authority is given willingly and maintained by good will. The informally recognized leader is restrained by a lack of positional authority. Should he provoke the others, they will rise up to take back the authority that is as rightfully theirs as his.

But I'm guessing. What we know is that Paul and Peter's churches had multiple elders who are all bishops, while John's churches, the churches in Asia Minor, had monarchial bishops. Eventually, by the mid-second century, all churches had monarchial bishops.

Priests

Now we must address priests. It seems almost out of place here because there is no mention of priests in the New Testament, nor any in the writings of second-century churches except in reference to all believers.

It seems unavoidable that the role of the bishop and elders in the churches was going to be compared to the role of the high priest and priests of Israel, especially as the church grew larger and clergy grew in authority. I can tell you from modern experience that as churches grow larger, it becomes harder and harder to include all members in the activities of the church. Paul talked about every member speaking at meetings in his letter to the Corinthians,[623] but this is impossible once a church has two or three hundred members or more. More and more, the speaking and leading is left to those with position or exceptional gifting.

---

[623] Several places in 1 Corinthians 14.

> One common answer to this problem today is to break larg-
> er church up into smaller groups. "Cell group" churches are
> popular in America today because they allow better participa-
> tion of all members, something the apostle Paul said was essen-
> tial to the growth of the church.[624]

The early churches were unable to avoid this problem. Even
before Constantine converted to Christianity and most of the Roman empire converted with him, it is easy to see the people of
God being treated more and more as "the masses." In such a situation, it is easy to picture the leadership of the church increasingly
being seen as having a priestly role, intervening between God and
his people.

But let's look briefly at the facts.

Even as early as *1 Clement* (AD 96), there is a comparison,
though only a comparison, made between the leaders of the
church and the priests of Israel. The Corinthians had removed at
least a couple of their elders from their position due to disputes
over either personality or minor doctrines. Either way, the church
at Rome was appalled and considered the expulsion of the elders
to be an act of division, not an act of purification. Clement writes:

> Our sin will not be small if we eject from the office of
> bishop those who have fulfilled its duties in blamelessness
> and holiness.[625]

That quote, by the way, is one of the clearest references that
those early churches established by Paul or Peter were still using a
system of multiple bishops. Clement is speaking of the removal of
elders from their position, yet he comments that they are being
removed from the office of bishop.

Clement tries to call the Corinthians away from their selfish-
ness by pointing out to them the proper limits of their authority.

---

[624] 1 Corinthians 12 & 14. Ephesians 4:11-16.
[625] *1 Clement*. 44.

It behooves us to do everything in order, which the Lord has commanded us to perform at stated times. He has enjoined offerings and service to be performed ... at the appointed times and hours. Where and by whom he desires these things to be done, he himself has fixed by his own supreme will, so that everything done piously and according to his good pleasure may be acceptable to him. Those, therefore, who present their offerings at the appointed times are accepted and blessed. ... For his own unique services are assigned to the high priest, their own proper place is prescribed to the priests, and their own special services devolve on the Levites. The layman is bound by the laws that pertain to laymen.[626]

Clement is simply using the Old Testament system as an example, as he should. According to the apostle Paul, the things that were written before were written as examples for our learning,[627] and all the early Christian writers were in the habit of using the Old Testament writings in this way.

Later though, these examples would become reality. Rather than being *compared* to priests, the elders would *be* priests, and there seemed to be little thought taken for the apostolic teaching that God's people are to be a kingdom of priests.[628]

The earliest use of the term "priest" to refer to Christian ministers that I can find is in Hippolytus, who wrote in Rome around the year 225. He refers to "bishops, priests, and deacons" in his *Refutation of All Heresies* IX:7. He also writes:

But we, since we are their successors and participators in this grace, high-priesthood, and office of teaching, as well as being reputed guardians of the Church, must not be found deficient in vigilance or disposed to suppress correct doctrine.[629]

---

[626] *1 Clement.* 40.

[627] Romans 15:4

[628] 1 Peter 2:5,9. Revelation 1:6.

[629] *Refutation of All Heresies.* Introduction.

The reference here is to bishops and elders taking the lead in defending against heresy.

Despite this earlier reference, the 19th-century historian Philip Schaff attributes the origin of the idea of elders as priests to Cyprian:

> [Cyprian] may therefore be called the proper father of the sacerdotal[630] conception of the Christian ministry as a mediating agency between God and the people.[631]

Cyprian wrote from Carthage in north Africa, and he was bishop there from AD 249 until his death in 258.

Schaff says that Tertullian, writing around AD 210, was the first to "expressly and directly" assert priestly claims for the Christian ministry, referring to *sacerdotium*. He doesn't reference this, and he goes on to point out that Tertullian "strongly affirms the universal priesthood of all believers."

This is true in many places, and especially in *On Monogamy*, which he wrote as part of the Montanist sect. He wanted the rules that apply to old covenant priests to apply to all Christians so that he could require, as all Montanists did, that Christians have only one wife after becoming Christian, even if their previous wife died.

The connection between Tertullian, Hippolytus, and Cyprian is that they all wrote in Latin. References to the clergy as priests in Greek would have to wait until later in the third century. Even the canons of the Council of Nicea do not refer to bishops or elders as priests.

There can be no doubt, however, that by the fourth century the idea of the priesthood of all believers was lost for practical purposes, and a sacerdotal clergy became accepted practice.

---

[630] Having to do with priests.
[631] *History of the Church*. Vol. II. Section 42.

Appendix D:

Arius' Letters

The letters that we have from Arius are only those preserved by his enemies.

Does this mean that they are corrupted or changed?

It is highly unlikely that Arius is not quoted accurately. Arius had four years to repent and speak differently than he had been speaking before Alexander excommunicated him. Afterward he did not repent or try to change his doctrine. Instead, he went to Nicomedia to be with the bishop Eusebius and continued to teach things that put the church in an uproar.

What need was there for his enemies to change his words? Arius' words were condemned at Nicea. With the Council of Nicea backing him, Athanasius, the main opponent of the Arians, had no need to put negative words in Arius' mouth. Arius is not charged with moral misbehavior but with teaching something novel.

Thus, scholars are confident that what is found in the writings of Athanasius, Theodoret, and Sozomen are accurate excerpts of what Arius wrote.

Three letters and one excerpt are appended below:

- Unknown excerpt quoted by Athanasius (c. 319)
- To Eusebius of Nicomedia (c. 319)
- To Alexander of Alexandria (c. 320)
- To Constantine (c. 327)

Excerpt found in Athanasius

This particular excerpt from Arius is composed in verse with meter, so it can be a little stilted. I have not corrected the unusual word order, which is due to the meter. Arius was known for writing songs to support his theology.

From Athanasius, *On the Councils of Ariminum and Seleucia* 15.

God himself, then, in his own nature, is ineffable[632] by all men.
Equal or like himself, he alone has none, or one in glory.

Ingenerate we call him, because of him who is generate by nature.
We praise him as without beginning because of him who has a beginning.
And adore him as everlasting, because of him who in time has come to be.

The Unbegun made the Son a beginning of things originated
And advanced him as a Son to himself by adoption.
He has nothing proper to God in proper subsistence
For He is not equal, no, nor one in essence with him.

Wise is God, for He is the teacher of Wisdom.
There is full proof that God is invisible to all beings
Both to things which are through the Son and to the Son He is invisible.

I will say it expressly, how by the Son is seen the Invisible
By that power by which God sees, and in his own measure
The Son endures to see the Father, as is lawful.

Thus there is a Triad, not in equal glories.
Not intermingling with each other are their subsistences.
One more glorious than the other in their glories unto immensity.
Foreign from the Son in essence is the Father, for he is without beginning.

Understand that the Monad was
But the Dyad was not, before it was in existence.
It follows at once that, though the Son was not, the Father was God.

Hence the Son, not being (for he existed at the will of the Father)
is God Only-begotten, and he is alien from either.
Wisdom existed as Wisdom by the will of the Wise God

---

[632] Unnamable. Pre-Nicene and Nicene Christians commonly commented that God is beyond being named by humans.

Hence he is conceived in numberless conceptions:
Spirit, Power, Wisdom, God's Glory, Truth, Image, and Word.
Understand that he is conceived to be Radiance and Light.

One equal to the Son the Superior is able to beget
But one more excellent, or superior, or greater, he is not able.
At God's will the Son is what and whatsoever he is.

And when and since he was
From that time he has subsisted from God.
He, being a strong God, praises in his degree the Superior.

To speak in brief, God is ineffable to his Son.
For he is to himself what he is, that is, unspeakable.
So that nothing which is called comprehensible[633] does the Son
know to speak about.

For it is impossible for him to investigate the Father, who is by
himself.
For the Son does not know his own essence
For, being Son, he really existed at the will of the Father.

What argument then allows
That he who is from the Father should know his own parent by
comprehension?
For it is plain that for that which has a beginning
To conceive how the Unbegun is, or to grasp the idea, is not possible.

Letter to Alexander of Alexandria

From Athanasius, *On the Councils of Ariminum and Seleucia*
16. This letter is written to Alexander, bishop of Alexandria, who
excommunicated Arius.

Our faith from our forefathers, which also we have learned
from you, blessed father, is this:

---

[633] This probably means that there is nothing in the Father that is comprehensible to the Son, which is the context of this section of the poem.

We acknowledge one God—alone ingenerate, alone eternal, alone unbegun, alone true, alone having immortality, alone wise, alone good, alone sovereign; Judge, Governor, and Providence of all, unalterable and unchangeable, just and good, God of Law and Prophets and New Testament—who begat an only-begotten Son before eternal times, through whom he has made both the ages and the universe. He begat him, not in illusion, but in truth.

[We acknowledge] that he made him subsist at his own will, unalterable and unchangeable; perfect creature of God, but not as one of the creatures; offspring, but not as one of the things begotten; nor as Valentinus pronounced, that the offspring of the Father was an issue; nor as Manichaeus taught, that the offspring was a portion of the Father, one in essence; nor as Sabellius, dividing the Monad, speaks of a Son-and-Father; nor as Hieracas, of one torch from another, or as a lamp divided into two; nor that he who was before was afterwards generated or newly created into a Son.[634] You yourself also, blessed father, in the midst of the church and in session have often condemned these things.

Instead, as we say, at the will of God, created before times and before ages and gaining life and being from the Father, who gave subsistence to his glories together with him. For the Father did not, in giving to him the inheritance of all things, deprive himself of what he has ingenerately in himself, for he is the fountain of all things.

Thus there are three subsistences. And God, being the cause of all things, is unbegun and altogether sole, but the Son being begotten apart from time by the Father and being created and founded before ages, was not [i.e., did not exist] before his generation. But being begotten apart from time before all things, he alone was made to subsist by the Father. For he is not eternal, co-eternal or co-unoriginate with the Father. Nor has he his being together with the Father, as some speak of relations, introducing two ingenerate beginnings, but God is before all things as being Monad and beginning of all.

Therefore also he is before the Son, as we have learned also from your preaching in the midst of the Church. So far then as

---

[634] Though he attributes these thoughts to known heretics, Arius is specifically rejecting several tenets held by the pre-Nicene churches. The illustration of one torch to another was used by Justin Martyr, and the idea that "he who was before was afterwards generated" is exactly what *homoousios* means.

from God he has being, glories, and life, and all things are delivered to him, in such sense is God his origin. For he is above him, as being his God, and before him. But if the terms "from him," "from the womb," and "I came forth from the Father and I am come"[635] be understood by some to mean as if he were a part of him—one in essence or as an issue—then the Father is according to them compounded, divisible, alterable, and material, and, as far as their belief goes, has the circumstances of a body, yet he is the incorporeal God.

To Eusebius, Bishop of Nicomedia

From *The Ecclesiastical History of Theodoret* I:4. This letter is to Eusebius of Nicomedia.

To his very dear lord, the man of God, the faithful and orthodox Eusebius.

Arius, unjustly persecuted by Alexander the pope,[636] on account of that all-conquering truth of which you also are a champion, sends greeting in the Lord.

Ammonius, my father, was about to depart for Nicomedia, and I considered myself bound to salute you by him and to inform as well that natural affection which you bear towards the brothers for the sake of God and his Christ, that the bishop [*i.e., Alexander of Alexandria*] greatly wastes and persecutes us and leaves no stone unturned against us.

He has driven us out of the city as atheists, because we do not concur in what he publicly preaches: "God always, the Son always; as the Father so the Son; the Son co-exists unbegotten with God; he is everlasting; neither by thought nor by any interval does God precede the Son; always God, always Son; he is begotten of the unbegotten; the Son is of God himself."

Eusebius, your brother bishop of Cæsarea, Theodotus, Paulinus, Athanasius, Gregorius, Aetius, and all the bishops of the East have been condemned because they say that God had an existence prior to that of his Son. Exceptions are Philogonius, Hel-

---

[635] Romans 11:36. Psalm 110:3. John 16:28.

[636] Alexandrian bishops were, along with several others, referred to as pope—meaning "father"—since perhaps the mid-third century.

lanicus, and Macarius, who are unlearned men, and who have embraced heretical opinions. Some of them say that the Son was belched out,[637] others that he is a production, others that he is also unbegotten. These are impieties to which we cannot listen, even though the heretics threaten us with a thousand deaths.

But we say, believe, have taught, and do teach that the Son is not unbegotten, nor in any way part of the unbegotten. We say that he does not derive his subsistence from any matter, but by his own will and counsel he has subsisted before time and before ages, as perfect God, only-begotten and unchangeable, and that before he was begotten, created, purposed, or established he did not exist. For he was not unbegotten.

We are persecuted because we say that the Son has a beginning, but that God is without beginning. This is the cause of our persecution. Similarly, we are persecuted because we say that he is of the non-existent. And this we say, because he is neither part of God nor of any essential being. For this are we persecuted; the rest you know.

I bid thee farewell in the Lord, remembering our afflictions, my fellow-Lucianist[638] and true Eusebius.[639]

Recantation to the Emperor Constantine

From *The Ecclesiastical History of Sozomen* II:27.

Arius and Euzoïus, elders, to Constantine, our most pious emperor and most beloved of God.

---

[637] "Belched out" is the literal meaning of Psalm 45:1 in the LXX: "My heart has 'belched out' a good word." This is symbolic, and it doesn't carry quite the unsocial stigma in its original language that it does in ours, but Arius is making the best negative use of the term that he can here.

[638] Lucian was an elder from Antioch in the late third and early fourth century who trained all the leading Arianists. Little is known about his personal view of the relationship between the father and son. He was out of fellowship with the church in Antioch for at least 16 years, and perhaps up to 35, but was readmitted and died a martyr, for which he is honored by both Roman Catholics and Orthodox to this day. See Chapter 4.

[639] Eusebius means "godly"; Arius is referring to him as truly godly.

Just as your piety, beloved of God, commanded, oh sovereign emperor, we here furnish a written statement of our own faith, and we protest before God that we and all those who are with us believe what is here set forth.

> We believe in one God, the Father Almighty, and in his Son, the Lord Jesus Christ, who was begotten from him before all ages; God the Word, by whom all things were made, whether things in heaven or things on earth. He came and took upon him flesh, suffered and rose again, and ascended into heaven, from where he will come again to judge the living and the dead. We believe in the Holy Spirit, in the resurrection of the body, in the life to come, in the kingdom of heaven, and in one catholic Church of God, established throughout the earth.[640]

We have received this faith from the holy Gospels, in which the Lord says to his disciples, "Go forth and disciple all nations, baptizing them in the name of the Father, of the Son, and of the Holy Spirit."[641] If we do not so believe this, and if we do not truly receive the doctrines concerning the Father, the Son, and the Holy Spirit, as they are taught by the whole catholic Church and by the sacred Scriptures, as we believe in every point, let God be our judge, both now and in the day which is to come.

Therefore we appeal to your piety, oh, our emperor most beloved of God, that, as we are enrolled among the members of the clergy, and as we hold the faith and thought of the Church and of the sacred Scriptures, we may be openly reconciled to our mother, the Church, through your peacemaking and pious piety, so that useless questions and disputes may be cast aside and that we and the Church may dwell together in peace. Then we all in common may offer the customary prayer for your peaceful and pious empire and for your entire family.

---

[640] As pointed out in Chapter 8, there is nothing in this creed by Arius that rejects any of his views.

[641] Matthew 28:19

Appendix E:

Constantine's Letter to Alexander and Arius

When Constantine first heard about the disruption in the churches, he tried to resolve it by letter. He sent the letter by Hosius, an aged and respected bishop from Cordova, Spain, who was a personal advisor.

This letter did not restrain Alexander or Arius.

Taken from Eusebius, *Life of Constantine* II:64-72.

Victor Constantinus, Maximus Augustus, to Alexander and Arius:

I call that God to witness, as well I may, who is the Helper of my endeavors and the Preserver of all men, that I had a twofold reason for undertaking that duty which I have now performed.

My design then was, first, to bring the diverse judgments formed by all nations respecting the Deity to a condition, as it were, of settled uniformity; and, secondly, to restore to health the system of the world, then suffering under the malignant power of a grievous distemper.[642] Keeping these objects in view, I sought to accomplish the one by the secret eye of thought, while the other I tried to rectify by the power of military authority. For I was aware that, if I should succeed in establishing, according to my hopes, a common harmony of sentiment among all the servants of God, the general course of affairs would also experience a change corresponding to the pious desires of them all.

Finding, then, that the whole of Africa was pervaded by an intolerable spirit of mad folly, through the influence of those who with heedless frivolity had presumed to rend the religion of the people into diverse sects, I was anxious to check this disorder. I could discover no other remedy equal to the occasion, except in

---

[642] A reference to renewed persecution by his co-emperor Licinius.

sending some of yourselves[643] to aid in restoring mutual harmony among the disputants, after I had removed that common enemy of mankind[644] who had interposed his lawless sentence for the prohibition of your holy synods.

For since the power of divine light and the law of sacred worship—which through the favor of God proceeded first from the bosom, as it were, of the East—have illumined the world by their sacred radiance, I naturally believed that you would be the first to promote the salvation of other nations. I resolved with all energy of thought and diligence of inquiry to seek your aid. As soon, therefore, as I had secured my decisive victory and unquestionable triumph over my enemies, my first inquiry was concerning that object which I felt to be of paramount interest and importance.

But, oh glorious Providence of God! How deep a wound did not my ears only, but my very heart receive in the report that divisions existed among yourselves more grievous still than those which continued in that country![645] So now you, through whose aid I had hoped to procure a remedy for the errors of others, are in a state which needs healing even more than theirs. And yet, having made a careful inquiry into the origin and foundation of these differences, I find the cause to be of a truly insignificant character and quite unworthy of such fierce contention. Feeling myself, therefore, compelled to address you in this letter and to appeal at the same time to your mutual wisdom, I call on Divine Providence to assist me in the task, while I interrupt your dissension in the character of a minister of peace. And with reason! For if I might expect, with the help of a higher Power, to be able without difficulty, by a judicious appeal to the pious feelings of those who heard me, to recall them[646] to a better spirit, even

---

[643] This would be a reference to Hosius and whichever other clergy Constantine sent with him to bear this letter.

[644] i.e., Licinius

[645] The Donatist schism in north Africa, centered in the area around Carthage. It is not covered in this book. Although it's an important split, it was local to north Africa.

[646] The catholics and Donatists.

though the occasion of the disagreement were a greater one,[647] how can I refrain from promising myself a far easier and more speedy adjustment of this difference, when the cause which hinders general harmony of sentiment is intrinsically trifling and of little moment?[648]

I understand, then, that the origin of the present controversy is this: When you, Alexander, demanded of the elders what opinion they each maintained respecting a certain passage in the Divine law — or rather, I should say, that you asked them something connected with an unprofitable question — then you, Arius, inconsiderately insisted on what ought never to have been conceived at all, or if conceived, should have been buried in profound silence. Hence it was that a dissension arose between you, fellowship was withdrawn, and the holy people, torn into diverse parties, no longer preserved the unity of the one body. Now, therefore, both of you, exhibit an equal degree of forbearance, and receive the advice which your fellow-servant righteously gives.

What then is this advice? It was wrong in the first instance to propose such questions as these or to reply to them when propounded. For those points of discussion which are enjoined by the authority of no law, but rather suggested by the contentious spirit which is fostered by misused leisure, even though they may be intended merely as an intellectual exercise, ought certainly to be confined to the region of our own thoughts and not hastily produced in the public assemblies, nor unadvisedly entrusted to

---

[647] The Donatists split over very similar reasons to the Novatianists and Melitians. Apparently, a lot of Christians did not want to allow repentance to those who denied Christ or offered sacrifices during persecution.

[648] No one, or almost no one, would agree with Constantine on this issue today, but he almost certainly obtained that opinion from Hosius, bishop of Cordova. Historians, both modern and ancient, express the opinion that many bishops barely understood the issues involved, nor did they even want to. Personally, I consider the issue itself important, but the greatest problem of all was the willingness to innovate and the unwillingness to submit shown by Arius and Eusebius (of Nicomedia). Apparently, a number of bishops had held Arian opinions since the time of Lucius and without controversy. With a better attitude, the fathers would have been consulted, and the issues easily resolved in council long before Nicea. The writings of the pre-Nicene Christians are clear and consistent on the issues raised by the Arius.

the general ear. For how very few are there able either accurately to comprehend or adequately to explain subjects so sublime and abstruse in their nature? Or, granting that one were fully competent for this, how many people will he convince? Or, who, again, in dealing with questions of such subtle nicety as these, can secure himself against a dangerous declension from the truth? It is incumbent therefore on us in these cases to be sparing of our words, lest, in case we ourselves are unable, through the feebleness of our natural faculties, to give a clear explanation of the subject before us, or, on the other hand, in case the slowness of our hearers' understandings disables them from arriving at an accurate apprehension of what we say, from one or other of these causes the people be reduced to the alternative either of blasphemy or schism.

Let therefore both the unguarded question and the inconsiderate answer receive your mutual forgiveness. For the cause of your difference has not been any of the leading doctrines or precepts of the Divine law, nor has any new heresy respecting the worship of God arisen among you. You are in truth of one and the same judgment; you may therefore well join in communion and fellowship.

For as long as you continue to contend about these small and very insignificant questions, it is not fitting that so large a portion of God's people should be under the direction of your judgment, since you are thus divided between yourselves. I believe it indeed to be not merely unbecoming, but positively evil, that such should be the case. But I will refresh your minds by a little illustration, as follows.

You know that philosophers, though they all adhere to one system, are yet frequently at issue on certain points and differ, perhaps, in their degree of knowledge. Yet they are recalled to harmony of sentiment by the uniting power of their common doctrines. If this be true, is it not far more reasonable that you, who are the ministers of the Supreme God, should be of one mind respecting the profession of the same religion?

But let us still more thoughtfully and with closer attention examine what I have said, and see whether it be right that, on the ground of some trifling and foolish verbal difference between ourselves, brothers should assume towards each other the attitude of enemies and the august meeting of the synod[649] be rent by profane disunion because of you who wrangle together on points so trivial and altogether unessential? This is vulgar and rather characteristic of childish ignorance than consistent with the wisdom of priests and men of sense.

Let us withdraw ourselves with a good will from these temptations of the devil. Our great God and common Savior of all has granted the same light to us all. Permit me, who am his servant,[650] to bring my task to a successful conclusion, under the direction of his Providence, that I may be enabled, through my exhortations, diligence, and earnest admonition, to recall his people to communion and fellowship. For since you have, as I said, but one faith and one sentiment respecting our religion, and since the Divine commandment in all its parts enjoins on us all the duty of maintaining a spirit of concord, let not the circumstance which has led to a slight difference between you, since it does not affect the validity of the whole, cause any division or schism among you.

And this I say without in any way desiring to force you to entire unity of judgment in regard to this truly idle question, whatever its real nature may be. For the dignity of your synod[651] may be preserved, and the communion of your whole body maintained unbroken, however wide a difference may exist among you as to unimportant matters. For we are not all of us likeminded on every subject, nor is there such a thing as one disposition and judgment common to all alike. As far, then, as regards the Divine Providence, let there be one faith and one understanding among you, one united judgment in reference to God. But as to your subtle disputations on questions of little or no significance, though you may be unable to harmonize in sentiment, such differences should be consigned to the secret custody of your own minds and thoughts.

And now, let the preciousness of common affection, let faith in the truth, let the honor due to God and to the observance of his

---

[649] A general reference to the bishops who would constitute a synod in that area. Constantine is not referring to a specific synod.

[650] Constantine represented himself as a Christian. Whether he was one in truth is discussed in Chapter 14.

[651] Again, this is a general reference to the bishops of the area, not a specific synod.

law continue immovably among you. Resume, then, your mutual feelings of friendship, love, and regard; restore to the people their desired embraces; and once you have purified your souls, as it were, once more acknowledge one another. For it often happens that when a reconciliation is effected by the removal of the causes of enmity, friendship becomes even sweeter than it was before.

Restore to me then my quiet days and untroubled nights, that the joy of undimmed light, the delight of a tranquil life, may be my portion from now on. Otherwise I will need to mourn with constant tears, nor shall I be able to pass the residue of my days in peace. For while the people of God, whose fellow-servant I am, are thus divided amongst themselves by an unreasonable and pernicious spirit of contention, how is it possible that I shall be able to maintain tranquility of mind?

And I will give you a proof how great my sorrow has been on this behalf. Not long ago I had visited Nicomedia and intended immediately to proceed from that city to the East. It was while I was hastening towards you and had already accomplished the greater part of the distance that the news of this matter reversed my plan, so that I might not be compelled to see with my own eyes that which I felt myself scarcely able even to hear.

Open then for me from this time forward, by your unity of judgment, that road to the regions of the East which your dissensions have closed against me. Permit me speedily to see yourselves and all other peoples rejoicing together, and render due acknowledgment to God in the language of praise and thanksgiving for the restoration of general concord and liberty to all.

Appendix F:

Constantine's Speech to the Council of Nicea

This was Constantine's opening speech when the bishops began to meet in session at Nicea.

From Eusebius, *Life of Constantine* III:12.

It was once my chief desire, dearest friends, to enjoy the display of your united presence. Now that this desire is fulfilled, I feel myself bound to render thanks to God the universal King because, in addition to all his other benefits, he has granted me a blessing higher than all the rest, in permitting me to see you not only all assembled together, but all united in a common harmony of sentiment. I pray therefore that no malignant adversary may henceforth interfere to mar our happy state; I pray that since the impious hostility of the tyrants[652] has been forever removed by the power of God our Savior, that spirit who delights in evil may devise no other means for exposing the divine law to blasphemous defamation.

For, in my judgment, internal strife within the Church of God is far more evil and dangerous than any kind of war or conflict, and these our differences appear to me more grievous than any outward trouble. Accordingly, when, by the will and with the cooperation of God, I had been victorious over my enemies, I thought that nothing more remained but to return thanks to him and sympathize in the joy of those whom he had restored to freedom through my instrumentality. As soon as I heard that news which I had least expected to receive—I mean the news of your dissension—I judged it to be of no secondary importance, but with the earnest desire that a remedy for this evil also might be found through my means, I immediately sent to require your presence.

---

[652] His fellow emperors over the last 20 years, who had all persecuted Christians.

And now I rejoice in beholding your assembly. But I feel that my desires will be most completely fulfilled when I can see you all united in one judgment, with that common spirit of peace and concord prevailing among you all, which it becomes you, as consecrated to the service of God, to commend to others. Do not delay, then, dear friends; do not delay, you ministers of God and faithful servants of him who is our common Lord and Savior. Begin from this moment to discard the causes of that disunion which has existed among you and remove the perplexities of controversy by embracing the principles of peace. For by such conduct you will at the same time be acting in a manner most pleasing to the supreme God, and you will confer an exceeding favor on me who am your fellow servant.

Appendix G:

The Nicene and Constantinopolitan Creeds

Here is the text of the Nicene Creed as reported by the primary sources. You may see modern renderings that include extra wording. This is because there were additions approved by the Council of Chalcedon in 451, which they attributed to the Council of Constantinople in 381. That creed is known as the *Nicaeano-Constantinopolitanum Creed*, and it is given below. Also, a version of the creed known as the Apostles Creed, which is the official creed of the Reformed churches.

The anathemas at the end of the Nicene Creed were included by the Council of Nicea, but they are not part of later creeds.

The original creed was written in Greek. This translation is from *The Nicene and Post-Nicene Fathers*, series 2, volume I. I have made minor updates to the punctuation, and I have formed sections for easier memory.

The Nicene Creed

The Father

We believe in one God, the Father Almighty, Maker of all things visible and invisible.

The Son

And [we believe] in one Lord Jesus Christ, the Son of God, the only-begotten of the Father.

That is, of the substance of the Father; God of God and Light of light; true God of true God; begotten, not made, consubstantial with the Father.

By [him] all things were made, both which are in heaven and on earth: who, for the sake of us men and on account of our salvation, descended, became incarnate, and was made man; suffered, arose again the third day, and ascended into the heavens, and will come again to judge the living and the dead.

The Holy Spirit

[We] also [believe] in the Holy Spirit.

Anathemas

But the holy, catholic, and apostolic church anathematizes those who say, "There was a time when he was not" and "He was not before he was begotten" and "He was made from that which did not exist," and those who assert that he is of other substance or essence than the Father, that he was created, or is susceptible of change.

The Nicaeano-Constantinopolitanum Creed

This is a slightly expanded version of the Nicene Creed that is still the official creed of the Roman Catholic Church. It is found in the proceedings of the Council of Chalcedon in 451,[653] where they attribute it to the Council of Constantinople. There is no evidence that it was formulated or approved there, but it remains known as the *Nicaeano-Constantinopolitanum Creed.*

If you ever see a version of the Nicene Creed published in modern times, it will usually be this one, though that is changing as the internet becomes more popular.

The Father

We believe in one God, the Father Almighty, Maker of heaven and earth and of all things visible and invisible.

The Son

And [we believe] in one Lord Jesus Christ, the only begotten Son of God, begotten of his Father before all worlds, Light of Light, very God of very God, begotten not made, being of one substance with the Father, by whom all things were made. Who for us men and for our salvation came down from heaven, was incarnate by the Holy Ghost and the Virgin Mary, was made man, and was also crucified for us under Pontius Pilate. He suf-

---

[653] *Nicene and Post-Nicene Fathers.* Series II. Vol. XIV.

fered and was buried. The third day he rose again according to the Scriptures, ascended into heaven, and sits at the right hand of the Father. He shall come again with glory to judge both the living and the dead. His kingdom shall have no end.

The Holy Spirit

And [we believe] in the Holy Spirit, the Lord and Giver of Life, who proceeds from the Father; who with the Father and the Son together is worshipped and glorified; and who spoke by the prophets.

And [we believe] in one, holy, catholic, and apostolic Church. We acknowledge one baptism for the remission of sins. We look for the resurrection of the dead and the life of the world to come. Amen.

Appendix H:

The Letter of the Council of Nicea to Alexandria and Egypt

This letter is found in *Ecclesiastical History of Socrates Scholasticus* I:9.

In preparation, you need to know the following about Melitius.

Melitius

Melitius was the bishop of Lycopolis in Egypt and as such would have been under the authority of the bishop of Alexandria.

Even while the Great Persecution was going on, Melitius refused to commune with those who had lapsed during persecution even if they repented later. He was not the first to take such a stand. The *Cathari*, or Novatianists, had taken the same stand in the mid-third century.

Melitius, like Novatian before him, let his opinion carry him into schism. He appointed a number of bishops who agreed with him, and he did so in areas where the metropolitan[654] of Alexandria should have had authority.

Apparently the council considered this a more local issue than the Novatianist schism. The Novatianists are directly addressed in Canon 8,[655] while Melitius is not mentioned except in this letter to Alexandria, written after the council.

The council's solution was not successful. The Melitians remained in schism and continued as a separated sect for another century. As with the Novatians, it was hard to stay in schism over an issue that involved the persecution of Christians when the per-

---

[654] A bishop of a major city that had authority over bishops of surrounding towns or even whole provinces and countries.

[655] Chapter 7

secution of Christians, for the most part, stopped after Constantine.

The Letter of the Council of Nicea to the Alexandrians

To the holy, by the grace of God, and great church of the Alexandrians, and to our beloved brethren throughout Egypt, Libya, and Pentapolis, the bishops assembled at Nicea, constituting the great and holy synod, send greeting in the Lord.

Since, by the grace of God, a great and holy synod has been convened at Nicea, our most pious sovereign Constantine having summoned us out of various cities and provinces for that purpose, it appeared to us indispensably necessary that a letter should be written to you on the part of the sacred synod so that you may know what subjects were brought under consideration and examined and what was eventually determined and decreed.

In the first place, then, the impiety and guilt of Arius and his adherents were examined in the presence of our most religious emperor Constantine, and it was unanimously decided that his impious opinion should be anathematized, with all the blasphemous expressions he has uttered, in affirming that "the Son of God sprang from nothing" and that "there was a time when he was not." He said moreover that "the Son of God, because possessed of free will, was capable either of vice or virtue," and he called him a creature and a work. All these sentiments the holy synod has anathematized, having scarcely patience to endure the hearing of such an impious opinion — or rather madness — and such blasphemous words.

But the conclusion of our proceedings against him you must either have been informed of already or will soon learn, for we do not wish to seem to trample on a man who has received the chastisement which his crime deserved. Yet so contagious has his pestilent error proved as to drag into perdition Theonas, bishop of Marmarica, and Secundus of Ptolemais, for they have suffered the same condemnation as himself. But when the grace of God delivered us from those detestable dogmas, with all their impiety and blasphemy, and from those persons who had dared to cause discord and division among a people previously at peace, there still remained the rebellion of Melitius and those who had been ordained by him.

We now state to you, beloved brethren, what resolution the synod came to on this point. It was decreed, the synod being moved to great clemency towards Melitius, although strictly speaking he was wholly undeserving of favor, that he remain in his own city but exercise no authority either to ordain or nominate for ordination and that he appear in no other district or city on this pretence, but simply retain a nominal dignity; that those who had received appointments from him, after having been confirmed by a more legitimate ordination, should be admitted to communion on these conditions: that they should continue to hold their rank and ministry, but regard themselves as inferior in every respect to all those who have been ordained and established in each place and church by our most-honored fellow-minister, Alexander, so that they shall have no authority to propose or nominate whom they please or to do anything at all without the concurrence of some bishop of the Catholic Church who is one of Alexander's suffragans.[656]

On the other hand, such as, by the grace of God and your prayers, have been found in no schism, but have continued in the Catholic Church blameless, shall have authority to nominate and ordain those who are worthy of the sacred office and to act in all things according to ecclesiastical law and usage. When it may happen that any of those holding preference in the church die, then let these who have been thus recently admitted be advanced to the dignity of the deceased, provided that they should appear worthy and that the people should elect them, the bishop of Alexandria also ratifying their choice. This privilege is conceded to all the others indeed, but to Melitius personally we by no means grant the same license, because of his former disorderly conduct and because of the rashness and levity of his character, in order that no authority or jurisdiction should be given him as a man liable again to create similar disturbances.

These are the things which especially affect Egypt and the most holy church of the Alexandrians. If any other canon or ordinance has been established, our lord and most-honored fellow-minister and brother Alexander, being present with us, will on his return to you enter into more minute details, inasmuch as he has been a participant in whatever is transacted and has had the principal direction of it.

We have also gratifying information to communicate to you relative to unity of judgment on the subject of the most holy feast of Passover, for this point also has been happily settled through

---

[656] A bishop that is under a higher bishop, such as a metropolitan.

your prayers. The result is that all the brethren in the East who have previously kept this festival when the Jews did will conform from now on to the Romans and to us and to all who from the earliest time have observed our period of celebrating Easter. Rejoicing therefore in these conclusions and in the general unanimity and peace, as well as in the extirpation of all heresy, receive with the greatest honor and more abundant love our fellow-minister and your bishop, Alexander, who has greatly delighted us by his presence, and even at his advanced age has undergone extraordinary exertions in order that peace might be reestablished among you. Pray on behalf of us all that the things decided as just may be inviolably maintained through Almighty God and our Lord Jesus Christ, together with the Holy Spirit, to whom be glory for ever.

Amen.

Appendix I:

Eusebius' Letter to His Home Church at Caesarea

From *The Ecclesiastical History of Socrates Scholasticus* I:8.

You have probably had some intimation, beloved, of the transactions of the great council convened at Nicea in relation to the faith of the Church, since rumor generally outruns true account of that which has really taken place. But lest from such report alone you might form an incorrect estimate of the matter, we have deemed it necessary to submit to you, in the first place, an exposition of the faith proposed by us in written form, and then a second which has been promulgated, consisting of ours with certain additions to its expression. The declaration of faith set forth by us, which when read in the presence of our most pious emperor seemed to meet with universal approbation, was thus expressed:

> As we received from the bishops who preceded us, both in our instruction and when we were baptized; as also we have ourselves learned from the sacred Scriptures; and in accordance with what we have both believed and taught while discharging the duties of elder and the bishop's office itself; so now we believe and present to you the distinct avowal of our faith. It is this:
>
> We believe in one God, the Father Almighty, Maker of all things visible and invisible.
>
> And [we believe] in one Lord, Jesus Christ, the Word of God—God of God, Light of Light, Life of Life—the only-begotten Son, born before all creation, begotten of God the Father before all ages, by whom also all things were made; who on account of our salvation became incarnate, lived among men; who suffered and rose again on the third day, ascended to the Father, and shall come again in glory to judge the living and the dead.
>
> We believe also in one Holy Spirit.

We believe in the existence and subsistence of each of these: that the Father is truly Father, the Son truly Son, and the Holy Spirit truly Holy Spirit; even as our Lord also, when he sent forth his disciples to preach the Gospel, said, "Go and teach all nations, baptizing them in the name of the Father, and of the Son, and of the Holy Spirit" [*Matt. 28:19*].

Concerning these doctrines we steadfastly maintain their truth and avow our full confidence in them. These also were our sentiments in the past, and such we shall continue to hold until death in an unshaken adherence to this faith. We anathematize every impious heresy. In the presence of God Almighty and of our Lord Jesus Christ we testify that thus we have believed and thought from our heart and soul since we have possessed a right estimate of ourselves and that we now think and speak what is perfectly in accordance with the truth. We are moreover prepared to prove to you by undeniable evidences and to convince you that in time past we have thus believed and so preached.

When these articles of faith were proposed, there seemed to be no ground of opposition. No, even our most pious emperor himself was the first to admit that they were perfectly correct and that he himself had entertained the sentiments contained in them.[657] He exhorted all present to give them their assent and subscribe to these very articles, thus agreeing in a unanimous profession of them—with the insertion, however, of that single word, *homoousios*,[658] an expression which the emperor himself explained as not indicating corporeal affections or properties. Consequently the Son did not subsist from the Father either by division or by cutting off. For, said he, a nature which is immaterial and incorporeal cannot possibly be subject to any corporeal understanding; hence, our conception of such things can only be in divine and mysterious terms. Such was the philosophical view of the subject taken by our most wise and pious sovereign, and the

---

[657] It is simply astounding that Eusebius felt it important to have the emperor's approval of the articles of faith, rather than informing the emperor of what the church approved.

[658] "One in substance." See Chapter 15.

bishops, because of the word *homoousios*, drew up this formula of faith:

We believe in one God, the Father Almighty, Maker of all things visible and invisible;

And [we believe] in one Lord Jesus Christ, the Son of God, the only-begotten of the Father, that is, of the substance of the Father; God of God, Light of light, true God of true God; begotten not made, consubstantial with the Father, by whom all things were made, both which are in heaven and on earth; who for the sake of us men and on account of our salvation, descended, became incarnate, was made man, suffered and rose again on the third day. He ascended into the heavens, and will come to judge the living and the dead;

[We believe] also in the Holy Spirit.

But those who say, "There was a time when he was not"; or, "He did not exist before he was begotten"; or, "He was made of nothing"; or assert that he is of other substance or essence than the Father; or that the Son of God is created, mutable, or susceptible of change, the catholic and apostolic Church of God anathematizes.

Now when this declaration of faith was propounded by them, we did not neglect to investigate the distinct sense of the expressions "of the substance of the Father" and "consubstantial with the Father." When we did, questions and answers were put forth, and the meaning of these terms was clearly defined. At that point it was generally admitted that *ousios*[659] simply implied that the Son is of the Father indeed, but does not subsist as a part of the Father. To this interpretation of the sacred doctrine—which declares that the Son is of the Father but is not a part of his substance—it seemed right to us to assent. We ourselves therefore concurred in this exposition. Nor do we cavil at the word *homoousios*, having regard to peace, and fearing to lose a right understanding of the matter.

On the same grounds we admitted also the expression "begotten, not made." "For 'made,'" said [the council], "is a term applica-

---

[659] Substance or essence.

441

ble in common to all the creatures which were made by the Son, to whom the Son has no resemblance. Consequently he is no creature like those which were made by him, but is of a substance far excelling any creature. The Divine Oracles teach that this substance was begotten of the Father by such a mode of generation as cannot be explained nor even conceived by any creature."[660]

Thus also the declaration that "the Son is consubstantial with the Father" having been discussed, it was agreed that this must not be understood in a corporeal sense, or in any way analogous to mortal creatures; inasmuch as it is neither by division of substance, nor by abscission,[661] nor by any change of the Father's substance and power, since the underived nature of the Father is inconsistent with all these things.

That he is consubstantial [*homoousios*] with the Father then simply implies that the Son of God has no resemblance to created things, but is in every respect like the Father only who begat him; that he is of no other substance or essence but of the Father. To this doctrine, explained in this way, it appeared right to assent, especially since we knew that some eminent bishops and learned writers among the ancients have used the term *homoousios* in their theological discourses concerning the nature of the Father and the Son.[662]

Such is what I have to state to you in reference to the articles of faith which have been promulgated and in which we have all concurred—not without due examination, but according to the senses assigned—which were investigated in the presence of our most highly favored emperor and, for the reasons mentioned, approved.

We have also considered the anathema pronounced by them after the declaration of faith inoffensive because it prohibits the use of illegitimate terms, from which almost all the distraction and commotion of the churches have arisen. Accordingly, since no divinely inspired Scripture contains the expressions, "of things which do not exist" and "there was a time when he was not" and

---

[660] While we would all agree with the sentiments expressed in this paragraph, the council did ban a term which they all understood to be used in Scripture. (Proverbs 8:22, LXX. See Chapter 15.)

[661] Cutting off.

[662] See Chapter 15.

such other phrases as are included there, it seemed unwarrantable to utter and teach them. In addition, this decision received our sanction from the consideration that we have never before been accustomed to employ these terms.

We deemed it incumbent on us, beloved, to acquaint you with the caution which has characterized both our examination of and concurrence in these things and [to inform you] that on justifiable grounds we resisted to the last moment the introduction of certain objectionable expressions as long as these were not acceptable. We received them without dispute when, on mature deliberation as we examined the sense of the words, they appeared to agree with what we had originally proposed as a sound confession of faith.

Appendix J:

The Letter of Constantine Regarding the Decisions of the Council of Nicea

Eusebius records a copy of this letter in *Life of Constantine* 17-20. He ends it by saying:

> The emperor transmitted a faithful copy of this letter to every province, in which those who read it may discern, as in a mirror, the pure sincerity of his thoughts and of his piety toward God.

Eusebius was, needless to say, very impressed with Emperor Constantine. Perhaps this letter will help in forming your own opinion of him.

Constantine, Early Christianity, and the Jews

Constantine's extremely negative attitude toward the Jews in this letter is a product of the Christians' attitude toward the Jews, and there is no justifying it.

When Jesus came, he confined all of humanity under sin, not any one race. It is the sins of mankind that put Jesus on the cross, not Jewish or Roman hands.

Constantine's Letter to the Churches

Constantinus Augustus to the Churches:

Having had full proof, in the general prosperity of the empire, how great the favor of God has been towards us, I have judged that it ought to be the first object of my endeavors, that unity of faith, sincerity of love, and community of feeling in regard to the worship of Almighty God might be preserved among the highly favored multitude who compose the Catholic Church. Because this object could not be effactually and certainly secured unless all, or at least the greater number of the bishops, were to meet together, and a discussion of all particulars relating to our most holy religion were to take place; for this reason as numerous an assembly as possible has been convened.

I myself was present at the assembly, as one among yourselves—far be it from me to deny that which is my greatest joy, that I am your fellow-servant—and every question received due and full examination until that judgment which God, who sees all things, could approve, and which tended to unity and concord, was brought to light, so that no room was left for further discussion or controversy in relation to the faith.

At this meeting the question concerning the most holy day of Passover was discussed, and it was resolved by the united judgment of all present that this feast ought to be kept by all and in every place on one and the same day. For what can be more becoming or honorable to us than that this feast, from which we date our hopes of immortality,[663] should be observed unfailingly by all alike, according to one ascertained order and arrangement?

First of all, it appeared an unworthy thing that in the celebration of this most holy feast we should follow the practice of the Jews, who have impiously defiled their hands with enormous sin, and are, therefore, deservedly afflicted with blindness of soul. For we have it in our power, if we abandon their custom, to prolong the due observance of this ordinance to future ages by a truer order, which we have preserved from the very day of the passion until the present time. Let us then have nothing in common with the detestable Jewish crowd,[664] for we have received from our Savior a different way.

A course at once legitimate and honorable lies open to our most holy religion. Beloved brethren, let us with one consent adopt this course, and withdraw ourselves from all participation in their baseness. For their boast is absurd indeed, that it is not in our power without instruction from them to observe these things. For how should they be capable of forming a sound judgment, who, since their parricidal guilt in slaying their Lord, have been subject to the direction, not of reason, but of ungoverned passion

---

[663] Because Jesus, our Passover, died on that day.

[664] What a different attitude the apostle Paul showed towards the Jews when he said, "I could wish myself accursed from Christ for the sake of my brothers, my kinsmen according to the flesh, who are Israelites, to whom pertains the adoption, the glory, the covenants, the giving of the Law, the service, the promises, to whom belong the fathers, and from whom, in regard to the flesh, Christ came" (Rom. 9:3-5). He obviously did not find them "detestable."

and are swayed by every impulse of the mad spirit that is in them?

Hence it is that on this point as well as others they have no perception of the truth, so that, being altogether ignorant of the true adjustment of this question, they sometimes celebrate Passover twice in the same year.[665] Why then should we follow those who are confessedly in grievous error? Surely we shall never consent to keep this feast a second time in the same year.

But supposing these reasons were not of sufficient weight, still it would be incumbent on your judgments to strive and pray continually that the purity of your souls may not seem in anything to be sullied by fellowship with the customs of these most wicked men. We must consider, too, that a discordant judgment in a case of such importance and concerning such a religious festival is wrong. For our Savior has left us one feast in commemoration of the day of our deliverance; I mean the day of his most holy passion.[666] He has willed that his Catholic Church should be one, the members of which, however scattered in many and diverse places, are yet cherished by one pervading spirit; that is, by the will of God.

Let the wise judgment of Your Holinesses reflect how grievous and scandalous it is that on the self-same days some should be engaged in fasting, others in festive enjoyment; and again, that after the days of Passover some should be present at banquets and amusements, while others are fulfilling the appointed fasts. It is, then, plainly the will of Divine Providence, as I suppose you all clearly see, that this usage should receive fitting correction and be reduced to one uniform rule.

Since, therefore, it was needful that this matter should be rectified, so that we might have nothing in common with that nation of parricides who slew their Lord; and since that arrangement is

---

[665] Due to the Jewish lunar calendar, Nisan 14 sometimes fell before and sometimes after the vernal equinox. So if a Passover fell after the beginning of spring one year, but before it the next, Constantine accuses them of celebrating two Passovers in the same year. The charge is obviously absurd, as Passover was originally a Jewish feast scheduled according to a Jewish, not a Roman calendar.

[666] Constantine is reporting what was handed to him, not establishing a new practice. All indications are that Passover was the only feast celebrated by Christians.

consistent with propriety which is observed by all the churches of the western, southern, and northern parts of the world—and by some of the eastern also; for these reasons all are unanimous on this present occasion in thinking it worthy of adoption.

I myself have undertaken that this decision should meet with the approval of your wise judgment, in the hope that Your Wisdoms will gladly admit that practice which is observed at once in the city of Rome, in Africa, throughout Italy, in Egypt, in Spain, the Gauls, Britain, Libya, the whole of Greece, in the dioceses of Asia and Pontus, and in Cilicia with entire unity of judgment. You will consider not only that the number of churches is far greater in the regions I have enumerated than in any other, but also that it is most fitting that all should unite in desiring that which sound reason appears to demand and in avoiding all participation in the perjured conduct of the Jews.

In conclusion, that I may express my meaning in as few words as possible, it has been determined by the common judgment of all, that the most holy feast of Passover should be kept on one and the same day. For on the one hand a discrepancy of opinion on so sacred a question is unbecoming, and on the other it is surely best to act on a decision which is free from strange folly and error.

Receive, then, with all willingness this truly divine injunction, and regard it as in truth the gift of God. For whatever is determined in the holy assemblies of the bishops is to be regarded as indicative of the divine will. As soon, therefore, as you have communicated these proceedings to all our beloved brethren, you are bound from that time forward to adopt for yourselves and to enjoin on others the arrangement above mentioned, the due observance of this most sacred day, that, whenever I come into the presence of your love, which I have long desired, I may have it in my power to celebrate the holy feast with you on the same day and may rejoice with you on all accounts, when I behold the cruel power of Satan removed by divine aid through the agency of our endeavors, while your faith, peace, and concord everywhere flourish.

God preserve you, beloved brethren!

Appendix K:

The Rule of Faith of the Church in Caesarea

The following rule of faith was presented to the Council of Nicea by Eusebius, the historian and bishop of Caesarea. It was then discussed and used as the basis for the Nicene Creed.

Eusebius himself, in his letter to Caesarea, testifies that "when these articles of faith were proposed, there seemed to be no ground of opposition." [667]

The Rule of Faith of the Church in Caesarea

We believe in one God, the Father Almighty, Maker of all things visible and invisible;

And in one Lord, Jesus Christ, the Word of God; God of God, Light of light, Life of life; the only-begotten Son, born before all creation, begotten of God the Father before all ages, by whom also all things were made; who on account of our salvation became incarnate and lived among men; and who suffered and rose again on the third day, ascended to the Father, and shall come again in glory to judge the living and the dead.

We believe also in one Holy Spirit.

We believe in the existence and subsistence of each of these: that the Father is truly Father, the Son truly Son, and the Holy Spirit truly Holy Spirit; even as our Lord also, when he sent his disciples out to preach the Gospel, said, "Go and make disciples of all nations, baptizing them in the name of the Father, of the Son, and of the Holy Spirit."

---

[667] Appendix I.

Appendix L:

Canonical Lists Before the Council of Nicea

The Muratorian Canon is given here in full because it is the earliest, dating from AD 170 (or thereabout). It is a fragment of an ancient manuscript, so it starts and ends abruptly.

After that I will simply give you the lists of books plus a reference to where the list is found.

Beyond what is listed here, we have the evidence supplied by Scripture quotations by the various pre-Nicene and Nicene authors, as well as discussions they provide concerning disputed books. Dionysius, for example, discusses the Book of Revelation, and Tertullian has a discussion on both *The Shepherd of Hermas* and Hebrews, the latter of which he believed to have been written by Barnabas.

Muratorian Canon (Fragment)

... those things at which he was present he placed thus.

The third book of the Gospel—the one according to Luke, the well-known physician—was written by Luke in his own name, sequentially, after the ascension of Christ at the time when Paul had associated him with himself as one studious of righteousness. [Luke] himself did not see the Lord in the flesh. As he was able he began his narrative with the birth of John [the Baptist].

The fourth Gospel is that of John, one of the disciples. When his fellow disciples and bishops pleaded with him, he said, "Fast with me for three days, and then we'll tell each other whatever may be revealed to any of us." That very night it was revealed to Andrew, one of the apostles, that John should write everything in his own name as they remembered them.

As a result, although different points are taught to us in the various books of the Gospels, there is no difference as regards the faith of believers. In all of them, under one imperial Spirit, everything is told which concerns the Lord's birth, his suffering, his resurrection, his conduct with his disciples, and his twofold coming: the first in the humiliation of rejection, which is now past, and the second in the glory of royal power, which is still in the future.

What a marvel it is, then, that John presents these various things so consistently in his letters, too! He says in his own person, "What we have seen with our eyes, heard with our ears, and our hands have handled, that have we written" [1 Jn. 1:1]. For in this way he testifies that he is not only the eyewitness, but also the hearer. Besides that, he is also the historian of all the wondrous facts concerning the Lord in their order.

In addition, the Acts of All the Apostles are comprised by Luke in one book and addressed to the most excellent Theophilus because these events took place when he was present himself. He shows this clearly—that the principle on which he wrote was to give only what fell under his own notice—by the omission of the suffering of Peter, and also of the journey of Paul when he went from the city of Rome to Spain.[668]

In regard to the epistles of Paul: again, to those who will understand the matter, they give their own indication of what they are, from what place or with what purpose they were directed. He wrote first of all, and at considerable length, to the Corinthians to check the schism of heresy; then to the Galatians to forbid circumcision; then to the Romans on the rule of the Old Testament Scriptures, and also to show them that Christ is the first object in these, which it is necessary for us to discuss separately.

The blessed apostle Paul, following the rule of his predecessor John, writes to no more than seven churches by name, in this order: the first to the Corinthians, the second to the Ephesians, the third to the Philippians, the fourth to the Colossians, the fifth to the Galatians, the sixth to the Thessalonians, the seventh to the Romans. In addition, though he writes twice to the Corinthians and Thessalonians for their correction, still it is apparent by this sevenfold writing that there is one Church spread abroad through the whole world. John, too, in the Revelation, although he writes only to seven churches, yet addresses all.

[Paul] wrote, besides these, one to Philemon, one to Titus, and two to Timothy, in simple personal affection and love indeed.

---

[668] It seems to have been a universal belief of the early churches that Paul went west to Spain, and possibly even to Britain, after his release from the imprisonment described at the end of Acts.

Nonetheless, these are holy in the esteem of the catholic Church and in the regulation of church discipline. There are also [letters] in circulation, one to the Laodiceans and another to the Alexandrians, forged under the name of Paul and addressed against the heresy of Marcion. There are also several others which cannot be received into the catholic Church, for it is not suitable for gall to be mingled with honey.

The Epistle of Jude, indeed, and two belonging to the above-named John, or bearing the name of John, are reckoned among the catholic epistles along with the book of Wisdom, written by the friends of Solomon in his honor.[669]

We also receive the Revelation of John and that of Peter, though some among us will not have this latter read in the church. The Pastor, moreover, did Hermas write very recently in our times in the city of Rome, while his brother, bishop Pius, sat in the chair of the church of Rome. Therefore it also ought to be read, but it cannot be read publicly in the church to the people, nor placed among the prophets, as their number is complete, nor among the apostles to the end of time.

Of the writings of Arsinous, also called Valentinus, or of Miltiades, we receive nothing at all. Those are also rejected who wrote the new Book of Psalms for Marcion, together with Basilides and the founder of the Asian Cataphrygians.

Melito of Sardis, c. AD 170

Old Testament only. Cited by Eusebius, *Ecclesiastical History* IV:26.

- Of Moses, five books: Genesis, Exodus, Numbers, Leviticus, Deuteronomy
- Jesus Nave [*i.e., Joshua of Nun*]
- Judges
- Ruth

---

[669] *The Wisdom of Solomon*, or *Wisdom*, is one of the seven "apocryphal" books that are in the Roman Catholic Bible, but not the Protestant Bible. It is interesting that the Muratorian Canon treats it as a New Testament book, when it would be considered Old Testament by modern Christians.

- of Kings, four books [*1 & 2 Samuel; 1 & 2 Kings*]
- Of Chronicles, two
- The Psalms of David
- The Proverbs of Solomon
- Wisdom[670]
- Ecclesiastes
- Song of Songs
- Job
- Of Prophets, Isaiah, Jeremiah
- Of the twelve prophets, one book
- Daniel
- Ezekiel
- Esdras[671]

Origen, c. AD 240

From *Commentary on Psalms*, cited in Eusebius, *Ecclesiastical History* VI:25:1-2.

- Genesis
- Exodus
- Leviticus
- Numbers
- Deuteronomy
- Joshua
- Judges & Ruth in one book

---

[670] It's hard to tell whether this is the Wisdom of Sirach, also known as Ecclesiasticus, or the Wisdom of Solomon, both of which are among the Roman Catholic "apocryphal" books not regarded as canonical by the Protestants.

[671] Esdras is our Ezra, and in this case it may have included Nehemiah as well. See, for example, Origen's list, which is next.

- 1 & 2 Kings in one book
- 1 & 2 Samuel in one book
- 1 & 2 Chronicles in one book
- Ezra and Nehemiah in one book
- Psalms
- Proverbs
- Ecclesiastes
- Song of Songs
- Isaiah
- Jeremiah and Lamentations in one book
- Daniel
- Ezekiel
- Job
- Esther
- The Maccabees

Eusebius, AD 323

From *Ecclesiastical History* III:25:1-4.

Accepted Writings:

- Four Gospels
- Acts
- Letters of Paul
- 1 John
- 1 Peter
- Revelation of John

Here, concerning the Revelation, Eusebius writes, "After [these accepted writings] is to be placed, if it really seem proper, the Apocalypse of John, concerning which we shall give the different opinions at the proper time. These, then belong among the accepted writings." At the end of his list of all three sets of books, he adds, "And besides, as I said, the Apocalypse of John, if it seem proper, which some, as I said, reject, but which others class with the accepted books."

Disputed Writings:

- James
- Jude
- 2 Peter
- 2 John
- 3 John

Rejected Writings:

- Acts of Paul
- Shepherd of Hermas
- Apocalypse of Peter
- Letter of Barnabas
- Didache

Augustine, AD 397

From *On Christian Doctrine* II:8:13.
- Genesis
- Exodus
- Leviticus
- Numbers
- Deuteronomy
- Joshua
- Judges
- Ruth
- Four books of Kings [*includes 1 & 2 Samuel*]
- Two books of Chronicles
- Job
- Tobiah

- Esther
- Judith
- 1 & 2 Maccabees
- Ezra and Nehemiah
- Psalms
- Proverbs
- Song of Songs
- Ecclesiastes
- Wisdom [*of Solomon*][672]
- Ecclesiasticus
- 12 Minor Prophets
- Isaiah
- Jeremiah
- Daniel
- Ezekiel
- Matthew
- Mark
- Luke
- John
- Romans
- 1 & 2 Corinthians
- Galatians
- Ephesus
- Philippians

---

[672] Augustine writes, "For two books, one called Wisdom and one called Ecclesiasticus, are ascribed to Solomon from a certain resemblance of style, but the most likely opinion is that they were written by Jesus, the son of Sirach. Still, they are to be reckoned among the prophetical books, since they have attained recognition as being authoritative."

- 1 & 2 Thessalonians
- Colossians
- 1 & 2 Timothy
- Titus
- Philemon
- Hebrews
- 1 & 2 Peter
- 1, 2, & 3 John
- Jude
- James
- Acts
- Revelation of John

Bibliography

These are in alphabetical order by book or web site title. I found it more useful to reference book titles than authors in the footnote. Thus, alphabetizing the bibliography by book or web site title was necessary for your reference.

- Coxe, A. Cleveland, ed. *The Ante-Nicene Fathers*. Grand Rapids, MI: Christian Classics Ethereal Library, 1890. Accessed 21 Jun. 2008 <http://www.ccel.org/fathers/>.

- Davies, Stephen, Translator. *The Apocryphon of John*. 2005. The Gnostic Society Library. Accessed March 17, 2011. <http://www.gnosis.org/naghamm/apocjn-davies.html>.

- "Apostolic Succession." *Catholic Answers*. 10 Aug. 2004. Accessed 20 Mar. 2011 <http://www.catholic.com/library/Apostolic_Succession.asp>

- *The Catholic Encyclopedia*. New York: Robert Appleton Company, 1910. New Advent. Ed. Kevin Knight. 2009. <http://www.newadvent.org>.

- Hardon, Fr. John A. "Cyprian Teaches Papal Primacy." *Challenge*. Vol. 16. Oct. 1989. *The Real Presence Association*. Inter Mirifica, 1998. Accessed 20 Mar. 2011 <http://www.therealpresence.org/archives/Papacy/Papacy_017.htm>.

- McBrien, Richard P. *The Church: The Evolution of Catholicism*. New York, NY: HarperOne, 2008

- Luther, Martin. *Complete Sermons of Martin Luther*. Grand Rapids, MI: Baker Books, 2007.

- Schaff, Philip. *Creeds of Christendom*. 6th ed. Harper & Brothers, 1877.

- Brown, Dan. *The Da Vinci Code*. 1st ed. New York: Random House, 2003.

- Gibbon, Edward. *Decline and Fall of the Roman Empire*. 1781. Sacred Texts. Evenity Publishing INC. Accessed 24 Mar. 2011. <http://www.sacred-texts.com/cla/gibbon/02/daf02030.htm>.

- Brenton, Sir Lancelot C.L. *English Translation of the Greek Septuagint Bible*. 1851. The Common Man's Prospective. Marsh, Ernest C. Accessed 19 Mar. 2011 <http://www.ecmarsh.com/lxx/Proverbs/index.htm>.

- Pagels, Elaine. *Gnostic Gospels*. Vintage Books 1989 ed. New York: Random House Digital, 1989.

- "The Gospel of Judas, the Hidden Story of the Betrayal of Christ." National Geographic. YouTube. Accessed 23 Mar. 2011. <http://www.youtube.com/watch?v=ywJdMezcqio>.

- Lambdin, Thomas O.; Grenfell, B.P.; Hunt, A.S.; Layton, Bentley. *Gospel of Thomas*. Sacred-Texts. Accessed March 17, 2011 <http://www.sacred-texts.com/chr/thomas.htm>.

- Schaff, Philip. *History of the Christian Church*. fifth ed. Grand Rapids, MI: Christian Classics Ethereal Library, 1882.

- Orr, James, ed. *International Standard Bible Encyclopedia*. Wm. B. Eerdmans, 1939. The International Standard Bible Encyclopedia Online. Accessed 2 Apr. 2011. <http://www.internationalstandardbible.com/>.

- *Jewish Virtual Library*. The American-Israeli Cooperative Enterprise. 2011. Accessed 4 Apr. 2011. <http://www.jewishvirtuallibrary.org/jsource/History/deadsea.html.>

- Keating, Corey. "Explanation of John 1:1." *Learning New Testament Greek*. Corey Keating. 2010. Accessed February 15, 2011 <http://www.ntgreek.org/answers/answer-frame-john1_1.htm>.

- Jenks, Philip E. "Catholics, Mormons, Assemblies of God growing; Mainline churches report a continuing decline." 12 Feb. 2010. *National Council of Churches*. National Council of the Churches of Christ in the USA. Accessed 15 Feb. 2011 <http://www.ncccusa.org/news/100204yearbook2010.html>.

- Schaff, Philip, ed. *The Nicene and Post-Nicene Fathers*. Grand Rapids, MI: Christian Classics Ethereal Library edition. New York: Christian Literature Publishing Co., 1890.

- Mead, G.R.S., Translator. 1921. *Pistis Sophia*. Sacred-Texts. Accessed March 17, 2011 <http://www.sacred-texts.com/chr/ps/ps005.htm>.

- *Watchtower*. 2011. Watch Tower Bible and Tract Society. Accessed Feb. 15, 2011 <http://www.watchtower.org>.

Thank You!

Thank you for reading *Decoding Nicea*! I hope that you have been encouraged, educated, entertained, and above all, provoked to love and good works in fellowship with Jesus Christ, the Son and eternal *Logos* of God.

Reviews

Reviews of this book are encouraged and greatly appreciated!

Please review at http://www.amazon.com; search for *Decoding Nicea*.

Author Contact

You may contact the author at: *admin@christian-history.org*

Future books by Paul Pavao and all books published by Greatest Stories Ever Told® can be found at:

http://www.GSETpublishing.com

Other books published by:

Greatest Stories Ever Told
P.O. Box 307
Selmer, TN 38375
admin@christian-history.org

The Apostles' Gospel (2013)
How to Make a Church Fail (2009)
Slavery During the Revolutionary War (2013)

  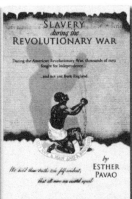

Made in the USA
Coppell, TX
16 December 2023

26402903R00262